Live Flesh

The Male Body in Contemporary Spanish Cinema

Santiago Fouz-Hernández
and
Alfredo Martínez-Expósito

I.B. TAURIS

LONDON · NEW YORK

Published in 2007 by I.B.Tauris & Co. Ltd
6 Salem Road, London W2 4BU
175 Fifth Avenue, New York NY 10010
www.ibtauris.com

In the United States and Canada distributed by Palgrave Macmillan,
a division of St. Martin's Press, 175 Fifth Avenue, New York NY 10010

ISBN (Hb) 978 1 84511 449 7
     (Pb) 978 1 84511 450 3

A full CIP record for this book is available from the British Library
A full CIP record for this book is available from the Library of Congress
Library of Congress catalog card: available

Typeset in Garamond by Dexter Haven Associates Ltd, London
Printed and bound in Great Britain by TJ International, Padstow, Cornwall

Contents

List of illustrations

All illustrations except 4, 5, 10 and 12 were provided by the graphics
department at the Filmoteca Española in Madrid and we are grateful to the
staff there for their help and attention. Still 4 (used also on the front cover) was
provided by Sonia Lázaro Arriola at Lola Films, Still 5 by Beatriz Morillas at
Amiguetes Entertainment (photograph by Mónica de Pascalis and Paola
Ardizzoni) and Still 12 by Ventura Pons, for which we are very grateful. Every
reasonable effort has been made to contact copyright holders in order to
acquire the necessary permissions.

Preface and acknowledgements

The idea for this book originated in 2000, when we initiated email correspondence about a film that we had both separately written about. The film was Almodóvar's *Live Flesh* (fatefully, its title has turned out to be an ideal one for this book too). Having identified a clear compatibility in our research interests, we organized a six-month teaching exchange in 2002 (between the Universities of Durham in the United Kingdom and Queensland in Australia). We then brought together our shared research interests (Spanish cinema and men's studies) in an extended project. This book is its main outcome.

Spanish director Bigas Luna once confessed that his fascination with the concept of 'Spanishness' had been stimulated by a visiting English friend. Those national customs and everyday objects that we take for granted in our own culture were perceived as surreal by the visitor. Our experience as Spanish nationals who have spent most of our formative years in Spain but most of our professional lives as academics in English-speaking countries has also given us a new perspective on our own culture. We feel privileged to have been exposed to the Anglophone theory and criticism on Spanish cultural studies and film studies and, at the same time, to have kept in touch with the ongoing academic discourses around this ever-growing field in Spain. The rapid changes that have taken place in our country of origin since we both left it over ten years ago have been all the more surprising and noticeable for us from abroad, particularly in what relates to issues of gender and sexuality and their representation in Spanish film and media. One of our main purposes when conceiving this book was to use such experience as the basis for the analysis of Spanish filmic texts produced during the last three decades. Scholarly work in the fields of Spanish gender and film studies has been immensely productive during that time in both the English-speaking and Spanish-speaking worlds. Parallel to this, the growing attention paid to the representations of masculinity and the male body in English-language films has prepared the ground for a study dedicated to the representation of the male body in Spanish cinema.

This project would not have been possible without the support of various institutions that funded periods of research leave and various research trips during 2004–6. We would like to start by thanking our institutions (Durham University and University of Queensland) for making the 2002 teaching exchange possible in the first place and for supporting our research project with their respective research leave schemes. The Ministerio Español de Asuntos Exteriores y de Cooperación and Agencia Española de Cooperación Internacional funded Alfredo Martínez-Expósito's stay in Madrid in late 2004. The British Academy funded a two-month stay in Madrid for Santiago Fouz-Hernández in early 2005 and also a six-week stay in Queensland later that year, whilst the University of Queensland Travel Award for International Collaborative Research covered his travel expenses to Queensland. Extended periods of research leave were funded by AHRC, The Arts and Humanities Research Council (Fouz-Hernández) and by the University of Queensland Research Development Grant and Centre for the History of European Discourses Research (Martínez-Expósito). The British Academy also granted an overseas travel award that subsidized a trip to Spain to present material of this book at a conference. Our thanks also go to the anonymous readers of the grant proposals for the invaluable feedback that helped shape the content and structure of the book.

At I.B.Tauris we would like to thank our editor Philippa Brewster for her help, encouragement and confidence in this project, Gretchen Ladish and everyone else involved in the production of this book. At the Filmoteca Española we thank all staff that assisted us in the library, graphics department and screenings, but especially Margarita Lobo and Trinidad del Río for their advice and for facilitating the daily viewing of films during December 2004, February and March 2005. We would like to thank the following colleagues for their advice and feedback on earlier drafts of various parts of the material included here: Mark Allinson, Ian Biddle, Roy Boyne, Joe Hardwick, Barry Jordan, Peter Lehman, Morris Low and Chris Perriam. We have presented versions of different parts of the book at conferences and research seminars held at universities in Australia (Adelaide, Flinders, Monash, Queensland, Sydney, University of Technology Sydney), Ireland (Limerick), Portugal (Braga), Spain (Valencia, Sevilla), UK (Bath, Cambridge, Institute of Romance Studies and Queen Mary and Westfield London, Newcastle upon Tyne, Glasgow) and USA (Chicago, University of California Los Angeles, University of California Santa Barbara) and we would like to thank the organizers for inviting us and the audiences for their feedback.

Ian Biddle, Christian Mieves and Tony Roberts very kindly proof-read drafts of the manuscript and Christian Mieves designed the concept and artwork for the book cover. Special thanks go to Sonia Lázaro Arriola at Lola Films for providing us with a high-resolution reproduction of the exact still that we wanted for the cover and for granting us permission to reproduce various stills on behalf of Lola Films. We are also grateful to Pedro Costa, Marta Esteban (at Messidor Films), Jason Leaf (at Avatar), Beatriz Morillas (at Amiguetes Entertainment), Ventura Pons and Christina Sutherland (Tessela) for granting us copyright permissions for the reproduction of various stills. Earlier versions of the analysis of *Jamón, Jamón*, *Barrio*, *El Bola*, *Krámpack*, *Live Flesh* and *Mar adentro* were published in the following books and journals: *Revisiting Space: Space and Place in European Cinema*, ed. by Wendy Everett and Axel Goodbody (Oxford: Peter Lang); *Youth Culture in Global Cinema*, ed. by Timothy Shary and Alexandra Seibel (Austin: Texas University Press); *Symbolism: An International Annual of Critical Aesthetics 7* and *Proceedings of the AHGBI Annual Conference 'Antes y después del Quijote: en el cincuentenario de la Asociación de Hispanistas de Gran Bretaña e Irlanda'*, ed. by Robert Archer, Valdi Astvaldsson, Stephen Boyd and Michael Thompson (València: Biblioteca Valenciana). We are grateful to the editors of those publications for their permissions. Finally, we would like to thank our students of Spanish cinema at the Universities of Durham and Queensland and our families and partners for their support and encouragement.

Film titles are given in the original Spanish and in their commercial English translation when available (we have provided our own translation in all other cases). Release dates, audience and box-office takings figures are based on data available at the electronic film database published in the Spanish Ministry of Culture website (www.mcu.es), consulted throughout 2005 and checked in August 2006. All translations from Spanish sources are ours, unless otherwise specified. English subtitles available in commercial releases of the films were followed only if they literally conveyed the meaning of the Spanish or in ways that satisfied the authors of this book.

Introduction

Traditionally regarded as the object of biology, the body has become increasingly prominent in a number of other disciplines, from anthropology to medicine and, more recently, sociology and cultural studies. Much European art from the fifteenth century onwards has focused on human anatomy, bringing together the disciplines of art and medicine. Medical literature and illustrations contributed to the emergence of a strong discourse of the body and to the emergence of the body as spectacle. This discourse remains largely intact today in the shape of successful serialized hospital dramas, as well as sensationalist television programmes that show footage of cosmetic surgery operations and dramatic 'make-overs', not to mention the more rare but extremely popular televised dissections such as those by doctor von Hagens shown on British television. The invention of photography and the moving image contributed to the dissemination of and curiosity in body images. The Hollywood epics from the 1920s onwards took the representation of the male body on the screen to another level, whilst present-day consumer-oriented societies have placed the body even more in the spotlight, with a clear shift from the nineteenth-century stress on clothing and the 'hiding' of the body to a culture that celebrates and displays the human form, prompting scholars from a wide range of disciplines to explore the social dimensions of the body, especially in relation to gender. The use and abuse of bodies (male and female) in advertising and other forms of media has also been widely discussed (Bordo 1999 is a key reference of such discussions with regards to the male body) as part of the ongoing debate arguably sparked by Mulvey's 1970s influential essay on the male gaze and the female star as spectacle in classic Hollywood cinema. Mulvey's controversial argument inspired a productive debate that initially resulted in major publications about femininity and the female body on the screen during the 1980s. In the years that followed, emphasis was diverted to cinematic representations of the male body, resulting in important publications such as those usefully summarized in the introduction to Powrie, Davies and Babington's own volume on masculinities in European and Hollywood cinemas (2004: 1–5) (see, for example, Shaviro 1993; Tasker 1993; Jeffords 1994; Cohan and Hark 1995 or Lehman 1993 and 2000).

Writing in the mid-1990s, Cohan and Hark regret that mainstream film theory has generally tended to equate masculinity with activity, voyeurism, sadism, fetishism and story, and femininity 'with passivity, exhibitionism, masochism, narcissism, and spectacle' (1995: 2). They denounce what they consider as a system based on 'monolithic', 'homologous differences' that attributes only 'power, stability, and wholeness' to masculine subjectivity in a seemingly axiomatic, universal distribution, and then reclaim for the masculine a symmetrical position to the feminine. In short, they are arguing that issues of spectacle, masochism, passivity, masquerade and the body – traditionally explored in female contexts – must be part of the purview of masculinity studies. A more critical masculine paradigm will necessarily have to consider men as spectacle-driven, exhibitionist, masochist, passive and narcissist; it will have to consider their masquerades and their bodies. One of the primary aims of this book is to contribute to this critical turn, by engaging specifically with the Spanish cinematic context.

In Spain, despite a self-declared focus on women and femininity, the early films of Pedro Almodóvar constitute an anticipation of the noticeable centrality that masculinity and the male body would have in the Spanish cinema of the last two decades (see Allinson 2001 or Smith 2000a). In that period, the Spanish male body has been both celebrated and problematized most notably by directors such as Bigas Luna, Álex de la Iglesia or Santiago Segura. Using a wide range of genres and styles, their films have drawn on Iberian stereotypes, on the commercial appeal of graphic violence and on the long tradition of the grotesque in Hispanic culture to both criticize and glorify older and alternative prototypes of Spanish masculinity. In *Stars and Masculinities in Spanish Cinema*, Chris Perriam (2003) mapped out one of the most relevant and revealing innovations in the field of Spanish cinema studies by (re)discovering masculinity as a marked, non-neutral and controversial aspect of a wide range of films beyond Almodóvar and placing Spanish cinema in the field of stars studies – a field usually associated with Hollywood productions. The list of actors whose careers Perriam examines could be seen as a canonic gallery of men who in some important ways have come to embody the values of contemporary Spanish masculinity, most of whom are also studied in various sections of this book, although in different contexts. In the case of Antonio Banderas, who now plays mainly Latino roles in Hollywood, the embodiment of masculinity has been associated for international audiences with the more controversial embodiment of a racial maleness often identified with alterity and otherness. Arguably, offshore readings of Spanish masculinity tend to emphasize elements of difference and otherness along racial and broadly defined cultural lines. Such readings draw on discourses often built on the acceptance of a national identity or racial determinism or a cultural specificity that allegedly dictates the authenticity of representations.

In this book we have explored a wide range of Spanish films from the last three decades with two main questions in mind: how the bodies of male characters are represented, and how those representations mediate the perceptions that different audiences obtain of Spanish masculinity. The first question is related to issues of visual rhetoric and the politics of the body, but also to more general questions of filmic discourse such as the gaze, spectacle and stardom. The second question is closely connected with issues of readership and spectatorship, and, in the context of an increasingly transnational Spanish cinema, with the question of stereotypes. We are also interested in exploring how recent developments in Spanish cultural studies, rooted in the Anglo-American and French traditions but rapidly developing within the Spanish academic discourse, can contribute to new understandings of Spanish masculinities. Thus, in the pages that follow, we will investigate the mechanisms by which hegemonic masculinities (for example, the *macho ibérico*, the young athletic ideal, the muscular hero) have made claims to public discourse and how those mechanisms have been contested in recent times. We will ask, furthermore, whether there is evidence to suggest that marginalized masculinities (such as those represented by disabled men, homosexuals, transsexuals and 'foreign' men) have made a contribution to the contestation of those conventional male hegemonic types. Our work is indebted to existing research in the field of Spanish masculinities and the Spanish male body in Spanish cinema by authors such as Paul Julian Smith, Peter Evans or, in Spanish language, Ricardo Llamas and José Miguel García Cortés but, at a more subject-specific level, to the essential volumes by Chris Perriam (2003) and Tatjana Pavlović (2003). Needless to say, key works that have focused on issues of femininity in Spanish cinema, such as those by Susan Martin-Márquez (1999), Isolina Ballesteros (2001) or the various essays on gender collected by Marsh and Nair (2004) have also been major reference points. The 'national' element that underlies this book is influenced by important readings of national and transnational identities in Spanish cinema such as those by Marsha Kinder (1993), Barry Jordan and Rikki

Morgan-Tamosunas (1998), Núria Triana-Toribio (2003) or Isabel Santaolalla (2005) amongst others.

The eight thematizations of the male body we propose in this book are related to established paradigms in film and cultural studies such as gender and sexuality (in Chapters 5, 6 and 8), stereotypes and issues of national representation (in Chapters 1 and 7), youth cultures (in Chapter 2), and the representation of particular aspects and parts of the body (in Chapters 3, 4 and 8). Rather than attempting a systematic account of the virtually limitless fields of sexuality, gender, class, age and nation, we have deliberately chosen critical intersections of these paradigms with the most revealing trends in contemporary Spanish cinema and we have thus chosen to focus on stereotypical, young, muscular, (dis)abled, homosexual, transformed and foreign male bodies in ways that will reveal as much about their opposites.

The first chapter introduces the concept of the 'Spanish' male body by revisiting some of the most memorable images of Spanish masculinity in the cinema of the democratic period. The often ridiculed 'average Spaniard' of the 1970s 'sexy comedy' exemplified by the '*landismo*' phenomenon (named after Alfredo Landa, the most popular actor starring in that type of comedies) is the starting point, leading to the ambiguously portrayed *macho ibérico* famously embodied by Javier Bardem in Bigas Luna's trilogy of 'Iberian Portraits' in the early 1990s (especially in *Jamón, Jamón* (1992), which is one of the central case studies of the chapter). We argue that, whilst such stereotypes run counter to the more Europeanized and sexually ambiguous types that abound in more recent films, the relatively recent commercial success of the politically incorrect *Torrente* saga (dir. Santiago Segura, 1998, 2001 and 2005), with their bald, overweight, grubby and reckless antihero played by the director himself, questions the relevance of the so-called 'metrosexual' or 'new' man in the Spanish context. This grotesque sub-genre (which includes another historic box-office success, *Airbag* (dir. Bajo Ulloa, 1997) and many others that followed) draws on scatological humour and on the commercial appeal of graphic and gratuitous violence which manifests growing anxieties about the demands of the body beautiful as well as a certain nostalgia provoked by the inevitable abandonment of more familiar models of Iberian masculinity.

Chapter 2 explores iconic representations of young bodies in democratic Spain, from Eloy de la Iglesia's *Colegas/Pals* (1982) to the more recent *Historias del Kronen/Stories from the Kronen* (dir. Armendáriz, 1995) or Cesc Gay's *Krámpack/Dani and Nico* (2000). In *Kronen* the emphasis is on hedonistic pleasure: a group of *madrileños* in their early twenties seek ever more extreme stimulation by experimenting with sex, drugs and alcohol or speeding and joy-riding. In *Krámpack*, the attention paid to the incipient transformation of the boys' bodies serves not only as an explicit reference to their growing-up but also as one of the keys to the exploration of their gender and sexual identities. The marginal settings of other recent Spanish films such as *Barrio/Neighbourhood* (dir. León de Aranoa, 1998) or *El Bola/Pellet* (dir. Mañas, 2000) seem to suggest that cinematic representations of contemporary Spanish youth are more closely related not only to their European contemporaries but also to previous iconic representations of youth in Spain in films such as *Colegas* or the earlier Saura film *Los golfos/The Delinquents* (1962). Their fragile, often abused and damaged bodies work as a metaphor for their social exclusion. Yet, the hospital drama *Planta cuarta/The Fourth Floor* (dir. Mercero, 2003) uses the very real physical vulnerability of a group of young cancer patients as a way to highlight the strength and resilience of the new generations. The scenes of group masturbation and the prominence of violence and risk-taking activities in many of the films studied illustrate the relevance of the body as a site of resistance but also as a tool of gender-identity formation from an early age, a key to the masculine identities in the adult characters explored in other chapters.

Questions of muscularity are examined in Chapter 3. The chapter starts with a review of key debates of screen 'musculinity', to use Tasker's term (1993), and highlights the relative absence of muscular bodies in Spanish cinema before the 1990s. After a brief review outlining relevant exceptions that go back to the Crusade films of the 1940s, we then focus on *El corazón del guerrero/Heart of the Warrior* (dir. Daniel Monzón Jerez, 2000) as an example of the presence of superheroes which is relatively infrequent in Spanish culture and film and tends to be mediated by someone else's fantasy. The chapter explores some of the ways in which the excessively muscular body enters the pantheon of accepted body images and how its reception is undeniably mediated by forms of popular art such as the Hollywood blockbuster and the superhero comic. Indeed, the muscular hero is a long way from the 'average Spaniard' discussed in the first chapter, or the struggling teenagers of the second. Notably, the ever-elusive 'hyper bodies' are often foreign characters and are frequently played by foreign actors. The figure of Philip the Handsome (Felipe I of Castile) (Daniele Liotti) in Vicente Aranda's *Juana la Loca/Mad Love* (2001) is also analysed in this chapter as an example of 'imported muscle', but also as an exceptional case which avoids both the superhero genre and, to an extent, the parodic intention that is often associated with 'heroic' bodies.

In Chapter 4 we use recent literature on filmic representations of disability to propose new readings of modern Spanish films. Álex de la Iglesia's disabled cyborgs (especially *Acción mutante/Mutant Action*, 1993), Amenábar's troubled men (from the sadist of *Tesis/Thesis* (1996) to the disfigured face of *Abre los ojos/Open Your Eyes* (1997) or the tetraplegic man that wants to end his own life with dignity in *Mar adentro/The Sea Inside* (2004)) or Almodóvar's battered lovers – especially *Carne trémula/Live Flesh* (1997), which we use as a case study – exemplify a common tendency to use the disabled body as a script. Most instances of broken and disabled bodies in contemporary Spanish film are marked in one of three ways: as diseased, as incapacitated, or marked by violence. Although these categories often overlap, each of them conjures up a well-defined epistemological landscape: disease as metaphor, disability as monstrosity, violence as bodily inscription. The chapter considers the enormous influence of Freudian theories of disability as castration and the Oedipus complex in the production and exegesis of contemporary films. However, it is proposed that the feminist-originated concept of 'body as text' might help explain more clearly issues of bodily technologies, scarification, bodily disorders (from obesity to bulimia), sensory deprivation, disfigurement and normalcy. This set of conceptual tools is also useful for a timely re-evaluation of the male body as an eventful locus of action, as opposed to a dynamic motor for the action plot. If the female had traditionally been the main site of bodily discourse, in the Spanish cinema of the last three decades or so, it is the man who becomes blind, lame, ill, hospitalized, physically attacked and even raped.

Recent and drastic changes in the Spanish legal system with respect to homosexuality (from incarceration during the dictatorship to equal rights including marriage and adoption since 2005) have undoubtedly contributed not only to improve visibility but also the gradual integration of the homoerotic gaze into mainstream film and media (although not always in a very favourable light, as Llamas (1997) argues). In the long path from Eloy de la Iglesia's tormented homosexuals to seamlessly integrated queers of Albacete/Bardem/Menkes or the adult types of Vera's *Segunda piel/Second Skin* (1999) or Pons's *Amic/Amat/Beloved/Friend* (1999), it is possible to identify a thorough investigation of the means by which a gay character can be visually constructed in mainstream Spanish film. The influence of Almodóvar both in terms of the stylization and character development (especially in *La ley del deseo/Law of Desire* (1987)) cannot be underestimated, as shown in our study of *Perdona Bonita, pero Lucas me quería a mí/Excuse Me Darling, but Lucas Loved Me* (dirs Félix Sabroso and Dunia Ayaso, 1997). In this generally poorly received but, for our purposes, highly relevant film, the male body takes centre-stage and becomes the recipient of many of the physical anxieties usually associated with gay men (fatness versus fitness, promiscuity, vanity and so on). Drawing on queer theory and existing studies of gay representation in Spanish cinema (such as Smith (1992b); Llamas (1995); Martínez-Expósito (1998b); Fouz-Hernández and Perriam (2000); Alfeo Álvarez (2000) or Mira (2004a)), Chapter 5 focuses on recent developments perhaps best illustrated by the controversial *Cachorro/Bear Cub* (dir. Albaladejo, 2004), where the naked large bodies of the so-called 'bear' men (often middle-aged, overweight and hairy) are boldly displayed and celebrated. Rather than attempting a history of the problematic representation of homosexuality on the screen, this chapter explores the visual rhetoric of such representations. Hence we focus on the strategies devised to organize and structure the bodies being shown as well as the means by which they influence the audience. Inevitably, the chapter draws on queer theory and scholarship, but it does so on the understanding that this theoretical body needs to be appropriated (and sometimes even reformulated) by the culture-sensitive critic if it is going to be used for the analysis of a non-Anglo-Saxon cultural object, and must therefore inevitably take into account recent developments in queer discourses from Spain.

In Chapter 6 we propose that the way the topics of sex change, transgenderism and cross-dressing are dealt with and presented to the audience depend largely on the pragmatics of genre. Whilst we would be reluctant to argue that high-brow genres offer a deeper, better articulated critique of the body, we can deduce from the cases studied that 'high' genres tend to focus on the character and 'popular' genres tend to exploit the (comic, sometimes farcical) situation. Early classic representations of transvestites and transsexuals such as those seen in *Mi querida señorita/My Dearest Senorita* (dir. Armiñán, 1972), *Cambio de sexo/Forbidden Love* (dir. Aranda, 1977) or *Ocaña, retrat intermitent/Ocana, an Intermittent Portrait* (dir. Pons, 1978) are compared with more recent examples in Fernando Trueba's *Belle Epoque/The Age of Beauty* (1992), Albacete and Menkes's *I Love You Baby* (2001) or Salazar's recent *20 centímetros/20 Centimetres* (2005). The chapter also revisits key episodes in Almodóvar's filmography, such as the influential *La ley del deseo/Law of Desire* (1987), *Tacones lejanos/High Heels* (1991), *Todo sobre mi madre/All About My Mother* (1999) or the more recent *La mala educación/Bad Education* (2004), which is used as an extended case study. The sexy comedy of the 1970s (exemplified by the box-office success *No desearás al vecino del quinto/Thou Shall Not Covet Thy Fifth Floor Neighbour* (dir. Ramón Fernández, 1970)), seems to be the origin of certain 'battle-of-the-sexes' comedies of the 1990s such as *Pon un hombre en tu vida/Put a Man in Your Life* (dir. Eva Lesmes, 1996) or *Corazón de bombón/Sweetheart* (dir. Álvaro Sáenz de Heredia, 2000). The high/low divide is a crucial factor in any attempt to understand the profound differences, both aesthetic and ideological, in the presentation of the male (and female) bodies in these titles. However, the more recent examples studied would seem to reflect an evolution towards a more 'positive representation' like the one experienced by the homosexual character, as suggested in the previous chapter.

Chapter 7 focuses on the representation of foreign bodies (tourists, migrants, nomads), whose presence is increasingly visible both in Spanish cinema and in its academic consideration (notably in Santaolalla's monograph on the subject – 2005). The relevance of the related topics of migration, nomadism and tourism is considerable for a country like Spain, with high levels of activity in the three areas. Not surprisingly, recent Spanish cinema is generous in the cultivation of them all. The intersection of national, class and gender identity can be used in order to queer those bodies' regimes of presence/absence, but also to invoke a cultural framework which is no longer that of modern radical subjectivity. The chapter analyses in detail two recent and representative migration films that until now have had less prominence in academic discourses on the subject: *Ilegal/Illegal* (dir. Ignacio Vilar, 2003) and the controversial *La fuente amarilla/The Yellow Fountain* (dir. Miguel Santesmases, 1999), famously denounced by the Chinese community in Madrid as racist and xenophobic. The chapter also examines mixed romances involving a foreigner and a Spaniard in films such as *La niña de tus ojos/The Girl of Your Dreams* (dir. Fernando Trueba, 1998), *La pasión turca/Turkish Passion* (dir. Aranda, 1994), *Hola, estás sola?/Hi, Are You Alone?* (dir. Icíar Bollaín, 1995) or *Torremolinos 73* (dir. Pablo Berger, 2003).

Peter Lehman (1993, 2000) and Susan Bordo (1999) amongst others have argued that the centrality of the phallus in patriarchal society is paradoxical. In Chapter 8 we explore the politics of male frontal nudity in Spanish cinema. Whilst the glimpses of the male genitals in films at the beginning of the democratic period such as Gutiérrez Santos's *Arriba Hazaña/Long Live Hazaña*, Ventura Pons's *Ocaña, retrat intermitent* or Eloy de la Iglesia's *El diputado/Confessions of a Congressman* and *El sacerdote/The Priest* (all released only months after the abolition of censorship in 1978) or even Almodóvar's *¿Qué he hecho yo para merecer esto?/What Have I Done to Deserve This?* (1984) seemed unusual and even shocking; the penis has become increasingly visible in Spanish films of the last three decades. In 1997 the total nudity of heartthrobs Jordi Mollá and Liberto Rabal (in Franco's *La buena estrella/ Lucky Star* and Almodóvar's *Carne trémula* respectively) attracted much attention as did the sight of an erect penis in Medem's *Lucía y el sexo/Sex and Lucía* (2001). More recently, films such as *Cachorro* (dir. Albaladejo, 2004) or *Amor idiota/Idiot Love* (dir. Ventura Pons, 2004) have included notorious close-up shots of penises that have attracted much media attention (but little or no controversy) whilst others such as *XXL* (dir. Sánchez Valdés, 2004) or *20 centímetros* (dir. Salazar, 2005) teasingly place the male organ at the centre of the narrative. The chapter questions the notion that this new visual investment in the male genitals has contributed to a 'decentring of the phallus' in the narratives of these films and ends with a detailed study of the phallic discourse in Pedro Almodóvar's filmography that supports the chapter's overall argument.

It is interesting that one of the most representative actors of contemporary Spanish cinema, Javier Bardem, features quite prominently in five very different chapters of this book, embodying very different types of men. Still regarded by some as the epitome of Iberian *macho* masculinity through his long-abandoned but still prominent roles in the first two installments of the Bigas Luna 'Iberian Portraits' trilogy, Bardem has struggled to be disassociated from the muscular heterosexuality and overt physicality that characterized much of his early work. Yet, his performances as a disabled man in Almodóvar's *Carne trémula* (1997) or Amenábar's *Mar adentro* (2004), or as an overweight and powerless unemployed man in León de Aranoa's *Los lunes al sol/Mondays in the Sun* (2002) as well as some of his gay roles (although not so much in Vera's *Segunda piel* (1999), as we argue in Chapter 5), are equally convincing. The malleability and adaptability of Bardem's body is a good illustration of the evolution of the representation of masculinity in Spanish cinema. The iconic image used on the cover of this book invites a careful reflection on the body and construction of masculinity on the screen. The posture and facial expression of Bardem's character in this still from Bigas Luna's *Jamón, Jamón* (1992) could suggest that the old *macho ibérico* type has been defeated by the new consumerist society. The muscular build and confident swagger have not prevented the commodification of his body, that, in this shot, is intensified: used by the newly financially powerful woman first as a vehicle to get her own way with her son and then as a toy-boy, his nude upper body is now marked by one of the utmost symbols of his consumerist ambition (the unmistakable Mercedes-Benz emblem). At a narrative level, he has been brought to the ground by his excessive sexuality and competitive instinct; yet, his lower body could also suggest that the defeat is only temporary. The legs are only partially spread and ready to get up and reclaim agency in the face of the malign erosion of his authority by late modernity. The question that we will be asking in the pages that follow is whether the apparent changes in the visual representation of masculinity described above are thorough-changing or only skin-deep.

1

Stereotypical bodies

MEET 'THE AVERAGE SPANIARD'

When considering the stereotypical representation of the Spanish male in Spanish cinema, most national audiences would inevitably think of the characters played by actors such as José Luis López Vázquez, Andrés Pajares, Fernando Esteso or, especially, Alfredo Landa in the 1970s. The so-called 'average Spaniard' of the Francoist *comedia celtibérica* and the *destape* films that followed has been unflatteringly described retrospectively as 'a eunuch proud of his excessive body fat', 'with depressing soft dicks' (Satué 1996: 57); 'a mediocre Spaniard, with various sexual traumas (…) short, ugly, a bit bald, funny, repressed and shy' (Freixas quoted in Pavlović 2003: 81) or a male 'responding to a realistic typology: short, horny, shy and poor' (Ponce 2004: 24). As Jordan and Allinson note, through a long series of roles in the 'Iberian sex comedy' in the 1970s, actor Alfredo Landa (born 1933) became 'the epitome of Spanish maleness' (2005: 127): he was 'short (…), balding, a little overweight and not good-looking' (126) and when stripped down to his underwear, the sight of his bent legs always guaranteed a good laugh. As Pavlović has argued, his legs became a symbol of the 'surface of embarrassment' that revealed the contrast between 'fantasies of endless sexual activity' and 'the reality of anxious and incompetent lovers' that characterized these narratives (2003: 82).

Yet, these films were also a celebration of the perceived interest in the *producto nacional* (literally 'the national product') expressed by the invariably foreign and blonde females (usually Swedish or French) that started to populate the Spanish holiday resorts from the 1960s. In these films, the lady visitors from Northern Europe brought their liberated ways into a demure society which, despite a shy *apertura* (economic and moral liberalization), was still under the influence of a dictatorial system that promoted the role of women as saintly wives and devoted mothers whilst their husbands made trips to France to watch erotic films banned in Spain (see Triana-Toribio 2003: 98 or Melero Salvador 2004: 93). After a carnivalesque encounter with the liberal female Other, the Spaniards of these films usually went back to their 'honest' wives, rediscovering their preference for the autochthonous female and moral values and thus conveniently restoring the status quo (see Pavlović 2003: 83–84). Beneath a thick layer of humour, as Pavlović has also noted, these films reveal some of the anxieties surrounding the regime's demands on national masculine identity which, within a strict gender division, asked that Spanish men were 'proper men, not queers'. Nowhere else are these anxieties more obvious than in what became the most representative film of the so-called *landismo* (a group of films starring Alfredo Landa in very similar roles and with the type of narrative that we have just described), *No desearás al vecino del quinto/Thou Shalt Not Covet Thy Fifth Floor Neighbour* (dir. Ramón Fernández, 1970), in which Landa's character leads a double life (see Chapters 3 and 5). It turns out that his camp persona, working as a dress-maker in his town, was only a cover story to ensure that his customers' husbands did not get jealous and disguised his 'real' *macho* playboy outlook and lifestyle in the capital.[1] Yet, as Pavlović argues, in their 'eagerness to perform both masculinity and national identity', the protagonists of these films 'destroy the desired effect' (2003: 82). It is important to note that, despite a marked emphasis on sexuality, these films, constrained by censorship, were more about guessing or hearing than actually seeing (Ponce 2004: 22) and teased audiences that never got to see 'what the tourists were up to', nor did the *macho ibérico* 'ever manage to consummate the act, despite the opportunities offered by those girls from the other side of the Pyrenees' (Lloréns and Uris 1996: 36).

Whilst the *destape* films that followed the end of censorship in 1977 were unashamedly generous with the exposure of female bodies ('*destapar*' literally means 'to uncover' or to 'undress'), male actors usually kept most of their clothes on, thus accentuating the objectification of women and the self-confidence of men, who rarely had to expose their own bodies or put under scrutiny their physical adequacy as sex symbols. The poster of *Los chulos* (dir. Ozores, 1981), a late example of the genre, typically illustrates this: the male protagonists (played by Pajares and Esteso) are fully dressed in suits, shirt, tie and smart shoes but are surrounded by drawings of three females, two of them blonde and fully naked and one brunette, topless and wearing revealing lingerie including black stockings and suspenders. Ponce has noted that, in theatre, Juan Ribó was made to wear a leotard that matched his skin colour during the censored play *Equus* and it is believed that he was the first male to be nude on a Spanish stage in the uncensored version of that play during the transition (2004: 54). It is revealing that in his book on *destape* films Ponce devotes only two illustrated pages to the section 'shirtless Spanish men' but 32 to the three-part section 'topless Spanish women'. Actors such as Patxi Andión (who, according to Ponce, was the first Spanish male to be nude in a film – in 1974 – 2004: 17), or Sancho Gracia (better known for his work on television) stand out as males who were more willing to take their clothes off on the screen and, even more remarkably, for special magazine spreads.

Things have certainly changed since then. The arrival of Pedro Almodóvar (and, before him, Eloy de la Iglesia – see Aliaga and García Cortés 1997: 152) onto the Spanish cinema scene introduced a male homosexual perspective in which the display and objectification of the male body was much more commonplace, as we will see in Chapter 5. Actors such as Antonio Banderas became famous for their attractive physique – in his case from his very first film role (for Almodóvar) in 1982 (see Perriam 2003: 45–69 for a detailed analysis of Banderas's Spanish career). Others like Imanol Arias or Jorge Sanz (both also discussed at length in Perriam 2003) took advantage of their sex appeal in roles that often involved (semi)nudity and which, especially in the case of Sanz, arguably helped to transform the public imagination of the Spanish male. In films such as *Amantes/Lovers* (dir. Aranda, 1991) or *Belle Epoque* (dir. Trueba, 1992), to mention two of the titles most familiar to non-Spanish audiences, Sanz's body is visibly inscribed – through its dressing in various uniforms – within some of the most traditional Spanish institutions (the army in *Amantes*, the Civil Guard in *Belle Epoque*) and thrown into relief against important episodes of Spanish history (Francoism and the Second Republic respectively). In both films, his characters seem to accept man's new position as an object of the gaze and yet, as Perriam notes, at times this objectification empowers Sanz's characters, enabling them to restore 'the male norm' (2003: 152) with gestures such as his gaze back at the camera (as in Figure 1).[2] Some of the characters played by Sanz during the late 1980s and 1990s are a more literal illustration of the commodified male body that, as we shall see in Chapter 8, has almost become commonplace in Spanish cinema.[3] Both in *Si te dicen que caí/If They Tell You I Fell* (dir. Aranda, 1989) and in the comedy *¿Por qué lo llaman amor cuándo quieren decir sexo?/Why Do*

They Call It Love When They Mean Sex? (dir. Gómez Pereira, 1993), his characters are paid for performing sex for an audience (thus directing the cinema audience's gaze at his body); in *Hotel y domicilio/In Calls and Out* (dir. del Río, 1995) he plays a rent-boy and, as we shall see in Chapter 6, in *I Love You Baby* (dirs Albacete and Menkes, 2001) he plays the love object of a homosexual man and a heterosexual woman.

Spanish cinema of the late 1980s and throughout the 1990s tended to blur the differences between the Spanish male and his northern European counterpart, placing the Spanish man within a modernized global (or at least pan-European) context of 'metrosexuality' in which men are aware of their appearance and look after it. Interestingly, the successful *Torremolinos 73* (dir. Pablo Berger, 2003) – discussed in Chapter 7 – recaptures the atmosphere of 1970s Spain and emphasizes the differences between the old-type 'average Spaniard' (ironically played by Javier Cámara, fresh from his role as sensitive 'new man' in Almodóvar's *Hable con ella/Talk to Her* (2002) and his Northern European counterpart (played by Danish actor Mads Mikkelsen), a contrast that some contemporary audiences have found laughable (such a reaction, if anything, illustrates our point).

It has been widely suggested in Spanish cultural studies (the edited volumes by Graham and Labanyi 1995; Kinder 1997; Jordan and Morgan-Tamosunas

1. Returning the gaze: Victoria Abril and Jorge Sanz in *Amantes*.

2000 and Labanyi 2002 being perhaps the most comprehensive and representative works) that Spanish society has radically revised its identity in the last three decades, following the end of the dictatorship. One important aspect that has transformed the 'Spanish stereotype' is its double re-positioning, on the one hand within Europe since entering the Union in 1986 and, on the other domestically with the instigation of the new *autonomías* (devolved administrative territories with Spain) that came with the democracy. José Luis Sangrador García, one of the key sociologists in the study of Spanish stereotypes, corroborates this: 'Spanish identity can be questioned at two levels: from within by some of the autonomous regions and from outside by the European Community' (1996: 20). One of the most commercially successful films of the 1990s, *Airbag* (dir. Bajo Ulloa, 1997) – with over two million spectators and with a box-office take of over seven million Euros – exemplified this, mixing actors and cultural references of several parts of Spain (including the historic regions of Galicia and the Basque Country) and Portugal. The use of regional stereotypes was defended by the director during the promotion:

> Any 8-year-old [Spanish] kid knows that a guy from Oklahoma wears a hat and takes care of cows and that it is cold in Boston. But they [Americans] don't know anything at all about us, they don't know the difference between a Galician and a Portuguese, they don't know that the Basque exist, that we are trustworthy people, very stubborn and party animals. (Triviño 1997: 8)[4]

As Sangrador García notes, stereotypes are, 'not only a reflection of reality, they help to create it' (1996: 96), and the mass media are one of the most effective ways of spreading them (see Mazzara 1999: 65). Mazzara explains how, apart from socio-historical reasons that have contributed to the formation of stereotypes (some artificially created for various interests, others with a 'kernel of truth'), we have a cognitive necessity to simplify reality and recognize 'others', as well as an anxiety of belonging to a group that shares some of our characteristics, even if these are the product of generalizations (1999: 93). In her analysis of the Andalusian stereotype in the cinema of the dictatorship, Jo Labanyi usefully applies Bhabha's (1994) study on stereotype and the colonialist discourse to explain how the gypsies exploited their own stereotype – first with the Spanish bourgeoisie then with the tourists – because it was in their interest, adding that 'the colonized subject can subvert the stereotype projected over it by imitating it to the point of excess, in a parodic way, in a type of transvestism that demonstrates its falsehood' (Labanyi 2004b: 10).

The films chosen as case studies for this chapter are iconic in their portrayal of stereotypical Spanishness. Special attention will be given to *Jamón, Jamón* (1992), the most well-known film of Bigas Luna's trilogy 'Iberian portraits', and arguably a major filmic representation of Spanish masculinity abroad.[5] As the title of the trilogy suggests, it engages in a self-confessed conscious effort to scrutinize 'Spanishness' from the perspective of a foreigner and to explore it with the earnestness of an 'outsider'. Aware of the blind familiarity with one's own culture, Bigas Luna famously declared that his fascination with everything Spanish was inspired by an English friend who was visiting the country and was shocked by the sight of 'animals' legs hanging from the ceiling of most bars' (Pisano 2001: 181–182). The emphasis placed on the male star of the first two films of the trilogy (Javier Bardem) also invites a careful study of the use of the actor's body as a site where issues of national identity can be contested. The films could be regarded as a cultural effort to exaggerate the *macho ibérico* stereotype and thus demonstrate its falsehood (in line with Bhabha's argument). The anti-hero of *Huevos de oro/Golden Balls* (dir. Bigas Luna, 1993) falls prey to the fantasies and overconfidence that characterizes the *macho* stereotype, at least on the surface, and his personality and dress-sense (if not his physique) draw on the tradition of those 'average' Spaniards of earlier times. Arguably, the politically incorrect and financially hugely successful *Torrente* saga (already a three-part phenomenon) that we will analyse later in this chapter also draws on this tradition, although it takes the stereotype further with its bald, overweight, grubby and reckless anti-hero played by the media personality Santiago Segura. The *Torrente* saga banks on the type of scatological humour and the commercial appeal of graphic and gratuitous violence that made *Airbag* or *El día de la bestia/The Day of the Beast* (dir. de la Iglesia, 1995 – starring Segura) box-office successes and that has continued to be exploited in films such as *Una de zombis/Zombie Adventure* (dir. Lamata, 2003) or *Isi & Disi: Amor a lo bestia/Isi & Disi: Beastly Love* (dir. de la Peña, 2004) and *Isi & Disi: Alto voltaje/Isi & Disi: High Voltage* (dir. Lamata, 2006), all starring Segura.[6] The excessive representation of the body, and of the male body in particular, in these films manifests a growing anxiety about the body beautiful and those Europeanized, beauty-conscious and pristine types that abound in recent Spanish cinema. Arguably, these films use irony and black humour to reclaim older and alternative prototypes of Spanish masculinity in what Jordan has called 'a conservative moral backlash' and a return to the *cutre* aesthetic of the 1980s with a certain anti-feminist and misogynistic tendency that has its roots in Buñuel.[7] The bodies analysed in this chapter provide a bridging reference to the past and an appropriate contextualization for some of the more 'modern' types studied in the chapters that follow. Icons of Spanishness including typical Spanish food such as paella, tortilla or *jamón*, the tourist industry, the Spanish flag or the national *fiesta* of bullfighting (seen by reformist thinkers such as Joaquín Costa as a key obstacle for the modernization and Europeanization of Spain – see Shubert 1999: 2–4) feature prominently in their visual narratives and are part of the exaltation of bodily pleasures such as food and sex that characterizes these films. Of all these symbols, it is the concept of the *macho ibérico* that most strongly stands out and that is common to both trilogies. An article published in the Spanish national daily *El País* in the days prior to the legalization of gay marriage in Spain offered a sarcastic but perhaps accurate explanation of the opposition that the law encountered amongst the most conservative (and nationalist) sectors of society: 'people will forgive ZP [the Spanish PM José Luis Rodríguez Zapatero] many things (…) but not to have put the *macho ibérico*'s reputation into question' (Martínez 2005: 15), adding that it was one of very few 'myths' left to Spanish identity – fittingly the article ends with a inappropriate line from the film *Torrente* which is too crude to cite here.

PORTRAIT OF AN IBERIAN *MACHO* OF THE 1990s

The iconic status achieved by the stereotypical representation of Spanish masculinity made in Bigas Luna's 'Iberian trilogy' owes as much to the director and scriptwriters as it does to the actor who played the central male roles of the first two films. As Perriam notes, Javier Bardem (born 1969) has become a key figure in recent discussions of the *macho ibérico* (2003: 93). Today one of the most representative and well-respected actors in Spain, he is also one of the most international (in 2001 he was nominated for a Golden Globe and an Academy Award for his first English-language role in Schnabel's *Before Night Falls* (2000)).[8] His first role, in Bigas Luna's *Las Edades de Lulú/Ages of Lulu* (1990), was as a male prostitute and the spectacular display of his naked muscular body in a scene of S&M was an important highlight of the film's visual narrative. Such spectacular emphasis on the male body seemed remarkable in a film that, as Ballesteros has argued, largely neglects the female voyeuristic pleasure and control of the narrative that the protagonist Lulú enjoyed in the original novel by Almudena Grandes (Ballesteros 2001: 194).

The sexualization of Bardem's body in that early appearance initiated a career that in its early stages was arguably built upon a visible corporality and *macho* attitude paraded in his next two roles with Bigas Luna but which, since then, has been proactively re-written with roles such as those discussed in Chapters 4 and 5 of this book. Despite acknowledging the crucial importance that the Bigas Luna films had had for his career in the early 1990s, half-way through that decade Bardem was openly trying to resist his typecasting as a 'cocky macho' (Rigalt 1997: 19). Aware of the importance of his appearance for his acting, he has admitted that his broken nose (due to the practice of boxing in his early days) was a key factor for Bigas Luna when choosing him for *Las Edades de Lulú* (Castellano and Elola 1997: 40) and that, beyond his strong performance in *Jamón*, it is his nose and rugged looks that are partly to blame for his typecasting as a 'hard male' (Rigalt 1997: 19). Yet, in the early part of his career at least, Bardem the actor actively encouraged the perceived attention to his well-developed physique. Happy to pose semi-naked for many photo sessions at the time, he has admitted that his first press conference (for *Lulú*) was a frustrating experience 'because nobody took pictures of me' (Rigalt 1997: 20). In the booklet that accompanied an early video edition of *Jamón, Jamón* Maruja Torres introduced Bardem as a 'young *macho*', adding that, in him, Bigas Luna 'saw the expressive force of his virility and the "deep Spain" that it represents' (1992: 28). Another piece in the same booklet stressed the centrality of his body to this film, saying that the actor 'filled with his physique a character written specially for him' (26).

Bardem has often spoken publicly about being famous for his screen nudes: of his role in *Jamón, Jamón* he says, 'I wonder why people keep talking about Penélope Cruz's breasts. I guess that it is at least as important that I am naked in it, isn't it?' (Mericka Etxebarría 1994: 4); of his role in *Perdita Durango/Dance with the Devil* (a film that originally was going to be directed by Bigas Luna but was finally directed by Álex de la Iglesia in 1997) he says, 'I was prepared to undress a lot more, but with the Americans (…) I ended up very frustrated' (Castellano and Elola 1997: 40). In an interview promoting *Perdita Durango* (another very 'physical' role) published in the Sunday magazine of the Spanish daily *El Mundo* (Rigalt 1997), the accompanying pictures of the actor wearing his half-opened bathrobe by the swimming-pool seemed to reinforce this point. The use of the bathrobe also invites a glance of his half-hidden naked body underneath and it also implies a level of domesticity whilst also suggesting post-coital relaxation (Bingham (1993: 172–173) makes this point when reading a similar picture of Warren Beatty). In the magazine, Bardem's 'powerful and potent body' is not only reflected in the pictures – the title page and the main text also insist on this. The interview is introduced by the (female) journalist with a detailed description of the actor's body and strong presence, describing his legs as 'two cement columns, two firm and Herculian towers' adding that 'each of them is about as large as two average ones put together: Javier Bardem has four legs (...) they emerge from the floor and feed the hardness of his masculine power' (Rigalt 1997: 16). Similarly, the journalists (one male, one female) who interviewed him two months later for *El País* also describe at length Bardem's sporty appearance and his unshaven face (Castellano and Elola 1997: 38). Ironically, for an actor that at one time was regarded as the epitome of male chauvinism, Bardem regards himself as more of a feminist, thinks that machismo is absurd and values greatly the influence that his mother (Oltra 1993: 99) and the family's gay friends have had on him (Rivera 1994: 5). Yet Bardem's entry in a short dictionary of new Spanish cinema focuses on his photogenic face and his 'electric' look (Fernández Santos 1998: 37), an aspect which, with hindsight, more recent studies emphasize (see, for instance, Perriam 2003: 93 or Evans 2004: 77) but which was already recognized in the interviews earlier mentioned. As Castellano and Elola put it, 'behind this big man with a hard look there is a delicate man hiding, with a certain defenseless look and a special sensitivity' (1997: 38). As we shall see, this perceived contrast between his 'sweet' look and his hard body is arguably one of the keys not only for a change of the perception of his public persona later on in his career but also to the complexity of his early roles (see Perriam (2003: 93–119) for a detailed study of Bardem's career throughout the 1990s).

One of the defining features of Bigas Luna's 'Iberian trilogy' is the representation of masculinity as excessive and in tune with the traditional traits of physicality, competitiveness and aggression. In *Jamón, Jamón* (1992) and *Huevos de oro/Golden Balls* (1993) (referred to as *Jamón* and *Huevos* hereafter), the characters played by Bardem are defined in clear physical opposition to his various rivals. In the first of these films, recently described as 'a gift for those who want to deconstruct notions of both gender and national identity, because it presents prototype characters, situations and cultural icons in an overblown form' (Jordan and Allinson 2005: 169), Raúl (Bardem) is pitted against José Luis (Jordi Mollà), and in *Huevos*, Bardem's Benito is contrasted at various stages of the film with men of other nationalities: a Moroccan – actually played by an Italian actor – (Figure 2), a North American and a Cuban in symbolic parallelisms with the film's spatial narrative that travels from Melilla (a Spanish enclave in the North of Africa) to Benidorm (tourist location in South West Spain popular with Anglo-American and German 'package' holidaymakers) and finally to Miami (perhaps the most markedly Hispanic location in the USA). As D'Lugo (1995) notes, the two male protagonists of *Jamón* embody the opposition between the old (Raúl) and the new (José Luis) Spain: whilst the former is initially associated with typically Spanish symbols (the ham leg – in a dream sequence he is seen hanging like a ham – and bullfighting) the latter is linked to materialist imagery, often non-Spanish, globalizing symbols of capitalism, such as the Coke ring that he gives to Silvia (Penélope Cruz) to mark their engagement or his mother's broken pearl necklace.[9] Such

2. National bodies:
Alessandro Gasmann and
Javier Bardem in *Huevos
de oro*.

opposition is thus literally embodied by the two male protagonists of the film in the way they dress, move or relate to their bodies. Notably, as Evans observes (2004: 72), José Luis spends large parts of the narrative within enclosed spaces (his car or the (over)protective environment of his parental home and family business) whilst Raúl spends most of his screen time outdoors, practising bullfighting, riding his new motorbike or, even when at work, sitting outside his ham factory – aptly named 'Los Conquistadores', further establishing the character's status as a symbol of national identity and perhaps nostalgia for the old Empire. Equally, the emphasis that the camera places on José Luis's clothing and well-groomed appearance is replaced in the case of Raúl by a focus on his body, often semi-naked and sometimes naked. Perhaps the most character-defining feature of Raúl is his independence and (apparent) control of his surroundings.[10] His familiarity with and control of the outdoors, coupled with the representation of his sexuality as overt and domineering, are factors that insist on the symbolic representation of this stereotypical '*macho*' as somewhat animal-like. This aspect is emphasized visually through the various matching shots established between him and two animals closely related to Spanish culture and gastronomy, the bull and the pig. As Barry Jordan and Rikki Morgan-Tamosunas have put it, Raúl represents, 'the clichéd, excessive embodiment of (heterosexual) male "Spanishness", asserting this identity by eating garlic, gulping wine, belching, riding motorbikes, engaging in naked bullfighting and famed for having inordinate amounts of sex' (1994: 61).

The rivalry between the two male leads is also built spatially with a number of establishing shots that sustain the visual association of Raúl with the arid and open land of Los Monegros (in North-Eastern Spain), and of José Luis with the sheltered and more artificial setting of the family home, defined by external symbols of purchasing power. The oft-commented opening sequence of the film (by, amongst others, D'Lugo 1995: 75; Deleyto 1999: 273; Evans 2004: 40 and Jordan and Allinson 2005: 168), in which Raúl rehearses a bullfight with a friend (who pushes a cart posing as a bull) establishes this association between Raúl and the Spanish land. A travelling shot across the dry land is followed by an extreme long shot that further emphasizes the framing of Raúl in these hostile surroundings. This integration of man and nature is achieved by first blurring the separation from the land of the human figures seen in the distance, and then combining long shots of the characters surrounded by the immediate landscape with cross-cutting close-up and extreme close-up shots of patches of land and parts of Raúl's body (notably his crotch and erection – almost refusing to hide under his bursting shorts). The focus on the land (which shares agency in the film with the bull silhouette) and the body in the opening scene draws attention to their interdependence. By contrast, in one of the scenes that most visually defines the character of José Luis, the focus is on the confined space of his stuffed bedroom: the camera travels on a medium shot barely focusing on all his possessions (drums, computer, hi-fi, light dumbbells) only to eventually pause by his bed, where his mother is undressing him, visually and verbally recalling images of his safe and sheltered childhood (the notable presence and interference of his family contrasts with the lack of information provided about Raúl's background, which stresses the latter character's self-sufficiency). The physical opposition between the two men is also clearly stressed in those scenes: the apparently naturally achieved hard body of Raúl (presumably the result of a physical demanding job) is compared to the lighter build of José Luis who, it is suggested, builds his body with the help of the remarkably light dumbbells that can be seen in the background.

Amongst masculine symbols of traditional Spanishness associated with Raúl (garlic, ham), the so-called Osborne bull is, without a doubt, the predominant one. This giant bull-shaped billboard used to serve as an advert for a well-known Spanish brandy (produced by the classic Osborne wineries – founded in 1772) is closely associated to Iberian masculinity through its most famous slogan: 'Soberano: it's a man's thing'. The bull itself as an animal is intrinsically related to Spanish culture and economy through the 'fiesta nacional' and later reinvented during Francoist times as a commercial icon for the brandy and also the jeans brand Lois.[11] Dozens of the 'Osborne' billboards (over 12 meters tall and 150 square meters in surface area), designed by Manolo Prieto in 1956, were dotted throughout the Spanish landscape during the 1960s and 1970s (Navarro 1999: 12) and were nearly withdrawn with the introduction of traffic laws that banned advertising outside urban spaces during the late 1980s and early 1990s, to considerable controversy. On one side were competitor companies that argued that even the blank billboards were unconsciously associated with the brand, supported by those Spaniards who wished to disassociate bullfighting from Spanish identity; on the other, those like Bigas Luna who claimed that the silhouette had not only become an integral part of the Spanish landscape but also of contemporary national culture and identity and a symbol of pride and incalculable value for future generations of Spaniards.[12] These words were echoed in the final legal ruling which resolved that the bull silhouette had transcended its original commercial connotations to become an integral part of Spain's cultural landscape.[13] The cultural association of the bull with 'old' Spain is so well established that *The New York Times* used it on the front cover of the issue that announced the death of Franco in 1975. It seems therefore justified to interpret Bigas Luna's visual investment in this icon as an homage to its autochthonous cultural historical value and perhaps even a celebration of those intrinsically 'vintage Spanish' characteristics that the film ambiguously presents.

At a more general level, bullfighting itself is generally recognized as a symbol of a particularly Iberian masculinity. Adrian Shubert describes how those in favour of bullfighting have historically defended it as an 'eminently masculine spectacle that contributed to the virility of the nation' (1999: 92), a feeling that was especially acute after what was perceived as a 'feminization' of the country following the military defeat in the Spanish-American War of 1898. As he notes, those against bullfighting were often accused of attempting to feminize Spain (1999: 94) and at the turn of the century it was not uncommon to find statements such as this in bullfighting magazines: 'we believe that it is even humanitarian to support those spectacles that tend to maintain the innate energies of a virile nation, such as Spain has always been' (Editorial from *El Toreo Chico* quoted in Shubert 1999: 93). Some anthropologists have seen the *corrida* as 'an embodiment of Spanish gender relations' in which the bull would symbolize the fate of women under the Honour Code, or even as symbolic rape (Shubert 1999: 4). In a graphic account of the sexuality inherent in the bullfighting ritual, Mexican writer Carlos Fuentes writes:

> The effrontery of the suit of lights, its tight-hugging breeches, the flaunting of the male sexual organ, the importance given to the buttocks, the obviously seductive and self-appraising stride, the lust for blood and sensation – the bullfighting authorizes this incredible arrogance and sexual exhibitionism. (quoted in Stavans 1998: 230)

This phallic metaphor of bullfighting has been exploited in many artistic forms and, in film, famously by Almodóvar in his classic *Matador* (1986), also recognized as a problematic dramatisation of the Spanish national *fiesta* – see Chapter 8. However, it is important to note that, despite all its implications of physical strength and sexual potency, the bull is also a symbol of vulnerability: the spectacle consists of its gradual weakening through deadly penetrations into its body and both the bull and the bullfighter are also exposed to the castrating, blood-hungry gaze of the audience. In *Jamón*, Raúl's portrayal is equally ambiguous, and he appears to be powerful (in so far as his body and sexual potency allow him to seduce various female characters and, through them, to traverse class boundaries),[14] but his body is also used, manipulated, objectified and hated by others at different points in the narrative (notably Conchita and José Luis) and, as Evans argues, the final fight between the two antagonists recalls the setting of a *corrida* (2004: 43).

Raúl's objectification is emphasized visually through shots of his body parts. The first instance of this ambivalence is offered in the opening scenes, where close-ups of his genitals, legs and arms overwhelm the less abundant long shots of his whole body. In the scene that follows, at an underwear factory, further close-up shots of Raúl's genitals (this time wearing tight underpants) are used in a casting session for an underwear ad campaign, which is being filmed on video. Interestingly, the video camera films his 'package' first, then his face, whilst his voice is heard (mostly off-camera) saying his name and what he does for a living. Although the cross-cutting of close-up shots of Raúl's (and the other candidates') crotch and shots of the face humanizes the genital shots and validate the men's phallic power (as Aguilar argues – 1998: 125–126), these shots also dissect their bodies, negating their wholeness and puts them in an equal position to the more usually fragmented female bodies (as indeed Aguilar also admits – 1998: 127).[15] He is chosen for the campaign and photos of his package are posted on dozens of billboards which underline the metonym (Raúl's photo and the Osborne silhouette) and further problematize the gender ambivalence suggested above. Like the bull, the picture of Raúl's genitals will become just another cultural motif and a modern icon of the new, commercialized Spain in what has been described as the Spanish equivalent of Warhol's Campbell's soup can (D'Lugo 1995: 74). Thus, the bodies of the Osborne bull and Raúl are objectified for consumption in a materialistic culture where photogenic and easily reproducible images make money. In his study of men's underwear advertising in the twentieth century, Paul Jobling argues that underwear could be regarded 'both as a way of concealing the phallic power of the male subject, and as a form of protection from his own (potential) unveiling and castration' (2003: 153). Raúl is apparently aware and in control of his own objectification.

If we consider nudity as 'an affirmation of the body as a subject in its own right' (Clark 1960: 3) the display of Bardem's body during the casting and throughout the film could be regarded as not simply the response to a purely economic need but as more of a narcissistic exercise – and indeed he will later use the impressively dimensioned poster as a way to demonstrate his worthiness to Silvia. However, in the two naked scenes, the *macho's* genitals are obscured: in the first instance (clandestine bullfight at nighttime), and despite the arguably beauty-enhancing and romanticizing value of the moonlight, the body is blurred by darkness and distance, whilst the genitals are covered by the cape most of the time. Later, during the unexpected visit to Silvia's house that follows, Raúl's genitals are covered again, first with his hands (see Figure 3) and then by markedly phallic imagery (the pointy legs of the stool that he holds horizontally to cover his bare genitals), which serve as a reminder of the penetrative potential of this body. This reminder was perhaps necessary after the previous scene offered more than just a glimpse of his backside, by far the most vulnerable part of the male body both because it reveals its more prominent fissure (hence it is often strategically hidden in filmic male nudes) and also due to its symbolic association with non-phallic bodily functions.[16]

Dyer's study of the male pin-up (1992) explained how the covering of the male body through lighting, phallic imagery or the emphasis on activity and action (in this case bullfighting, riding bikes, handling hams) could reveal a certain awareness and concern with sexual objectification and castration. As noted earlier, the bull itself is a vulnerable being, and, as Strick points out, even the bull silhouette is 'at risk from every

3. Vulnerable: Javier Bardem and Tomás Penco in *Jamón, Jamón*.

strong breeze' on the top of the hillside (1993: 58). In fact, the all-important genitals are clearly cracked at the beginning of the film, revealing its diminished stature as a blank icon of global consumerism.[17] In the end, Raúl's 'Iberian' body (like the bull's) is forcefully re-inscribed into an economic global context. In the final scene, he pulls out the Mercedes logo from his coveted car and rests it against his abdomen, suggesting that the body itself is used as a site of resistance against such re-inscription (as shown in Figure 4).

For Evans, Raúl's reaction in the final sequence of *Jamón* (he does not approach his girlfriend Silvia but his victim's mother) reveals that 'the child triumphs over the man in Raúl's subjectivity and makes us see in flashback all the signs of his immaturity which were hidden behind a mask of manliness' (2004: 82). Such observations are consistent with Bardem's version of the *macho ibérico* in the next film of the trilogy. In *Huevos*, we are constantly reminded of Benito's (Bardem) manhood with a plethora of phallic symbols, only to see them dramatically collapse one by one (notably the inescapably phallic tower, the construction of which had come to represent Benito's upmost ambition). With all its emphasis on images of erections and phalluses, it is the images of collapse and impotence, including the anti-climatic sex scenes involving Benito, which have a longer-lasting effect. Benito's body is mutilated (visually by the camera and physically as a result of an accident) and in the last scene he is shown crying and distraught (see Fouz-Hernández 1999). The

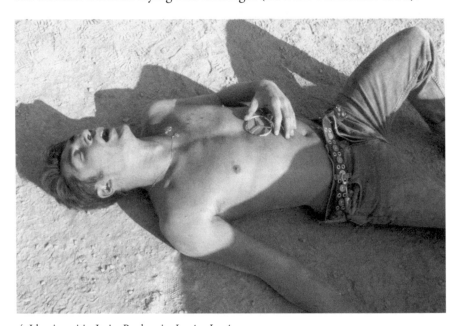

4. Identity crisis: Javier Bardem in *Jamón, Jamón*.

final scenes of both *Jamón* and *Huevos* could thus be interpreted as a nostalgic farewell to the *macho ibérico*, a figure unable to survive in a newly globalized and at the same time de-centralized Spain. And yet, only a few years later, the average Spaniard would be back with a vengeance.

TORRENTE: THE RETURN OF THE SPANISH HERO[18]

Whereas it would be impossible to comprehensively illustrate the stereotypical cinematic representation of the Spanish male in just a few pages, this chapter must nonetheless deal with what is perhaps the most important meta-filmic event of recent Spanish cinema as well as the most commercially successful, the so-called *Torrente* phenomenon (see Esquirol and Fecé 2001: 28–31 or Lázaro-Reboll 2005: 220–222 for a discussion of *Torrente* as an 'event film'). Nor can we ignore the impact that Santiago Segura's star persona ('possibly the most ubiquitous figure in Spanish popular culture' as Triana-Toribio aptly describes him – 2004: 147) has had on current configurations of Spanish masculinity. As noted by critics, the overwhelming use of local jokes and references as well as the highly politically incorrect humour of the *Torrente* saga make it a product hard to export (see Triana-Toribio 2003: 154 or Jordan 2003b: 196). Yet, as these same critics also acknowledge, at home these films are responsible for reviving Spanish audience's interest in national productions (the genre is remarkably popular with younger generations) and for positioning them in direct competition with big blockbusters, 'a lesson in how to develop a form of national cinema able to compete with dominant American action cinema whilst retaining clear signs of its own local identity' (Jordan 2003b: 205). Indeed, the credit sequences evidence the Hollywood connection with spoofs of the foreign product as if suggesting that *Torrente* is their Spanish more realistic counterpart. In *Torrente, el brazo tonto de la ley/Torrente, the Stupid Arm of the Law* (1998, henceforth referred to as *Torrente 1*) the presentation of the Spanish ex-policeman (expelled from the police force and now working clandestinely as a private detective) has been read as 'the physical and behavioural antithesis' of Dirty Harry, one that replaces the 'tall, "in shape", and healthy, clean, neutrally dressed, macho, expert marksman' American super-cop with 'a flabby, balding, drunken, cowardly grease ball, dressed like a pimp and hopeless with firearms' (Jordan 2003b: 201). The opening credit sequence of *Torrente 2: Misión en Marbella/Torrente 2: Mission Marbella* (2001: *Torrente 2* hereafter) mocks the familiar opening of the Bond series with Torrente playing a 'grotesquely re-shaped (or mis-shaped)' version of James Bond (Lázaro-Reboll 2005: 223), and there is a spoof of the Rocky films in the scenes of physical training in *Torrente 3: El Protector/Torrente 3: The Protector* (2005: *Torrente 3* hereafter), except here, the 'Spanish hero' trains in the *Valle de los Caídos* (Valley of the Fallen) – where Franco is buried – and uses a genuinely national *Serrano* ham instead of an all-American punch bag for kick-boxing. Segura was well aware of the market potential of his creation even before the release of his phenomenally successful directorial debut with *Torrente 1*, claiming that '*El día de la bestia* and *Airbag* have opened the door for *Torrente* to be a success: we are no longer afraid of Spanish cinema' (Calleja 1998: 37). To put things into perspective, according to the official data recorded by the Spanish Ministry of Culture (www.mcu.es) the aforementioned *No desearás al vecino del quinto*, for many years the highest-grossing Spanish film at home, attracted an audience of over four million spectators over the years. The first three installments of *Torrente* put together surpass the 11 million so far, whilst the spectators of the entire trilogy of '*Retratos Ibéricos*' have reached just over one million (*Jamón* had 673,467 spectators).[19] Hence, if we are to accept the thesis discussed at the beginning of this chapter with regards to the power of mass media for the spreading of stereotypes, the *Torrente* films are of crucial importance here. As Esquirol and Fecé (2001: 31–33) argue, the relatively scarce academic attention paid to them in Spain so far is possibly due to a hegemonic discourse still firmly grounded on the 'high' and 'low' culture divide in which *Torrente* and other 'neo-vulgar comedies' (to use Triana-Toribio's term – 2003: 151) would be dismissed as 'only entertainment'. For scholarship oriented to a cultural studies approach, this is a text of unquestionable value and its relevance is doubly justified here given the films' ironic reclamation of older models of markedly Spanish masculinity and stereotypes as well as the importance of the protagonist's body for his characterization. In that sense, the *Torrente* films provide interesting connections with those discussed so far in this chapter and, at a wider level, they are an important part of an effort to build and legitimize 'a Spanish cinema tradition' (Esquirol and Fecé 2001: 38) that has had the backing of the Spanish Academy of Film Arts and Sciences (*Torrente 1* received two Goya awards: one to Segura as the best directorial debut and one to Leblanc for his supporting role). The references to the 1960s Spanish comedy are abundant and the saga also draws on a wider Spanish grotesque cultural tradition that, as Segura proudly claims, goes 'from the Picaresque novel (…) to the Valle-

Inclán *esperpento*' (Muñoz 1998: 36; see also Jordan 2003b: 198 and Rabalska 1999). The representation of gender, the frequent use of sexual innuendos, some of the settings and even the cinematic style are highly reminiscent of the 1960s and 1970s Spanish films described at the beginning of this chapter. One could even see in Landa, as Triana-Toribio has done (2004: 150), the model for Segura's own star persona. The cross-referential casting of Iberian sex-comedy regular Toni Leblanc for all three installments so far (he returned to the screens in 1998 with *Torrente 1* after more than two decades incapacitated due to an accident) and of José Luis López Vázquez and Juanito Navarro for *Torrente 2* also reveals a conscious effort to establish a meta-fictional link with such tradition. The films also share an excessive exaltation of Spanishness with the Bigas Luna films discussed here: the Osborne bull is replaced with badges of the Atleti football club or Spanish flags; where we had Benidorm we now have Marbella, and where we had the music of Julio Iglesias we have El Fary, whilst *tascas* (old-fashioned Spanish bars that serve food and drink) and *puticlubs* (topless bars and brothels) feature prominently in both. The 'Iberian trilogy' and the *Torrente* series also share an arguably 'ironic homage' to the *macho ibérico* (particularly with the character Benito in *Huevos*) although, in its Santiago Segura impersonation, the physical effect is rather different. As mentioned at the beginning of this chapter, and as argued by Triana-Toribio, the popularity of the overweight and unattractive character played by Segura 'seems to indicate the appeal of (…) the refusal to the media's imposition of the beautiful, clean and healthy body which other Spanish stars display' (2004: 152) as well as 'the resilience of a representation of masculinity and virility that some hoped would be put to rest (…) by means of the Socialist legislation on cinema popularly known as the *Ley Miró*' (152).[20] For Triana-Toribio, Segura's success 'indicates that this version of masculinity is alive and well, and accepted by Spanish audiences, perhaps because it is more familiar and believable than the "good-looking" masculinity of the *guapos* like Javier Bardem' (2004: 155). Interestingly, Bardem himself appears in *Torrente 1* with a cameo role as a rough man with what we might euphemistically term 'learning difficulties', a scarred face and a damaged eye; a far cry from his sexually appealing appearance in *Jamón*.[21] The physical contrast between Bardem and Segura is further developed by Triana-Toribio in a passage about the excessive representation of the body in *Torrente* that is worth quoting at some length given its usefulness here:

> This excess is best illustrated in comedy through the body of Segura, which is
> the exaggerated obverse of the traditional galán or male lead of Spanish cinema.

> If we look at the actors that have recently represented Spanishness and maleness for foreign and local audiences, we find that the most common type is that of the photogenic lead exemplified by Antonio Banderas, or Javier Bardem. In contrast with the bodies of these male actors, Segura's body is, by traditional standards of male beauty, unappealing, unglamorous and famously short (…) In the Torrente incarnation, the Segura body is smelly, unhygienic, fat, and with a fast-receding hairline (…) If Bardem made his own the role of the 'macho ibérico' in Bigas Luna's *Jamón, jamón* (…) then Segura's characters present the off-putting obverse 'would-be macho ibérico', who in the Torrente incarnation behaves as though his body is that of a Javier Bardem, even though this is real only to him. (2004: 150)

Segura has carved himself a reputation as someone acutely aware of his unconventional physique in a long series of appearances on Spanish television before, during and after the *Torrente* releases, to the point that it is rare not to hear or read some self-depreciating remarks about his body in his many interviews, especially those that relate to his characterization as the grotesque detective. By now most people know that for the *Torrente* roles he puts on up to 40 kilos, Robert de Niro style ('only' 20 in *Torrente 3* – see Figure 5), and reaching 110 kilograms for the first installment of the series. During the promotion of *Torrente 1*, he confessed to a journalist: 'It is not that I had to gain weight for the role, I have a tendency to do so (…) but it was the perfect pretext [and] I have lost 15 kilos since filming wrapped up' and added: 'all this obesity was great for the characterization [of Torrente] but it is no good when you go out on the pull' (Salgueiro 1998: 50). Famously, in the run-up to the release of *Torrente 2*, the actor accepted – and won – a public challenge in the now defunct but then sensationally popular late-night show of Tele 5 *Crónicas Marcianas* (in which he had been a regular) to lose 20 kilos before the film's première. The audience could witness his progress with regular Weight-Watchers-style public weigh-ins. Had he lost the challenge, he would have had his characteristic long hair (balding on top) and beard shaved by the show's host. For Segura, this would have been a great loss: his hair was the only part of his body that he refused to alter for the role, hiding it instead underneath a toupee: 'If you have a character like Mickey Mouse you don't cut off the ears (…). I wanted to do the promotion as Santiago Segura, so I simply could not have had my hair cut' (Nieto 1998: 4).

It is no surprise in this context that the abject body and the representation of Spanishness (both of crucial relevance to this chapter) are the two aspects that have attracted more critical attention. The films' treatment of national identity created considerable controversy: as Esquirol and Fecé note, some reviewers saw in the films' nostalgic 'appropriation of the *españolada*' a conscious revalorization of the Francoist values embodied by the older films (2001: 28).[22] Such a clear-cut judgement of the films' highly ambiguous politics could be based on a literal interpretation of some of the lines made newly famous by the films and which were reminiscent of the old regime (such as Torrente's supposed 'last words' in the first film: 'there is one thing more important than being a policeman: being Spanish', which are also reiterated in parts 2 and 3).[23] Esquirol and Fecé have argued that, even if we are to read in the films' ironic register an attempt of disassociation from older political agendas, we should also consider how these texts have contributed to the celebration of a particular kind of 'Spanishness' which, in their view, had been circulating 'in certain cultural and political sectors of Spanish society since 1996' – clearly referring to the start of the eight-year Aznar conservative government (2001: 37). Aware of this, Segura was quick to distance himself and his work from politics as well as from the kinds of reprehensible ideologies embodied in the Torrente figure's world view. Thus, in the promotional interviews of *Torrente 1*, Segura emphasized the fact that the film was not meant to promote nationalist ideas, nor to condone racist or male chauvinistic attitudes: 'I hope people realize that I am not making fun of ethnic difference, rather I am laughing at racists' (Nieto 1998: 4). According to its creator, we

5. Spanish hero? Santiago Segura in *Torrente 3: El Protector*.

should see Torrente as a 'freak', a character 'to laugh at', 'the classic *macho* that you can find at billiard halls' because 'if a human being such as this exists, the only point of making a film about him is to portray him as a monster (...) for me Torrente is like Frankenstein' (Nieto 1998: 4). He even coined the term '*freakler*' to define the genre: 'a mix between freak and thriller' (1998: 4) and argued that the film was meant as 'a sort of exorcism of Spanishness (...) so that we can have a good laugh [at ourselves]' (Muñoz 1998: 36). However, he also took every opportunity to warn the public that 'Torrente represents that part of us all because of the country we have had to live in' (1998: 36). The saga playfully and provocatively uses a Francoist concept of nationalism, pushing all the buttons of Spain's sense of national identity by offering a politically incorrect take on the 'big' ongoing political debates around this subject, such as immigration and nationalisms within Spain. *Torrente 3*, released in the midst of a heated political debate about the Catalan *estatut* (finally approved in a referendum in 2006), acts out what can only be described as the worst nightmare of any old-fashioned 'Spanish hero': in one (bad) dream scene Torrente wakes up surrounded by Barcelona Football Club memorabilia and is horrified to find himself thinking and speaking in Catalan.

With regard to the films' body politics, Jordan convincingly reads the saga in the context of Bakhtin's grotesque, highlighting what he sees as their 'celebration of the lower body in its most basic forms' and 'the depths of de-sublimation and degradation of the body, captured graphically through the language and behaviour of *Torrente*'s monstrous, lower-order stereotypes' (2003b: 193–194). The films' overwhelming commitment to a certain abject logic of physicality can be seen in a short scene where Torrente's neighbour (played by Almodóvar regular Chus Lampreave) compares the burden of her children with having 'hemorrhoids, diarrhoea or bunions'. There are many episodes of graphic violence such as the torture scene in which a Chinese man has one of his ears cut off and his knee punctured with a corkscrew in *Torrente 1* (clearly indebted to Tarantino's *Reservoir Dogs* (1992) or Lynch's *Blue Velvet* (1986)) or where, in the same film Torrente feeds his handicapped elderly father (played by Leblanc) a cold soup made by mixing in a food-processor the leftovers gathered from his local bar including various animal bones and even cigarette butts.[24] Equally unpleasant is the vision of the character making himself presentable for his first date with his voluptuous and nymphomaniac young neighbour Amparito (Neus Asensi). This involves squeezing a spot (the contents of which land on the mirror) and fixing his toupée, which is kept on a dirty bathroom cabinet full of cockroaches (this image is compounded by his farting and his filthy fingernails). Importantly, despite his unattractiveness and very much like the 'average Spaniard' of the Iberian sexy comedy, Torrente still manages to seduce Amparito in an elaborate fantasy scene that plays out using a combination of provocatively sexist and nationalistic imagery: in Torrente's imagination she performs a striptease for him and reveals that her knickers have a Spanish flag imprinted in the crucial place and her nipples are covered by Atleti football club crests.[25] Despite the expectation created by such a scene, Torrente comically ruins the erotic potential of the quick sexual encounter that follows by ejaculating prematurely, leaving her frustrated but boasting that for him this was 'one of [the] best "free" shags ever', in another manifestation of his/the film's retrograde sexual politics, which unashamedly disregard women's needs, treating them, in Torrente's words, as 'bitches, livestock'.[26]

The way in which Torrente relates physically to his male 'work' partners is also interesting. The sort of physical comparison established between the Bardem characters and their antagonists in the Bigas Luna films is here established between the detective and the young males that, in line with the Quixote/Sancho classic relationship, decide to assist him in his 'altruistic' adventures and become his pupils. The overt homoerotic element that can be found in the working relationships between policemen and civil guards on patrol – at least in the homosexual imaginary – is played out rather explicitly in all the instalments of this saga and in ways that recall frustration and immaturity that are not dissimilar from those seen in the youth-themed films that will be discussed in the next chapter. Torrente's casual invitations to his partners to mutually masturbate while on duty are reluctantly accepted, but then truncated at the key moment by an unexpected event in the main action narrative. In *Torrente 1* they are caught by one of the criminals, in *Torrente 2* a sudden gunshot prevents Cuco (Gabino Diego) from performing fellatio on the detective and in *Torrente 3* the detective and his assistant Solís (Javier Gutiérrez) are interrupted by a barman (Cañita Brava) demanding that Torrente pays off his large debt of whisky drinks. The buddies are also seen together in various sexual scenarios. *Torrente 1* and *3* enact the classic rite of passage setting in which a younger man is taken to a brothel by an adult 'guardian' so that he 'becomes a man'. In *Torrente 3* a flashback reveals a young Torrente (Carlos Latre) scared by the prospect of sleeping with a woman but actually discovering sexuality with one of the male clients in the toilet instead. Retrospectively, a similar scene in *Torrente 1* can be interpreted as a repetition of the same pattern, with the detective now in the adult role and his assistant and neighbour Rafi (Javier Cámara) as the inexperienced protégé whose first encounter with a prostitute is never consummated. The homoerotic overtone is more explicit in *Torrente 2*, where the detective and his assistant accidentally find themselves in a gay sauna (where, it is suggested, Cuco perhaps naively accepts an old gay man's sexual advances).

Also interesting are the observations that these characters make about each other's bodies. In *Torrente 1* the detective seems shocked by the sight of Rafi's large penis in a public urinary. Such revelation becomes symbolic of the surprise also caused by the other discovery that, behind a façade of extreme physical awkwardness, and deficient eye-sight meant to suggest a certain mental ineffectualness, Rafi hides excellent reflexes, pays attention to detail and is a crack shot. In this phallic economy, the apprentice's mental superiority over his mentor is explained in terms of his large penis. *Torrente 3* offers further evidence that this 'Spanish *macho*' is a precocious ejaculator who will use a Viagra pill to attempt to seduce the film's heroine (an Italian MEP played by Yvonne Sciò whom he had been hired to 'protect' during her visit to Spain). In *Torrente 2* Cuco, understandably taken aback by the sight of Torrente in a G-string, tells him: 'Sir, I had not realized that you have tits.' In a humorous but typically overconfident manner that reveals his lack of self-awareness Torrente replies angrily: 'These are called pectorals.' The same visual joke is taken a step further in the opening of *Torrente 3*: a dialogue between two characters at the start of the film suggests that Torrente has lost a lot of weight and is now extremely fit due to an intensive exercise regime. The next scene reveals that he is as fat as ever: the sight of the overweight sweaty man skipping vigorously and topless but still wearing a golden chain around his neck is unforgettable and revealing of the saga's anxieties about the inadequacy of the so-called Spanish hero's male body. In his usual and pathetically overconfident manner, Torrente declares 'I have always been an athlete: check out these pectorals' (...) 'I have transformed my body into a combat machine.' Yet, the real human combat machine of the film is a Northern European-looking body-builder hired by the villains. The appropriately named Coloso ('Colossus', played by former gay porn star Martin Czehmester) is Torrente's physical antagonist: blond, blue-eyed and remarkably tall and muscular. Torrente, in awe of him, describes him as 'Swedish-looking' and 'huge', 'like four men put together'. The film's villain Montellini (Fabio Testi) – the head of a non-ecological oil company that the female MEP wants closed – is also foreign: an older but fabulously turned out Italian man whose lifestyle would be Torrente's dream (he regularly receives sexual favours from his – mostly willing – female staff and various other exuberant ladies). The film's playful re-creation of those transnational narratives of the *destape* films described at the start of this chapter is clearly staged: even though, unsurprisingly, the Italian MEP fails to fall for Torrente, her female assistant (also Italian) falls for Torrente's own assistant Solís (an unlikely *macho ibérico*, named after a well-known 'Spanish' tomato sauce brand, who has a markedly Galician accent). Significantly, when Solís tries to arrest Coloso, he points a gun at his head and announces that he is now under the custody of the special forces of the (Spanish) state. The word used for 'forces of the state' in Spanish is '*el cuerpo del estado*' (literally 'the body of the state'). Coloso leaves little doubt about his opinion of the Spanish '*cuerpo*': with incredible precision he catches Solís's gun and sends him flying across the room with a series of spectacular punches, hits and swings.

As in the Bigas Luna 'Iberian trilogy', the *Torrente* saga's phallic imagery is profuse and hyperbolic, often related to guns and oversized weaponry such as the all-important missile of *Torrente 2* that a band of criminals wanted to use to destroy Marbella[27] but that Torrente manages to re-direct to Gibraltar, a feat that gets him readmitted into the police force at the end of the film. Given the ongoing dispute between Great Britain and Spain about the sovereignty of the rock, this is clearly another sarcastic twist on the films' nationalist discourse – and of its fetishization. Like Benito in *Huevos*, the male genitals feature prominently in Torrente's vocabulary as a signifier of anything that he finds 'great' (*cojonudo*). It is no accident that he compensates for his physical inadequacy for the job with a reflex to kick an opponent's genitals. This phallocentric discourse is nowhere clearer than in Torrente's only mention of personal hygiene:

> There are two types of men: those who wash their hands before peeing and those who wash *afterwards*. I wash them before. Why? Because my dick is sacred. It has to be venerated. It is the centre of the universe. The old good hose of happiness. You have no idea of the amount of growths and macrobiotic micro-organisms out there in the street to then go and touch it. I can't stand those queers that run to wash their hands as soon as they touch their dicks, as if they were disgusted by it (emphasis ours).

In the Bond-style credit sequence of *Torrente 2* the detective teases the audience by dropping his pants, but not revealing his 'famous' penis. Perhaps in compensation for this, his whole body becomes a giant, fat penis that appears to enter (head first) one of the 'Bond girls' with a jump (it turns out to be a visual effect: he was in fact holding on to a giant machine gun *behind* the girl (we will return to this in Chapter 8 with a more detailed analysis of a similar instance in Almodóvar's *Hable con ella* (2002)). It is not a surprise that in the opening of *Torrente 3* Madrid's own Twin Towers (less of a phallic symbol and more of a female crotch in this case) are blown up by a plane: not only could they be read as a symbol of male impotence – the towers lean towards each other – they are also known as 'the gates of Europe', a symbol of the 'new Spain' that Torrente would despise.

Interestingly, a psychoanalytic Spanish review of the first two installments found in Torrente 'the ugly adolescent, insecure, ungraceful and clueless with women, the adolescent who abandons his hygiene because he is unable to take charge of his unsettlingly sexualized body' (Dora Liébana quoted in Esquirol and Fecé 2001: 32 n 16).[28] Some of the episodes discussed here clearly support this argument and provide a further link with the infantilized *macho ibérico* that we recognized in the Bigas Luna narratives, also applicable to the Iberian sex comedies discussed at the beginning of this chapter. Perhaps what these stereotypical texts have in common is an overwhelming feeling that, contrary to public belief, it is not as much that the mythical *macho ibérico* is dead, rather, behind the tough and overconfident cover, there is a child that refuses to grow up. In the meantime, the children of democratic Spain would seem to be evolving rather differently, as we will see in some of the films discussed in the next chapter.

2

Young bodies

YOUTH AND ADOLESCENCE IN RECENT SPANISH CINEMA

In a memorable scene of the film adaptation of Elvira Lindo's novel *El otro barrio/The Other Side* (dir. García Ruiz, 2000), the plump and shy teenage protagonist that finds himself accidentally involved in the tragic events that lead to the death of two people (an elderly neighbour and one of his friends) is asked by a psychologist what he dislikes about himself. 'Perhaps I would like to have a bit of stubble. I would also like to be thinner. Have no spots. Being blond would be nice too,' he says. This short dialogue articulates the importance that body issues have for teenagers, and is an illustration of their presence in recent Spanish cinema. Self-image issues and the other physical challenges that relate to the transformation of the body during adolescence are just some of the problems that young people have to face and that, as Quart observes, have been compounded since the 1980s with the increasing social pressure now for boys, as well as girls, to look good. As she argues, whilst there is an expectation for girls to be 'small' (thin), it is expected that boys will be 'big' (muscular), a tendency that could have come as a result of the much publicized (and demonized) increase in childhood obesity in America and in the Western world as a whole (2002: 129–135).

As a short, transitory stage of personal/social development, youth tends to be regarded as problematic because it somehow destabilizes the boundary between childhood and adulthood. Teenagers face the shock of having to manage without parental guidance and protection that they had during childhood and enter the 'real' world, often struggling to learn and negotiate the rules of adult society. Hence, as Shary argues, 'delinquency becomes the means through which many teens achieve not only an identity (…) but also a sense of who they are in relation to the structured world around them and the adult life ahead of them' (2002: 81), and this tendency is dramatized in films about delinquent youths that were common in 1980s Hollywood – and, as we shall see, also in Spain. The social pressure brought to bear not only by the family but also by institutions like schools adds to the anxieties of youth. Male teenagers, for example, feel pressured to 'perform' their assigned gender role and establish a firm male identity in front of their peers, as well as reaffirm the heterosexuality that is taken for granted by the social majority. The pressure for them to enter the adult world and to be emancipated often results in a temporary identity crisis, which many youths struggle with, in many cases finding an alternative refuge in one or more of the so-called 'youth subcultures'. In this chapter we will refer to youth in the widest sense of the word. We will not be focusing strictly on any sub-cultural groups as such ('gangs' marked by class, clothing and linguistic codes), but more on male youth in general. References to 'youth culture' are also used in the broadest sense of the word (sub-culture only in so far as it is built as an alternative to the adult mainstream).

The cliché runs that adults often react negatively to the values and lifestyle of the younger generations, as they often subvert adults' rules and thus pose a threat to that adult hegemony. In recent years, however, there has been a shift in the perception of 'youth' culture in the Western world. New generations of adults seem more interested in glamorizing the young aesthetic and lifestyle (as noted by Pomerance and Gateward 2005: 2–3 and 9). It seems that younger generations at the end of the twentieth century became less overtly political and therefore less threatening to the mainstream. Indeed, as Tim Shary notes, Hollywood 'teen films' since the early 1990s have tended to almost erase the delinquent school character that characterized the school films of the previous decade (2002: 42 and 2005). His view is that, in the North American context in particular, this might be due to the real-life violent events that made the news headlines during that decade, providing sufficient warning as to the dangers of violence (the famous Columbine shooting was dramatized in 2003 by Gus Van Sant in *Elephant*), and making violent protest more politically difficult. On a global scale, as Quart (2002) notes, there is also a tendency for adults and the media to glamorize youth: advertising and new media directed specifically at this market (such as music channels or, at an even earlier age, the cartoon channels and computer video games) have contributed to providing a more affluent and less violent image of youth than in previous generations. In other words, perhaps as a result of their potential as consumers in the global market, the young have been commodified. From the late 1980s, the mass media have been drawing attention to (and have often exploited) images of young people, not just to target the strictly 'young' market (the under-25s, who supposedly do not have the 'buying power'), but those new generations of young professionals who aspire to remain looking and feeling young for as long as possible (the controversial Calvin Klein underwear ad campaign in the early 1990s is a clear example – see Quart 2002: 133 and Bordo 1999: 179–225), or even to those who are no longer 'young' but who would like to look younger by following certain 'street' fashions, using anti-ageing cosmetics, not to mention taking advantage of the increasing accessibility of cosmetic surgery. As a result, as Lury (2000: 104) and others have noted, it is becoming increasingly difficult to delimitate the concept of 'youth'. This is partly due, as Pomerance and Gateward argue, to the development of capitalism, given the interest in extending adolescent boyhood 'in a kind of unending consumer dream state, with a vast population of physically mature males being denied the full responsibilities of adult citizenship in order that their activities might be the more predictable, the more controllable and the more exploitable' (2005: 3). This chapter will investigate how the 'young' male body is represented in five films about 'youth' (here regarded in a wide age range that goes from the teens to the mid-twenties) that have been particularly well known in contemporary Spain.

Films about youth have been prominent in Spanish cinema of the last three decades. Trenzado Romero has found that, from the early 1990s in Spain, youth went from media under-representation to over-representation and that the 'profession' most widely represented by male characters in the Spanish cinema of the 1990s was that of the 'student', even if the narrative was completely unrelated to the world of education (1997: 99–100).[1] Young people between 15 and 29 years of age represent almost a quarter of the Spanish population,[2] and, judging by the *Revista de estudios de juventud* (*Journal of Youth Studies*) published quarterly by the *Instituto de la Juventud* (The Youth Institute), the field of youth studies is enjoying a period of considerable productivity in Spain.[3] According to a survey carried out by the CIS (Spanish Centre of Sociological Research) in 2005, 68% of young Spaniards between the ages of 15 and 29 live at their parents' home – 10% less than in 1999 but still an extremely high proportion in relation to their Northern European neighbours (see Aguirre Gómez Corta 2005 and CIS

1999), and studies suggest that the age of emancipation of young people in Spain continues to rise due to the high cost of housing and the instability of job markets (Requena 2002). This perhaps explains the prominence of the family settings in Spanish films about 'the young experience', something to be expected in films that deal with teenagers but which seems surprising in films about people in their early twenties such as *Historias del Kronen/Stories from the Kronen*. Further social dynamics might also explain it: Monterde (1993) and Trenzado Romero (1997) have argued that the family setting is also useful since its multifunctional narrative potential can serve as a way of generating narrative richness in film. Indeed, as Trenzado Romero puts it, the family setting provides a setting for the exploration of discourses of 'power, submission and transgression (…) emancipation, maturation, initiation to sex, confrontation of old and new customs and economic cell of production and reproduction' (1997: 100–101), although the more recent trend seen in films such as *Gente pez/Fish People* (dir. Jorge Iglesias, 2001) or *El año de la garrapata/The Year of the Tick* (dir. Jorge Coira, 2004) seems to resort to the setting of the shared student (or recent graduates) household that had worked so well in the French-Spanish co-production *L'Auberge espagnole/Una casa de locos/Euro Pudding/The Spanish Apartment* (dir. Cédric Klapisch, 2002).

Amongst the most widely recognized post-Franco cinematic representations of Spanish youth are the iconic *Tigres de papel/Paper Tigers* (dir. Colomo, 1977) or Almodóvar's debut film *Pepi, Luci, Bom y otras chicas del montón/ Pepi, Luci, Bom and Other Girls on the Heap* (1980), both set around the time of the first democratic elections.[4] The early 1980s films of Eloy de la Iglesia which focused on the world of drugs and delinquency or, in the 1990s, Montxo Armendáriz's *Historias del Kronen* (1995) are also generational landmarks from their respective decades.[5] Narratives about young people and teenagers also have a long and successful history in Spanish television. The early 1980s hit series *Verano Azul* (*Blue Summer*, TVE-1) or more recent and equally successful series such as *Compañeros* (*Peers*, Antena 3), *Un paso adelante* (*One Step Ahead*, Antena 3) or *Al salir de clase* (*After School*, Tele 5) illustrate the topicality of the fictionalization of youth on Spanish television. Reality shows such as the various editions of *Gran hermano/Big Brother* (Tele 5) or *Operación Triunfo* (*Fame Academy*, TVE-1 and later Tele 5) have also contributed to the increase of media representation of youth and its spectacularization. The emphasis that these series place on the display of young and usually fit bodies (of women and men alike) – often provoked by means of challenges that test their physical ability or by the tempting availability of sun-bathing decks or outdoor Jacuzzis – deserves a separate study for which there is little room here. There is, however, an important connection to be drawn between the television serials and films: many directors of 'youth' films have filmed some of these series – Antonio Mercero who directed *Planta cuarta/The Fourth Floor* in 2003 became famous for his direction of *Verano Azul/Blue Summer* in the 1980s – and some of the actors that started working in these television series later starred in some of these films (the earlier mentioned *El año de la garrapata* is a good example of this). The films recently directed by Miguel Martí (*Slam* in 2003 and *Fin de curso/School is Out* in 2005) exploit the Hollywood teen-movie formula of classics of the genre such as the Porky's series in the 1980s or the *American Pie* films of the new millennium much more directly. Familiar ingredients include the school setting, the obsession with masturbation and sexuality in general, the opposition between different 'tribes' (the posh kids versus the alternative pomo hippies), or the emphasis on music and sports and the final challenge (typically a car race in *Fin de curso*). Remarkably, though, the Spanish films are not as sexist in the formal imaging of girls' bodies as their Hollywood counterparts. According to Shary, girls' bodies in the Hollywood teen film are 'held up for voyeuristic pleasure by the male gaze in much greater proportion than the number of boys who are photographed for the opposite purpose' (2002: 214). It is noteworthy that, in *Fin de curso*, a boy and not a girl becomes the centre of attention of (and competition between) two girls (belonging to very different groups of the class). Jaime (Jordi Vilches – who plays Nico in *Krámpack*, one of the films that will be discussed later in this chapter) becomes a toy-boy who will have to change his appearance (clothing and hair style) on several occasions to match the much more clearly defined styles of the two girls.

Even though, in keeping with the scope of this book, we will be focusing on recent films, it is worth noting that, although earlier iconic representations of Spanish youth such as Buñuel's *Los olvidados/The Young and the Damned* (1950), Saura's *Los golfos/The Delinquents* (1962) or de la Iglesia's *Colegas/Pals* (1982), to give a significant example from each of these decades, focused on an older model of representation of the young as delinquents (as the titles suggest), these films share many features with the most recent ones discussed below. *Los golfos*, *Los olvidados* and *Colegas* all have tragic endings not dissimilar from that of *Barrio/Neighbourhood* (dir. León de Aranoa, 1998), as we shall see: in all these films, a young delinquent presented as a victim of his social circumstances dies at the end in the hands of a figure that represents the law (or a subversion of it). The older films are also remarkable in their representation of the male body. The places in which the boys' corpses end up in the films by Buñuel and Saura (a rubbish dump and the sewer system respectively) serve to graphically emphasize the victimization of the boys as well as a perceived social worthlessness of their bodies. Both films also include scenes that emphasize the physicality of the male protagonists. The sexual implications of bullfighting discussed in relation to *Jamón, Jamón* in the previous chapter or *Matador* in Chapter 8 are also applicable to *Los golfos* (see Kinder 1993: 96–111). There are scenes of very physical wrestling between the boys and the clothing (body-hugging sleeveless t-shirts) or activities such as sunbathing that favour the display of their bodies. Much more explicit and interesting for this book is de la Iglesia's film because of its unusually high visual investment on the young male characters' bodies.

In *Colegas* not only do Antonio (Antonio Flores) and José (José Luis Manzano) appear completely naked at several points (in bed, in sex scenes or in the shower), they are also seen masturbating (perhaps one of the most commonly depicted activities in the post-1990 youth films discussed later as we shall see) and they negotiate with their bodies through prostitution (with a mature woman and at a gay sauna) and drug-trafficking (they work as drug mules). These are all ground-breaking steps in the representation of the young male body and homoeroticism in Spanish cinema. Even more remarkable is the visual reference to sodomy in the way in which the men are asked to carry the drugs: these are not introduced through their mouth but through their anuses. Significantly, the drug is kept in condoms and introduced by lubricating it with a popular brand of moisturizing cream. The scene highlights the pain of the act of anal penetration. Further to this, the striking photography enhances the display of the extremely fit bodies of the men by means of homoerotic aesthetics and frequent close-ups of various body parts, often as they are examined by their potential consumers. The athletic appeal of the young gipsy bodies is highlighted in contrast with the older and flaccid naked bodies of the gay men that they encounter at the sauna. The inclusion of a 'youth' film-within-the-film is explicitly self-reflective about the politics of youth representation. One of the boys is offered a contract to take part in a film about 'young delinquency', thus provoking a discussion amongst his friends about the misrepresentation of youth in the media. Besides the further layer of commercialization of the young body that this film-within-the-film constitutes, there is also a level of meta-fictional reflexion about the film's own exploitation of the fame of the Flores brothers (their mother was the late flamenco dancer Lola Flores, widely recognized as a symbol of national identity 'the Lola of Spain' through a successful career as a dancer but also as a 'folkloric' actress through the 1940s, 1950s and 1960s). In retrospect, Antonio's tragic death in *Colegas* was a premonition of his real death by drug overdose only two weeks after his mother's in 1995. The film's spectacularization of his funeral (the glass-top coffin culminates the display of his body by means of Christian imagery) would be duplicated in reality 13 years later with the media frenzy that surrounded his tragic death.

REBEL BODIES IN THE 1990s

Following the success of José Ángel Mañas's novel *Historias del Kronen* (1994), the film adaptation by Montxo Armendáriz one year later (referred to as *Kronen* hereafter) has become one of the most iconic films of 1990s Spanish youth. The novel and the film (often discussed together, given their chronological proximity and joint cultural impact) have attracted significant critical attention in Spain and abroad, particularly in the context of so-called 'Generation X'.[6] The film depicts the hedonistic lifestyle of a largely affluent group of friends in their early twenties who live in the Spanish capital. The summer break and a generous cash flow from their well-to-do families allows them to live mostly at night and sleep for most of the day. The apparently never-ending possibilities of the nightlife in Madrid (although with some restrictions imposed by the then newly introduced European laws – as angrily noted by the protagonists of this film) provide plenty of opportunities for these young men to get high on drugs or alcohol, have sex and socialize in bars and clubs until closing time.[7] Although these freedoms were far from newly available to Spanish youths by the mid-1990s, the novelty of this text lies in the fact that the youth of *Kronen* are the first 'proper' post-Franco generation, born with the democracy and now starting to discover the flaws of the new society. The ubiquitous television and the lunch-time news (*Telediarios*) work as a striking reminder of the pessimistic socio-political background to *Kronen* (the post-1992 economic recession and political scandals that grounded the first socialist government – as noted by Moreiras Menor 2002: 219–220).

For the purposes of this chapter, we will focus on the physical characterization of the triangle of friends formed by Carlos (Juan Diego Botto), Roberto (Jordi Mollà) and Pedro (Aitor Merino). Male identity in

Kronen is constructed by opposition (as also seen in the films discussed in Chapter 1). As Ballesteros notes, the film portrays three kinds of masculinity, which are embodied by Carlos ('a hyperbole of the strong and manipulative leader whose transgression of hierarchies and the inherited bourgeois values does not stop him from being a male-chauvinist, homophobe and racist'), Pedro ('the prototype of the weak "loser" who cannot survive the competition of those stronger than him') and finally Roberto (who 'represents moral and sexual ambiguity: ethical but cowardly, transgressor but in awe of taboo and authority, fascinated by violence but needy') (2001: 259). However, if the Bigas Luna characters mentioned in Chapter 1 were obsessed with bettering their financial position, the young men of *Kronen* all but take material possessions for granted and the thrill comes from daring to break the rules. Carlos is obsessed with speeding and unconsciously identifies it with virility and sexual potency. As argued by Stanley joyriding is an activity 'often undertaken by adolescent males either to impress adolescent females or as a mark of "dare" which expresses courage in the presence of other adolescents' (Stanley 1995: 102).[8] In *Kronen*, Carlos speeds when driving, especially when he is in the presence of his various girlfriends or with his close friend Roberto, whose sexual orientation is a mystery for the audience but, as we discover at the end, a suspected threat to Carlos's own. References to the male genitals abound: it is Carlos's way to push his friend's gender/sexual insecurities further: 'you have no balls, have you? You are such a queer boy!', 'Come on, queer boy, drive against the traffic!' For Roberto this challenge is a risk worth taking, as Carlos will reward it in ways that significantly increase their physical intimacy: a 'manly' kiss on the lips as they brag about it with their mates and, as proposed by Roberto, a double blowjob by a prostitute. The (female) prostitute becomes a convenient mediator of the sexual tension that had been obviously mounting between the two friends, the usual 'talismanic figure against the possibility of sexual love between men' (Troyer and Marchiselli 2005: 271). In her queer reading of the Anglo-American literary canon, Eve Sedgwick (1985: 21–27) notes that women are often used as a convenient displacement of sexual desire between two men.

Carlos's sexual encounters with women are shot in ways that compliment his well-defined body and his sexual skill. All three experiences occur outdoors (at a backyard, in a car and in a building site) and finish quickly, suggesting the protagonist's preference for fast and intensive pleasure-seeking with no foreplay and no apparent concern for anything beyond the physical. In one occasion, Amalia (Núria Prims), Carlos and Roberto go to the cinema to watch Carlos's favourite horror film: *Henry, Portrait of a Serial Killer* (dir. John McNaughton, 1986). Carlos is clearly turned on by the extreme violence seen on the screen and directs Amalia's hand to his crotch whilst Roberto's own arousal is the result of his awareness of his friends' sexual game. Later Carlos and Roberto watch the same film on video at Amalia's house while she goes out to get a pizza. Although the two friends (both wearing boxer shorts and a shirt, sitting next to each other on the couch) do not touch each other, the mise-en-scene is reminiscent of the earlier scene, except now Roberto has replaced Amalia. The sexual triangle is symbolized by the triangular pizza slices that they eat together whilst watching the film. Interestingly, both the relationship between Carlos and Roberto and the illicit triangle with Amalia are associated with a sick pleasure in physical violence. The film they so much enjoy is rich in scenes of damaged and bleeding, dismembered bodies of women. As Linda Williams notes, this type of film 'like pornography, (…) pries open the fleshy secrets of normally hidden things' (1999: 191) and the frequency with which violence is directed towards women in this genre has earned it a reputation as misogynistic (190): 'The human "monsters" of such films rarely rape, they more often kill, but killing functions as a form of rape' (191). Indeed, a real story of rape and violent murder is heard on the background news during one of Carlos's family lunches. On one occasion he tries to force Amalia to have sex with him in her own home and when that fails, he later tries to take advantage of his own sister late at night in the lift whilst confessing that he used to think about her when masturbating as a kid. As we will discuss later, Carlos's violent nature will culminate in a symbolic rape (and accidental murder) of the friend that he perceives as 'the weakest': Pedro.

The parallelism between the protagonist of *Henry* and Carlos is played out visually by association between McNaughton's film poster – shown in close-up as the three friends leave the cinema. In the poster, the film's protagonist is seen looking at himself in the mirror and Carlos's moral and physical deterioration is sign-posted through at least four key moments in which he is doing just that. The first of these instances occurs as he wakes up from a long siesta after 7 p.m., he observes his reflection in the mirror as he ingests two pills, presumably to get rid of the hangover. Later, at the nightclub he and his friends snort cocaine in the toilet, again in front of the mirror. He seems to take a narcissistic pleasure in witnessing the signs of his physical excess (such as nose-bleeding). Later, one of the clearest signs of his moral decay (the attempted abuse of his sister in the lift) is also reflected in a mirror. Finally, as we will discuss below, a static close-up shot of a mirror is chosen to close the film, just as Roberto and Carlos are faced with the consequences of the most tragic of their actions. Beyond the possible Lacanian readings of these scenes, the mirror, then, is a powerful metaphor for the protagonist's physical and moral decay, but it also symbolizes his unhealthy relationship with Roberto, which, as we have seen, is characterized by the kick found in suicidal driving, drugs, prostitution and violent films, all very physical ways of channelling the sexual tension that exists between them.

Although Carlos seems indifferent to Roberto's feelings, there are two instances in which the homoerotic tension is explicitly addressed: a late-night nude swim at Roberto's neighbourhood outdoor pool (which is deserted at that time) and a scene of mutual masturbation at Pedro's tragic birthday party. In the first of these instances, the nudity and drunkenness give Carlos the perfect excuse to comment on Roberto's 'large instrument' (a comment once again defused with a reference to Roberto's female neighbours – the ones who, for Carlos, would be impressed with such a sight). At Pedro's party, their mutual masturbation is recorded by a hand-held video camera which Carlos had dropped on the floor whilst filming (and which, perhaps on purpose, he forgot to turn off). Interestingly, this sense of visual mediation (but also spectacularization) is also used to film Pedro's death.

Before discussing the film's ending, the figure of Pedro deserves some attention. He is a diabetic, and this, combined with his history of being bullied at school, make him the most vulnerable character in the film. Carlos had made this perception clear early on in the film, when breaking into a building site. Pedro was the only one reluctant to access it, the only one 'with no balls', to use Carlos's words. Carlos had also challenged him with references to his gender ('Come on, go faster, don't act like a little girl') and sexual identity ('Come on, don't be queer'). His friends ask him to leave Pedro alone, but Carlos argues that 'he likes it', thus making an unconscious link between homosexuality and masochism (this link is critically explored in depth in Edwards 1994: 74–89). The assumption is backed up with childhood memories of abusing Pedro: 'Don't you remember when we caught him at school and left him hanging from the staircase?' The film plays out the association between sickness and lack of manhood. When Pedro leaves, Manolo (Armando del Río) asks Roberto: 'Why is he always fucked-up?' Roberto explains that Pedro is diabetic and has had a kidney removed. Manolo replies: 'Fuck, now they only have to rip off his dick.' The abuse is repeated at the bar, although this time at the hands of another group of guys who are drinking there (including an anonymous youth played by Eduardo Noriega). They also question his sexuality: 'He enjoys being fucked,' they say, as if justifying their abuse when confronted by Carlos. The group defies him to hang from the bridge in a head-to-head contest with his homophobic opponent (Noriega), to see who can hang for longer and survive. At the bridge, Pedro's physical weakness is all but confirmed: close-up shots of his face reveal his struggle to hold on to the bridge whereas his opponent seems to laugh it off. Luckily, the police arrive before tragedy ensues in bitter anticipation of Pedro's tragic death later in the film, where the follow-up scene at the police station will be replaced by one at a hospital – these institutions, together with the family and homes, work as a reminder of 'adult' and organized society.

Carlos's rejection of any physical contact with Pedro is apparent throughout the film. Whilst he seems to be quite tactile with his other male friends (Roberto in particular), he half-jokingly rejects Pedro's pat on the shoulder: 'Are you feeling me up again?' The abuse and questioning of his sexual and gender identity as well as the suggestion that he is a masochist during the building-site episode (reinforced when Pedro leaves: 'Don't piss yourself with pleasure on the way down') is repeated at Pedro's birthday party even before it starts. Whilst touching Pedro's bottom Carlos tells his friends about the drug-related arrangements for the party: 'Manolo will get the pills and "this beauty" will do the rest.' At the party, when Manolo mentions that it is a shame that there are no girls, Carlos says (in front of Pedro): 'Don't worry, if you get horny you fuck Pedro's butt. I'm sure he'll love it,' and then proceeds to dance with him, holding him as if he were a girl and agitating his body, forcing Pedro to lose his grip. The assumption that Pedro will enjoy being raped, although meant as a joke, underlines Carlos's male chauvinism and internalized homophobia (as discussed in relation to his obsession with *Henry*). Pedro is eventually raped, although not quite literally. Carlos (really high on a lethal mixture of cocaine, pills and alcohol) forces a bottle of whisky down Pedro's throat, resulting in his almost instantaneous death (being a diabetic he cannot drink excessively). The act of tying him up ('He loves it,' Roberto says) holding him to the chair and forcefully pushing the (phallic) bottle into his throat, ignoring his verbal and physical attempts to resist it, serves as a metaphoric reminder of rape, where his mouth works as a substitute for his anus and the bottle as a penis held by his supposed friends.[9] As observed by Sedgwick (1985) in relation to the Gothic novel, there is a tendency to associate homosexual inclinations and desires with murderous instincts

(Ballesteros also observes this association in *Kronen* – 2001: 260). This is suggested visually in the film through the use of the same filming technique for the masturbation scene and the death of Pedro. In the final scene of the film we find out that Carlos was always aware of Roberto's feelings, accusing him of being a coward, never wanting to face up to reality, comparing his refusal to show the video evidence to the police with his refusal to accept his attraction to men (particularly Carlos). In the fight, the mirror mentioned earlier gets broken, perhaps as symbolic rupture with the false reality in which these characters lived. If one is to believe that the film version of Carlos is redeemed at this point (see Ballesteros 2001: 257), the broken mirror could then mark the end of that Henry-like Carlos who, as we have seen, was constructed visually by the mirror image that replicates the *Henry* film poster. Yet, the static camera now fixed in the mirror and thus hiding what is going on out of frame also offers a connection with the masturbation scene and the death of Pedro. The soundtrack gives the only clue to what is going on between the two friends: they are moaning, almost out of breath, presumably fighting for the video (that Carlos took from Roberto in order to hand it in to the police) but maybe having sex. Carlos's final acknowledgement of Roberto's feelings seems to suggest that the underlying homosexual tension between the two main characters was in fact one of the main preoccupations of both men, an interesting reflection on the importance of the homosexual panic that surrounds many of the typical behaviours (the speeding, the violence, the power struggle, the need to prove oneself) in this crucial stage of sexual and gender-identity formation that is youth; a tendency that seems to underlie (as an ever-present threat but also a reference against which to establish 'the norm') the narratives of Mañas's novel and Armendáriz's film.

VULNERABLE TEENAGE BODIES

The protagonists of the films chosen for discussion in the next two sections are younger than those of *Kronen* and share a patent focus on the maturation process of male teenagers. First, we will look at three films that share aspects of context, narrative and production thus producing a cohesive unit of analysis. All three films have been commercially successful in Spain and have been well received by the critics and by the Spanish Academy.[10] Furthermore, these three films were produced at the end of the millennium (1998–2000) and, importantly, by young directors in their early thirties, a factor that sets them apart from *Kronen* (although Mañas was of the same generation as the characters of his novel, Armendáriz was 45 at the time of filming) and from *Planta cuarta*, discussed in the final section of this chapter (it was directed by Antonio Mercero at the age of 67 but written by a 29-year-old).[11]

In *Barrio/Neighbourhood* (dir. Fernando León de Aranoa, 1998) three teenagers from a depressed area of Madrid suffer the consequences of their families' poor, tragic and, in one case, repressive and violent background. *El Bola/Pellet* (dir. Achero Mañas, 2000), also set in Madrid, focuses more closely on the tragically familiar issue of domestic violence in Spain, here affecting a 12-year-old boy who becomes a victim of the extreme physical and psychological violence exerted by his repressive father (a reminder of the 'old' Spain of the dictatorship), but who finds refuge in the warmth of a new school friend and his liberal, young parents (representative of the 'new democratic Spain'). Finally, the two young protagonists of *Krámpack/Dani and Nico* (dir. Cesc Gay, 2000) come from a much better-off (and Catalan) background. The luxurious surroundings of Dani's family's beach house and a few ephemeral moments of sexual pleasure with his friend Nico (they engage in mutual masturbation – which they call 'krámpack') help to make their sexual-identity struggle more bearable.[12] Yet, while Dani is in love with Nico, Nico is in love with a local girl. Eventually, and partly due to Dani's friendship with an adult gay man, the summer proves a beneficial, life-changing experience for both boys, and their different sexual tendencies do not seem to get in the way of their friendship.

Like most of the films analysed so far, the male protagonists of *Barrio* are defined by opposition to each other. As one reviewer graphically put it, each friend stands for one different part of one body: 'Manu is "the chest": he is driven by his feelings; Javi is "the head": the most cerebral and Rai would be "the balls" since (…) he has a blind trust in his luck' (Belategui 1998).

Steven Schneider (2005) has noted that scenes of frustrated masturbation are crucial elements of the representation of male adolescents in recent Hollywood cinema. His articulation of what he calls the 'paradox of masturbation' is based on the apparent contradiction of this act, which, 'on the one hand (…) signifies the teenage boy's entrance into the pangs and pleasures of pubescence (i. e., physical manhood); while on the other hand (…) is widely perceived as a symptom of spiritual and social immaturity' (2005: 381). In fact, this paradox is the perfect symbol of the messy status of adolescence that we described at the start of this chapter. The masturbation scenes that take place in *Barrio*, *Krámpack* and *Planta cuarta* are of particular relevance here as these are not the kind of solitary acts that are interrupted by an adult to the embarrassment of the youngster that Schneider has seen in Hollywood films. In these Spanish examples, masturbation is a rite-of-passage that transgresses the limits of the private to become an act of pleasure and friendship.

In *Barrio*, the scene is but a confirmation that, for the boys, sex is experienced as an anticlimactic and out-of-reach fantasy. First, they use up all their cash on a frustrating call to a sex phone line only to suddenly get cut off. The unavailability of sex and romance is also symbolized by Rai's (Críspulo Cabezas) dance with a cut-out cardboard lady stolen from a travel agency that ends up being accidentally beheaded by one of his friends; the unavailability of sex/romance is also symbolized by Javi (Timy Benito), who is seen sleeping with a giant and dirty teddy bear found on a skip.[13] If in *Kronen* the masturbation scene between Carlos and Roberto is mediated by the hand-held camera and immediately followed by tragedy, here Javi and Manu (Eloy Yebra) masturbate whilst looking at CCTV live images of Rai's brother getting intimate with his girlfriend, and they are suddenly interrupted by Rai's gun-in-mouth Russian roulette game. The Russian roulette is an anticipation of Rai's real death by gunshot, but the flirtatious play with the phallic gun in his mouth and its visual reference to fellatio contributes to the kind of association between sex and violence/destruction or reality and fantasy seen in *Kronen*. Yet, it is also part of a process of feminization enacted on Rai's body throughout *Barrio*, not dissimilar from one discussed also in relation to Pedro and the bottle of whisky in Armendáriz's film. Were it not for the arrest and police interrogations about drug-dealing, one would be led to assume that Rai's dark dealings with the mysterious middle-aged man that follows him around in a car could be of a sexual nature. Indeed, his arrest in front of his friends also contributes to his feminization: whilst his friends are frisked whilst standing up, he, as the main suspect, has to bend over a car and undergo a thorough search that, to an extent, violates him. Yet he offers little resistance and the close-up shots of his face, showing concern about his friends, overwhelm those of his body (similar close-ups of his face during the interrogation that follows further contribute to his characterization as a defenceless character). As Carlos did with Pedro in *Kronen*, here both Manu and Javi refer to Rai in feminine terms in several occasions calling him '*guapa*' (nice-looking girl) when he wears a wreath around his neck at the cemetery, or touching his long hair and jokingly suggesting that he sell it to be made into wigs or sex-dolls' hair. If we accept one of the precepts of Mulvey's theory of the gaze (1992), the feminization of Rai would be consistent with his objectification throughout the film: the vulnerability of his body is made clear by the way in which he seems drawn to risky behaviour (through his delinquent activities) but also metaphorically with the Russian roulette and his walks on tightropes (actually walls or wires found lying on the floor), in one case working as a premonition just before his death. This vulnerability is also heightened by his continuous references to death, such as his jokes about Manu's mother or his stories about seeing a drowned man in *Baywatch* and about his having been born dead and then 'resuscitated'. Drowning becomes a metaphor for his inability to escape the claustrophobic *barrio* and also for his powerlessness and eventual death. The symbolic sense of enclosure is also established by the mise-en-scene in several medium shots of the three friends holding on to the railings of a bridge above a busy road – see Figure 6 (the boys go there to spot cars and fantasize about owning them) and which resemble prison bars (this effect is emphasized by the metal bars that protect windows in various buildings). On one occasion Javi and Manu get up and leave whilst Rai stays alone, behind the railings, in anticipation of a prison sentence for drug-dealing that he will never live to serve.

6. Behind bars: Eloy Yebra, Críspulo Cabezas and Timy Benito in *Barrio*.

The secondary but striking presence of death and ageing also present in *Kronen* (in the figure of Carlos's sick grandfather (André Falcón)) is a key reminder of the futility of youth in both *Barrio* and *El Bola*. In *Barrio*, the sick (deaf) grandparent living under the family roof is an important source of tension at Javi's home. In *El Bola*, Pablo (Juan José Ballesta) helps his mother wash his grandma (here suffering from incontinence) but looks away whilst he holds her in the shower. The grandma's comments ('You should not help me shower in the presence of the boy') reflect Pablo's family's attitude to the body and death, very different to his new friend Alfredo's (Pablo Galán), who discuss his godfather's illness and at one point the whole family and some friends joke about farting in the car. They have a tactile relationship with the boys, that contrasts with Pablo's father's distant nagging and aggression. Pablo's father's behaviour reveals perhaps a repression of his emotional ties with his son but also a certain crisis of the old patriarchal model.[14] Despite the lack of scenes of any sexual nature in this film, Alfredo's father's job as a tattooist and Pablo's physical suffering provide many opportunities for the boys to discuss and draw attention to their own and others' bodies. Pablo is seen staring at photographs of Alfredo's dad (Alberto Jiménez) tattooing a client, spellbound in fascination. As Mañas has explained (in the interview included in the Spanish DVD released by Tesela in 2000), Alfredo's tattoo (done by his dad in a loving ritual) offers a sharp contrast with Pablo's bruises, also done by his father but in a very different context. When Alfredo's dad invites Pablo to witness how he tattoos his son, Pablo's gaze at his friend's shoulder (Figure 7) mirrors that of Alfredo when he accidentally discovers Pablo's bruises earlier on: close-up shots of the boy looking are cross-cut with shots of the body parts in question. When Pablo has to miss school due to a particularly bad battering, his father says he has tonsillitis, associating his action and its physical consequences with illness.

Like Rai in *Barrio*, Pablo talks about the inescapability of death and even his desire to be cremated (he does not want to be buried in a hole like his brother). Pablo's vulnerability is also marked by powerful metaphors, such as his calling himself 'Pellet'. The physical precariousness of the kids is also symbolized by the game of chicken that they play (they have to remove a bottle from the rail track as a fast train approaches). The film opens with close-up shots of the feet of children walking on the tracks, as if on a tightrope (like Rai in *Barrio*): close-ups of the kids' body parts, their feet but also their hands as they make preparations for the game are a visual reminder of the real slashing that their bodies would suffer if anything went wrong. The pellet (the small metal ball that he carries around as an amulet) symbolizes Pablo's being kicked around and abused by his father and his school friends, his lack of control over himself and his destiny. In one of the final sequences of the film, his chase (by Alfredo's dad) is filmed like an animal hunt: lamed by his father's latest attack he tries to run away but finally falls to the ground. Notably, he drops the pellet whilst he is being checked up at the hospital towards the end of the film, marking an unlikely awakening (the pellet drops just as the anaesthesia kicks in). Nowhere in the film are we more aware of physicality than during Pablo's final declaration. The description of his father's abuse includes references to being kicked, his hair pulled, his skin burned with cigarettes, being forced to drink urine and to take laxatives as well as being spat on. Close-up shots of his face still bearing the marks of his father's abuse (he has stitches next to his right eyebrow) are cross-cut with close-up shots of the pellet, now abandoned at the rail track (the scene of the suicidal games of his old self) and melted by a passing train: Pellet himself could have easily died on the tracks but, instead, the metal pellet is destroyed as if to mark the end of his tragic childhood and a new, braver and brighter start as Pablo.[15]

In *Krámpack*, the family background of protagonist Dani (Fernando Ramallo), is closer to the well-off twenty-something guys of *Kronen* and, in that sense, provides a contrast with *Barrio* and *El Bola* (Dani's father is a

7. Love marks: Pablo Galán, Juan José Ballesta and Alberto Jiménez in *El Bola*.

university professor; they have a huge summer house with a swimming pool and a maid). Dani's parents conveniently go on holiday at the very start of the film, leaving their son and his visiting friend Nico (Jordi Vilches) – whose parents we never see – to their own devices. Whilst other adults fill the parental roles, they have a rather open approach to life. The maid (a liberated French woman – Myriam Mézières) asks Dani's friend Nico to take her out to parties with them; the English teacher (actually Spanish – Ana Gracia) admits to Dani that she had a lesboerotic friendship in her adolescence and has liberal views on sex, reluctantly consenting to Dani's intimate encounter with her gay friend (who is about twice the boy's age). In the meantime, the 'real' parents are on a trip to Egypt, thus further separating the world of the adults from that of the boys and yet, the 'foreign' and feminine influence of the maid and the teacher contributes to the boys' critical reorientation away from the *macho* and conservative ways of Francoist Spain and their further integration into the more modern gender attitudes of Northern Europe.

In this film, the boys' bodies serve as explicit reference to their growing-up process: the summer and coastal setting favours the constant display of flesh. Nico (Jordi Vilches is a real-life acrobat) wears muscle shirts and is often seen topless or just wearing shorts. As Dani's maid remarks, he looks thin but also grownup and 'handsome'. He is a master of performing masculinity: when meeting the girls for a party he stresses the fact that he has just shaved and wears shirt, tie and braces. One of his first conversations with Dani is about how proud he is of his pronounced Adam's apple. In a close-up profile shot he is seen feeling it whilst remarking 'It's grown,' adding: 'Women like this: it is a sign of strength, virility and potency (...) a large Adam's apple suggests other things... and girls like those things.' In response, Dani points out that his feet have also grown, perhaps unconsciously drawing attention to his own manhood but Nico is unimpressed: 'Ok but girls can't see that' and touching his neck again he adds: 'When you order a drink at the bar, when you drink girls notice that, they look at it.' Once again, the reference to women defuses the homoerotic threat posed by such mutual admiration of their growing bodies.

The mutual masturbation scenes of the film's title are noteworthy as, in the pattern discussed with regards to Carlos and Roberto in *Kronen*, they clearly define the heterosexual boy as the one in control and also the one who would adopt the 'active' role sexually. In the first of these scenes, Dani explains that he has learned to send his hand to sleep by sitting on it before masturbating, so that it feels like someone else's hand. Nico seems adamant to defuse the palpable homoerotic tension by saying that he was thinking it is the hand of a famous female newscaster. In the next krámpack, Dani switches the light off for intimacy. What for Nico is a mechanical act of pleasure seems an intimate affair for Dani: the camera shows him from behind, with soft lighting drawing attention to his backside, then he switches the light off before performing fellatio on his friend. Nico seems surprised at first but lets him proceed. References to sexual roles are more explicit in the third erotic scene between the two boys, which takes place just after Dani interrupts Nico's sexual adventure with Elena. After Nico confesses that he is fed up with the krámpacks and with spending so much time with Dani, Dani suggests they have penetrative sex and immediately adopts the receiving position (although the act never materializes as Nico reaches the orgasm before penetration). Selfishly, Nico then turns around, refusing to help Dani reach a climax. His excuse ('I now have a headache') is part of the spoof of the married couple routine that seems to be shaping up between them. Whilst the bodies of the two boys are equally exposed and presented as attractive, Nico, the heterosexual, is seen as the one in phallic, penetrative control and Dani, like Pedro and Roberto in *Kronen*, Rai in *Barrio* or Pablo in *El Bola*, as the vulnerable passive Other.[16]

The physical homology of the two boys' bodies is further emphasized by the mise-en-scene on several occasions. The boys' farewell scene at the end

8. Performing adulthood: Jordi Vilches and Fernando Ramallo in *Krámpack*.

of the film mirrors the one at the beginning, thus confirming that the sexual tensions between them have been overcome and their friendship remains untouched after what has clearly been a process of maturation for Dani. Both scenes take place at the train station and, with the train about to leave in the background, the two friends pretend to wrestle and then hug each other. This harmony is particularly palpable at a carefully choreographed scene at the beach party: in medium-close shot, the two boys light a cigarette at the same time and with the same gesture (see Figure 8), then they follow exactly the same rhythm both when dancing on their own and cheek-to-cheek with the girls. The type of medium-close shots that we saw repeatedly in the urban setting of *Barrio* framing the three friends together (at the bridge, on an underground train) and that we will see also in *Planta cuarta*, occur in *Krámpack*. Ground-level medium and medium-close shots show the two boys sunbathing next to each other on the swimming pool deck or at the beach, often on occasions in which Dani tries to discuss their relationship. The filming of these two scenes: ground-level and from behind the boys' heads whilst they lie on the ground insists on the impossibility of discussing their physical intimacy and contrasts with other frames in which the two boys are seen together cycling or hunting.

THE TEENAGE VULNERABLE BODY STRIKES BACK

The imagery of the final film chosen for this chapter is the most physically charged of all those discussed so far. *Planta cuarta/The Fourth Floor* (dir. Mercero, 2003) is a remarkable film based on the real-life experiences of playwright and scripter Albert Espinosa (born 1974) who, like the kids in this film, also had to face cancer and live in a hospital during part of his early teens (in the film his persona is represented by Izan – Luis Ángel Priego). The interest for our analysis lies in the relative novelty of focusing on a group of very young terminally ill boys (all in their early teens) and the camera investment on the boys' sick bodies. Yet the most remarkable element of the film is the way in which, despite the apparent focus on illness, there is an overwhelming sense of normality and health to these boys' lives, to the extent that the film adheres to the format and narrative structure of the American teen movie with the only notable change of the setting: the school is replaced with the hospital. In many ways, the sick children of this film appear to be much less vulnerable than those discussed in the previous section.

Most of the usual ingredients are intact: this is a story of adolescent friendship with elements of romance, transgression and a strong presence of popular music and sport.[17] *Planta cuarta* has many things in common with the three films discussed in the previous section. Apart from the coincidence in casting (Juan José Ballesta – main protagonist of *El Bola* – also leads here as Miguel Ángel), this film also celebrates the importance of male friendship in the face of unfavourable circumstances. Like in the other films, there is an element of tragedy (one of the boys dies of the illness) that will speed up the boys' maturation process. One of the film's most repeated lines summarizes the boys' (and the film's) attitude to their condition: 'no somos cojos … somos cojonudos' a pun that does not translate very well to English: 'we are not lame, we are top of the game' (subtitles used in the Spanish commercial DVD published by Bocaaboca) but that in Spanish effectively transforms what could be perceived as a demeaning adjective that reduces lame people to their condition ('*cojo*') with an assertive (albeit male-chauvinistic) adjective that refers to the male genitals to describe something that is great ('*cojonudo*') (the line might be better translated as 'we might be lame but we have a lot of balls').

The film starts with a long shot of a group of boys gathered by a hospital bed talking about a basketball game. As Miguel Ángel excitedly tells his friends, this was no ordinary contest: all the players were missing at least one limb: 'There were two with one leg, three with one arm against us three with one arm, one with one leg and a Kotz prosthesis. Their one-armed players had better hook shots than Michael Jordan.' The comparison with the famous basketball star sets out the mood for the film: these boys can be as good as, or even better than, any 'able' and famous sportsman. From the outset, as in Almodóvar's *Carne trémula/Live Flesh* (1997) (see Chapter 4), the film draws our attention to the fact that these apparently 'disabled' bodies are capable of delivering a high physical performance. Furthermore, the spectacularization of the disabled body here is framed not in terms of its 'freakiness' but in terms of its value as a commodity. These boys' bodies are displayed on the sports pitch and also on the catwalk. The story about the 'brilliant match' is abandoned when another boy approaches the group to announce that he has got a hydraulic false leg fitted and has been discharged from hospital. Now the room is turned into an improvised catwalk: the boy is asked to show-off his new leg and take a stroll 'for his fans'. Suddenly a mixed group of patients and hospital staff line up both sides of the room, improvising an imaginary catwalk for the boy to strut his stuff. He rolls up his trousers and proudly reveals his brand-new artificial leg. Miguel Ángel starts a fashion-parade type of commentary that becomes a parody of the fetishist discourse of the sequence: 'Ladies and gentlemen: here we have Antonio Valle wearing a super hydraulic false leg: the style for the Spring-Summer season will be the *Terminator 2*, very different from last winter's Robocop model.' The commodification of the cyborgesque implements is reminiscent of Ferreri's *El Cochecito/The Wheelchair* (1960) (see Kinder 1993: 113–115), which will be briefly examined in Chapter 4. In *Planta cuarta*, the camera zooms in to show in detail the features of Antonio's leg at key moments: he swivels on it and even turns it around in a complete circle as a grand finale.

From the outset the film presents what could be regarded as a tragic situation not only as fun but as a real spectacle. The relocation of the so-called disability into the sports arena or onto the catwalk is an invitation to see disability in a new light. Furthermore, these boys seem to be living in a rather happy and mischievous environment not radically different from other boys their age. The hospital becomes a playground with endless possibilities for fun. There are many opportunities to transgress the apparently perfectly organized world of the institution, which becomes a metaphor for the organized world of adults, a microcosm to be subverted just as the school in the typical North-American teen movies. For these kids, going out at night ('*ir de marcha*') means cheating the hospital security, leaving their rooms and going for a wander in their wheelchairs, exploring other floors. This could involve going down to the maternity wing and trying to make the other 'baldies' (babies) laugh. If they decide to go on the pull, they can take the lift up to the sixth floor and meet the girls in the Psychiatry ward. If they fancy a take-away they can pretend to order a pizza using the intercom system. The subversion of adult space that was so apparent in *Kronen* or *Barrio* and especially in *El Bola* is symbolized here by their breaking the hospital rules, having clandestine meetings in rooms, 'joyriding' with their wheelchairs along the corridors or breaking into diagnosis rooms and using the X-ray machine as if it were a fun photo booth. The usual car race of the American teen movie (seen in *Fin de curso*) is replaced with a frantic wheelchair race, filmed in a dynamic way that emphasizes the agility of the boys' bodies and their skill managing the wheelchairs. The scene is reminiscent of the classic chariot race in *Ben-Hur* (dir. Wyler, 1959) (the head doctor notes this connection when discussing it at a disciplinary board): close-up shots of the wheels (at one point dangerously rubbing against each other) are cross-cut with close-up shots of the boys' faces. The soundtrack (percussive noises made by the hospital's electrician – he does them to cheer up the boys several times in the film) adds a nostalgic note to the scene's focus on competition whilst also increasing the sense of dynamism. The *Ben-Hur* reference brings into focus issues of male identity and power implicit to the chariot race of the classic film (an instance of the type of aggression meant to 'disavow any explicitly erotic look at the male body' in Steve Neale's view (1992: 285)). The wheelchair race in *Planta cuarta* thus endows the boys' bodies with a mythical and spectacular element that is reminiscent of the masculine ideal favoured in Hollywood's version of Imperial Rome. The reference also contributes to the film's discourse on the ability and strength of these apparently disabled bodies. Apart from the wheelchair, other orthopaedic aids are also reinvented by the boys as musical instruments or sports gear. The crutches in particular are used as a guitar and, at the end of the film, as bowling lanes. Other scenes invite a reflection on the morbid side of the medical discourse on disability and disfiguration. Miguel Ángel is visited by a group of student doctors and one of them is asked to describe his case ('cancer of the tibia and amputation') while the others take notes in front of their 'subject'. The scene is a good reminder of the spectacular side of the medical discourse that characterized a considerable part of its history. For centuries, the dissection of the human body has surpassed the strictly medical or indeed private domain. This spectacular element of the body in medicine is encapsulated in the idea of the operating 'theatre' open to the public that was a popular form of entertainment in the sixteenth century as described by Kemp and Wallace:

> the opening up of a body was a ritual act, a performance staged for particular audiences within carefully monitored frameworks of legal and religious regulation (…). The audience was as likely to consist of curious non-specialists as aspiring or actual members of the medical profession, and the interior wonders of the body were rendered open to view in sequence according to a pre-determined choreography. (2000: 23)

The appeal of this type of spectacle remains today as evidenced by a number of very successful serialized hospital dramas. There is also an increasing number of reality shows that, in the name of medical or scientific interest, manage to introduce cameras into emergency rooms and operating theatres, giving the audience full access to just about every part of the human body, internal organs included. The high audience ratings of cosmetic surgery programmes or the famous public dissection of a corpse by doctor von Hagens broadcast by the British Channel 4 in 2002 (and then serialized in anatomy programmes in 2005 and 2006) are very telling (see Méndez 2004: 35–36).

Whilst *Planta cuarta* seems to go out of its way to downplay any element of sickness or abnormality in these boys, then, the film does not shy away from the physical matter at stake. Miguel Ángel's body is fetishized further in a scene in which he exercises his stump by trying to lift with it a weight that hangs from the ceiling. His friends put extra weights on the machine for a laugh, making Miguel Ángel's whole body hang from the ceiling 'like a pig about to have his throat cut', as one of his friends remarks. Despite the humorous element of that vision (apparently meant as comic relief) and an attempt at normality through humour (the boys act with naturalness and find a fun and funny side to their condition), the scene is also a reminder of the animal side of humans. Later, a child who was visiting another patient is drawn to Miguel Ángel's maimed limb and asks if he can touch it and then comments on its 'softness'.

The type of medium-close shots that frame the friends together that we saw in *Kronen, Barrio* and *Krámpack* are also notable here. The boys' independence from their wheelchairs is highlighted with a medium shot of four empty wheelchairs followed by an overhead shot of the four friends sunbathing with no shirts on, next to the chairs, and wearing cool dark sunglasses on the hospital's yard (reminiscent of those seen in *Krámpack*). An almost identical shot of only three of the boys later on emphasizes the absence of the one who dies. As in most of the films discussed in this chapter, there is a group masturbation scene, which in this case makes it clear that their condition has not challenged their sexuality and that they have a healthy level of sexual curiosity normal at their age. As in the other cases discussed so far, a reference to a female object of desire is introduced to defuse the potentially homoerotic potential of this intimate moment (here it takes the shape of a poster showing a nude female model who is supposed to live in the building opposite the hospital). POV close-up shots of the poster are inserted in between shots of the boys masturbating (emphasizing their gaze). The humorous way in which the scene is shot (their movements are synchronized to the rhythm of Classical music) all but eliminates the erotic tension altogether – already diminished by the type of shot: medium and from the waist up.

The films discussed in this chapter illustrate how the body is used as vehicle of the anxieties that underlie narratives of adolescence and youth. The very nature of these narratives often facilitates the display of the male body in the context of violence, rebellion, and the discovery of sexuality and one's own (changing) physique. Interestingly, male friendship is a central part of these stories and in almost all the cases discussed here (perhaps more explicitly in *Kronen* and *Krámpack*), girls are used both as mediators of underlying homoerotic desire and as a means to deny that desire, given the homosexual panic that seems common at that stage of a man's life and which is present in one way or another in all these films. Other strategies used include the singling out and harassing of an individual who represents 'the Other' (Pedro in *Kronen*, Rai in *Barrio*, Dani in *Krámpack* or, to a certain extent, Pablo in *El Bola*) by drawing attention to his 'female side' (gestures, appearance, feelings) as a way to reaffirm the others' own masculinity and heterosexuality. Interestingly, such difference is often represented with visual references evocative of penetration and/or rape, such as those discussed in our analysis of *Colegas*, *Kronen*, *Barrio* or *Krámpack*. Remarkably, in the first three cases, those perceived as weaker are killed and yet those who remain alive are portrayed as equally vulnerable. Scenes of group masturbation are also seen in most of these films (*Kronen*, *Barrio*, *Krámpack*, *Planta cuarta*), something that is not common in Hollywood, where, as Schneider (2005) has argued, scenes of solitary masturbation do abound but are consistently interrupted when a second character accidentally walks into the scene. In the Spanish case, those scenes are a celebration of male friendship and a means of escapism from tough realities, although in *Krámpack* and *Barrio* they are sexually charged and draw attention to the homoerotic component that underlies such friendships. The noticeable visual investment on the young male body in all these films also reflects the tendency to commodify youth (and the young body in particular) that we referred to at the start of this chapter and that is by now well-established in most Western societies.

3

Muscular bodies

BUILDING THE PERFECT BODY

For centuries, the muscular male body has represented the ideal masculinity that in the Western tradition soon became synonymous with impenetrability, rigidity and solid hardness. In his detailed study of visual and literary representations of the muscular body throughout history, García Cortés identifies the Greek origins of this tradition (*Discobolus, Farnese Herakles*) to be closely linked to Michelangelo's sculptures in the Renaissance Period (2004: 16). The representation of the muscular body has been uninterrupted until today. García Cortés mentions examples from different historical epochs across a variety of media, including drawings by Johan Heinrich Füssli and Pierre-Paul Prudhon, poems by Walt Whitman, sculptures by Auguste Rodin, and the literary (and later cinematic) figure of Tarzan (Edgar Rice Burroughs's 1912 story was first filmed by Scott Sidney as *Tarzan of the Apes* in 1918). The Nazi glorification of the muscular body influenced sculptures by Josef Thorak and Arno Breker, as well as the imagination of Herbert List, Jean Cocteau and Jean Genet amongst many others. In our time, superheroes such as Flash Gordon, Superman and Batman (and their sub-cultural correlates, such as the hyper-muscular gay men in Tom of Finland's drawings) were soon followed by a plethora of Hollywood superheroes incarnated by actors such as Clint Eastwood, Arnold Schwarzenegger and Sylvester Stallone. These superheroes' main function, according to García Cortés, was not only 'the constitution of an individual heroic male body', but also 'the representation of a nation and the national collective imaginary' (García Cortés 2004: 18).

Historically, it can be observed that the muscular male actors of classical Hollywood cinema, such as Charlton Heston in the epic films of the 1950s (*The Ten Commandments* (dir. Cecil B. DeMille, 1956); *Ben-Hur* (dir. William Wyler, 1959); *El Cid* (dir. Anthony Mann, 1961) and Johnny Weissmuller in his Tarzan series (starting with *Tarzan the Ape Man* (dir. W.S. van Dyke, 1932)) were presented to the audience as extreme cases of developed bodies belonging to heroic characters. According to Bou (2000), the Hollywood superhero adventure genre was, and still remains, heavily dependent on the male muscular body, as demonstrated, amongst others, in the cases of the actors Arnold Schwarzenegger (*Conan the Barbarian* (dir. John Milius, 1982) and *Conan the Destroyer* (dir. Richard Fleischer, 1984); *The Terminator* (dir. James Cameron, 1984) and its sequels), Sylvester Stallone (*Rocky* (dir. John G. Avildsen, 1976) and its sequels; *First Blood* (dir. Ted Kotcheff, 1982); *Rambo: First Blood Part II* (dir. George P. Cosmatos, 1985)), Bruce Willis (*Die Hard* (dir. John McTiernan, 1988) and its sequels), Jean-Claude Van Damme (*Cyborg* (dir. Albert Pyun, 1989); *Kickboxer* (dirs Mark DiSalle and David Worth, 1989)), Russell Crowe (*Gladiator* (dir. Ridley Scott, 2000)), Brad Pitt (*Troy* (dir. Wolfgang Petersen, 2004)) and Mel Gibson (*Mad Max* (dir. George Miller, 1979) and its sequels; *Lethal Weapon* (dir. Richard Donner, 1987) and its sequels; *Braveheart* (dir. Mel Gibson, 1995)). During the 1980s, the 'hard body' in the American superhero film was, according to Susan Jeffords, closely related to Ronald Reagan's patriotic ethos, at least, in the open and obvious contrast with other, softer bodies: 'The errant body containing a sexually transmitted disease, immorality, illegal chemicals, "laziness" and endangered fotuses [was opposed to] the normative body that enveloped strength, labour, determination, loyalty and courage – the "hard body" (…). The depiction of the indefatigable, muscular, and invincible masculine body became the linchpin of the Reagan imaginary' (Jeffords 1994: 24–25).[1] Therefore, the reception of action Hollywood films outside the USA was associated with America's military and foreign policy. As Tasker has put it, the pumped-up figures of muscular action heroes were more than just a metaphor; they functioned 'as the literal embodiment of American interventionism' (1993: 92). However, in more recent times, cultural constructions of masculinity as predominantly muscular ('musculinity', to use Tasker's term – 1993: 149) have been criticized for imposing unreachable body standards – along the lines of the feminist contestation to female slenderness (Powrie, Davies and Babington 2004: 12–15).[2] The much-publicized accident of Christopher Reeve (1952–2004) (associated with the heroic body of *Superman* (dir. Richard Donner, 1978) and its sequels during the 1980s) and the resulting quadriplegia that reduced him to the wheelchair contributed to stir a debate about the superhero muscularity of the Reagan years.[3]

The emergence of the bodybuilder as a new, readily recognizable type in the 1980s gave muscular masculinity a new edge. Muscularity was no longer reserved for the gods and the heroes: the implicit message seemed to be that anyone with a desire to obtain a more muscular body could have it, thanks to a combination of weightlifting, aerobic exercise and special nutrition. It was soon discovered that a large percentage of males were dissatisfied with their body image, in particular with their muscular tone. A 1994 survey found that 91% of US college men and 78% of women desired to be more muscular (Jacobi and Cash 1994: 383). It was also discovered that dissatisfaction with one's own body image has rapidly grown over the last two decades: the percentage of men dissatisfied with their muscle tone rose from 25% in 1972 to 45% in 1996 (Cash 1997). Amongst the cultural consequences of this raised bodily awareness, the gym made its appearance in the lifestyle of the average man, the cultural industry introduced ever-increasing levels of muscularity in male characters and toys, and the media pressure on men to strive for muscularity became oppressive and ubiquitous. Clinical problems, such as eating disorders and body dysmorphic disorder, associated with the muscularity fuss were described (Thompson, Heinberg, Altabe and Tantleff-Dunn 1999: 30–41). Body dysmorphic disorder affects men who have the following characteristics: excessive preoccupation with an aspect of appearance, intense obsessive-compulsive activities centred around the site of concern (that is, checking, weighing, grooming and so on), and behavioural avoidant features (refusal to engage in social activities because of disparagement of own appearance). Thompson suggests that any aspect of appearance may become the focus of this level of dissatisfaction, leading to severe interference with social and occupational functioning (Thompson, Heinberg, Altabe and Tantleff-Dunn 1999: 2–8; Thompson 2004). Alissa Quart has found a connection between the super-size body culture that has become prevalent amongst American adolescent boys in the last decade and the marketing interests of nutritional-supplement companies and preppy clothing manufacturers:

> In just five years, these firms have created a greater sense of inadequacy among boys about their bodies than ever before. Not so coincidentally, this has produced a whole new market for underwear and powdered drinks that teen boys now buy in an attempt to end this inadequacy. An astronomical and younger-than-ever

use of steroids accompanies it all, along with a trade in dubious, over-the-counter nutritional supplements. The drive to grow big, like the drive for youthful plastic surgery, goes beyond becoming big or becoming perfect; it's the sort of self-construction that Generation Y understands. It's self-branding as an emotional palliative. (Quart 2002: 129–130)

The most worrying side of Quart's analysis is the possibility, which she abundantly documents, that many of the most problematic body-changing behaviours could actually be prompted and planned by private interests and that films could be used, together with television and videogames, as a mass brain-washing tool. In an image-driven world, the construction of the self would have devolved into an urge to conform to commercially approved models. In the case of teen weightlifters, Quart concludes that 'the line between self-betterment and a morphic pathology is a blurry one' (2002: 135). A similar contrast between personal triumph and body hysteria frames Tasker's analysis of the bodybuilder in Hollywood cinema, 'whose over-developed and over-determined body has been taken by some to indicate the triumphal assertion of a traditional masculinity, defined through strength, whilst for others he represents a hysterical image, a symptom of the male body (and masculine identity) in crisis' (1993: 109). Whilst recognizing that this ambivalence is not exclusive to the male bodybuilder (1993: 119), Tasker chronicles some of the media manipulations of Schwarzenegger's and Stallone's public personae that presented them as problematic, underdeveloped children, suffering from various disabilities, who found in bodybuilding 'the key to the successful achievement of a masculine identity' (1993: 122). These before-and-after stories are located at the very centre of the teenager excesses described by Quart (2002).

SCREENING SPANISH MUSCLE

In sharp contrast to this tradition of masculine muscularity that can be traced throughout most of Western civilization, it is surprising that Spanish culture, with its deeply entrenched masculine values, has been so slow, one would even say reluctant, to develop a filmic imagery of muscular man. Images of *galanes* or heartthrobs, paterfamilias and cute boys seem somehow to compensate for the absence of the images of muscular men. As we discussed in Chapter 1, with the exception of a few background and secondary figures, Spanish male actors prior to the 1990s were extremely unlikely to unveil their bodies for the camera. The muscular male body, conspicuously absent from most Spanish cinema, could be back-tracked to the Crusade films of the 1940s, where war settings provided the right atmosphere for displays of athletic bodies: *¡Harka!* (dir. Carlos Arévalo, 1941), *Raza/Race* (dir. José Luis Sáenz de Heredia, 1942), *¡A mí la legión!/Follow the Legion!* (dir. Juan de Orduña, 1942). The military and war genres were associated in the Franco years with the ideals of the 'new' fascist man and the associated values of discipline, honour and loyalty. In *Novios de la muerte/The Betrothed of Death* (dir. Rafael Gil, 1975), the same spirit was still associated with the athletic body of 35-year-old Juan Luis Galiardo, an actor whose physicality would quickly turn from the sturdy to the bulky. It seems that modern-day examples of the genre have definitely abandoned muscular and athletic models. In *Guerreros/Warriors* (dir. Daniel Calparsoro, 2002), the cast is made up of lean, unmuscular actors, such as Eloy Azorín, Rubén Ochandiano and Jordi Vilches,[4] with a more developed Eduardo Noriega holding back his physicality. *Historias de la puta mili/Tales of the Stinking Military Service* (dir. Manuel Esteban, 1994) goes even further to sarcastically display an overtly unfit and overweight sergeant (Juan Echanove) leading a command of unlikely soldiers (Jordi Mollà, Achero Mañas, Marc Martínez, David Gil and Carles Romeu).

The muscular male body also features in Spanish cinema as a fantasy of desire in the comedies of the 1960s, being strongly influenced by the presence of foreign tourists on the Spanish beaches. In Pedro Lazaga's comedies, fit foreign-looking bodies were looked at by Spanish women and men, and the comparisons with the 'national product' were immediate. The comical side of the physical comparison was then taken to the sexual terrain in the sexy comedies of the 1970s, when, as discussed in Chapter 1, the body of Alfredo Landa (short, flabby, unfit) became the standard of national masculinity, very often in explicit contrast to the toned-up and desirable body of some foreign characters. In Chapter 7 we shall see that the contrast of the unfit Spaniard and the fit foreigner was sometimes an extradiegetic matter and was used as an apt metaphor for the Spanish crisis of self-esteem as an underdeveloped nation. In the 1970 hit *No desearás al vecino del quinto/Thou Shalt Not Covet Thy Fifth Floor Neighbour* (dir. Ramón Fernández, 1970) the two leading male roles were performed by Landa and the French actor, Jean Sorel, although both characters were supposed to be Spaniards.[5] The film is a comedy based on the simulated homosexuality of Landa's character – and on his visual comparison with the openly heterosexual character of Sorel. Both men embark on a frantic search for sex using the relative security of a city apartment where they bring their (usually foreign) female conquests. Whilst preparing one of these parties, Sorel's character comments on the beauty of a new couple of sexual partners, and then Landa replies that what they really like and are looking for is 'Sunshine, oranges, and Spanish men like you.' It is interesting that he says 'like you' and not 'like us', because the visual construction of both characters carefully contrasts Sorel's good looks – toned body, tight but not beefy muscles and generally pleasant attire – with Landa's short and unfit body. A common feature of the times was that non-Spanish women felt sexually attracted to non-Spanish men, even if, as in this case, some were foreign in the fiction and others were foreign in reality (Martínez-Expósito 2004a).

During the 1980s and 1990s, the imagery associated with muscularity and perfect bodies became ubiquitous in the Spanish visual media. Television commercials that stressed the importance of possessing a perfect body, epitomized by the early 1990s Danone campaign that coined the expression *un cuerpo Danone* ('a Danone body'),[6] planted the idea that the perfect body was not the exclusive domain of Hollywood hunks and superheroes (Rambo, Terminator, Superman) and that any regular bloke could and should aspire to having one.

Muscular masculinity is one of the most frequent devices to create parodies of Hollywood films (and more generally of American mass culture) and its stereotyped models of bodily perfection, which in Spanish cinema tended to adopt scornful overtones (Triana-Toribio 2003: 155). *¡Dame un poco de amor!/Bring a Little Lovin'* (dirs Forqué and Macián, 1968) is presented as a precedent to the superhero parodies of the 1990s, such as Father Beriartúa (Álex Angulo) in *El día de la bestia/The Day of the Beast* (dir. Álex de la Iglesia, 1995) and Lucas (Alonso Caparrós) in *Perdona Bonita, pero Lucas me quería a mí/Excuse Me Darling, but Lucas Loved Me* (dirs Sabroso and Ayaso, 1997) – this final example is discussed in Chapter 5. A well-known example of Spanish attempts to domesticate popular images of the muscular superhero tradition, and one that has enjoyed unprecedented attention in the media, is the *Torrente* saga. As we discussed in Chapter 1, the sort of excessive muscularity that some audiences take seriously when displayed by leading male actors in Hollywood action films is displaced in the *Torrente* films to the periphery of secondary characters, such as watchmen and bodyguards, played by little-known actors. Some of the muscular bodies in the films are black, and some are assumed foreign. These bodies and the characters they represent are obvious caricatures (the films themselves are caricatures) of types whose origins could be identified in the Hollywood action genres. The caricature does not focus on their muscularity, which, incidentally, is kept at optimal levels; instead, it takes on their absolute uni-dimensionality, which makes of them only muscles, with no potential whatsoever for action or dialogue. Furthermore, the films seem to conflate this gallery of ideally muscular males with a gallery of anti-ideal bodies, which include chubby Torrente (Santiago Segura), his assistants and a number of characters with physical impairments and also wheelchair-bound. In fact, muscular men seem to be, if possible, even thicker and dumber than the rest. There is nothing innocuous or innocent in this; whilst some commentators have preferred to dismiss the *Torrente* saga as an example of bad-taste popular cinema, Barry Jordan has perfectly identified the nature of the Spanish/Hollywood diatribe signified by the film (Jordan 2003b: 205) whilst Núria Triana-Toribio (2004) has discussed at length the saga's very relevant gender politics.

Muscularity is not the only attribute of the type of bodies we are examining in this chapter. Whilst in the Hollywood genres most heroic males have been represented as having muscular bodies, suggesting, not very subtly, an analogy between muscle tone and ethical will, it would be incorrect to infer a strict correlation between heroism and muscularity. For instance, one particular Hollywood stereotype of the male villain requires more muscle than the corresponding hero. In Spanish cinema, the physical signal corresponding to the favoured ethical will has traditionally been a combination of good health and neat looks, instead of the upright muscularity that would have been rarer in the local talent than in Hollywood. Constructing heroic bodies in Spanish cinema has, therefore, been more a matter of translating the abstract (psychological, ethical, ideological) heroic qualities of the hero into a set of conventional visual bodily attributes (one of which is, sometimes, muscularity; but also an appropriate hairstyle, a low and masculine voice pitch, clean and neat clothes, a shaved face, masculine movements that denote spotless heterosexuality and so on).

There is a long list of recent Spanish films, particularly comedies, which present groups of men in troubling circumstances. Some films can be read as discourses on masculinity, such as *Los lunes al sol/Mondays in the Sun* (dir. Fernando León de Aranoa, 2002), *Días de fútbol/Football Days* (dir. David Serrano, 2003) and *El penalti más largo del mundo/The Longest Penalty in the World* (dir. Roberto Santiago, 2005). It is difficult, however, to find muscular or merely toned-up bodies in these films, because they focus on the skinny, the flabby and the unfit. In the context of Spanish cinema, in the last two decades a group of young actors have represented something of an exception to the general absence of muscularity. Javier Bardem and Antonio Banderas are arguably the two most internationally recognizable Spanish hunks (see Perriam 2003). Bardem set the visual standards of his prototypical masculinity with Bigas Luna's 'Iberian trilogy' in the early 1990s (as discussed in Chapter 1). At the same time, Banderas had been building his own cinematic persona, with Pedro Almodóvar,[7] amongst others, since the early 1980s. Both Banderas in the 1980s and Bardem in the 1990s marked an evident departure from previous models of seductive masculinity in Spanish films, which had been represented by soft-faced *galanes* such as Imanol Arias and old-day *donjuanes* such as Arturo Fernández. Unlike Arias and Fernández, the new masculine models represented by Bardem and Banderas are strongly dependent on their physicality, making their bodies both a statement of virility and an object of desire. It must be remembered that prior to Banderas and Bardem, these bodily values were invested almost exclusively in foreign actors in imported (mostly Hollywood) films. *Boca a boca/Mouth to Mouth* (dir. Manuel Gómez Pereira, 1995) is a film that makes an explicit and direct attempt to acknowledge and redress the domestic/foreign paradigm in relation to the construction of muscular masculinity against the backdrop of a contemporary Spanish urban setting. A US film crew discovers in the character played by Bardem (an aspiring actor by the name of Víctor Ventura, who is on the verge of giving up his professional ambitions owing to a lack of opportunities) the stereotypical Latin lover they need for their next film. Víctor's transformation from ordinary boy into extraordinary man slavishly follows the Latin-lover stereotype, taking it to ironic extremes (see Perriam 2003: 112). In one particular scene, Víctor complains that the character he is being forced to create for the Americans is totally artificial because it no longer represents anybody in Spain. His agent's pragmatic reply is that it does not matter as long as the Americans buy it. The resulting character bears some resemblance to Bardem's role in *Huevos de oro/Golden Balls* (dir. Bigas Luna, 1993) in his annoying self-confidence, arrogant demeanour, and his old-fashioned clichéd set of gestures and stock sentences (Berthiers 2001). However, whilst in *Huevos de oro* the audience is simply annoyed by the character's arrogance and chauvinism, in *Boca a boca* there is a thrilling complicity in the artificial creation of the character because it is intended to somehow cheat on the Americans.[8]

Banderas's and Bardem's hunk roles have been followed by similar attempts by, amongst others, José Coronado in *Yo soy ésa/I'm the One* (dir. Luis Sanz, 1990), *Salsa rosa/Pink Sauce* (dir. Manuel Gómez Pereira, 1992) and *Anita no perd el tren/Anita Takes a Chance* (dir. Ventura Pons, 2001); Carmelo Gómez in *Vacas/Cows* (dir. Julio Medem, 1992), *La ardilla roja/The Red Squirrel* (dir. Julio Medem, 1993) and *El portero/The Goalie* (dir. Gonzalo Suárez, 2000); Liberto Rabal in *Carne trémula/Live Flesh* (dir. Almodóvar, 1997) – discussed in Chapter 4; David Selvas in *Amic/Amat/Beloved/Friend* (dir. Ventura Pons, 1999) – discussed in Chapter 5 – and *Pau i el seu germà /Pau and His Brother* (dir. Marc Recha, 2001); Eduardo Noriega in *El espinazo del Diablo/The Devil's Backbone* (dir. Guillermo del Toro, 2001) and *El Lobo/Wolf*(dir. Miguel Courtois, 2004); and Pablo Puyol in *20 centímetros/ 20 Centimetres* (dir. Salazar, 2005) – this last example is discussed in Chapters 6 and 8.

The muscular hunk is typically associated with roles that combine erotic interaction and violence in the Hollywood genres. In contemporary Spanish films, however, this kind of character is often associated with a rhetoric of allusion whose referent is displaced from the screen into an intertextual space of (mostly American) classic film heroes and superheroes. As we shall see in our analysis of *El corazón del guerrero* later in this chapter, in fantasy genres these intertextual links are explicit. In comedy genres, one can usually discover an implicit wink to the audience as soon as the male muscles are displayed on screen; for example, Coronado's first appearance in *Anita no perd el tren* is shot as a POV through the eyes of Anita (Rosa María Sardá), an aged single lady who is about to (comically) discover love in a younger, attractive bricklayer.[9]

While muscularity does not occupy a prominent place in Spanish film studies, Chris Perriam acknowledges in his groundbreaking study on Spanish male actors as stars, that contemporary Spanish cinema is particularly insistent on the display of the erotic male body, but as far as the actors are concerned, that does not immediately translate into a 'better commodification of their bodies by becoming spectacularly quick, lithe or muscled (even Banderas had to wait for the gyms of America to change that)' (Perriam 2003: 11). Apart from Banderas, Perriam singles out Carmelo Gómez for his 'solid rather than dynamic' (2003: 12) athletic role in *El portero/The Goalie* (dir. Suárez, 2000); Jorge Sanz for his image of 'smooth compactness' and 'energetic sex scenes' – and Imanol Arias for his image of 'tormented interiority', which is more immediate than any 'orthodox, exhilarating (or terrifying) physicality' – to conclude that:

> With the notable exception of Noriega in more recent roles the generality of Hollywood buffed ideal is set aside in favour of sharper stabs at looking and

acting like a Spanish – or perhaps European – man. Bardem is probably the nearest to being the physically dominant screen male of the twentieth-century Hollywood type (…). He is a hefty presence, is involved early on in his career in a famous fight scene (in *Jamón, jamón*), and has an admirable record of athletic sex scenes (and revelations of his buttocks). (Perriam 2003: 12)

Jordan and Morgan-Tamosunas make the point that 'the stronger female protagonists of a number of contemporary Spanish films are registering their rejection of the traditional *macho* male and a preference for the socially and emotionally reconstructed "new" Spanish man who displays gentleness, sensitivity, tolerance' (1998: 153). Feminine males are promoted, and non-masculine characters are favoured. Jorge Sanz, equated with innocence and inexperience, is cited as an example, as are Coque Malla, Pere Ponce, Gabino Diego – and even Javier Bardem in many of the performances that followed the early 1990s Bigas Luna trilogy. Jordan and Morgan-Tamosunas rightly point out that the undermining of the traditional masculinities (based on ideals such as bravery, superiority and virility) occurs frequently in comedies (Jordan and Morgan-Tamosunas 1998: 141), such as *Los peores años de nuestra vida/The Worst Years of Our Lives* (dir. Emilio Martínez Lázaro, 1994), where the oppositional looks of Gabino Diego and Jorge Sanz are used to highlight all sorts of different values associated with successful and alternative masculinities. Similar exploitations of the handsome/ugly couple have a long history in comedic genres and, for the purposes of a discussion on masculine muscularity, one could mention titles as diverse as *No desearás al vecino del quinto* and the Schwarzenegger and DeVito coupling in *Twins* (dir. Ivan Reitman, 1988).

MUSCLES AND FANTASY IN SPANISH CINEMA OF THE NEW MILLENNIUM

El corazón del guerrero/Heart of the Warrior (dir. Daniel Monzón Jerez, 2000) represents an unusual combination of the teenager fantasy film with derivations of the thriller, the political conspiracy and other topical sub-themes, such as the impossible love, the special boy and parallel universes. On the one hand, it is a teenage film that managed to attract the attention of a much wider audience, perhaps because it was a well-finished Spanish product partially derived from the 'sword and sorcery' sub-genre – very rare in Spain's film history – perhaps because of its Quixotic combination of reality and fantasy or perhaps because of its rich intertextuality or perhaps, one might even argue, because the film does not take itself very seriously.[10] On the other hand, the conflation of a modern-day reality and a mythical fantasy is aptly expressed by different generic strategies: a Conan-inspired romantic epic as the fantasy and a teen role-playing game story that suddenly turns into a modern-day political conspiracy narrative.[11] Under its teen-flick surface, *El corazón del guerrero* has a complex story to tell; one that goes well beyond the expectations of the fantasy genre viewer.

The film has failed to attract the attention of serious critics because of its strong generic association with Hollywood fantasy films and their innocuous imitations. However, it also departs from the strict conventions of the sword-and-sorcery sub-genre in several interesting ways. The best-known character hero of the sword-and-sorcery sub-genre is Conan the Cimmerian, created by author Robert E. Howard in the 1930s and, through the mediation of influential visual renditions such as those by Frank Frazetta for the paperback editions of Howard's novels in the 1960s and Barry Windsor-Smith and John Buscema for Marvel Comics in the 1970s, adapted to the silver screen in titles such as *Conan the Barbarian* (dir. John Milius, 1982), *Conan the Destroyer* (dir. Richard Fleischer, 1984) and a long list of sequels and imitations. In this type of film the protagonist is defined as strong and shrewd, barbaric and ambitious; more often than not, he finds himself in remote, primitive worlds ruled by magic and the occult. The hero's final triumph over dark forces is always made possible by his physical prowess. The structure of these stories is usually deceptively simple: the hero must overcome some kind of obstacle, which he does after a series of thrilling episodes.

'La realidad es mentira' ('Reality is A Lie'), the poster slogan of *El corazón del guerrero*, provides an interesting inflection on the theme of the alternative worlds typical of the genre. Incidentally, the slogan can be used as a key to the plot, which could be read in two opposite directions: either 16-year-old Ramón (Fernando Ramallo) falls victim to a role-playing game and takes his game character (Beldar, a Conan-like mythic hero) as true, or else, Beldar (Joan Joel) finds a bewitched heart-shaped stone, and upon getting hold of it is transformed into a 16-year-old boy living in a future world (corresponding to Spain in 2000). In clear contravention of the usual narrative order of events – reality first, fantasy second – the film opens up with a fantasy underworld sequence strongly reminiscent of Conan's visit to the cave where he finds the sitting skeletons of Crom and other warriors and gets his sword. In *El corazón del guerrero*, Beldar enters a hidden cave, 'la Cueva de los Mil Ojos' ('The

Chamber of the Thousand Eyes') and finds the highly protected, powerful and sacred Warrior's Heart stone. When he tries to escape the place, which has become too dangerous, the first transition between the worlds takes place: the muscular, oversized mythic hero finds himself in the tiny bed of a modern-day boy. The sharp, unexpected contrast between both worlds is emphasized by the pressing presence of what must be the boy's mother, giving him all sorts of instructions for the day, before leaving for work. Both worlds are seamlessly connected by the imposing presence of Beldar, dressed in full epic attire, in the otherwise perfectly ordinary modern-day boyish bedroom. The fact that Beldar's story frames that of the boy Ramón, rather than the other way round, is intended to confuse the audience even more and advance the proposition – made clear in the last scene of the film – that the relationship between reality and fantasy is far from stable and univocal. The Quixotic lineage of this proposition is never far from the surface in *El corazón del guerrero*; the truly Quixotic character of Ramón, for instance, maintains the same symbiotic relation with the sword-and-sorcery stories that Alonso Quijano had with the chivalric romances in Cervantes's novel, to the extent of 'losing his marbles' in the unanimous opinion of those who knew him.[12] What is more relevant to our interests, though, is the choice of actors to incarnate Beldar the hero and Ramón the boy, and the way their bodies are allowed to speak to the spectator. Fernando Ramallo (Madrid 1980) made his debut in *La buena vida/The Good Life* (dir. David Trueba, 1996) playing a troubled teenager who survives the death of his mother, father and a grandparent whilst trying to make sense of his own existence. The vulnerability of his character was emphasized by his thin, smallish body, the dreamy quality of his look and his child-like demeanour.[13] Trueba's film plays out a similar adolescent fantasy involving the same actors, although without the element of schizophrenia that defines *El corazón del guerrero* (Ramallo's character was the sore loser in the disparate competition with Joel's for the sexual favours of a female character). The spectacularly muscular body of Joan Joel (Barcelona 1971) is magnified in Monzón Jerez's film by a visual presentation that makes him a clone of Conan. It is his body's presentation that signals the film's generic link with the Conan adventure genre, whilst simultaneously borrowing its masculine muscular identification from that genre.

El corazón del guerrero, unlike some Hollywood action films, makes it clear from very early on that its intended audience is made up of adolescent males. The complicity between the narrative and the visual aspects of the film, and the fantasies and anxieties typical of the male teenager is never understated.

There are school and after-school, home-alone, impossible-love and save-the-world narratives. There are dangerous games, rock concerts and global conspiracies. There is the perfect embodiment of ideal femininity in the double character of Sonja/Sonia (Neus Asensi). And there is the split personality of the main character, which allows for that teenager's favourite narrative, the misfit (Shary 2002: 50–61). After a long first sequence entirely set in the epic world (Beldar getting the heart-shaped stone), Beldar wakes up in the world of a present-day middle-class teenager, with its admonitory mother who proffers her last orders before rushing out for work. Having survived the most extreme dangers in his latest adventure, Beldar is speechless and stunned in this utterly incongruous setting – corresponding to the most innocuous morning routine of everyone else in the audience. The incongruity of this scene, which is visually stressed by oppositions (Beldar's large-framed body and the small bed he lies on, his combat-built body and the cosy bedroom atmosphere, his petrified immobility and the mother's rushing around), signifies the pleasure of the adolescent spectator who feels vindicated and *understood*. After all, the adolescent is a dreamer whose dreams are simply not understood by those who, in his opinion, should be the most understanding – his own parents. Teenage fantasies are extremely complex because of the libidinal brain activity and very often the communication codes that have served the adolescent so well during his infancy are unable to cope with the latest needs. The typical communication breakdown between teenager and parents is humorously represented in this scene, where the mother blatantly fails to see the adult body that lies on the bed and that that person lying on the bed patently fails to open his mouth. It would be hard to imagine a more apt scene to capture the fantasy-genre principles that the presence of superheroes is usually mediated by a subjective fantasy (be it a person who dreams or makes things up in his imagination, a manuscript or a legend) and that perfect bodies haunt the imagination of men with imperfect or inadequate bodies. However, the wake-up scene is ambivalent. Since no other contextual hints are provided, it could well be that the only real thing in the present-day bedroom is Beldar, put under a mysterious spell after taking possession of the heart-shaped stone. This ambivalence fits well with the teenage genre: ambivalence is, after all, the very essence of adolescence – a transitional growing period in which infantile and adult traits can coexist for a period of time (see Chapter 2). The double reading of this scene provides the spectator with some added self-identificatory pleasure, which is only compounded by the second part of the scene: a bewildered Beldar rushes to the bathroom for some fresh water; he looks at his image in the mirror, he throws some water over his face, and when he looks at the mirror again he does not see his own image any more, but that of a young boy. It is well known that the problem with mirrors in films is that the audience can never be sure which side is real and which is the reflection. In this case, the ambivalence is maintained for a few seconds, until the image of Beldar is definitely replaced by that of Ramón the boy, on both sides of the mirror. Those few seconds, however, play a crucial role in the film's libidinal economy, because they offer the most explicit comparison between the boyish, bony, pale and vulnerable body of Ramón, and the glorious, muscular, toned, powerful body of Beldar (Figure 9).[14] Both bodies remain ecstatic for a while, staring at each other. A staring gaze at the mirror is necessarily construed as a sexual exercise, especially if it is the body (semi-naked in this case) rather than just the face that the mirror reflects. Again, the spectator is offered an identifying hint by being shown the sexual inadequacy of the adolescent facing the commanding power of the adult. The resulting bruised self-esteem of the boy will stay with him for the rest of the film and will become one of the engines of the narrative by providing the main character with a reason to act: by becoming in his own world as sexually adequate and commanding as Beldar is in his. This, of course, translates into a number of goals to be achieved (finding a partner, having sexual intercourse, behaving in a protective manner, defeating sexual competitors) and a number of difficulties to be overcome – the bread and butter of romantic adventure.

Interestingly, the contraposition of Ramón and Beldar, which is initially presented at the bodily level, is not further developed in the rest of the film. As the story unfolds, we learn that Beldar and his world belong to the script of a role-playing game Ramón is involved in over several days with his friends. Each player has a character assigned, and their deeds are largely determined by the dices. Ramón's obsession with the game keeps growing until he becomes unable to tell the game from his real life. That is when he starts to believe that he and Beldar are the same person or, more precisely, that he is Beldar, who has just been trapped in the body of a child by some powerful spell. He then sees the surrounding reality of his present-day world as a coded version of the game's reality. Ramón believes himself to be Beldar: his feeble teen-boy body is not his, it is just his humiliating prison. This hallucination allows Ramón to consider his lacklustre body and his sexual underperformance as mere accidents of his highly heroic and adventurous misfortune. The perception of his muscular body makes him feel superior, different and special.

IMPORTED MUSCLES

As we mentioned in the second section of this chapter, there are a number of Spanish films where a foreign actor embodies the muscular male, usually but not necessarily representing a foreign character. Such are the cases of French-born George Corraface (who plays Yaman, a Turkish gigolo, in *La pasión turca/Turkish Passion* (dir. Vicente Aranda, 1994)); Albanian Dritan Biba (who plays Kyril, a Bulgarian bisexual man, in *Los novios búlgaros/Bulgarian Lovers* (dir. Eloy de la Iglesia, 2003) – discussed in Chapter 5), or Italian Daniele Liotti, whose performance as Philip the Handsome in *Juana la Loca/Mad Love* (dir. Vicente Aranda, 2001) we are about to discuss. These are very different films in many ways, from genre to ideological stance, but in all three a foreign actor embodies a male muscular character.

The figure of Felipe 'the Handsome' (Daniele Liotti) in Vicente Aranda's historical film *Juana la Loca* (2001) combines the muscular body on display with a subdued characterization of the historical figure of Felipe of Habsburg.[15] The semi-legendary love story between Queen Juana I of Castile and her husband Felipe – given an almost definitive dramatic form by Romantic playwright Manuel Tamayo y Baus in *Locura de amor* (1855) and then adapted for cinema first by Ricardo de Baños (*Locura de amor/Love Crazy*

9. Seeing Double? Fernando Ramallo and Joan Joel in *El corazón del guerrero.*

(1909) silent) and then Juan de Orduña in *Locura de amor/The Mad Queen* (1948) – owes much of its modern appeal to the nicknames of the protagonists, that is, *la Loca* or Madwoman and *el Hermoso* or Handsome (Donapetry 2005; see also Mira 2004b). There can be little doubt about the historical instability of these terms: madness in late fifteenth-century Flanders and early sixteenth-century Castile was probably equivalent to modern-day verbal incontinence or extravagance,[16] and male beauty was probably more related to class and decorum than to physical traits. Whatever the precise meanings that madness and beauty had in those historical times and locations, Aranda is not too concerned about them. Instead, he deliberately intends to invest them with modern meanings, hence making the Juana and Felipe story more palatable to modern-day audiences. He was reported as saying that Queen Juana was mad according to sixteenth-century values and beliefs, but not by today's standards; and that her madness was about having her own identity and being aware of her own sexual needs (Fernández Santos 2000: 76). This conscious decision might have been based on the ideological uses of the story and the tiredness and boredom now associated with it. In this regard, it should be noted that the film was released shortly after the electoral victory of the Popular Party in 2000, which meant, amongst other things, an invigoration of the historical vindication of figures traditionally associated with right-wing values (see Mira 2004b). The most significant of these vindications would have been in 2005 with the fifth centenary of Queen Isabella's death – frustrated by the electoral win of the Socialist Party in the tumultuous 2004 poll, and the subsequent decision in 2005 to mark the fourth centenary of the publication of Cervantes's *Don Quixote*. Aranda's attempt to render a modern interpretation of Queen Juana is based on a careful avoidance of ideological debates (barely mentioned in the film are the questions of the legitimacy of Felipe's ambitions to the throne of Castile and the role played by King Fernando) and the insistence on the sexual element as the key to understanding Juana's love for Felipe. Unlike the romantic love that features in Tamayo y Baus's mid-nineteenth-century play and also unlike the political overtones present in Orduña's 1948 film – which made of Juana a symbol of Spanish resistance against foreign traitors and therefore a figure cherished by Franco's regime (Martín Pérez 2004: 72) – the main theme in Aranda's 2001 film is physical and sexual love, almost animal in its representation of jealousy.[17] The image of Juana sniffing the bed where Felipe has just played his adulterous games (and then comparing it with the bodily odours of all damsels in the court) suggests an exacerbation of her senses that goes beyond the rational in ways that transcend the humorous excess of Almodóvar's *Laberinto de pasiones/Labyrinths of Passion* (1982). Aranda's point seems to be that Juana, being in love with Felipe, behaves as a possessive lover who would hate to lose her man to another woman. This approach to the story obviates the husband/wife dimension as much as the king/queen, both of which become mere backdrop elements to the passionate story of sex and co-dependency. This reduction to the sexual is clearly evident in the portrayal of an elderly Juana who, at 74, reminisces of Felipe: 'When I close my eyes he approaches, I feel his skin on my finger tips, I feel his voice in my ears, I perceive the scent of his armpits, my desire arouses.' According to Martín Pérez, 'the intention here is to link Juana directly to her sexuality rather than to offer a 74-year-old woman the opportunity to reflect on her role as a Queen' (2004: 75), concluding that Aranda's Juana is over-sexualized and that 'the outcome of his representation of Juana is that of an "uncontrolled" woman who lives and breathes just for sex, which is evidently undermining of her image as a public and *political figure*' (2004: 82–83, original emphasis).[18]

Despite the film's title focusing exclusively on Queen Juana and the media's promotion of actress Pilar López de Ayala, the character of Felipe is equally central to the story. Aranda, an experienced director of films on extremely troubled couples – after *Amantes/Lovers* (1991) and *El amante bilingüe/The Bilingual Lover* (1993) – is clear about the centrality of Felipe's character: he is the object of Juana's desire. But far from being a passive object (which would tie in well with his consort political status), Felipe becomes a promiscuous sexual predator and is discovered by Juana on the same day he becomes King Consort of Castile. It looks like the over-sexualization of Felipe responds to the need to over-sexualize and animalize Juana. Felipe's character evolves according to a three-stage script: first, Juana's loving husband, then a sexual and political machinator, and finally a sick and dying man unable to perform either sexually or politically. To achieve some kind of audience identification with the story, the figure of Felipe is constructed alongside modern-day values. If Juana's love is presented as sexual, Felipe's beauty is visual and corporeal, rather than symbolic and behavioural. Any notion of Felipe as a well-mannered, well-groomed man is lost in favour of an immediate and incontestable bodily presence. The choice of Italian actor Daniele Liotti must have responded to the need to build the character around an impressive, muscular body, a limited range of emotional expressions through face and voice, and a vague sense of foreignness, thus avoiding the temptation to domesticate the historical figure of Philip of Habsburg as Spanish.

Juana and Felipe first lay eyes on each other with a very obvious sexual interest. In a short preamble, the audience is informed of Juana's anxious desire to find true love (and her disappointment on hearing from her mother, Queen Isabella, about the primacy of politics over sentiments). Felipe is first seen in a bust portrait in Juana's room; and then in a typically masculine hunting scene, where he receives the news of Juana's arrival in Flanders for the wedding. The eminently sexual character of their relationship is defined from the moment they encounter each other in Felipe's palace. The highly formal occasion is broken by Juana's evident trepidation over the fixity and intensity of Felipe's eyes, and by the utterly inappropriate passionate kiss Felipe gives her. Breaking all sense of etiquette and protocol, Felipe insists in getting a priest's blessing to consummate their marriage immediately. He then takes Juana in his arms and disappears with her into his private rooms, and 'fare thee well' to all present until the official ceremony to take place a week later. The screen fades out to black, suggesting that some time, perhaps a few days, have elapsed before fading in again to the next scene: the naked, uncovered bodies of Felipe and Juana lie on a bed, resting after having had highly satisfactory sex. The composition of this scene is crucial for the sexual definition of both characters. The camera slowly zooms in towards the lovers' bodies; contrary to the convention of allowing the female body to occupy more screen space than the male, Felipe's body is closer to the camera, with his legs, buttocks, back, left arm and long hair in full display. The camera zooms over him and focuses on Juana's face, which is now looking pensively at Felipe. There is a cut to the next shot, with the camera positioned behind Juana and offering a semi-POV shot of Felipe's awakening face from Juana's perspective. Two more cuts interpose close-up shots of Felipe from Juana's perspective and medium shots of Juana from the original camera position established at the end of the zoom-in. The audience is clearly invited to identify with Juana's gaze, which is focused on Felipe. Felipe then rises from bed; the camera, still focused on the central area of the bed, gives only a slightly blurred image of Felipe's muscular torso, just before Juana asks him not to leave. A new Juana-POV shot frames Felipe's shoulders and head from a lower angle; he turns his head back to the camera/Juana. There is a new cut to the previous shot of Juana on the bed with Felipe's unfocused body occupying the right half of the screen; he stands up, turns around and faces Juana, but we can only see the dimly lit, blurred movements of his arm and part of his back. Juana can see Felipe in full-frontal nude, and we can see, in the left half of the screen, with lateral dimmed lights and perfect focus, her reaction to the sight of

Felipe's genitalia. She gets closer, her eyes glued to what they see and we can only imagine from her fascinated expression. Juana looks upwards and smiles at Felipe. Felipe is then shot from the lower angle position from Juana's perspective – who is looking at his genitalia. Felipe's sombre face is kept in the dark, in contrast with Juana's well-lit figure. Juana's smile is now replaced with a rather anxious expression as she lies down again; the frame includes now her face and her breasts. She gasps. Felipe is shown again from a Juana-POV shot: he is looking down at her, then he bends down and her head and torso ascend into the camera/Juana, darkening the screen. The rest of the action is sex, but it is not enacted on screen; instead, a group of damsels who happened to be dancing and singing in a nearby room (the dancing song in the background) are shown as overhearing Juana's loud groans and screams. The careful visual composition of this first love scene establishes Juana as an ardent lover who has just found her perfect match, and Felipe as a potent stud who enjoys sex but probably not always with the same partner. The naked bodies are instrumental in conveying a sense of the virginal candour associated with Juana's paleness and of hot experience in excessive lust with Felipe's darker tones. In addition, the scene succeeds in constructing Felipe's muscular body as a synecdoche of his powerful sexual drive, thus making his body the visual emblem of Juana's fixated love. Felipe's heroic body, which from today's perspective could be read as both athletic and fashion-sculpted, is morosely described by the camera, but, probably for reasons related to the commercialization of the film as mainstream, his penis is never displayed (in consistency with strategies of representation of male genitalia, as we shall see in Chapter 8). This love scene is also important because it is the only one of its kind in the first stage of Juana and Felipe's relationship.

The second time Felipe is seen having sex corresponds to the moment when the courier arrives at the Brussels court with the news of Isabella's death; Juana runs to tell Felipe, only to find him with another woman. Juana's out-of-focus darkened body fills up the left half of the screen (in a way that is visually reminiscent of the first sex scene), while on the right half we see a general shot of the bedroom and Felipe fastidiously getting up and finding some clothes whilst a naked woman jumps from the bed and runs out of the room. 'Traitor!' Juana utters repeatedly. 'You're mad,' Felipe replies. 'It must be madness to love someone as despicable as you!' is her unmistakably modern conclusion. This will have found a receptive audience in the followers of the cheated-lover popular genres. The dialogue, shot in lower camera angles for Felipe and upper angles for Juana, contributes to reinforce the notion that somehow Felipe still has the upper hand in sexual matters at the same time as it visually idealizes further his heroic muscular body.

The naked body of Felipe is next seen, not with Juana, but with a Moorish prostitute (Italian actress Maria Gracia Cucinotta) who will use her sexual attraction and black magic to secure Felipe's favour.[19] The sex scene between her and Felipe is shot in the traditional close-ups and, more than the sex, this matters because of the conversation the lovers hold during the sex scene, regarding her ambitions to become his permanent lover. Felipe's body will not be shown naked again. As his political schemes develop and his extra-marital sexual affairs (apparently) prosper, his relationship with Juana goes awry and the role of his body becomes less central to the story. Perhaps it is not entirely a coincidence that, from this point onwards, Felipe's face appears clean-shaven, in contrast to the half-grown facial hair he had displayed since the very beginning of the film. Before the heroic echoes of Felipe's body are allowed to disappear, a new male character is developed in clear contrast to him. Juana makes an attempt to regain Felipe's attention by simulating a love affair with Captain Álvaro de Estúñiga, a close friend from her childhood. The choice of the boyish and lean Eloy Azorín as Captain Álvaro could not be more dramatic in contrast to the overtly virile Liotti. Felipe is then seen drinking a glass of iced water after coming back from hunting, and that marks the beginning of his physical malaise. The last part of the film is about the political manoeuvres around the throne of Castile and the possibility and consequences of declaring Queen Juana unfit because of her madness. The body of Felipe in this part is the body of a sick man whose health is rapidly deteriorating. It is always shown fully dressed, and in resting or sitting positions. He then dies. A narrating voiceover brings the story to a closure. 'Although Parliament never took away her title of queen, Juana, at the age of 28, was shut away in the castle of Tordesillas. Felipe's body was laid to rest in a nearby monastery, which Juana was allowed to visit from time to time.' Felipe's heroic body is not a parody of fantastic superheroes, and he is not a superhero himself but a highly sexualized body as seen through the eyes of someone who is in love with him.

As it has emerged in this chapter, masculine muscularity seems to be a concept with strong foreign connotations in contemporary Spanish cinema. From the unavoidable intertextual links with Hollywood superhero genres to the use of foreign actors and characters in muscular roles, the association of muscles with foreignness seems to be constant. However, it has become increasingly difficult since the early 1990s to argue that muscularity is culturally disassociated from the Spanish imagination, as the case of Javier Bardem, just to mention a most eminent example, demonstrates. Increased levels of male bodily self-awareness and the popularization of a gym culture, produced during the 1990s a more visible presence of the muscular man in Spanish society, which has encountered different reactions, from sympathetic views in some sectors to ironic responses from those who still consider domestic muscularity an uncritical reproduction of US models. The string of ironies that we have explored in this chapter could be read as a defence strategy against some kind of perceived threat. It is unclear where this threat is thought to come from: as we have argued, muscularity combines elements of excessive masculinity, potential physical violence and foreignness, and the general sense of 'threat' ascribed to these elements remains vague and ubiquitous. In Chapter 7 of this book we will discuss the modes of representation of the male foreigner and the way muscularity is subsumed in the more frequent strategy of hyper-sexualization. An interesting corollary of the intersection of muscularity and foreignness (which will be discussed in more detail in Chapter 7) is that both the muscular man and the foreigner are frequently used in contemporary Spanish cinema as reflections of the average Spanish male. This inverted-mirror effect is one of the most powerful devices of non-realist genres such as the fantasy film, the *esperpento* and the period drama, precisely those where the muscular man is more often represented. Muscles, it seems, find their way into Spanish cinema through some kind of libidinal activity and it is through the gaze of others (a skinny teenager, a female lover, a flabby mate) that the audience gets to visualize them. The muscular body, therefore, is no longer a metaphor for the nation, as it was often the case in some heroic films of the 1940s, and is not a sign of ethical goodness or physical perfection, as the examples of Joan Joel in *El corazón del guerrero* and Daniele Liotti in *Juana la Loca* eloquently demonstrate. Instead, it frequently indicates the presence of a powerful and often sexualized gaze characterized by strong subjective elements such as anxiety or desire.

4

(Dis)abled bodies

(DIS)ABILITY, DISFIGURATION AND 'THE NORMAL IDEAL'

Disabled bodies have become one of the most versatile tools of contemporary Spanish cinema in its relentless attacks on traditional, patriarchal masculinities and in the formulation of alternative, decentred, non-hegemonic masculinities that reflect changes in the perception of gender power relations within Spanish society. An unproblematic, fully functional body was one of the attributes of the traditional representation of the ordinary man. In the Spanish film industry, the dismissal of discredited patriarchal masculinities (initiated, arguably, by García Berlanga) has been followed by the popularization of certain prototypes of manliness, such as the 'new', soft-mannered man, the gay virile and more recently the so-called 'metrosexual' (an already outdated version of the ever-evolving 'new' urban man who is both virile and in touch with his feminine side). All these prototypes depart in various degrees from the traditional masculine values of virility, masculinity, vigour, strength, muscularity, ruggedness, toughness, robustness, powerfulness and brawniness. In this context, it might be useful to remember that, up until the 1990s, the consideration of masculinity in film was limited to a set of models that rarely included the wounded, diseased or disabled male. Despite some instances of men in wheelchairs, in hospital beds, paralysed and seriously injured or diseased,[1] the theoretical gaze was somewhere else (namely in the empowerment of the female and the deconstruction of patriarchy), and the masculine field was simplistically reduced to patriarchal models (see, for example, Benito Gil 1987; Norden 1994 or Alegre de la Rosa 2003). Spanish cinema in the

1990s has consistently explored the crisis of traditional masculinities and their alternatives.

Using the feminist notion of body as text, we will argue that many Spanish film industries of the 1990s have marked a departure from the previous modes of representation of the male body as 'rigid', illegible and invisible. In contrast, it has become writable and readable; it has been made the object of the cinematic gaze; declared open to interpretation and subject to varying and conflicting interpretations. Thus, the family man as the hero of the paradigmatic films of the 1960s such as *La gran familia/The Big Family* (dirs Palacios and Salvia, 1962) and its sequels offered a portrayal of the man as the person 'by default': the physicality of his body was taken for granted, never allowing it to interfere with his daily business, nor to become too explicit – never to allow female or gay spectators to become too involved with it. All characters in *La gran familia* are defined in contrast to the Father (Alberto Closas), including his wife, children, aged father and emasculated best friend (López Vázquez). In post-patriarchal times, however, the textualization of the male body, which requires it to be objectified, dissected and manipulated, is more eloquently expressed by means of visual disfiguration – hence, the abundance of disfigured men and narratives of disease, disability and violence in the contemporary Spanish film industry.

The films discussed in this chapter are more akin to the sort of physicality proposed in *El Cochecito/The Wheelchair* (dir. Ferreri, 1960) in a sui-generis neo-realist line that was unfortunately short-lived (Hopewell 1986: 238–239). In *El Cochecito*, a retired Don Anselmo (José Isbert) must choose between his family and his friends. Whilst his friends are a group of physically handicapped people who use motorized wheelchairs, his extremely conservative family is tyrannically headed by Don Anselmo's son. The audience sympathizes with the group of physically disabled friends to the extent that Don Anselmo, who has no disability, ends up purchasing his own wheelchair and joining them. As Marsha Kinder has pointed out, the ambiguity of the eventual poisoning of the family can be read both as an overthrow of Francoism and as a critique of consumer capitalism embraced by an increasingly dehumanized Spanish society (1993: 113). The film could then be interpreted as a premonition of capitalist anxieties (and the individual responses they generate) in the globalized Spain of today.

Social sensibility in Spain towards the representation of disfigured bodies has been influenced by sources other than the Spanish film industry. An excess of violence in American films and TV news footage in an era of international terror have contributed to create a special mood against visual excesses on the coverage of the terrorist attacks in New York (2001), Madrid (2004) and London (2005) or the Iraq war and the Middle East conflict.[2] Concurrently, the growing social awareness of violent crimes has been fed by the notorious episodes of violence that have been promptly echoed in films, migrant bashing in *Bwana* (dir. Imanol Uribe, 1996) (see Chapter 7), village massacres in *El séptimo día/The Seventh Day* (dir. Carlos Saura, 2004), sexual kidnapping and murder in *Tesis/Thesis* (dir. Alejandro Amenábar, 1996), domestic violence in *Te doy mis ojos/Take My Eyes* (dir. Icíar Bollaín, 2003), political killings in *Yoyes* (dir. Helena Taberna, 2000), and all sorts of bodily violence in the films of Jess Franco (Pavlović 2003: 107–122).

Questions of physical normalcy and disfiguration are central to our understanding of the body, and as a result, to our understanding of modern subjectivities. An initial difficulty in the study of body distortion is posed by the seemingly endless multiplicity of disfigurations, mutilations, disabilities, wounds, illnesses, affections and conditions that we can find in a body. Tetraplegia or scars, for instance, are radically different subjective experiences linked to different stories that are susceptible to very different social interpretations. The cases of disfiguration discussed in this chapter might have different causes and might have very different meanings attached to them, but they all point towards the lost nature of an original, ideally healthy body. In his attempts to describe the nature of that ideal, lost model, Lennard Davis (1997) suggests a genealogy to the idea of the normal that is prevalent in our age. Normalizing the body into a set of standard proportions and measurements became an aesthetic convention of Renaissance art and an economic necessity of early capitalism. The too-short, too-tall, too-fat or too-thin would be a potential hazard in the workplace and were therefore put aside. The normal, in a mass-market economy, also became the norm for ready-made clothing, and also for the setting of architectural and design standards that would determine the size of beds and bedrooms and all sorts of everyday objects. Before the norm, Davis reminds us, the model was the ideal body, the perfect, proportionate, splendid bodies fabricated by the visual artists and proposed to us as impossible, albeit desirable, bodies (1997: 10). He goes on to suggest that, in our time, the norm has been replaced by a different model, which he calls 'the normal ideal': a highly perfect body, corresponding to the top statistical percentile of the general population, which is proposed as a 'hegemonic vision of what the human body should be' (Davis 1997: 17). This is the ideal body used by publicists to convey normalcy – or at least, an optimal level of normalcy – to which everyone ought to aspire. This discourse generates anxieties and conformity crises because of the impossibility inherent in its own definition. Many teenagers and many bodybuilders have learned this the hard way, through anorexia and steroid abuse. The aporia inherent in the normal ideal is that it offers, as the only acceptable model, an idealization that excludes any visible physical condition, most skin colours, old-age symptoms and poor body management. The personal demands of this model are so strict, and at the same time so useless in the pursuit of the ideal, that they remind us of totalitarian regimes based on a rigid discipline for the sake of it. Of course, we know, after Foucault (1991), that strict body regimes respond to the necessity for maintaining and controlling the mechanisms that regulate power. Davis's normal ideal model, as transmitted and reinforced by visual representations of model males and females in films, fashion, visual arts and the media is a model based on the constant repression of nearly all body forms. The history of cinema offers eloquent images that could be readily added to Davis's pictorial and sculptural examples from the pre-twentieth-century European visual arts. Spanish post-war cinema is rich in idealized bodies, mainly through the visual construction of the fascist hero in the *crusade* films in the early 1940s (see Chapter 3), a male prototype that was later adapted to the varying social and economic conditions of the country, re-emerging in the 1960s as the modern paterfamilias exemplified, as we have seen, by Closas in *La gran familia*, 'the National-Catholic representation of blissful lower-middle class life' (Triana-Toribio 2003: 127).[3]

In his study of the American action film, Peter Lehman describes the typical corporeal visual clues that conventionally signal the character's loss of power, control or influence (Lehman 1993: 61). In female characters, this loss is signalled by a physical mark related to facial beauty; in male characters it is typically marked by a crippling, which is literally and symbolically a limitation of the ability to act and therefore a limitation of their phallic power. This scheme of gender roles seems only too appropriate in relation to the otherwise simple set of values governing the action genre, but in a culture decidedly critical of patriarchal values, like the Spain of the 1990s, Lehman's observation about the classic American action film requires a broader perspective. In a film like *Abre los ojos/Open Your Eyes* (dir. Amenábar, 1997), as we shall see later in this chapter, the male protagonist invests much of his personal drawing power, magnetism, seduction abilities and even self-identity in the beauty of his face. Losing his beauty in a car accident signifies an immediate disempowerment, a loss of phallic power.

The point of this particular film is precisely that the obsession with beauty is general in our society and cannot be attributed to women only. On the other hand, Lehman's assertion that, 'a scar on a man's face frequently enhances rather than detracts from his power' (Lehman 1993: 63) is perfectly coherent with the well-established tradition of the 'noble wound', typically acquired at war or in some manly duty. Moral and civic discourses about war mutilations have a long literary and film history. It is a fact that wounded men have managed to construct their imperfect bodies as embodiments of national virtues, as heroic testimonials, as narratives of selflessness, all of it inevitably leading to a phallic, and sometimes erotic, overvaluation of what is left of them. Thus, in today's Spanish cinema, the noble wound, the crippling and the scarred face are only three of the many possible ways to disfigure the male body.

Davis claims for the disabled the same minority community status granted to women, gays or blacks (1995; 1997). He observes that the disabled have traditionally been the object of continuous discrimination, marginalization, negation and control. Like homosexuals (see Chapter 5), those regarded as disabled are commonly reduced to their bodies, as if they were no more than a manifestation of 'the Other', since body normalcy, as Davis notes, is only defined negatively in relation to the abnormality characteristic of the disabled. Rod Michalko (1946) amongst others (Thomson 1997; Mitchell and Snyder 2000) draws attention to the fact that disabled people are still feared, and explores the social meanings associated with disability, not least the consistent exclusion of disabled people from the common understanding of what constitutes a good life. As Michalko argues, disability is a type of 'difference' that leads to a social identity, thus becoming a political issue.

Social perceptions of health and disease offer different nuances in relation to gender. A visible disease of the kind that leaves unhidden marks or signals in the body is likely to be interpreted by others according to various factors (is it contagious? Is it horrific? Is it permanent? Does it hurt?), including the unavoidable question as to whether the disease can interfere with the masculinity or femininity of the afflicted – in the broadest possible sense, sex ability, seduction capability, gender definition. One inference from recent literature on gender and health is that a perfect health is generally expected from men, while women's ill-health or a transitory disease is more easily forgivable. Mangan focuses on fitness as a key masculine concept, closely related to the social construction of men as outwardly oriented and women as oriented towards the home (Mangan 2000: 1). This model dictates that the man, as the impregnator, protector and provider must never become dysfunctional in any of those roles; he is defined by his sexual, physical and economical strength. To fail in those is to fail as a man. Understandably, pressure to perform at all these levels often leads to anxiety and depression. Paradoxically, the fear of failing as a man can lead to panic situations and the somatization of a purely mental activity can provoke the very same body dysfunction that was feared at the beginning. To make things worse, there is the destructive concept of 'true manhood', which venomously suggests that there are good ways and bad ways of 'being' a man. The conflation of different levels of manhood with different levels of body functionality generates the idea that the diseased male is, somehow, less male – that his masculinity has been diminished. The diseased male who feels vulnerable and diminished in his manhood generally activates the outward/inward duality evoked by Mangan (2000). Thus, the first typical reaction of a sick male character is to go private, to remain hidden from the public view. Women, in turn, tend to go public, to look for the support of friends or family, and to let everyone know what is going on (this tendency is parodied in Pedro Almodóvar's *Volver* (2006) in a scene in which a terminally ill female cancer patient is pushed to discuss her illness on live national television).

The film *Solas/Alone* (dir. Benito Zambrano, 1999) offers a magnificent example of the diseased male retractive behaviour. Set in a modern-day Andalucian city, the film features a dysfunctional, dismembered family torn apart by the irreconcilable drives of the authoritarian father (Paco de Osca) and the assertive daughter (Ana Fernández). The narrative is centred on the figure of the mother (María Galiana), caught between her violent, dominant husband and her uncompromising daughter. This three-fold conflict unfurls through a series of tense two-way situations along the storyline of the father's time in hospital (which generates visits from his wife, from his daughter, and from both together) and also the dialogues of the mother and daughter outside the hospital. In a way, the film is a family portrait: the three characters are characteristic of a very recognizable Spanish narrative, successfully portrayed here. The father, for instance, is represented as insultingly arrogant, bad tempered, bad mannered, obsessed with his own manliness and with the way others might perceive it, obsessed with his wife's loyalty and submission, and obsessed above all things with living his life according to some pre-existing script that determines with exacting precision what a man is and is not. Through the dialogues, we also learn that his marriage is based on a violent, aggressive relationship with his wife and that he hates to be in the hospital where 'they do with you as they please'. It is quite clear that the hospital experience, in his case, is the reversal of the domestic violence he has left at home: there, he was the aggressor; here, he is the victim. In the 'manliness script' that governs his life, becoming the recipient of any physical violence is similar to occupying the wife's position and, therefore, it becomes an unbearable affront to his masculinity.[4]

RESISTING 'THE BODY BEAUTIFUL' IN 1990s SPANISH CINEMA

The Spanish monster film is slightly different from its Hollywood counterpart, at least in its parodic overtones. Stated or not, the Spanish genre draws on its domestic audience's knowledge of the Hollywood canonical conventions such as the monster as evil, the gendering of good and evil, and the unhappy or sometimes tragic ending. Spanish monster films show a preference for happy endings, in a reversal of the Hollywood-coded genre that is most likely an effect of the parodic vein Spanish scriptwriters adopt in their response to the imperialistic and undesirable competence of the US films. The Spanish film industry, perfectly aware of its underdog market position in Spain, seems to have chosen, in the 1990s, not to compete directly with Hollywood in those genres and areas where Hollywood dominance is overwhelming. Instead, the Spaniards actively explore and exploit where Hollywood has a lesser role – Spanish topics, *auteurisme* and parodies of Hollywood genres. The connection between the topics of the monster, the dark humour and the grotesque on the one hand, and the demands of the market expressed in audience figures on the other, has been evidenced by Carmen Rabalska (1999).

Acción mutante/Mutant Action (dir. Álex de la Iglesia, 1993) is a fantasy film where disabled men are presented in relation to the issue of compulsory beauty. Openly parodying Hollywood sci-fi genres, and combining the elements of the western, the musical, the hijack film and the drawing-room comedy (Jordan and Morgan-Tamosunas 1998: 108), *Acción mutante* tells the story of how the young daughter (Frédérique Feder) of a wealthy businessman (Fernando Guillén) is kidnapped during her wedding party and taken to another planet where her father is asked to pay the ransom, and how in the process she falls in love with her (male) kidnapper (Antonio Resines) to finally elope with him. This topical storyline is built on a powerful ideological observation that rescues the film from total irrelevance: the kidnappers are a group of disabled men, marginalized in a (futuristic) society which is obsessed with physical perfection and the body beautiful. Their inability to get their rights back leads them to resentment and hence they decide to resort to terrorist means. Being just a parody, terrorism here is merely an allusion to real-life terrorist groups whose use of violence seems to be motivated by disgruntlement and acrimony.[5] The source of inequality, discrimination and symbolic violence in the film is corporeal imperfection. The gang comprises a pair of Siamese twins, a dwarf, a legless man who hovers around on a small flying saucer, a half-defaced man who holds his brains in with a metallic grid, and a man whose body depends on countless harnesses to hold it together. There is also a gigantic, deaf-mute man credited with having the lowest IQ in the universe. The members of the gang are annihilated one by one, until only the boss is left. Terms such as 'bad taste' (Jordan and Morgan-Tamosunas 1998: 108) and 'vulgarity' (Triana-Toribio 2003: 159) have been used in relation to the film as a whole. The all-male atmosphere is made even more masculine by the transformation of the kidnapped 'princess' from a defenceless, tied-up damsel into an aggressive, armed, female warrior, equally able to get rid of a rapist gang and to shoot down her own father. The unexpectedly happy ending is made possible by two amputations: the girl loses an arm, and the only surviving Siamese twin loses his brother's dead body. The armless look lovingly at each other and try, comically, a one-arm hug. However, the eventual success of the terrorist group fails to make any sense in relation to its stated goal to 'fight beautiful people'. In fact, this goal is lost early on in the film, being replaced with the ideologically innocuous cash ransom. It would have been interesting to see how a narrative articulation of that fight against the beautiful could have symbolized other few-against-many fights. It would also have been interesting to explore how a society of perfect bodies would have dealt with its minorities and what technologies would have been used to integrate the marginalized and the disempowered. Yet the film succeeds in suggesting totalitarianism as the main organizational principle of a civilization based on the perfect body, with terrorism being the only response left to its dissidents. Echoes of totalitarian dystopias that predict a society based on the fascist principles of the dismissal of the unfit and government through the TV image are quite clear throughout the film.

In her study of *Acción mutante*, Madeline Conway discusses the film as a modern-day freak show, where the 'normal' spectator pays to see 'abnormal' bodies; whilst in traditional freak shows the marketing was crucial, in *Acción mutante* the group of disabled men is first presented by means of a TV news bulletin (Conway 2000: 257). Nevertheless, she concludes that the film does not permit the spectator to rely on the catharsis usually associated with a freak show.[6] The introduction of a screen-within-the-screen very early on in the film could help to explain the phlegmatic reaction of the film's audience, because by means of a second-degree diegesis, the whole story of the disabled terrorists and their victims is framed as a refereed discourse mediated by TV. The prologue scene, including the TV news bulletin, contains three important elements that require some analysis: a discourse on the body, terrorism and the introduction of the gallery of male characters that make up the gang.

The film opens with a gory scene of torture and death. The components of the terrorist group, '*Acción Mutante*', display eminently unprofessional and incompetent behaviour with a kidnapped victim, who ends up dying at their hands. Then, the screen is filled with a futuristic version of present-day news or current affairs TV programmes: the image of the anchorman is digitally projected in various areas of the screen, against a backdrop of newsreels that occupy the whole screen, leaving no space for any display of a studio or any other analogue image. The audience is presented with the *Sucesos* (accident and crime reports) section of the news show in a TV channel called JQK, featuring the slaughter of Matías Pons, president of a Bodybuilders Association, attributed to the 'terrorist gang'. Credits roll whilst in the soundtrack a theme presenting the ideology of the group is sung in the first person plural; the lyrics contain a returning line '*Mens Sana in Corpore Tullido*'/'*A healthy mind in a crippled body*' and a direct allusion to Dalton Trumbo's *Johnny Got His Gun* (1971), a film often referred to in discussions of filmic representations of the disabled body. The visual background of the credits scene consists of a series of images of the terrorists, the members of '*Acción Mutante*', setting the farcical tone that will dominate the story – drawing on the discrepancy between their diversely disabled bodies and the assumed perfection of their guns and weapons.

The ideology behind '*Acción Mutante's*' terror campaign is spelled out in two different moments of the film, beyond the general idea of fighting the perfect body expressed in the TV show. When gang leader Yarritu (Antonio Resines), joins his cronies to prepare for the next action, the group chants a few slogans and their leader addresses them with a speech about the need to resist the imposition of the perfect body and perfect looks, using, if necessary, terrorism as an answer. He makes explicit the connection between body perfection and social enforcement, which in part helps to explain the true nature of the terrorists' 'mutation'. Whilst in science-fiction classics a mutation usually refers to a change in the genetic code, in *Acción mutante* it seems to signify an ideological change of seriously injured or maimed people who had lost all hope into radical activists who will fight society rather than being erased from it. Society, for these mutants, is controlled by advertising and the media that dictate a lifestyle based on a strict body discipline. For the mutants/terrorists, the act of refusing to follow the media edicts is subversive enough to marginalize them from mainstream society – a society preoccupied by the integrated elite of the posh, stylish and fashionable represented by the wealthy Orujo family and the glamorous party guests, which include familiar faces, such as Almodóvar regulars Rossy de Palma and Bibí Andersen (see Chapter 6), two unlikely representatives of conventional beauty.

The second ideologically important moment takes place in planet Axturias. Here, all signs of trendy sophistication are gone; there seems to be no TV and no media advertising activities; in fact, the planet seems to exist in a mix of the pre-capitalist and the post-nuclear age. The bodies of the Axturian population could be best described as 'dark, filthy, earthy, scabrous' (Jordan and Morgan-Tamosunas 1998: 108). Yarritu has killed all his peers, and now drags the kidnapped Patricia by her hair up a hill, whilst she declaims a speech about the need to change the world and create a new society of disabled and mutilated people. What Patricia is doing through this mutant/terrorist speech could be described as a revolutionary programme based on two Marxist principles: that capitalism is inhumane, and that another world is possible. She then justifies, à la Trotsky, recourse to violence in order to build a new, fairer world. But, instead of proposing the orthodox notion of fairness and the rule of law, she speaks of mutilation as the only equity principle. It is not, then, a case of beauty being discarded as social currency, but of mutilation – a state the healthy person should mutate towards – as the new currency. This grotesque deformation of a Marxian-inspired discourse is presented as pure comedy, but the point it makes about the excessive power of the media and its alienating role in a consumerist society is taken more seriously by the film.

La mujer más fea del mundo/ The Ugliest Woman in the World (dir. Bardem, 1999) is another good example of the parodic approach to the genre film, because it contains a conscious intertextual activity through the use of people's names (La Bella Otero,[7] Teresa of Calcutta and other names that resemble those of real Spanish celebrities), music (*pasodobles*), parodied television genres (New Year's Eve broadcast from Madrid's Puerta del Sol, news bulletins) and film genres (the metamorphosis and the double-life variants of the monster film), the republican parody of national Spanish institutions (flag, president,

Madrid DF, Federal Police), to mention but a few examples. Some of these intertextual and parodic games are in fact quite elaborate; for instance, the onscreen displays of the Spanish 'Other' self – the republican shadow – are in line with the two main characters' 'Other', more authentic self – the unpleasant, ugly appearance of their faces – and with the more general philosophy that only inner beauty counts. Whilst in the barbarous world of *Acción mutante*, only the visible is real (thus collapsing any difference between inner and outer beauty), in *La mujer más fea del mundo* there is a conscious effort to take that dichotomy to narrative and symbolic levels. At the narrative level, there are several instances of people wearing masks and fancy dress, of people showing their body enhancements (from wigs to high heels), of people talking about plastic surgery and other body modifications, and, importantly, of people being aware of the duplicitous nature of beauty, deceitful when superficial but rewarding when invisible. At the symbolic level, the film takes the ethical principle of inner beauty to propose a radical, albeit somehow diminished, critique of physical beauty as a source of social or interpersonal power. However, the film fails to point to the fact that inner beauty usually refers to moral perfection and a standard normalized virtue. This failure is even more regrettable since the concept is introduced by an aged blind nun who, as a helper to the female monster, is unmoved by and perfectly unaware of her physical ugliness, and is picked up by the Beautiful Otero herself on accepting the first prize at the Miss Spain contest. Any expectation that the ugly woman is going to be morally perfect is reversed as she turns out to be a serial killer. But, unlike the cash-motivated gang in *Acción mutante*, her only goal in life is 'to be loved'.

La mujer más fea del mundo contains, like *Acción mutante*, a futuristic depiction of the totalitarian ubiquitousness of television, but it is more restrained in generic conventions because it draws mainly on science fiction, the thriller and *film noir*. The apparent focus of the film is female beauty (the plot revolves around a Miss Spain beauty contest). The villain happens to be one of the contestants, by the name of Lola Otero (Elia Galera), a strong and phallic woman whose 'female avenger' dimension allows for intertextual links to other 1990s *noir* thrillers, such as *The Last Seduction* (dir. John Dahl, 1994) and *Batman Returns* (dir. Tim Burton, 1992), whilst at the same time invoking the 1940s Hollywood romantic *noir* film by means of a heterosexual happy ending (Parrondo Coppel 2004: 119). Not surprisingly, most studies of the film have focused on the central female figures. Eva Parrondo's psychoanalytic interpretation of the phallic woman takes into account not only Lola Otero's ability with weapons, but also her centrality in the narrative progression of the film and, importantly, the concept that physical beauty is not limited to women only. The trajectory of this female character is quite unusual: born with a monstrous face deformity, she presents a history of child neglect, abuse and rape before meeting a certain doctor whose experiments give her a perfect, beautiful face as long as she keeps taking a drug. She then becomes a famous and prominent member of the 'beautiful people' society, but at the same time she starts taking revenge on that society by killing every winner of the Miss Spain contest. Eventually, she is caught and put in jail, where, the drug being no longer available, she returns to her original monstrous condition. In an unexpected turn of events, she and the male detective, who has been able to stop her killing, fall in love. Our last glimpse of the monstrously disfigured Lola Otero, which contradicts all the conventions of the monster genre, is one of happiness and hope in personal fulfilment.

However, despite the centrality of the character of Lola Otero, the film possesses an all-male symbolic universe that is somewhat reminiscent of *Acción mutante*: in both stories, a multiplicity of men moves around a central female character. In *La mujer más fea del mundo*, all the main characters suffer the effects of unresolved issues of body and self. The figure of the male detective, Lieutenant Arribas (Roberto Álvarez) represents a perfect example of Lehman's (1993) point, discussed earlier in this chapter, about the effects of physical disfiguration in male characters. In a particularly revealing scene quite early on in the film, we discover that he leads a double life in terms of physical appearance. His moderately attractive looks at work turn out to be very unpleasant in the loneliness of his high-tech apartment. His home-theatre system is equipped with voice recognition, allowing him to give verbal commands, suggesting the Lieutenant's high degree of control over his own image. The scene utilizes alternating shots of the detective and shots of the TV screen. Each shot of the detective corresponds to a verbal command. For the first command ('*Start*'), he is shot from his right; the frame contains the human figure in the left-hand side and the wall-mounted plasma TV to the right. '*Back*' is shot from behind the detective; we can now see the TV screen he is watching. '*Stop*' corresponds to a medium shot of his face. '*Go*' is shot in close-up, as are the next commands: '*Stop*', '*Zoom in*', '*More*', '*Print*'. Up to this point, the soundtrack of this scene has been a *pasodoble*; then, a voice comes from the TV set which announces a 'Miss Spain' beauty contest that will hail the next beauty queen. Jokingly, the announcement suggests that the beauty queen would wear the only existing crown in the Republic of Spain. The notion that beauty is undemocratic receives, in this TV formulation, a sarcastic innuendo by suggesting that a super-democratic republican Spain would still recognize the aristocracy of the beautiful. Deciding to ignore this beauty-as-elite talk on television, Detective Arribas makes a point of going to the bathroom 'to get comfortable'. Against the uninterrupted backdrop of the *pasodoble*, he takes some delight in contemplating his own image reflected in the mirror before removing his wig, then his glass eye and finally his denture, revealing a burnt, scarred scalp, an empty eye socket, and an imploded cheek in the process. This 47-second fragment contains 15 shots, all of them close-ups of the detective, some frontal, some from behind (incorporating his image in the mirror), from his left and also close-ups of the prostheses he is using. Quite clearly, his looks would be intolerable to his peers if he did not use those prostheses or beauty supplements. Thus, the scene is a poignant reminder of the unreliability of appearances and on the possibilities of altering our own image to appear more attractive.

The scene of the detective in front of the television screen and then in front of the mirror highlights a connection between body and identity that is almost unparalleled for its powerful conciseness in contemporary Spanish cinema. Roberto Álvarez gives his character a tired demeanour, which can equally correspond to both the end of a hard day's work and to a more profound sense of weariness of his masculine condition in a world that no longer privileges masculinity. The succession of close-ups and medium shots of his face from all angles emphasizes the symbolic nature of his fatigued air. We will never know the origin of his facial disfigurations, but we witness his masterful control of his own looks, and the easiness with which he seems to wear his 'mask' – especially when compared to the traumatic approach to the prosthetic mask displayed by the disfigured male character in Amenábar's *Abre los ojos* (1997) discussed in the next section of this chapter.

None of Arribas's peers in the police headquarters has a good-looking or moderately attractive face (this is underlined with a notorious physical feature that defines each one – squint, obesity, stuttering). This world of the imperfect and the below-average-looking is by no means equated to the monstrosity of Lola Otero; instead, it is offered in contrast to it. There is, the film seems to propose, an abysmal difference between the non-conforming beauty of the moderately unattractive, and the transgressive ugliness of the abject monster. The former brings about a simple dispossession of the power given to the beautiful; the latter is punished with symbolic and actual marginalization. Interestingly, both the monster and the detective seem to share a common concern with not being loved. The primal fear of being cut off from the world surfaces here in the form of the modern world's paranoia with physical appearance, not only in relation to mating and sexual gratification, but also, primarily, in relation to social integration, self-acceptance and authenticity. It is hardly surprising that contemporary Spanish cinema has paid increasing attention to the question of authenticity, given that the evolution of the Spanish society has brought about a common Western obsession with the external, the physical and the bodily. The relationship between body and the inner-self permeates recent Spanish films in ways that would be unimaginable when Almodóvar was beginning to experiment with a post-modern aesthetic in his early films and with segmented bodies from *Kika* (1993) onwards.

BEAUTY IS ON THE INSIDE: THE SICK BODY IN THE FILMS OF AMENÁBAR

The films of Alejandro Amenábar provide an ideal case study for the representation of the sick body in recent Spanish cinema (Fouz-Hernández 2005b). His first short film, *La cabeza/The Head* (1991), ends with the severed head of a man whose face had been disfigured in a fatal accident. His first feature film *Tesis/Thesis* (1996) explored the dark depths of the so-called snuff films.[8] In his second feature film, *Abre los ojos/Open Your Eyes* (1997), the once-handsome protagonist tries to push the limits of cosmetic surgery, hoping to have his disfigured face reconstructed, but settles for cryotherapy. The little-known illness of photo-sensibility inspired his third film, *Los Otros/The Others* (2001), and his successful *Mar adentro/The Sea Inside* (2004) is based on the real-life story of a tetraplegic man and his fight for a dignified death. The fleshiness of Amenábar's work is palpable and crosses over into the way in which he experiences cinema and filmmaking. He describes as 'orthopaedic' those films in which the editing tricks are visible (see, for example, Rodríguez Marchante 2002: 72) and he is very fond of describing in length the painstaking process of putting on the character that his actors undergo. Thus, we know how the four-hour make-up sessions suffered by Noriega in *Abre los ojos* were complicated by real-life wounds caused by the strings that held the make-up together, and which became infected and painful (Rodríguez Marchante 2002: 104–106), or that Javier Bardem had to undergo daily five-hour make-up sessions prior to shooting in *Mar adentro* (Figueras 2004: 76) – these efforts were acknowledged with an Oscar nomination in the make-up category. Moreover, the director himself suffers physically when filming: the nerves make him rub his hands obsessively to the point that he often ends up with sores all over his hands (Rodríguez Marchante 2002: 150).

In *Tesis*, the deaths of several characters, including the two main villains, are recorded on a video camera. As in *Mar adentro*, the presence of the camrecorder is emphasized by shots of the machine (with the red light flashing) from the POV of the characters. For Amenábar, this technique 'despectacularizes' the act of dying (Rodríguez Marchante 2002: 98), but in this film at least it also has a moralizing effect, given that the two villains that we see die on camera made money out of filming other people's murders. In an interview that took place just after the 9/11 attacks in New York, Amenábar expressed his rejection of the way in which the images of violence and suffering (such as those who jumped to their deaths from the Twin Towers) were shown repeatedly and in slow motion on Spanish television (Rodríguez Marchante 2002: 52). In retrospect, the opening scene of *Tesis*, in which a Madrid Metro train is evacuated after someone had thrown himself to the tracks, has become all the more poignant following the Madrid train bombings on 11 March 2004, almost ten years after the film was shot. In that scene, based on a real-life experience of the director (Rodríguez Marchante 2002: 51), the guards repeatedly ask the passengers not to look at the tracks, where the dismembered body of the man lays. The announcement clearly increases the curiosity of some of the passengers, such as the female protagonist Ángela (Ana Torrent) who breaks away from the line of people leaving the train and approaches the tracks to have a look but is suddenly stopped by a guard just as she (and we) were about to see the mutilated body. Arguably, Ángela's investigation of snuff films for her undergraduate thesis stands for Amenábar's own *Tesis* on this subject (the film): the character and the director insist on declaring their dislike of images of violence (Rodríguez Marchante 2002: 51) and yet, like some of the passengers of that train and like many film audiences, they are fascinated by it. The film's ending takes us back to the beginning. Appropriately, the final scene takes place in a hospital where one of the protagonists is recovering from the final struggle with the killer. All the other patients in that hospital room (mainly elderly people) are eagerly watching a sensationalist television report on the university snuff films story of the film, their sickness being an allegory for the 'sick society' poisoned by media (as Amenábar has acknowledged in Rodríguez Marchante 2002: 51).[9] Just as a fragment from one of these films is about to be shown (the same footage that had been seen by the characters but only partly heard and partly seen by the audience), the film ends abruptly after the following warning is shown on the television screens: 'please beware that the images that you are about to see could be found to be offensive' (for a further discussion of violence in *Tesis* see Allinson 1997).

The fascination with seeing is clear in Amenábar's other films too. It is implicit in the title and the plot of *Abre los ojos*, a film that also ends with an abrupt cut to a blackout, just as the protagonist César (Eduardo Noriega) is about to crash to the floor having thrown himself from the top of a skyscraper. His broken body on the pavement is never shown, despite what some members of the audience would have been expecting. *Abre los ojos* explores the theme of narcissism but also encourages audiences to turn their gaze to the body whose transformation is shown, first by admiring it in its undamaged form, comparing it with the body of his less attractive friend and then, as Perriam suggests, 'by presenting a newly scarified image of Noriega [that] heightens by contrast the usual pleasure in his looks' (Perriam 2003: 175). We know that the effect works when we share a feeling of anxiety followed by one of relief when Sofía (Penélope Cruz) removes the plaques from his face after the final operation (one that had only taken place in virtual reality as we only find out later) and gradually reveals parts of his reconstructed face that now appears even more attractive than before the accident.[10]

Actor Eduardo Noriega who, as Rodríguez Marchante puts it, 'is, without a doubt, the actor who best represents the "*fleshy*" in the world of Amenábar' (2002: 208, our emphasis), had established a reputation as the convincingly attractive and self-confident male through his Bosco character in *Tesis* (Perriam 2004a: 209) – his good looks were instrumental in his killings. In that film, Bosco seduces Ángela, her sister, her mother and even the audience as he leads us to doubt whether the less attractive character Chema (Fele Martínez) was the killer. On one occasion he invites Ángela to 'take advantage' of him. Later we see how, despite apparently resisting his approaches and despising him, Ángela had erotic fantasies about him that are manifested in a dream and also in a secretly obtained video recording where she is seen touching and kissing Bosco's image on a television screen (the perfect metaphor for the objectified male).

The physical contrast established between the characters played by Noriega and Martínez is re-enacted in *Abre los ojos* by the characters César and Pelayo, but only to be turned inside out after an accident disfigures César's face. Initially, César is the rich kid who seems to have it all. Not only does he have a nice house in the centre of Madrid, three cars and all the girls that he wants, he is also the modern 'metrosexual' who takes pride in his appearance. This is suggested by his well-groomed aspect and the frequency with which he is seen in the bathroom and looking at himself in the mirror in the first half of the film – an action that he will fear after the accident, declaring that he wants to die every time he sees his reflection in the mirror.[11] By contrast, his average-looking friend Pelayo (Martínez) complains about his lack of sex-appeal and the fact that he only looks 'OK', and only when he is not seen next to César. The drastic change of circumstances marked by the character's change of looks after the accident (Pelayo would become attractive by comparison) provides a good opportunity to reflect on the excessive importance that our society places on appearances, a critique contained in César's words to the plastic surgeons at the clinic when they ask him to accept himself: 'Who will accept me?' he asks, 'Are you going to tell the people who stare at me in the street? Are you going to tell them all that looks are not important and that beauty is on the inside?' César's confrontations with the plastic surgeons and then with the representatives of the cryotherapy company, 'Life Extension', symbolizes a critique of those corporate powers that sell the idea of physical perfection (as seen in the films discussed in the previous section of this chapter), and which here is contained in the persistent close-up shots of corporate logos, something that Shaviro has also noted in Cronenberg's 1981 film *Scanners* (Shaviro 1993: 135).

Bardem's remarkable role in Amenábar's multiple-award-winning *Mar adentro* (it won a record 14 Goya awards and the Oscar for the best Foreign Film in 2005 amongst many other national and international recognitions) is based on the real story of Ramón Sampedro, a tetraplegic man from North-Western Spain who fought unrelentingly and quite publicly to end his life with dignity after almost 30 years prostrated in bed.[12] Sampedro's real-life battle is palpable in *Cartas desde el infierno* (*Letters from Hell*) (2004), a collection of letters published during his lifetime as a means to critique a legal system that, for Sampedro, unfairly 'appropriated' his body for 29 years and which were used as inspiration for the film's script. The choice of Javier Bardem for this role was an interesting one. As Amenábar has said, 'the casting of Bardem to play a man that renounces his body, his physique, of a different age and tetraplegic, could seem a complete mistake. Everything was against him' (Ponga 2004: 81). Yet, as Perriam has noted (2003: 93), the over-sexed '*macho ibérico*' types for which Bardem became known in the early 1990s have been compensated for and superseded by other well-known roles, such as the one in Almodóvar's *Carne trémula* (discussed in the next section of this chapter), in which his acting persona has been associated with disability. Perhaps there is an unconscious but powerful cross-referential link to one of those 'sick' characters (also based on a real person and one that in the fiction also dies through an assisted suicide) in the way in which Ramón's ambulance journey to the courts of A Coruña is filmed: the visual emphasis on the vignettes of Galician rural life is reminiscent of the taxi journey back home from hospital taken by Bardem's Reynaldo Arenas in *Before Night Falls* (dir. Schnabel, 2000). In that film, objective POV shots of the urban landscape of New York are mixed with fantasy shots of rural Cuba, Arenas's native land, and one that has strong connections with Galicia. Like Schnabel's Arenas, Amenábar's Sampedro is also subtly charged with Christian iconography, such as when he appears in bed with both arms outstretched (see Toro 2004: 35).

Bardem's impressive physical transformation (see Figure 10 and compare with Figures 2, 3 and 4) was one of the aspects of *Mar adentro* that attracted most attention and which Amenábar duly explained to *Fotogramas*: 'to *cancel out the physical* in Bardem, we used a harness so that he had to arch his back and tuck in his shoulders' (Ponga 2004: 81 – emphasis added). Elsewhere, the actor also explained that a special bed had been designed to hide part of his body and make it look 'the opposite of what it is' (Toro 2004: 39). This 'negation of physicality', as both Amenábar and Bardem graphically put it, is nowhere more evident than in the semi-nude television pictures that are shown early on in the film and that we will discuss later. For that long shot, Amenábar considered replacing Bardem's body with one of a real tetraplegic but instead decided to use Bardem's own body and digitally reduce his shoulders, arms and legs (Ponga 2004: 81).

The more the audience learns about Sampedro's life before the accident, the more acute his immobility becomes: an adventurous sailor, he had travelled around the world at the age of 19. Perhaps as a way of insisting on the contrast between the character's past mobility and his current situation, Sampedro's travels in the film are not shown through flashbacks of moving pictures but are contained in the close-up shots of the photographs seen by Julia (the solicitor played by Belén Rueda) whilst staying at his house. It is as if even the memory of movement had been impregnated with his current stasis. The mobility is only recovered in a series of romantic dreams inspired by some of his poems, in which he flies out of his bedroom window like a seagull (Sampedro 2004: 71), to fly over the Galician fields, down to the sea, often to reach out to an idealized lover. Notably, and as we shall see later, in contrast with Bardem's character in *Carne trémula*, Ramón refused to use a wheelchair and become semi-mobile. As documented in Sampedro's book, then in Amenábar's film and also explained by Bardem in interviews, Sampedro felt that accepting the wheelchair would be 'to accept that miserable freedom (…) the appearance of being a person when one is no more than a head' (Sampedro 2004: 85 – see also Figueras 2004: 78). However, his refusal to use a wheelchair does not make the character any weaker than David in *Carne trémula*. Bardem's Sampedro is equally determined and strong, although at a psychological level.

The introduction of a scene in which a tetraplegic priest visits him to try and persuade him not to end his life illustrates the limitations of Ramón's other choice: the priest's better economic means are made clear in a series of close-up shots of the car that brings him to the village and that also allow a meticulous scrutiny of his so-called assisted mobility: the back door opens up, a ramp assists his descent and two young men are needed to help him out. Yet, the sequence that follows is shot in a way that accentuates the limitations of this type of motorized mobility so detested by Sampedro. In other words, the sequence is an attempt to understand the protagonist's refusal to use a wheelchair and his choice of a 'dignified death' over what he seemed to regard as 'undignified living'. The stubbornness of both men in their non-negotiable ideological positions concerning paraplegia and

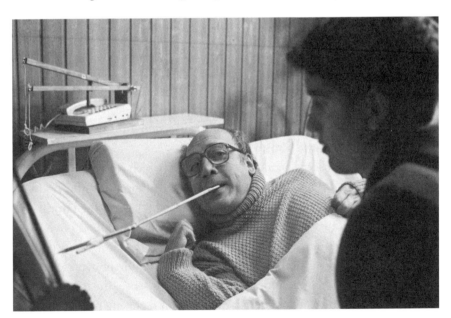

10. Transformed: Javier Bardem (with Tamar Novas) in *Mar adentro*.

euthanasia is illustrated in the priest's insistence to be taken up to Sampedro's room in his bulky wheelchair, despite the visible limitations of the steep and narrow staircase leading to the first floor (neither his chair, nor his ideas will get through to the bed-ridden man), as well as in Sampedro's refusal to be taken downstairs. On accepting the impossibility of making his way to Sampedro's room, Father Francisco (Josep María Pou) uses the young seminarist Brother Andrés (Alberto Amarilla) as an intermediary, in a memorable scene that sees Andrés going up and down the staircase trying to convey the opposing arguments to the two parties, metaphorically standing in the landing in between the two floors by the end of this awkward exchange, as if in the middle of the two opposing ideological standpoints. Clearly, he is the only one prepared to change his mind. Yet, close-up shots of his feet as he runs up and down the stairs serve not only to accentuate his mobility in contrast with the two men, but also perhaps to point out that his is a privileged physical situation that gives him more room for ideological flexibility. In his argument, Father Francisco resorts to barely sustainable moral issues to persuade Sampedro. These include accusations of the re-appropriation of the concept of private property (applied to our own bodies) or the self-affliction of the Nazi extermination tactics, all cleverly refuted by an increasingly sarcastic Sampedro who reminds the priest about the Catholic Church's own concept of property and their politics with regards to the death penalty. If there were any doubts about the film's positioning on this respect, Ramón's moral high-ground is emphasized by his spatial position upstairs or by the use of claustrophobic close-up shots with the priest and the medium shots of Sampedro. Furthermore, the generously and 'naturally' lit room of the latter contrasts with the darkness that surrounds Father Francisco. Nowhere else in the film is the contrast between these two differing positions so clearly established, an illustration of many such discussions that became commonplace in the Spanish media at the time of the film's release.[13]

In the television scene we mentioned earlier (which re-creates one of the iconic images of Ramón), television cameras are allowed into his home to film Ramón's shrivelled semi-naked body in bed. Beyond the ethical and political implications that this public display of his nude body may have had for his personal story, the 'spectacularization' of the tetraplegic's body in Amenábar's film insists on the need to question the dominant representations of the male body in contemporary cinema. In this sense, the images would seem to contribute to a destabilization of dominant representations of the male body in cinema. This is an aspect that Shaviro has highlighted in the context of Cronenberg and the so-called 'new flesh' films, arguing that 'by insisting on the gross palpability of the flesh, and by heightening (instead of minimising) our culture's pervasive discomfort with materiality, Cronenberg opposes the way in which dominant cinema captures, polices, and regulates desire, precisely by providing sanitized models of its fulfillment' (Shaviro 1993: 132). In the Spanish context, the increasingly common contestation of those aesthetic values favoured by dominant culture has also been described by José Miguel García Cortés as a tendency of contemporary art as a whole:

> We now find figures of clumsy men (…) weak (even impotent), docile (even passive), insecure (even scared) or deteriorated (even aged) that show in all their crudity the psychological vulnerability, the personal anxieties and physical mortality of a masculinity that was sold to us as invulnerable. (Garcia Cortés 2004: 56)

ALMODÓVAR'S APPROACH TO (DIS)ABILITY

As we have already mentioned, Almodóvar's *Carne trémula/Live Flesh* (1997) and Javier Bardem's performance in it offer a point of contrast with *Mar adentro* with regards to the metaphoric value of the wheelchair. Here, David (Bardem, who is wheelchair-bound for most of the film) takes up the challenge not only of using the wheelchair but of mastering its use, to the extent of becoming a Paralympic basketball champion. As in *Mar adentro*, Bardem's body is used as an important metaphor and a container for some of the main anxieties that underlie the film's narrative. His disabled body is defined in contrast to the other male lead played by Liberto Rabal (described by Almodóvar as the actor with 'the fleshiest lips in Spanish cinema' – Smith 2000a: 183),[14] and the importance of his character's physical attributes becomes apparent in his last-minute casting of Rabal over the then also famously handsome Jorge Sanz; because the latter actor 'did not have an adequate physique' for the role (Piña 1997: 18), he was controversially fired once shooting had commenced. The film's title itself ('*carne*' meaning both 'flesh' and 'meat' in Spanish and '*trémula*' having the extra 'connotations of trembling and pulsating' missed in the English translation) draws our attention to the equation drawn in the film between 'flesh' and 'meat' (Arroyo 1998: 51). The apparent coexistence of elements traditionally associated with 'masculinity' (such as the 'instincts' of competitiveness and the sexual 'hunt', the emphasis on sport, physical activity and muscularity) with less traditional 'masculine' values such as sensitivity or nurturing and the crucial presence of physical disability makes this film a particularly relevant one to end this chapter.

The initial erotic triangle established in the film between David (Bardem), Sancho (José Sancho) and Clara (Angela Molina) anticipates the triangular structure of the erotic narrative that, in each case, invites a comparison between the two men involved. Sancho will be involved in a second triangle with his wife Clara and Víctor (Rabal), when the latter comes out of prison. Although he only faces this at the end through the photographic evidence provided by David, the revelation will be an important and final blow to his already tarnished masculine identity because it reminds him once again that his wife has found, in the body of another younger, fitter man, the satisfaction that he can no longer provide. The interesting consequence of this second triangle is that, on the one hand, Víctor replaces David who, we assume, had stopped seeing Clara since the shooting and his consequent marriage to Elena. On the other hand, the triangle can be read both as a mirror of the one established when David married Elena (Víctor's object of desire) and in anticipation of the reconstitution of that same triangle when Víctor and Elena reunite, apparently for good. Notions of poetic justice could invite a conservative reading of the film where Víctor is compensated for his having served for a crime he did not commit and David is punished for a second time (the first being the shot that caused his lower-body paralysis) for his affair with Sancho's wife, which, in its turn, had indirectly caused Víctor's unfair imprisonment.[15] Víctor's self-confessed revenge plan, which consisted in becoming 'the best fucker in the world', gives a further indication of how a healthy body is seen as the ideal weapon to take revenge on disabled David (Martínez-Expósito 2000: 101, 2004b: 195–213).

Early on in the film, Víctor, still in prison, watches David in his wheelchair playing for the national basketball team in a Barcelona Paralympics match shown on television. The lyrics of the extra-diegetic music ('Suffer like I do') both adds to the loathing contained in Víctor's gaze and underlines the homo-erotic elements of the love triangle discussed earlier (as discussed by Perriam – 2003: 107). In a later scene, David witnesses Clara's arrival at Víctor's slum and fixes his voyeuristic gaze on the semi-naked body of Víctor, clearly about to have sex with the woman with whom he used to have an affair. To further emphasize the voyeuristic quality of his gaze, David photographs the couple unaware, hoping to use the evidence as revenge both for the shooting (for which Víctor had been – wrongly – blamed) and Víctor's interference with his wife Elena. The images of Víctor 'in action' contained in the photographs play a similar role to those of David playing basketball that Víctor had witnessed on television, and they symbolize the homoerotic, fetishizing gaze of the two men at each other. The running commentary of the Paralympic television coverage underlines the ability of David's body to 'shoot' ('*lanzar*') and 'score' ('*marcar*') with the precision of a machine, stressing that he is the best player and the one who scored the decisive shot. The commentator explains that he became a paraplegic 'on duty', suggesting that his victimization in the accident has turned partly to his favour, elevating him and enhancing his heroism. The footage also reinforces David's ability to shape, control and move his body. This, together with the sex scene that will follow suggests an even greater degree of physical self-control, because he has managed to shape an apparently disabled body into a machine capable of competing at a high standard and giving sexual pleasure. Moreover, the appreciation shown by the spectators at the stadium and the commentator's remarks in this footage make his (dis)abled body desirable to an extent that transforms him into a marketable commodity (as suggested by the iconic 'Champion' T-shirt that he wears later in the poster of a lavish advertising campaign of the famous sport brand).[16] Interestingly, the context of televised sports renders harmless the male-to-male gaze. Whilst the camera often focuses on the bodies of the sportsmen in action, voiceovers usually contribute to place the emphasis on the various techniques as well as on narcissistic identification and admiration for the sportsman, thus disavowing the potential desire (Trujillo 1995). Víctor's attentive gaze at David on the television is thus partly justified by the context and de-eroticized by Víctor's aggression and thirst for revenge. David's gaze at Víctor's naked torso (emphasized with his camera and glasses – both adding to his reliance on apparel and his cyborg-like image) is later justified both through his detective instinct and his sudden loyalty to his friend Sancho, but mainly through his own feelings of revenge and competition for Elena.

The first face-to-face encounter between the two men after Víctor's release from prison is preceded by a series of contrasting shots between Víctor inside the house doing strenuous press-ups and David, outside, struggling to get out of his car in his wheelchair and approaching the house.[17] Once inside, David confronts Víctor about his attempts to approach his wife, and Victor fights back by asking defiantly how is he going to defend himself (pointedly looking down at his wheelchair). David's responsive punch on Víctor's genitals is both a reminder of his physical ability (he can defend himself and also inflict pain on others) and also a way of emphasising their difference. Whilst Víctor's virility is trapped into a phallic economy, post-shooting David has learned to relocate his masculine identity beyond the phallic, as suggested by the oral-sex scene with his wife. On the day of the filming, Almodóvar described the scene of the encounter as one of 'exacerbated masculinity' where muscle and genitals play a key part:

> We will only see Víctor's torso and arms; below, a chair. Later on we will find out that Javier [Bardem] had crawled his way to the house (...) and can only see what the spectator sees: muscle and genitals. It is a classic masculine challenge, with all the good and bad elements of exacerbated masculinity. Víctor starts doing press-ups to demonstrate the might of those physical attributes that Javier lacks. Javier starts deftly maneuvering [his wheelchair] in a manner that is almost impossible for a paraplegic, as if saying: you do this if you have the balls! Two men confronting each other with what they have. (Alas 1997: 47)

During another face-to-face confrontation, David reminds Víctor that, after their first meeting (the shooting), his perspective on everyday life has changed: instead of looking upwards he now has to look downwards. Whilst earlier on David had threatened to crack Víctor's skull if he ever got anywhere near his wife again, he now turns that image against himself, shifting his active threat into a reminder of his own passive suffering: 'I look down (...) so that I do not break my skull (...) you have condemned me to look down.' Although both encounters seem to suggest irreconcilable animosity between the two men, in the first of these, a goal by the Madrid-based Atlético in the televised match against Barcelona (seen in the background) turns a moment of aggressive tension between the two men into one of intense and celebratory homosociality, which reveals that the men's rivalry was purely posturing (as argued by Morgan-Tamosunas 2002: 192). The aggression (see Figure 11) provoked by the masculine traits of competition and ownership (of Elena) is easily abandoned when, as Perriam puts it, stronger allegiances to 'birthplace, neighbourhood, home town and nation, and not the least to manhood' are brought to the fore by 'the commercialized and "mediatized" competition that is football' (Perriam 2003: 109).[18]

Although the contrast established between the bodies of the two men seems to favour Víctor's upright, fit and able body over David's disabled one restrained by the wheelchair, the prison scene discussed earlier would seem to suggest exactly the opposite. As Víctor points out in one of their confrontations, David has turned his disability to his advantage. As mentioned earlier, the Paralympic television coverage that Víctor watches from the confinement of prison implies that the paraplegic David enjoys not only the coveted company of Elena but also, ironically, the mobility and social recognition that is initially denied to the apparently more able Víctor during his imprisonment.[19] In that scene, the visual contrast between David's freedom of movement and enjoyment on the court and the oppressiveness of Víctor's confinement is made explicit through the sharp contrast in lighting; the low-angle shots of David from Víctor's POV (the television set is raised on the wall, contributing to elevate David's image); the distinctly opposed body language and facial expressions of the two characters and, as already mentioned, the non-diegetic music that illustrates Víctor's thoughts. It is in this ambivalent opposition between the bodies of the two main male characters that *Carne trémula* provides an interesting study of the contemporary understandings of masculinity as a whole. Both men are subjected to traditional masculine values, such as a high sexual drive and a competitive instinct. Their animalistic side is illustrated with David's 100% animal T-shirt and with the wolf mask that Víctor wears during his re-encounter with Elena at the children's home that she runs and where he wants to work. Both men have muscular bodies. But whereas for the paraplegic, David's muscular strength is of crucial importance, not only for his sporting ambitions but for the sake of movement and physical independence, Víctor built his body obsessively whilst in prison perhaps, as Morgan-Tamosunas argues (2002: 191), to compensate for the castration anxieties that Elena had triggered just before the shooting

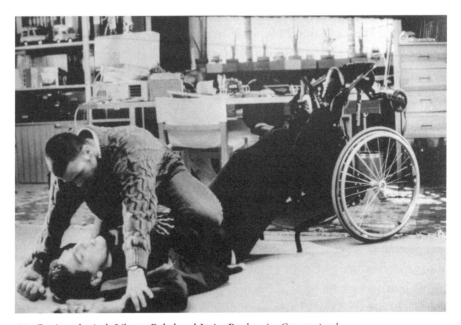

11. Getting physical: Liberto Rabal and Javier Bardem in *Carne trémula*.

(she had reminded him in a humiliating tone that what he regarded as a great sexual encounter had not even involved penetration). Yet, one should also bear in mind that Víctor's efforts whilst in jail also included learning a foreign language from an inmate, completing a distance university course on Education and reading the Bible, suggesting a spiritual and intellectual side to all his actions (including the physical training: necessary, as he says, to keep his mind busy). Also, his naiveté after the first sexual encounter with Elena, his humility on accepting his lack of sexual experience with Clara, and the good relationship he had with his mother, accentuate his nurturing and childlike side. These key qualities for his job as a child-carer will eventually help him win Elena over and are an essential part of his re-framing within the safe environment of the family setting that is exalted in the film's ending.[20] As Marsh has pointed out, it is interesting that 'while lacking the comforts, he is more at home in his particular domestic sphere than Clara is in hers' (Marsh 2004: 63).

Víctor's emphasis on the healthiness and cleanliness of his body, free from drugs and not contaminated by HIV during his time in prison, as he proudly writes in his letter to his mother and also tells Clara (with medical evidence to prove it) before their first sexual experience, contrasts with the apparent decline of both Sancho's and David's bodies. Yet, as mentioned earlier, David's body is glorified and presented as 'able' and in control, whereas Víctor's seems at times more vulnerable (confined to the space of the prison, less sexually experienced and precariously exposed to a menacing fire towards the end). Almodóvar's most radical approach to the male body in this film could be his blurring of the previously fixed differences between gender behaviour, sexual orientation and, especially, 'able' and 'disabled' bodies. The director has spoken publicly of his admiration for paraplegic players (whom he regards as heroes), and of how he refused to idealize Bardem's character, 'although I personally idealize those guys and I think that they are a real lesson' (Sánchez 1997: 9). In the film, David's wheelchair becomes part of his body. His masterful control over it proves that, like previous models of gender and sexual behaviour, certain standards and expectations of the male body are also becoming obsolete. David's example opens up new ways of imagining the body.[21] David can be read as a cyborg figure, not in the sense of a half-man half-machine futuristic 'creature' but as an iconic image that undoes the limits of what we are used to understanding as a human body (Haraway 1985). Hence, Bardem's role as the disabled David here has radically different connotations from the emasculating disability that he had embodied in *Huevos de oro* (dir. Bigas

Luna, 1993).[22] Interestingly, *Carne* was seen by some sectors of the press as a 'risk' to Bardem's heartthrob status: 'The (female) admirers of the muscular and attractive young Spanish actor Javier Bardem will go through a real test when they see their idol in a wheelchair' (*Diario 16* 1997: 47).

Yet, as we have seen, Almodóvar makes it quite clear that David is able to perform sexually and satisfy his wife. Paul Julian Smith has equated the naturalness of the scenes of 'casual domesticity' of gay and lesbian families in Almodóvar's early works with scenes like this in *Carne*, where 'the everyday lives of people with disabilities and those who love them are at once represented and respected' (Smith 2000a: 184). Disabled audiences who, as Smith notes, had been less than happy with the representation of the handicapped man in Rendell's novel, also welcomed the casting of Bardem and, in particular, the addition of the oral-sex scene that proves that David is able to satisfy his wife after the accident. In her study on the politics and representation of disability in contemporary Spain, Madeline Conway's reading of *Carne* stresses precisely the fact that 'given that Bardem is known for his film roles as macho studs, this was inspired casting' (Conway 2000: 256). The implications of this statement could be double-edged, because one could wonder whether he was chosen as a way to endow the disabled character with a desired level of sexual attractiveness and physical 'ability' (via personification of the actor well known to international audiences as the *macho* of the Bigas Luna 'Iberian Portraits' trilogy discussed in the first chapter of this book) or whether this role was seen by the actor as an opportunity to overcome such undesired typecasting. On the other hand, and whilst the separation of Elena and David may be 'in no way connected to his impairment' (Shakespeare 2001), one could also read David's final uprightness and strength as a way to reaffirm his damaged masculinity (Morgan-Tamosunas 2002: 191).

The films that we have discussed in this chapter reveal a deep-seated anxiety about questions of beauty and physical normalcy in recent Spanish cinema. Despite its very different approaches, it is refreshing to see how some of these narratives challenge the conception of the so-called 'normal ideal'. Whilst *Acción mutante* or *La mujer más fea del mundo* may be accused of exploiting those most unconventional and damaged bodies as a means of resistance in their narratives, the underlying political message of these films and their visual investment in 'the gross palpability of the flesh', to use Shaviro's term (1993: 132), arguably destabilizes the notion of ideal beauty or physical normalcy. The work of Amenábar and Almodóvar is much more nuanced in their respective representational approaches, as well as more gender-conscious.

Connell's study on the psychological effects of physical disability in males revealed that one of the most common strategies was 'to reformulate the definition of masculinity, bringing it closer to what is now possible, though still pursuing masculine themes such as independence and control' (1990: 55). In the context of this book, it is interesting to see how Bardem's body in these films has contributed to destabilize the notions of masculinity and virility that his iconic *macho* roles in the 1990s discussed in Chapter 1 of this book had helped construct. Still, as we shall see in the next three chapters, the concept of normalcy excludes many other types of bodies beyond those that may be perceived as somehow 'ugly', 'sick' or 'disabled'.

5

Homosexual bodies

HOMOSEXUAL BODIES

Foucault's work has drawn much attention to the ways in which, for centuries, social systems of discipline and surveillance (such as schools, prisons, hospitals, factories or the army) and other regulatory policies have been used as a means of controlling the population through the exercise of high levels of power and authority over the human body (Foucault 1990: 139 – see also Foucault 1991). As Ricardo Llamas states, the classification and categorization of people in terms of their bodies has been a recurring strategy of control and domination, and explains that the 'hyper-corporality' of certain human categories tends to coincide with those sectors of society that are 'discriminated, exploited and oppressed', such as homosexual men and women (1995: 153). By means of the Cartesian understanding of the body/mind binary opposition, the hyper-corporal specimen becomes one-dimensional, hence restricted to the physical:

> Being mostly a body means to stop being other things; to abandon the possibility of existence in spheres beyond the material. It means, at times, the inability to access the true human statute; the loss of the ethical, social or political dimensions of human existence (…) and also, perhaps, the loss of freedom and autonomy, in the benefit of those who do exercise a full humanity that enables them to make decisions and to determine their own life and those of others. (Llamas 1995: 154)

Llamas illustrates this argument with historical evidence of how this 'hyper-corporality' has been used to oppress slaves (and more generally, the manual workforce – also valued in terms of their physical strength) or women (as mothers), but (as he points out later), this concept is also behind the politics of racial 'purity' (such as that promulgated by the Nazi regime) and applies to some of the social sectors discussed in this book, the disabled (Chapter 4), the transsexual (Chapter 6), or the foreign 'Other' (Chapter 7).

The classification of human beings with regard to their physical features, appearance or body types (size of the skull and limbs) was relatively common in the nineteenth century. This type of categorization was often used in the criminal and medical discourses to underpin those members of society considered a threat or different, such as criminals or people with mental diseases. In 1801, the French psychiatrist, Philippe Pinel, wrote a treatise on 'mental alienation' that was based on the apparent degradation of the ideal Caucasian into 'lesser' types with Mongol characteristics. Photographic material and other sorts of visual records were held at hospitals and other institutions as a means of identifying the 'lower types'. In Britain, Francis Galton (Darwin's cousin) established a list of 'physiognomic classes' in the 1870s. Italian criminologist Cesare Lombroso gave a detailed portrait of the type that he believed to represent almost fifty per cent of criminals (in his famous *L'uomo delinquente* – 1876). His description of the criminal included a series of recognizable 'stigmata', which included not only physiognomy but also external decorations such as tattoos (Kemp and Wallace 2000: 94–147). According to Petersen (1998), this obsessive classification underlies medical discourses on sexuality until well into the twentieth century. In such discourses, it was common to assign homosexuals a particular kind of body, namely 'fragile' and 'effeminate', the opposite of what was expected from a man in the value system that equated masculinity with power and strength, and femininity with weakness. An essay published in the *American Journal of Psychiatry* in 1934 defined the homosexual male as:

> characterized by a feminine carrying of angle of the arm, long legs, narrow hips, large muscles, deficient hair on the face, chest and back, feminine distribution of pubic hair, a high-pitched voice, small penis and testicles and the presence of a scrotal fold (...) excess of fat on the shoulder, buttocks and abdomen. Occasionally the penis is very large and the hips are unusually wide. (Henry and Galbraith 1934: 1265; quoted in Petersen 1998: 60)

Richard Cleminson and Francisco Vázquez García cite an earlier example from a Spanish source published in Madrid in 1901, 'minuscule and closely shaven moustache or beard, dark brown hair, pale bluish iris, misshapen (*ondulosa*) nose. 1.6555m tall (...) smooth chest, large penis and testicles, funnel-shaped anus and post-wart scars' (2000: 176).[1]

According to Laqueur, moreover, an ancient text attributes sexual passivity in males 'both to an excess of semen and to a congenital defect that shunts this excess to an inappropriate orifice, the anus, instead of allowing it to simply build up in the proper male organ' (1990: 44). Others have ascribed to the active homosexual a thin and small penis and have described the passive homosexual as having a bent spine, sunken and bony facial features and a forward-leaning head, amongst other features (Llamas 1995: 163 – see also Arnalte 2003: 83–114 for further details of medical approaches to homo-sexuality in the Spanish context, including aversion therapy treatments and imprisonment during the Franco dictatorship).[2] This biological-determinist approach to sexual orientation (sometimes with more constructive means, such as Ulrichs's 1860s Third Sex theory – later developed by Hirschfeld) has persisted in our society in the shape of expensive research projects that try to determine the existence of a 'gay gene' (notably, the DNA research carried out by Dean Hamer, as noted by Petersen – 1998: 62–64).[3]

Llamas refers to the homosexual as a clear example of the 'hyper-body' mentioned above: often defined exclusively by sexual choice, he is seen as a 'prey of sexual bulimia' who 'consumes organisms immoderately, anxiously and desperately seeking pleasure as if (in fact) he could do nothing else' (1995: 168). Consequently, other assumptions followed that, as we shall see, have been and in some cases still are commonly applied to homosexual characters in cinema, such as promiscuity, sexual frustration, the inability to maintain a stable relationship or the notion that homosexuality represents an inability to approach the opposite sex, a tragic destiny which eventually leads to his death (Llamas 1995: 168–169). As Llamas also notes, in this context the moral degradation of the homosexual would be expected to be externalized with marks of sickness such as those caused by the STDs, including, of course, AIDS. Hence, despite the evidence of infection amongst the heterosexual population and the drug-related infections, in the years that followed the discovery of the HIV virus, 'a body with AIDS became a homosexual body' (1995: 179). It comes, perhaps, as no surprise that dominant cultural representations of the homosexual body as somehow feeble and diseased have abounded, and Spanish cinema is no exception (Martínez-Expósito 1998b). Even within the material studied so far in this book, we find examples that are alarmingly recent, such as Pedro in *Historias del Kronen/Stories from the Kronen* (dir. Montxo Armendáriz, 1995), whose suspected homosexuality, as we have seen in Chapter 2, was metaphorically marked by his illness and inability to drink 'like a man' as well as being a suspected masochist. Yet, as part of what could be considered as a Foucauldian 'reverse' discourse, 'gay men have often appropriated images of heterosexual masculinity to put into question the dominant definitions of homosexuality that locate it between genders' (Lahti 1998: 187). Thus, the body of a gay man can be considered as the setting of resistance to the oppressive notions of masculinity and power: the human ability to transform our bodies regardless of gender or sexual orientation evidences 'the performative nature of our identities [and] also the malleability of our bodies' (Lahti 1998: 187). The gay appropriation of post-war masculinist symbols of rebellion and bravery (such as leather and the motorcycle cultures) provided an alternative gay iconography that contrasted with the predominant understanding of the gay man as effeminate that prevailed at the time. Using Butler's theory of performativity ('a reiteration of a norm or set of norms... [that] conceals or dissimulates the conventions of which it is a repetition' (Butler 1993: 12)), Lahti has argued that the gay men's appropriation of symbols of heterosexual masculinity evidences further the performative character of such symbols (and hence, of 'heterosexual masculinity' itself) (1998: 195). Whereas this attitude could imply a rejection of anything 'feminine', and therefore a compliance with the dominant (masculinist) power structures, the *macho* look and attitude in gay men is often excessive and, as many have argued, equally camp and potentially subversive as excessive effeminacy (see Dyer 1983: 14; Llamas 1997: 227; Sinfield 1994: 194 or Spencer 1995: 375). As we shall see later, some Spanish critics have urged the gay community to reclaim and re-appropriate the national tradition of effeminacy as a means of avoiding the masculinization of the gay sub-culture (Aliaga and G. Cortés 1997: 159–161). The terms of that reclamation and, in particular, the extent to which it might, in turn, return the community to a more overtly homophobic image of gay men is still highly contested.

HIDDEN PLEASURES: INTRODUCING THE GAY BODY IN SPANISH CINEMA

As Alfeo Álvarez claims, José María Delgado's *Diferente/Different* (1962, re-released 1978) is probably the first filmic depiction of homosexual desire in a male protagonist in Spanish film history (2000: 138). In that film, the allegedly gay protagonist, Alfredo (played by the Argentinian actor, Alfredo Alaria), is presented as both a subject and an object of desire. His involvement in the world of performance (theatre and dance) allows for generous shots of his muscular, hairless body as he prepares for a show, as well as the tight-fitting costumes that draw attention to his muscles and genitals. Despite the dark message conveyed by the film (the tragic death of Alfredo's father on his way to the theatre is predictably blamed on the (homosexual) son's lifestyle – perpetuating the associations between homosexuality and tragedy or guilt that are constants in much filmic representation of lesbians and gay men, even to date – see Dyer 1983), the film should be credited for its brief acknowledgement of the homosexual gaze. As an object of desire, Alfredo will be voyeuristically observed by the camera whilst getting ready for a performance in his dressing room, whilst performing or even whilst asleep in his bedroom. As a gay subject, he is portrayed as highly narcissistic (as suggested by the way he looks at himself in the mirror or his hysterical laughter), but it is suggested that he also interacts with and desires other men. In one scene, he gazes intensively at the muscular body of a workman who is energetically drilling a hole into the ground. The workman's muscular arm (flexed with intensity whilst drilling) and the vibrating, penetrating machine itself are obvious sexual metaphors that illustrate not only Alfredo's admiration of the male body but also his desire for sexual intercourse with other men.

The period of political transition towards democracy was a productive time for cultural productions in Spain during which previously oppressed marginal identities were allowed to emerge and develop. As more recently noted by critics, *Diferente* was an exception that passed the Francoist censorship on its first release in 1962. Yet, in its post-censorship re-release, the re-designed promotional poster drew explicit attention to the character's previously 'veiled' homosexuality and the meaning of the film's title (Alfeo Álvarez 2000: 138; Arnalte 2003: 84–85). Trenzado Romero has explained how the media enjoyed an unprecedented level of prominence in the Spanish society of the transition, mediating between new (previously marginalized) voices and the more traditional social sectors such as family and school (1999: 327). This was a time in which male bodies would become eroticized in magazines for the first time, not only in the already-mentioned magazine *Nuevo Fotogramas* (see Chapter 1), but also in the first Spanish magazine, *Party*,[4] aimed at a gay readership.

The gay-themed films of Eloy de la Iglesia and Pedro Almodóvar deserve a special mention, because they stand out precisely for their exploration of the homoerotic gaze at the 'homosexual body'. Eloy de la Iglesia (1944–2006) is unanimously considered the first Spanish filmmaker to have consistently dealt with homosexuality in his politically engaged work. His films are realist dramas that seek to portray the social fabric of the late Franco period, the transition and, in his more recent work, the new realities of immigration in the 1990s. In the vein of the social denunciation genre, his focus tends to be on the underclass, the lower socio-economic echelons, the inhabitants of shanty-towns and marginalized subjects.

His three most explicitly gay films, *Los placeres ocultos/Hidden Pleasures* (1977), *El diputado/Confessions of a Congressman* (1978) and *Los novios búlgaros/Bulgarian Lovers* (2003) have, in common, a difficult relationship between a homosexual mature man and a much younger boy who is either heterosexual or bisexual and is of a lower social level. The asymmetry of these relations is constantly emphasized in the films, to the point that it has become the most distinctive feature of de la Iglesia's treatment of homosexuality, as identified by the most authoritative studies of his oeuvre (see Hopewell (1989: 164–178) or Smith (1992a: 129–162)). Whilst the younger boy has no financial stability, no job and is frequently seen wearing informal clothes or semi-naked, the mature homosexual men are invariably well-situated pro-fessionals (a bank office director, an MP, a well-off consultant) who wear relatively expensive clothes and are rarely seen undressed. The Greek-love model is made clear not only by these differences, but also by the fact that the youngster relies on the older man for financial improvement and a sense of direction; this is particularly clear in *Los placeres ocultos* (Tropiano 1997: 162–164). The Greek paradigm is further emphasized by the fact that the youngster's sexuality is kept deliberately ambiguous. Miguel in *Los placeres ocultos*, Juanito in *El diputado* and Kyril in *Los novios búlgaros* are clearly interested in women and have girlfriends or fiancées, but they also seem to have no difficulties in flirting with the older homosexual men from whom they expect to gain some material benefits. In the context of the military-driven scenario provided by the Greek-love model, it is interesting that de la Iglesia's homosexuals end up being the victims of physically violent attacks, which in turn leave visible marks in their bodies; significantly, the novel Eduardo keeps writing in *Los placeres ocultos* has the working title of *Los heridos* ('The hurt') (Tropiano 1997: 165–166).

The representation of the homosexual body as virile is undoubtedly one of the most relevant aspects of de la Iglesia's approach to homosexuality. As Alberto Mira has pointed out, the effeminate homosexual is consistently represented negatively in *El diputado* and *Los placeres ocultos* (Mira 2004a: 504), in contrast with the many films of the time that represented the effeminate homosexual humorously for the uncritical heterosexual audiences. Mira goes on to argue that *El diputado* represents a landmark in the process of raising the political awareness of gay men because the main character, a closeted communist MP, makes his own coming-out an ethical, socially responsible act and thus relocates homosexuality from the private into the public sphere (Mira 2004a: 509). Once out of the closet, the body of Roberto Orbea (José Sacristán) does not become the territory of fashion, body modification or exhibitionism; on the contrary, his body remains as sober, unassuming and clothed when he is a homosexual as when he tries to pass as a heterosexual. The film is clearly not about the displaying or showing off of a sexualized body or a sexual tendency, as the voyeuristic credit title sequence could suggest (Tropiano 1997: 172), but, as Mira convincingly states, about a political metaphor that links the repression of political ideologies with the repression of sexual identities against the moving backdrop of political transition. Orbea, still oppressed in his sexuality, if not any more in his communist militancy, does not inspire compassion or rejection, but maintains a certain dignity (Mira 2004a: 509–510). Something similar occurs in *Los placeres ocultos*, when Eduardo's homosexuality happens to be much less 'hidden' and much more respected than he would have expected; his own mother dramatically confides in him that she 'knew' all along – a confession echoed by the youngster, Miguel, when he declares that he 'respects' Eduardo's 'choice'. *Los placeres ocultos* is perhaps less obviously political than *El diputado*, but the ethical element is equally strong, with a climactic coming-out scene that encapsulates the essential difference between the 'revealed' homosexual and the many other homosexual types (such as hustlers, effeminates and promiscuous toilet loiterers) so negatively portrayed in the film.

In *Los novios búlgaros*, the contrast between the two men who engage in the homosexual relationship is stressed by all possible means: the oppositions of age, class, economic situations, legal situation, nationality, sexuality, physical attributes and degree of emotional involvement separate Kyril (Dritan Biba) and Daniel (Fernando Guillén Cuervo). The story is told from Daniel's perspective; the image of his upper torso, dimly lit by a lighter, frames the film in the first and last scenes: he is in a gay club's dark room. The isolation of his body in the frame is somehow indicative of his loneliness, the main aspect derived from the original novel by Eduardo Mendicutti (1993). Surrounded by friends and male prostitutes in the Madrid gay district of Chueca, Daniel's loneliness becomes symptomatic of a gay culture heavily focused on hedonism but not enough on meaningful relationships. Gildo (Pepón Nieto), Daniel's best friend, gives voice to this contrast when he asserts that 'Money can buy many centimeters of dick, but just a tiny fraction of love', thus pointing out yet another crucial opposition in the film – body versus sentiment. The film is rich in its visual representation of male bodies;

the three well-off Spanish friends are shot in a variety of gay scenarios such as dark rooms, gay clubs, parties and saunas, and they are seen fully naked at least once (in sharp contrast with Eduardo and Roberto Orbea in *Los placeres ocultos* and *El diputado*). Most of the young Bulgarian hustlers are seen in sexually provocative poses and their bodies are seen frequently semi-naked, including a full frontal. There are also full frontals of Kyril and two detailed gay sex scenes between Kyril and Daniel, in medium shots and close-ups, that do not, however, allow for a direct view of erect penises or anal penetrations. As was the case in *Los placeres ocultos* and *El diputado*, the camera frequently adopts the point of view of the older man and offers the audience his desiring gaze over the body of the youngster. This translates in frequent shots of a highly eroticized body of the youngster and fewer shots of a sexualized but not openly eroticized body of the older man. In one particular scene in *Los novios búlgaros*, Daniel uses a camcorder to capture images of young men (including Kyril) in openly provocative demeanours: the pleasure of his gaze is stressed by the screen-within-the-screen effect that helps the audience identify with the gay perspective of the narrative, and by the fact that Daniel's body is not revealed in any detail. But the sadism inherent in this voyeuristic setting, later confirmed by the client-costumer economic relationship he and Kyril engage in, does not translate into Daniel's active/penetrative role; sex scenes between him and Kyril reveal Daniel at the passive/receiving end, although he adopts an active role when having sex with another Bulgarian boy.

An interesting aspect of Daniel's visual presentation in the film is his relation to oneiric and imagined images of himself. There are several instances of such images: he imagines himself speaking in harsh terms to Kyril, he envisions himself as a child contemplating a painting and he has a dream involving a radioactive blast. These are important images for the construction of his libidinal imagination and his own body construction as ambiguous (versatile, flexible). In the first instance he sees himself adopting a position of control with Kyril: it is a position he could easily adopt if he wished, but he consistently refuses to do so. In the second instance, he sees his own adolescent body contemplating the image of a young man embracing a horse and grasping its penis, and the identification of the adolescent's gaze with the homoerotic content of the painting is made obvious by the deferred gaze of Daniel himself. In the third instance, the dream scene suggests a strong identification between the homoerotic horse and the cylindrical, phallus-shaped uranium stick, which is in turn identified with Kyril elsewhere in the narrative, and the nuclear blast leads to images of decaying flesh and catastrophic meltdown. The film is punctuated by these visions of desire and death. Simultaneously, Kyril's hands are seen scarred on several occasions, suggesting an ambiguous relation with dangerous materials whose nature is never ascertained.[5] Death is represented in the film as an unpleasant and undesired interruption of hedonism. It is shown literally in this way by the figure of the death child during Daniel's visit to Sofia, and implicitly in many other instances, such as, already mentioned dreams and visions and the anti-erotic remarks of one of Daniel's friends, a dermatologist obsessed with sexually transmitted skin conditions.

In several important ways, *Los novios búlgaros* represents a radical departure from the modes of representation of the homosexual body as seen in de la Iglesia's earlier films. Daniel's subjectivity, represented by the conspicuous POV shots and the narrative perspective used (that arguably derives from the first-person narrative of Mendicutti's novel), is heard more clearly than Eduardo's and Roberto's. He is also much more and better socialized than his predecessors and his social life seems to be fully rewarding in the gay Chueca district. Importantly, his homosexuality is utterly and unashamedly visible; there is no blackmail, no traumatic coming out, no need for political statements. Subjectivity, sociability, visibility and a lack of political engagement put *Los novios búlgaros* at a distance from de la Iglesia's earlier films and serve as indicators of the remarkable evolution of the modes of representation of the homosexual body in recent Spanish cinema. This evolution is symptomatic of the transformation of the legal framework, visibility (and, arguably, social acceptance) for Spanish lesbians and gay men in the thirty-year gap between *El diputado* and *Los novios búlgaros* (see Fouz-Hernández 2003 and 2004 and Martínez-Expósito 2004c).

Needless to say, the early films of Pedro Almodóvar should also be credited for the establishment of a more obvert acknowledgement of the male gay gaze at the male body which, as we shall see in some of the examples that we are about to analyse, had an enormous impact on gay representation in the Spanish cinema that followed. The opening sequence of *La ley del deseo/Law of Desire* (1987) (which will be analysed in detail in Chapter 8) and the shower scene of the same film (as well as the homoerotic gaze that stands out in various scenes of *Laberinto de pasiones/Labyrinths of Passion* (1982) and *Matador* (1986)) are paramount examples in any discussions of the homosexual male gaze and the 'homosexual body' in Spanish cinema. Indeed, the opening shots of *La ley del deseo* (reminiscent of the opening of de la Iglesia's *Los placeres ocultos*) have been examined internationally by gay film critics as an example of gay subjectivity beyond its significance for Spanish cinema history (see, for example, Alfeo Álvarez 2000; Arroyo 1992; Fouz-Hernández and Perriam 2000; Jackson 1995; Smith 1992b and 1997; Waugh 1993). As we will discuss in Chapter 8, in that sequence, an athletic man is asked by an anonymous voice to undress for him (and for the camera), kiss his own image on the mirror, touch his body, masturbate with his back to the camera and ask to be fucked. The voice that encourages the spectacular display of this attractive male object of desire speaks on behalf of the (mainly male gay) audience's unspoken desire. On the other hand, the depiction of penetrative sex between the two male protagonists (who, importantly, were major stars of Spanish cinema at the time: Antonio Banderas and Eusebio Poncela) also marked a 'before and after' in terms of the representation of 'the gay male body' in Spanish cinema.

SECOND SKIN: GAY BODIES IN RECENT SPANISH CINEMA

The Spanish film industry of the 1990s witnessed a considerable increase in the number of gay-themed films produced – particularly comedies such as those discussed in Fouz-Hernández and Perriam (2000) or Collins and Perriam (2000) – leading some critics to conclude that 'no Spanish comedy can be regarded as genuinely modern unless it includes a dose of so-called *petardeo* or gay humour' (Moreno 1997: 15). Both *Perdona Bonita, pero Lucas me quería a mí/Excuse Me Darling, but Lucas Loved Me* (dirs Félix Sabroso and Dunia Ayaso, 1997 – henceforth *Perdona Bonita*) and *Más que amor, frenesí/Not Love, Just Frenzy* (dirs Alfonso Albacete, Miguel Bardem and David Menkes, 1996) have many features in common, in terms of (co)-direction, production and narrative (as noted in most of the reviews cited here). Both films were released within a two-month period, both were co-directed and both are comedies set in Madrid. Certain aspects of their plots are also similar: the quest for a flatmate (who is murdered in both cases),[6] the competition amongst some of the main characters for the love of a man (in both cases a secondary character) and so on. Visually, there is also an element of gore in both films that culminates with the messy disposal of the dead male bodies (Lucas's body is burnt in the Police Academy headquarters and Luis/Pablo's body – badly wounded in the head and groin – is dumped in the rubbish truck, then finished off with a gunshot in a later scene). Finally, in terms of style and atmosphere, both films are indebted to Almodóvar, with a clear contrast between stereotypically strong (if at times also vulnerable) female characters and the equally predictable weaker men. Also, like in the early Almodóvar, humour is found in the mockery of the characters that traditionally stand for authority (in both films, members of the police force).[7]

Despite the undoubted value that these and other films of that time had for the Spanish gay community (they are arguably part of a move towards greater visibility and acceptance), the more attentive critics would have found some aspects of the narrative of these films highly problematic from the outset. Whilst the kind of physical stereotyping of the gay men that we will see in *Perdona Bonita* is happily avoided in *Más que amor, frenesí* (the only explicit scene of gay sex features two similarly shaped bodies – both well-toned and attractive), gay male desire in the latter film is also truncated. The two love-interests of the only character who defines himself as 'gay' (Alberto, played by Gustavo Salmerón) turn out to be both married and straight. On the other hand, the refreshingly explicit scene of gay penetrative sex, which takes place barely ten minutes into the film and which goes much further than the earlier-mentioned shower scene in Almodóvar's *La ley del deseo*, is mediated by a mirror. The reflection of the anal penetration (in long shot) mitigates the visual pleasure by establishing a break from the seamless editing of the close-up shots used during the foreplay, thus encouraging a distancing from the action by drawing attention to the act of looking. The mirror also metaphorically suggests that this brief encounter is just a mirage, destined to failure – as is later confirmed (see Fouz-Hernández and Perriam 2000: 107–108).

The depiction of the male body (and the gay male body in particular) in *Perdona Bonita* provides plenty of food for thought as a case study. In the publicity material used in the commercial release of the film, the three gay flatmates are introduced one by one as 'esoteric and hash-addicted; fragile and depressive and promiscuous and selfish' (the descriptions correspond to Alberto (Jordi Mollà), Carlos (Pepón Nieto) and Dani (Roberto Correcher) respectively). On the back of the video sleeve (released by Sogepac in 1996), the word '*loca*' (Spanish for 'gay queen' but also 'mad') is imprinted three times (once for each character), thus marking them in advance as nothing but crazy queens (Fouz-Hernández and Perriam 2000: 103; Perriam 2003: 129). Although, as Perriam notes, this film should be credited for being probably 'the first Spanish film to target itself explicitly in its marketing on a gay and gay-sympathetic audience' (2003: 129) and for its casual approach to gay living and gay friendship (or is it gay cat-fighting?) in 1990s Madrid, the film's construction of the homosexual gaze is extremely knotty, ultimately obtruding the visual pleasure of the characters and, indirectly, the male gay audiences'. The film does present the gay characters as desiring subjects, although not as desirable in themselves. In opposition, the three men portrayed as their objects of desire happen to be heterosexual: a stripper hired as a birthday surprise for Dani is unable to do the job claiming that he has only stripped once and only for a female audience; Alberto's love-interest, Miguel, is married to his friend Estrella and, crucially, the gay guys' new flatmate, Lucas, is sexually ambiguous on the surface but, as we find out only at the very end, so heterosexual at his core. Lucas is a long-haired stud (played by Alonso Caparrós) whose presence in the flat will create considerable tension and competition amongst the three '*locas*', as well as a great deal of frustration. He is everybody's object of desire.[8] In contrast with the insecure, over-gesticulating and hysterical gay men, their heterosexual hero is the picture of contentment and self-confidence, as well as remarkably attractive: much taller and stronger than his flatmates, he strides with confidence and his muscular body is frequently on display in life (whilst asleep, whilst watching television on the sofa, and so on)… and death. And what a pretty corpse he makes. Far from decreasing his appeal, it seems that death has increased it. One of the female inspectors investigating the murder takes the forensic photographs of his body parts with fetishistic pleasure and secretly kisses his lips. The three gay flatmates are also allowed a final group-gaze at his dead body, which they use to make remarks on his beauty and the added kinky appeal of the corpse.[9] Lucas's lifeless, naked body had been found by the flatmates lying on the apartment's floor, with a row of seven knives stuck in his body, ever so alluringly stained with blood. Even though his death had been caused by a jealous husband whilst awaiting a female lover, his dead body is unmistakably homo-eroticized via graphic reference to the iconic image of the 'gay saint' par excellence, Saint Sebastian. Yet, in maintaining Lucas's ambiguity and mystery whilst alive, the narrative had encouraged speculation about his sexual orientation, boosting the three gay characters' (and, through them, the audience's) expectations, only to eventually deceive the desiring gay subjects. It turns out that Lucas had dated both the policewomen involved in his own murder investigation and, at the time of his death, contrary to the audience's expectations, he was not having an affair with any of the gay flatmates, but with the female colleague of one of them. As a result, the straight audience might have had a laugh witnessing how these queens fantasize about 'them' but the gay audience's pleasure is truncated. The same could be said about Alberto's fantasy romance with Estrella's husband (Miguel) or, in *Más que amor, frenesí*, Alberto's (Gustavo Salmerón) overtures to straight nude model David (Liberto Rabal).

It is interesting that the heterosexual sex-object becomes a blank canvas where the three gay men project their fantasies and anxieties in each of their police interrogations, changing their attire and bodily features accordingly. For Dani, Lucas is an adventurous globe-trotter of Australian origin and wears a clingy, sleeveless t-shirt that accentuates his muscularity; for Carlos, he is a sensitive intellectual who wears shirt and glasses and for Alberto, he is an alternative-type but thoughtful partner who picks him up from work at the end of a long day. The film invites a Freudian reading of homosexuality as a regressive neurosis caused by an unresolved Oedipus complex (Hocquenghem 1993: 79–83, 106–109). This is implied in the way in which the gay flatmates relate to other adults. On one occasion (just after they meet Lucas for the first time), the three gay flatmates stare at him from the window as he leaves the building and Alberto remarks that 'he is like a father'. This adds to the confusion of gender identities and sexuality because, in that line of argument, the characters are identifying with (and desiring) a father figure (for the implications of 'the absent father' for the male sex-role identity, see Pleck 1987: 34–36; Simpson 1994: 8–19 and 36–37; Silverman 1992: 190–195 or Rutherford 1992: 143–172).[10] On another occasion, Carlos says that Juliana, their cleaning lady, 'is like a mother' (thus also reinforcing the stereotypical obsession of gay men with their mothers – Hocquenghem 1993: 79).

Perdona Bonita raises other issues of interest here: Dani takes pleasure in reminding his overweight and oversensitive flatmate Carlos that his body shape is one of the main catalysts of his mental-health issues and insecurity. Whilst doing some strenuous sit-ups, and as a revenge for having apparently lost Lucas to Carlos (this is according to Carlos's version of events and, by all accounts, unconscious self-flagellation), Dani would remind Carlos that his body size will be a major obstacle in finding a man, 'You have zero sex appeal, you can forget it, especially in the gay world, which is body-crazy.' There is no doubt that Carlos's obesity is used in the film as a mark of weakness that obliquely alienates him from his flatmates and, as Dani reminds him, from the gay community as a whole. As acknowledged in countless studies of gay representation (see, for instance, Llamas and Vidarte 2000: 55–70 for a Spanish perspective on this topic), there is an element of 'body fascism' in the gay community that is contained here in the physical contrast established between Dani and Carlos and the implications that their body shapes have in other aspects of their life and interests. Moreover, this opposition establishes the fat body as passive and victimized and the trim one as active and in control. As Llamas and Vidarte argue, the gay community has embraced the gym as an expression of success (personal and professional) and self-control, often sublimating sex (particularly in times of AIDS) (2000: 58–59 see also – Mira 2004a: 611). A gym-toned body has also resulted in a certain physical elitism that determines the type of bars, clubs and social spaces that one is allowed to enjoy, and as such, it could be read as isolating. It is no coincidence that in the film Carlos is associated with a mental illness as well as with physical deficiency and passivity. Dani is not the only character to treat him accordingly. Carlos himself perceives his shape as an external reflection of the difficulties experienced since childhood in having to learn to live with himself ('in our own skin', to use his words) and being treated as somewhat 'imperfect'. The struggle with his sexual identity has made him otherwise 'defective': he is now dependent on anti-depressants and therapy. It comes as no surprise that, when seeing blood stains on Carlos's shirt, the cleaning lady assumes straight away that his flatmates have hurt him, not that he has hurt anyone. Later, the policewoman dismisses his half-pretended panic attack as 'faked hysteria' easily overcome with the threat of calling his mother. Beyond the obvious misogynistic implications that are behind the equation of effeminacy and weakness, this character could be read as a cruel dismissal of the effeminate type that used to be common and accepted in what Guasch calls 'pre-gay' Spain and that are now highly stigmatized (1995: 93, see also Aliaga and G. Cortés 1997: 127–130). For Guasch, the 'gay' model (which he regards as a 'masculinization' and apparent 'politization' of the 'homosexual' – 1995: 75) favours the 'masculine' and 'young' types at the expense of the older ('*carroza*') or the effeminate ('*loca*').

Still, Dani himself and the type he stands for does not come out unscathed. He is portrayed as a stereotypical 'queeny bitch', as suggested by his affected facial expressions (permanently raised eyebrow), which craft an exaggerated one-dimensional 'evil' characterization. In contrast with Carlos, he is also a stereotypical gay 'bimbo', obsessed with his body and clothes, occasionally bumping into men he has slept with. In his defence of the so-called *musculoca* (literally a 'muscle queen', a pun with the Spanish word for 'musclely' in the feminine (*musculosa*) and the already discussed *loca*),[11] Mira argues that the proliferation of the *musculoca* came as a reaction against the stereotype of the gay man as 'thin, weak, curvy and young' that was abundant in illustrations of homosexual narratives in the 1920s, '[André] Gide wanted to show that the homosexual was not effeminate, and proposes the athlete and the warrior as models of the "good homosexual"' (Mira 2004a: 611). As he notes, this new model reproduces prejudices about effeminacy, and yet, as Niall Richardson (2004) argues, body-building and other physical practices devoted to the cultivation of one's body image have a lot in common with what is traditionally regarded as 'feminine' and, as such, it has enormous subversive potential (Llamas and Vidarte have similar views on this subject, 2000: 64–66).

Contrary to *Perdona Bonita*, the film *Amor de hombre/The Love of a Man* (dirs García Serrano and Iborra, 1997) does not take homosexuality for granted. It discusses it and problematizes it in various important ways. *Amor de hombre* is representative for a style of 'pedagogic' comedies that during the 1990s were intent in 'explaining' homosexual lifestyles to mainstream audiences whilst simultaneously trying to be attractive to the gay spectator. Firstly, the central character happens to be a single heterosexual woman (Esperanza, played by Loles León), in sharp contrast with the sexually hyper-active gay men whose romantic stories are the film's main thematic concern. Homosexuality is thus framed by a (sympathetic) heterosexual gaze. And secondly, the plurality of gay lifestyles is represented by a large number of gay characters with different and at times idiosyncratic understandings of their own sexuality. Apart from this obviously pedagogic subtext, the film displays some features that are typical of most Spanish gay narratives of the post-Franco period: there are thematic references to homosexual self-hatred, including the possibility (not realized) of suicide, and visual representations of disability and disease (for instance, a traffic accident, a wheelchair, a limb in a cast). There are also some innovative elements, such as the more than occasional display of naked male bodies (albeit not in full frontal nor having gay sex) and the sympathetic representation of gay foreigners: Esperanza's flatmate, Ramón (Andrea Occhipinti), is an Italian barrister specializing in (heterosexual) divorce cases, and one of the many secondary gay characters is a young Swedish guy who is introduced to Ramón in an utterly dehumanized way, as a mere (perfect and desirable) body – something that, as we have seen, de la Iglesia's *Los novios búlgaros* (2003) does much more eloquently and dispassionately. The heterosexual perspective of the film is visible in its tendency to represent gay men as sexually hyper-active (as pointed out by Llamas, 1995: 153, 168) and physically attractive. But the stereotyping heterosexual perspective also demands from the gay body a high level of performativity. In one particular scene of *Amor de hombre*, Ramón and Esperanza pretend to be a heterosexual couple dancing in a disco – the simulation is innocuous in its narrative context, but the possibility of visualizing the two characters as a happy couple is hinted at several times during the film (as in *Sobreviviré/I Will Survive* (dirs Albacete and Menkes, 1999) – see Perriam 2004b).

The equally didactic *Segunda piel/Second Skin* (dir. Gerardo Vera, 1999) was, unsurprisingly, received with suspicion by those gay critics who might have hoped for a glimpse of new horizons in terms of the gay representation in this semi-autobiographical piece. The film starred two of the biggest male stars of recent times (Javier Bardem and Jordi Mollà) providing, as Perriam (2003: 114) has noted, a good intertextual opportunity to re-create the frustrated gay desire between the characters played by the same actors that had been so contained in *Jamón, Jamón* (see Chapter 1). Although both actors had some experience playing gay or 'semi-gay' roles,[12] and, as Mira notes, teasingly exploited their fictional relationship during the promotion of the film (2004a: 596, see also Perriam 2003: 114), the acting was panned by critics as 'inauthentic' (see, for example, Perriam 2003: 113 or Mira 2004a: 596–600). Indeed, beyond the excitement raised by the sex scenes between these two key contemporary actors (both shown in different states of undress in the sex scenes) and despite the high levels of corporality implied by the film's title and the opening credits (during which highly homoerotic silhouettes of the naked bodies – presumably of the three protagonists – are superimposed on a background of human X-rays),[13] the approach to the 'gay male body' is far from ground-breaking. Although, as Perriam argues, *Segunda piel* renders visible 'the fragility of heterosexual as well as homosexual identities' (2003: 125) and does bring home the closeted reality of many homosexuals and the rampant homophobia that remains in certain sectors of contemporary Spanish society; it also revisits (and arguably perpetuates) some of the more negative elements of earlier gay-themed narratives. Apart from the apparently inescapable and by now highly predictable element of the collapse of the gay (bisexual?) body through tragedy and death, the narrative subtly conveys the idea of homosexuality as an illness (although not so much self-inflicted but as the result of a sick society). Closeted married man Alberto (Mollà) becomes physically sick when his wife Elena (Ariadna Gil) confronts him about the impact that his sexuality will have on their plans as a family. In their first discussion of the situation, she confesses that the discovery of his (homo)sexual goings-on made her vomit. Tellingly, during that first conversation, Elena (who had just accidentally discovered her husband's gay affair) is digging a large hole in the ground and planting some flowers in it. This is a premonition of Alberto's inexorable journey to his grave and the implication that his homosexual inclinations will form the driving force behind his tragic fate could hardly be any clearer. In that scene, Alberto offers to leave (home) and come back when he is 'well' (read: cured), thus implicitly associating his homosexual inclinations with an illness.[14] Comically, in the next scene, Diego (Bardem) – who is a surgeon – examines an X-ray of a 'serious fracture'.

Diego's profession and his confident sexuality have the potential to turn the negative metaphor inside-out: the gay surgeon's role would be to offer an alternative 'fix' for Alberto by making him come to terms with his real feelings and consider a future in a homosexual relationship (it is not a coincidence that the affair started after Diego 'fixed' Alberto's broken arm). Instead, Diego becomes desperate and weakened by Alberto's emotional inconsistency and lack of commitment. The evolution of this character comes as no surprise, given the stereotypically gendered construction of the narrative. Diego's passive role in their sexual relationship is complemented by his domestic role as the one who cooks a special dish for his lover and also by the red intensity of his apartment (a reflection of his equally intensive emotions) that contrasts with the sterile and cooler blue that dominates Alberto's family home (arguably reflecting similar associations with those colours and their respective characters in *Jamón, Jamón*). Predictably, Diego is also portrayed as the passive 'piggy-in-the-middle': waiting for the married man to make all the decisions, left to one side when Alberto is taken to hospital (despite his profession and his involvement with the patient) and later in the shadows at the funeral. And yet, his role in the triangle is portrayed as a distortion of the all-important (sacred) nuclear family, getting in the way of Alberto's 'proper' commitments such as his son's birthday. Both Diego and Alberto are portrayed as immature, Alberto in his 'childlike apprehension' (as Perriam notes (2003: 123)) and Diego in his hopelessness, clinging to his teddy monkey in a moment of crisis. In a rare moment of comic relief, Elena (now estranged from her husband) watches a morning television programme with her mother. The presenter (played by Ana Rosa Quintana – a television presenter in real life) addresses her (predominantly female) audience with a list of 'the greatest monsters of the twentieth-century'. The list includes well-known and markedly masculine monsters of popular culture: Gozilla, The Loch Ness Monster, the Wolf-man or the Bogeyman. As she pauses dramatically before introducing 'the most terrible of them all', audiences would be forgiven for expecting to hear 'the homosexual'. Instead, she introduces the only feminine term in the list: cellulite (a feminine word in Spanish). Undoubtedly, the presenter was about to offer a way to tackle the much-feared abject condition.

In contrast, in *Cachorro/Bear Cub* (dir. Miguel Albaladejo, 2004) gay men are portrayed from a gay perspective. There is no explicit pedagogic intention and it makes no apologies for representing bear gay men – a minority within a minority – without the hygienic precautions that were once deemed necessary preconditions for the filmic representation of homosexual men. This becomes overtly clear from the opening credits, a gay sex scene between two overweight, hairy men. An erect penis and the buttocks of one of them, together with the sexual act itself, are the most striking elements of the scene not only because they unambiguously go beyond the limits of the mainstream conventional representations of gay sex but also because the bodies of the two men do not conform to mainstream models of male beauty. The startling effect of the scene is helped by a careful cinematography: at the beginning, the camera zooms in on several posters and portraits, one of them showing two men (it will be revealed later that they are the film's main character and his French boyfriend), whose protective glasses reflect the blurry image of the two men having sex on the bed. The image of the men having passionate sex is then reflected in various pieces of furniture as the camera slowly scans the room, then dissolves into an unexpectedly clear close-up shot of both men kissing passionately. The men's naked bodies fill the screen in a series of medium shots as they lick each other, followed by a long shot of one of the men rimming the other, conveniently framed by the door. The close-up shots that follow all lead to the penetration as one of the men opens a condom and both apply lubricant to the relevant parts of their bodies, whilst medium shots are used during the penetrative sex. The set is properly framed when the film's main character, Pedro (José Luis García Pérez), enters the bedroom and asks the two men to finish off as he is expecting some visitors. At one point, the three men are framed together in the bed, in a mise-en-scene that celebrates their friendship.

The sense of placid normalcy that the three men instil into this early-morning sex scene will then extend to all the other gay sex scenes in the film – in parks, clubs and saunas. Homosexuality is not a problem for gay men in *Cachorro*, although, perhaps surprisingly for those familiar with the evolution of Spanish gay cinema, it is used for blackmail (a hot topic in the 1970s that featured prominently in Eloy de la Iglesia's films, but that became rare during the 1990s); in fact, Pedro is the victim of a double blackmail – as a homosexual and also as HIV positive. There are some other elements that relate this to other Spanish gay films, including, importantly, the topical representation of an illness associated with the main homosexual character. In this case, Pedro spends a time in hospital as a result of HIV-related pneumonia, thus confirming the already mentioned statements by Llamas about the equation of AIDS and homosexuality and the externalization of homosexuality as sickness (Llamas 1995: 179). The fact that Pedro is a dentist by profession and that he has not ceased practising despite his known HIV condition also contributes to the medicalization of homosexuality. The implicit pathologization of gay lifestyles, together with the blackmail narrative and the insistence on promiscuous sex scenes, are elements that seem to shed a negative light on gay representation. However, the conclusion of the film offers a more positive horizon with the death of the blackmailer and the visibly good health of Pedro.

Ricardo Llamas's concept of the homosexual 'hyper-body' could easily be illustrated with just the credit sequences of some of the gay-themed films that we have discussed so far. As in *Segunda piel*, the opening credits of Ventura Pons's *Amic/Amat* (*Beloved/Friend*, also released in 1999) clearly establish from the outset the centrality of the body in gay narratives, and place the gay/ bisexual male body as a locus of pleasure… and pain (X-rays and silhouettes of naked bodies in the opening credits of *Segunda piel*, a hustler changing into his S&M gear in *Amic/Amat*). As in Vera's film, the plot of *Amic/Amat* involves a triangle between a bisexual man, his female partner (pregnant in this case) and a gay man whose love for the bisexual (?) man remains largely unrequited. *Amic/Amat* also ends in death, although here the death is not a dramatic shock as in *Segunda piel* but announced from the start.[15] Interestingly, the gay character in Pons's film is terminally ill (as well as twice the age of his object of desire).

The opening credits of *Amic/Amat* present a series of close-ups and extreme close-ups of various body parts of a young, fit man getting undressed. The reddish lighting and the zebra bedding of the very first shot provide a slightly seedy context for the images that follow. A right pan takes us to the body of the man sitting on the bed, taking his boots off. Credits on a black background are cross-cut with further close-up shots of the man's body as he removes his shirt (chest), unbuttons his jeans (crotch) and applies a generous amount of massage oil to his back (hands, back). Medium shots then travel across his body again whilst he applies the oil to his legs, stomach and back. This fit, male body, already deconstructed as an impersonal object of desire by dissecting its parts in a succession of close-up shots and separating them from the head (the only part we do not see is his face, and later his head is covered with a leather mask), is then sexualized further as the anonymous man adjusts a black leather harness to his back and chest, then a leather jockstrap and then a black leather mask over his head, all recognizable symbols of S&M sex. In sheer contrast, the film proper opens with a bright daylight scene showing a young heterosexual couple (students) enjoying the sunshine lying on the grass just outside a university building. Little does the audience know at this point that the young man pictured in this blissful scene with his girlfriend is the same one in the opening credits. From the outset, the film plays out the malleability and performative potential of one of the male bodies at the centre of its narrative. The next scene shows the older gay man Jaume (Josép María Pou) discussing his inevitable death with his long-term friend and now also fellow university professor Pere (Mario Gas). The young man seen at the beginning is David (David Selvas) who happens to work as a 'part-time' male prostitute but who also dates Pere's daughter (as established in the opening credits and first scene, respectively). To further complicate matters, David was recently a student of both Pere and Jaume, and has made Pere's daughter pregnant (much to Pere's disapproval). In a further turn of the screw, Jaume has fallen desperately in love with his student, impressed by his confrontational personality in class and his strong ideas about the work of Ramón Llull, Jaume's specialist subject. Jaume's strong infatuation with his student is, therefore, both physical and intellectual, and the tension between the two will become a key part of their short-lived but extremely intense bond. Jaume first approaches David to ask for feedback on his recently finished book manuscript (a labour of love for the terminally ill academic) but, coincidentally and unknowingly, ends up hiring his sexual services. In line with the Greek model seen in the early films of Eloy de la Iglesia discussed earlier, a classic teacher/pupil, father/son age-structured dyad is established between the two characters: Jaume has the upper-hand in terms of experience (personal and intellectual) and also social position, whereas David is clearly superior in physical terms.[16] The former will use his manuscript and financial means as a defence strategy against the latter's sexual overconfidence. Hours before his death, Jaume proposes a deal: if David will abandon prostitution and support a family, he will provide financial support for David to finish his studies. For him it is important that David has the child that he could never have. In a triangular structure that is highly reminiscent of the Eduardo/Miguel relationship that we saw in de la Iglesia's *Los placeres ocultos*, the financial offer is presented as a 'sort of scholarship' and a payment for David's help with publishing his manuscript. The comparison established between David's still-unborn baby and Jaume's unpublished manuscript is intensively played out. Orphaned David has no interest in becoming a father, and favours the idea of abortion. Equally, he destroys the discs containing the only available copies of Jaume's manuscript, as well as his computer. Yet, as Jaume reminds him in his last conversation, after destroying the discs, David will remain the only person to have read his unpublished work, thus forever holding Jaume's legacy in his mind.

The visuals and dialogues of this film are a minefield not only for a study of the gay male body but also the ageing and decaying male body. Refreshingly, the two older men are also seen completely naked (Pere on his way to the shower, after what appears to be a sexually intensive night with his wife, and Jaume also in the shower). In a touching scene, whilst awaiting his rent-boy (still unaware that the boy would be David), Jaume looks at himself in the mirror, getting ready for his date, removing his glasses and undoing his shirt. David will take great pleasure in drawing attention to Jaume's ageing and overweight body, which he reads as feminized and thus, in the same value system described in the previous analyses of this chapter, weak ('I didn't realize that you were a grannie', 'you should really hit the gym'). Jaume puts up with the abuse with some dignity and is drawn to confess that he accepted an extension to his university contract because of him and that he is in love with him. David's response could not be less noble. Afraid of any sort of feelings and attachments, he takes the opportunity to express his disgust towards the

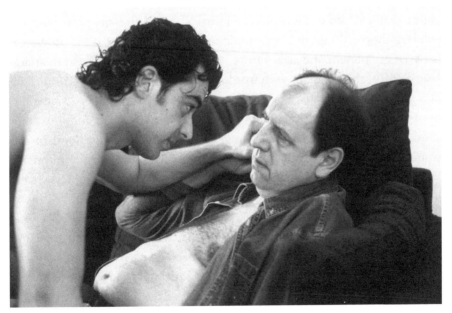

12. Father/son; teacher/student; hustler/client: Josep María Pou and David Selvas in *Amic/Amat*.

old man's body, in two cruel monologues that are worth quoting at length because of the binary oppositions established in it between young/old, fit/unfit bodies, which indirectly stand for the straight/gay body opposition (see Figure 12). As Thomas Waugh has argued, the 'gay subject' is often portrayed in Western cinema as older than his young object of desire. The 'subject' will also be seen dressed, in opposition to the nude object: clothing will connote class and cultural-racial privilege of the subject over the object (1993: 141). Gender roles are opposed and the body condition of the subject ('markers such as eyeglasses, makeup, obesity, disease and mortality') will be opposed to 'beauty, strength and health' of the object (Waugh 1993: 146).

> David: You are a sad man, you are finished. You will never be able to make anybody love you or desire you again. Never again. You will have to pay for sex and, if you are lucky, a good professional like me will make you have a good time (….) Nobody will tremble when you get close to them, nobody will tell you that they love you while their dick gets hard.
> (…)
> David: The day that I look at myself in the mirror and find my body half as repulsive as I find yours now, that day I will kill myself.

The old man's revenge is to remind David that one day he, too, will have a belly and he will still cling to his life. Furthermore, having suffered the humiliation of his physical inferiority with regards to the young hustler, Jaume reminds him of his own superiority, 'I am a university professor, you will be a shop assistant at a male underwear boutique: that is the difference between my present and your future.' These words prompt David to attack Jaume again, this time not with words but with brutal physical action. This new attack is two-fold: he first destroys the professor's computer (containing what he thinks is the last remaining copy of the manuscript) and then, in a similar – extremely physical and angry – fashion, kicks him hard in the stomach and face. He leaves Jaume lying on the floor, bruised and bleeding. Jaume's body is thus now doubly hurt: internally, his terminal illness affects his vital organs, and externally he is bruised and wounded. Scared, he runs to his friend Pere who, in a symbolic act of protective love and friendship, cleans his wounds and tells him that he would rather see him dead than behaving like a 'scared animal'. The internal and external damage to Jaume's body is an externalization of his hurt feelings, caused mainly by a tragic love life: he had earlier confessed to his heterosexual long-term friend Pere that he had been the love of his life and that the only two love stories in his life had been brief. This sense of tragedy is now heightened by David's rejection and his own humiliation (it is no coincidence that his last infatuation was also the cause of his final physical wounds). In a scene that follows, Jaume is shown having a shower at home. The camera travels down his aged and badly bruised body in close-ups, in sheer contrast with the close-up shots of David during the credit sequence. It is unclear whether all the blood that can be seen in the bath comes from his facial wounds or from some more major damage caused either by the kicks in the stomach or by his illness. The shower turns out to be a ritualistic cleansing in preparation for his assisted death with the help of Pere.[17] Once again, the homosexual body is damaged and associated with illness and sexual frustration. From the view of his beloved one at least, Jaume's is an undesirable body weakened by age and excess weight (and also by his illness). Yet, before his death, Jaume will have a final conversation with David and despite what it may appear then, the conversation will have a meaningful effect on the younger man. David's evolution and change of heart about fatherhood becomes Jaume's salvation, as suggested by the enunciation of Llull's words at the end – in a Jaume voiceover. When David returns home, he hesitates to return his girlfriend's message about whether she should have their baby. He is interrupted by a call from a client and accepts to see him, in his words, because he will have to bring up a child. The film closes with a scene that, on the surface, mirrors the opening credits: David is getting ready for a client. This return to the start could suggest a negative sense of circularity and lack of evolution of a character that would be stuck in his current lifestyle. Yet, in this final scene, there is a notable difference: whilst in the opening credits David's body was dissected in impersonal, objectified parts in close-up shots, here he is seen in a long shot and facing the camera before putting on the mask: the flesh-object seems to have become a thinking-subject as a result of his encounter with the not-so-powerless, dying gay man.

As we have seen in this chapter, Spanish gay-themed films have a tendency to emphasize the 'corporality' of gay men. The 1970s films of the recently deceased director Eloy de la Iglesia were ground-breaking in their portrayal of homosexuality, although they were also trapped in a Greek paradigm, which, as Waugh (1993) has noted, was prevalent in much gay representation in Western cinemas. In this model, the gay male subject is separated from the object of his desire in terms of age, class and experience. The gap between the subject and the object affects the representation of the gay body in so far as the elder subject tends to remain clothed and act as the vehicle of the audience's desire for the object. Some of the more recent films that still maintain this model, such as Pons's *Amic/Amat*, have broken new-ground in this sense, by disturbing the visual economy that separates the gay subject from the object and reflecting on such oppositions more overtly. The representation of the gay body in recent Spanish cinema is also hugely indebted to the homoerotic gaze encouraged by many Almodóvar films (discussed in Chapters 4, 6 and 8). However, as we have seen, some of the 1990s gay-themed comedies that tried to imitate the Almodóvar style were rather regressive in their representational politics, often reiterating some of the oppressive stereotypes that were more characteristic of those modes of representation of the democratic transition. Comedies such as *Perdona Bonita* are often made with the mainstream public in mind and tease gay audiences by encouraging a homoerotic gaze on the male body whilst often frustrating queer visual pleasure. Some more recent films such as *Cachorro* might still be unable to escape some of the tropes that have characterized much gay representation to date (emphasis on sexual activity, health narratives and so on), but they are also less afraid to address queer audiences. These new and more liberating modes of visualization of the gay male body in Spanish cinema are undoubtedly a reflection of the new status of the gay and lesbian community in Spain that, in a relatively short period of time, have emerged from the oppression of the dictatorship to the enjoyment of one of the most favourable legislative frameworks of the Western world.

6

Transformed bodies

TRANSFORMING THE BODY

Body modification has become one of the most visible features of post-modern radical subjectivity. Piercing, tattooing and implanting are now common amongst the affluent urban youngsters, as much as extreme hairdos, drag and unconventional clothing were for the previous generations. New or rediscovered practices such as scarification, and everyday sado-masochism have caught the attention of sectors of the mainstream media. As we discussed in Chapter 2, today's teenagers and young adults have unprecedented control over their bodies, which sometimes translates into the deliberate tactics of temporal or permanent transmogrification, masquerading or metamorphosis. Although body-modification theorists tend to focus primarily on the most 'primitivist' facets and consider gender issues as somewhat marginal (Featherstone 2000: 4–5), it is obvious that cross-dressing and sex change have an immediate impact on the way the body is perceived and that, from a filmic perspective, either phenomenon cannot be cut from a more general paradigm of deliberate somatic transformation. For Judith Halberstam, transgender film offers the best example of contemporary ('transmodern') fantasies of the morphed, fluid body:

> Whether it is the image of surgically removable faces in John Woo's *Face/Off*, the liquid-mercury type of slinkiness of the *Terminator* in *Terminator 2: Judgment Day*, the virtual bodies of *The Matrix*, or the living-dead body in *The Sixth Sense*, the body in transition indelibly marks late-twentieth- and early-twenty-first-century visual fantasy. The fantasy of the shape-shifting and identity-morphing body has nowhere been more powerfully realized recently than in trans-gender film. (Halberstam 2005: 76)

This putting of the gender-morphing body centre-stage could well be a consequence of the fact that, more than any other body-transformation practice, cross-dressing and transsexualism currently enjoy unprecedented levels of visibility and social acceptance. The Spanish 2004 edition of *Big Brother* included a female-to-male transsexual amongst the contestants, in what represented but one more example of the increased presence of trans-sexuals in mainstream media. In June 2006, the Socialist Government approved the project for the country's first Law of Gender Identity. This law, passed in 2007, allows for gender reassignment without the prerequisite of undergoing sex-change surgery. Despite the huge differences between identity disorders such as gender dysphoria at one end of the spectrum and the fashion-driven somatic strategies such as cosmetic body decoration at the other, all these manifestations of body modification reveal a common contemporary tendency to subject the body to a strict control. Surgery and other techniques are the instruments that make it possible to gain or, as Victoria Pitts puts it, 'reclaim' control over the body in ways that were unimaginable only a few decades ago (Pitts 2003). Richard Ekins considers cross-dressing and sex-changing practices as manifestations of a broader social process that he names *male femaling*:

> Male cross-dressers and sex-changers are genetic males who 'female' in various ways, variously adopting what they take to be the thoughts, feelings, attitudes, behaviours, accoutrements and attributes of genetic females (....) Male femalers wish to 'display' their femaling. When they do so they are 'displaying' – a major 'near core' variable of male femaling. Those 'male femalers' who wish to 'display' full time and in all contexts as female and never wish their male identities to be revealed have particular problems. Others may wish to disclose aspects of their identities in certain settings and not in others. (Ekins 1997: 48–49)

Examples of male femaling abound in cinema. Cross-dressing was the most-common formulation of conventional body-image modification in classic Hollywood films, such as *Some Like it Hot* (dir. Billy Wilder, 1959), *Psycho* (dir. Alfred Hitchcock, 1960), *Victor/Victoria* (dir. Blake Edwards, 1982), *Tootsie* (dir. Sydney Pollack, 1982), and has been constantly deployed up until today in more recent cases, such as *The Crying Game* (dir. Neil Jordan, 1992), *Mrs Doubtfire* (dir. Chris Columbus, 1993), *The Birdcage* (dir. Mike Nichols, 1996), *Boys Don't Cry* (dir. Kimberly Peirce, 1999), *She's the Man* (dir. Andy Fickman, 2006) or *It's a Boy/Girl Thing* (dir. Nick Hurran, 2006), to mention but a few well-known examples. In Spanish film, cross-dressing has a long tradition in comedy, with well-known examples, such as *El extraño viaje/Strange Journey* (dir. Fernando Fernán Gómez, 1964), *Una señora llamada Andrés/A Lady Called Andrés* (dir. Julio Buchs, 1970), *La liga no es cosa de hombres/League/Garter is Not For Men* (dir. Ignacio F. Aquino, 1972), *La tía de Carlos/Carlos's Aunty* (dir. Luis María Delgado, 1981), *Vestida de azul/ Dressed in Blue* (dir. Antonio Giménez-Rico, 1983), *La monja alférez/The Lieutenant Nun* (dir. Javier Aguirre, 1987) and, more recently, *Almejas y mejillones/Clams and Mussels* (dir. Carnevale, 2000), *Corazón de bombón/ Sweetheart* (dir. Álvaro Sáenz de Heredia, 2000) or *I Love You Baby* (dirs Albacete and Menkes, 2001). Examples abound in films where a character makes an occasional dress change, usually in the context of plot-driven deception scenes, costume parties and the like: a carnival dance party in *Belle Epoque* (dir. Fernando Trueba, 1992), detectives in disguise in *Tacones lejanos/ High Heels* (dir. Almodóvar, 1991) and *Torrente 2: Misión en Marbella* (dir. Santiago Segura, 2001) or cross-dressing bank robbers in *El palo/The Hold-Up* (dir. Eva Lesmes, 2001). There is also a smaller number of straight-passing-as-gay comedies epitomized in the early 1970s titles such as the already discussed *No desearás al vecino del quinto/Thou Shalt Not Covet Thy Fifth Floor Neighbour* (dir. Ramón Fernández, 1970) (see Chapters 1 and 5) and *A mí las mujeres, ni fu ni fa/Women Don't Do it for Me* (dir. Mariano Ozores, 1971).[1]

The theme of sex change is present in a smaller cluster of films. Time-honoured Hollywood titles such as *Glen or Glenda* (dir. Edward D. Wood, 1953) and *Goodbye Charlie* (dir. Vincente Minnelli, 1964) showed a penchant for the psychotic and the bizarre that was still present in the first Spanish attempt, *Mi querida señorita/My Dearest Senorita* (dir. Jaime de Armiñán, 1972). It has been toned down in more recent films such as *Willy/Milly* (dir. Paul Schneider, 1986), *Switch* (dir. Blake Edwards, 1991) and the closely thematically related *Pon un hombre en tu vida/Put a Man in Your Life* (dir. Eva Lesmes, 1996), and *Transamerica* (dir. Duncan Tucker, 2005), which bears some similarities to *20 centímetros/20 Centimetres* (dir. Ramón Salazar, 2005). The relative scarcity of examples in classic cinema could be explained by the fact that the transsexual acquired 'official' status only in 1949, when David Cauldwell diagnosed one of his patients as a 'psychopathic trans-sexual' (Prosser 1998: 9), and has taken even longer to constitute a narrative theme.

There is an interesting disparity between the so-called 'high' art cinema's tackling of cross-dressing and transgender themes, and that perpetuated by 'low' mass-oriented films.[2] Elitist, minority, high-brow films, usually associated with artsy and auteur cinema, tend to challenge commonly held assumptions.

Popular, mass-oriented, low-brow films, usually associated with the more predictable forms of comedy, tend to support and perpetuate those same assumptions. This distinction was contested and recycled into a new paradigm (the quality popular film) by popular auteurs such as Pedro Almodóvar. However, the aggregated topics of sex change, transgenderism and cross-dressing have been portrayed in contemporary Spanish cinema in ways that respond primarily to the dichotomous opposition we have just outlined.[3] More precisely, those films that are primarily intended for a potentially enlightened and ideologically progressive audience do portray these topics as inherently related to one particular character against the backdrop of a family or a society that is not always ready to support the character in his or her journey. On the other hand, those films that are primarily concerned with satisfying the audience's entertainment needs do seek to disembody these issues from the experiential realm of the character to render them readily understandable to the average spectator. This difference between challenge and avoidance as two opposite representation modes determines the two ideological approaches to sex change and to most issues related to sex and sexuality in Spanish film. The challenge to received conceptions leads to the formulation of new explanatory models and hence to a pedagogical function; avoidance leads to the perpetuation of fixed ideas and clichés, more often than not based on poor sexology and a morally conservative viewpoint on sexual matters.

If it is true that the way TG bodies (we will use this now widely accepted term henceforth to refer to cross-dressers, transsexuals, drags, gender fuckers, she-males and similar permutations) are represented in cinema depends largely on the genre, and that 'high' genres tend to focus on character building, whilst 'popular' genres tend to exploit situations (usually in comic or farcical modes). Thus it is not difficult to understand the general tendency in cinemas worldwide to privilege the popular approach. The sort of avoidance favoured by comedy allows for the reduction of a very complex psycho-sexual matter to a few effective representations that can be used contextually in a film. This avoidance could then be seen as a form of displacement that would attempt to divert attention from some complexity and direct it to accepted bodily forms. In classic psychoanalytical terms, cross-dressing and gender bending are related to a taboo behaviour and a consequent transgression that sometimes creates a fetish attachment. The complexity that comedy and popular genres try to avoid is the original taboo of the body in transit, epitomized by the experience of the transsexual who feels trapped in the wrong body; the transsexual is yet to '*constitute* a "body" that can be mobilized in relation to society for "him or her" to act as a subject' (Jagodzinski 2003: 38; original emphasis).

Representing a transitional body that does not yet quite embody a 'finished' subject constitutes a problem that the comedy has typically replaced with bodies that simply accumulate layers of gender excess. In the classic *Some Like it Hot* (dir. Wilder, 1959), as in all the films of the male-in-disguise sub-genre, the displacement is achieved by reducing the subversive potential of cross-dressing to an innocuous game of deception in which the bodies of Jack Lemmon and Tony Curtis are treated as palimpsests – one more layer of deception is always possible. The casting of the actors adds an important dimension; arguably, the natural choice for transgender roles should be transgender actors such as, in Spain, Bibiana Fernández (aka Bibí Andersen).[4] Transgenders playing transgenders would be a performing-arts version of the principle of transgenders theorizing transgenderism, offered by Susan Stryker as the most important milestone in the development of transgender theory in modern times (Stryker 2006).[5] Pat Califia emphasized the epistemological importance of rescuing transgenderism from those who have historically used it for their own purposes, in particular early gender scientists who defined transsexuality as a pathology and 'would have absolutely no ethical problem with genetically engineering trans-sexuals out of existence' (Califia 1997: 81), 'trans-phobe' feminists who decried sex-reassignment surgery, and gay male social scientists who appropriated historical instances of transgenderism and bisexuality in a 'drive to normalize homosexuality by simply documenting its widespread existence' (Califia 1997: 121).

TG in its many different forms has been traditionally linked to homo-sexuality and gay identity. For Garber, both histories 'constantly intersect and intertwine, both willingly and unwillingly [but] neither can simply be trans-historically "decoded" as a sign for the other' (Garber 1993: 131). In visual spectacles such as theatre and film, the transvestite often plays the role of controlling homosexual panic for the heterosexual audiences. Drawing on Garber, Ballesteros suggests that transvestism 'translates homosexuality into representation' (Ballesteros 2001: 109), something that the Spanish films of the 1970s, as we shall see, consistently offered their heterosexual audiences by means of humour and farce.

The conflation of homosexuality and TG represents the most visible case of the use of the latter for other purposes and interests (Tyler 1991: 32–33). But the narratives of body transformation we will be commenting on in this chapter demonstrate that TG can serve as an apt symbol for a myriad of thematic interests, whilst it is extremely rare to find a film focusing unambiguously on TG *per se*.[6] The transitional body, it seems, is an inexhaustible metaphor, which can work as a metaphor even when referring to itself. 'Trans-sexuality entered the cultural lexicon first as a form of extreme (body) transvestism, with the body's skin as the "clothing" that the subject needed changing' (Prosser 1998: 69). The metaphors used by transsexuals to refer to their own body (Prosser mentions in quick succession 'prison', 'diver's suit', 'suitcase full of clothing', 1998: 68) seem to suggest a form of subjectivity based on an experience of the body radically other and undecipherable to the conservative audiences and low genres. This intrinsic difficulty, which was identified in relation to homosexuality in earlier periods (Haste 1993: 287; Martínez-Expósito 1998a), could explain why the TG body is always something more, and often something else, than just a body.

STRANGE JOURNEYS: CROSS-DRESSING AND SEX CHANGES IN PRE-1990s SPANISH CINEMA

Instances of cross-dressing in Spanish films during Franco's dictatorship are very scarce, but for that very reason, they have attracted critical attention in more recent times. In *El extraño viaje/Strange Journey* (dir. Fernando Fernán Gómez, 1964, re-released in 1970), a small-village thriller based on a real-life story, Carlos Larrañaga plays Fernando, a week-end musician and double-life gigolo who on occasion tries on women's clothes for the pleasure of his mistress. Slightly surrealist and profoundly disturbing, *El extraño viaje* relies for effect on the suspense created by a lack of information about a crime, followed by the criminal's full confession. Fernando unwillingly enters a strange and furtive love relationship with wealthy Ignacia (Tota Alba), who asks him to buy her expensive clothes and lingerie, and then makes him wear them and pose for her in seemingly sadistic albeit inoffensive private evening encounters. When Ignacia is murdered by her idiotic brother and sister, Fernando cannot avoid being involved in the cover-up, in what later on becomes a convoluted whodunit plot. The film has been recently rediscovered and celebrated as a powerful allegory of the corrupt and dysfunctional socio-political atmosphere of Spain in the 1960s that draws on oppositions such as tradition versus modernity and city versus village to finally articulate a critique of totalitarian authority (Zunzunegui 1999; Pavlović 2003, 2004; Mira 2005b). In her despotic attitude towards her infantilized siblings,

Ignacia has been compared to Franco, 'whereas her brother and sister suggest that the people he [Franco] rules over are scared and childish, sexually castrated and always dreaming of something exciting that lies outside the house walls' (Mira 2005b: 125). Surprisingly for a film that was five years in the vaults for its allegedly poor commercial prospects (Mira 2005b: 119), modern critics have come to consider it as representative of its time (Pavlović 2003: 87) and of Spanish culture at large (Almodóvar in Strauss 2001: 55), whilst heavily drawing on Spanish genres and cultural references (Zunzunegui 1993: 56) and providing modern directors such as Almodóvar with ideas and inspiration (D'Lugo 2004: 292–295). In such an allegorical film, Fernando's drag asks to be taken as a representation of some symbolic journey. Whilst the modernization of Spain (and some of its social difficulties) is mentioned repeatedly in the film, Pavlović suggests that the psychoanalytic notion of the gaze can be used to sustain a broad interpretation of the film as social critique, '… with the disclosure of the crime we suddenly realize that the scene, the film, and the culture from which it emerges are complicated by the multiplication of gazes' (Pavlović 2003: 87). Ignacia's authoritarian gaze creates Fernando's submissive cross-dressing, and the audience is momentarily asked to identify with her sadistic and fetishistic drive. Fernando, a young and solid bloke, has been seduced and reduced by an older woman. As Mira suggests, 'the shots in which he walks in different female clothes whilst Ignacia looks on, placidly smoking a cigarette, are amongst the most remarkable in the film and the weirdest in Spanish cinema of the time' (Mira 2005b: 126). Modern audiences immediately detect Larrañaga's awkward air in these shots: his firm muscular tone, his large frame and his hairy chest contrast sharply with the female underwear and lingerie he is required to parade; he rehearses a few female gestures and body movements, but his stolid facial expression denies what little femininity his body manages to conjure up. Ignacia's pleasure is all that counts, and Fernando's cross-dressing is presented as perverse and humiliating. His is clearly not the body of a transvestite or a homosexual – the only two interpretive modes of cross-dressing in the Spain of the 1960s.[7]

Mi querida señorita/My Dearest Senorita (dir. Jaime de Armiñán, 1972) has become a classic of Spanish cinema and is seen by many as one of López Vázquez's finest works. Despite a poor mise-en-scene and infelicitous soundtrack (a repetitive orchestral version of *Tristesse d'Amour,* a Chopin piano etude), the script (co-written by Armiñán and José Luis Borau) contains numerous narrative ellipses and ambiguities, and therefore the film relies on the actor's ability to convey with few words the gist of the story. In its first half, the film focuses on Adela Castro (López Vázquez), a small-town spinster in her forties who lives in permanent conflict with her body (must shave her face daily), with her maiden (she feels jealous of her romantic outgoings) and with her social milieu (she persistently declines marriage propositions). The village priest listens to her problems but has no solutions; a city doctor is more helpful and unveils for her the truth about her body: she is a man. The spectator is spared the details of the physical transformation. Instead, there is a dissolve to black and the camera, from a train's POV, moves towards the end of a tunnel and then into a Madrid rail station. Provincial Adela Castro is now newcomer city-dweller Juan Castro. New to the male gender, Juan must learn to think and act as a man; the city provides for the necessary anonymity, but, true to the Spanish metaphor of the city as beehive, it is also a source of alienation. Juan's body becomes his main identity sign: he grows a moustache, he becomes aware of old-lady manners (walking, talking) and habits. His male body, though, allows for a comforting and conforming heterosexuality, which is given an interesting narrative twist when he meets Isabelita (Julieta Serrano), his maid from the village (who seems to know nothing of his *señorita*'s new life). The romance story unfolds with the usual ups and downs. Sex is ambiguously portrayed as mutually unsatisfactory, but when Juan tries to come clean to Isabelita and tell her the truth about his identity she replies: 'Hardly news to me!' ('¡Qué me va usted a decir, señorita!'). Her facial expression is more telling than her shocking words: it suggests that she unconsciously knew about Juan's identity, but she had never realized it consciously. For Juan, the epiphany of this anagnorisis represents the final stage of his transition towards full masculinity. In the second (male) half of the film, López Vázquez's movements, gestures and intonation are perfectly, mathematically measured in a slow progression from contention and rigidity to expansive flexibility. The same happens with his body, which goes from an initial obsessive veiling (by means of a slightly exaggerated gentleman attire) to a more relaxed, casual dressing (spring-time scenes at Casa de Campo park), to the final sex scene with the display of semi-naked bodies. However, contrary to popular-genre expectations, this progression fails to reinforce the static notions of the gendered body. Juan Castro remains a project 'in progress' during the second half of the film, as much as Adela Castro had been an unfinished project of a woman for most of her life. Juan's male body seems to have been perfectly reconstructed by the surgeon, to the point of being able to maintain sexual intercourse; but his is a body without a past, now living like many other migrants, in a hostile city. In one particularly telling scene, Juan's bags are inspected by the owners of the *pensión* where he lives on the suspicion that he is a pervert. The bags contain female clothes that confirm the owners' worst suspicions; but the old clothes are only a memento of his past life that keep reminding Juan that his masculinity is just another stage on a longer journey. The permanent transition of Juan's body and his vulnerable masculinity contrast vividly with all the other characters in the film, whose neatly (almost stereotyped) defined genders correspond exactly with their bodies and their identities. However, *Mi querida señorita* ends with an optimist note of recognition and self-acceptance, suggesting that transitional bodies could find a more propitious understanding in future times.

If, according to the novelist and journalist Francisco Umbral, Bibí Andersen embodied the spirit and pathos of Spanish transition to democracy (Umbral 1977), Paul J. Smith convincingly underlined Umbral's idea that in the 1970s, homosexuals (of the very early public species, mostly around the *Front d'Alliberament Gay de Catalunya*) offered the best metaphor for the political transformation of the country, but within the rather amorphous and generous category of the homosexual as it was understood at the time (vaguely synonymous with non-heterosexual, deviant, sexually other), the transvestite and in particular, the transsexual was the epitome of political change (Smith 2000b: 14, 2000a: 34). This conflation of categories should be hardly surprising: Bibí Andersen (or Bibiana Fernández as she now likes to be known), born Manuel Fernández Chica (Tangier, 1954), became the first successful transgender actress in the history of Spanish cinema at a time when popular knowledge and understanding of transgenderism was almost nil. Bibí Andersen's public persona was quickly built up in the public television of the 1980s, coinciding with the first years of the Socialist Party rule, as a perfect token of the spirit of progress and tolerance that were meant to symbolize the new Spain. Before that, however, Bibí had made her film debut in *Cambio de sexo/Forbidden Love* (dir. Vicente Aranda, 1977), playing herself in what could be interpreted as an early attempt to build a public persona. Interestingly, Bibí's character in the film was not only non-fictional, because she played herself, but it was also an eminently pedagogic role; in the story she becomes the guide and mentor of a younger transgender who, like most of the audience, is utterly confused by the conflict between his body and his feelings. In other words, from very early in her career, Bibí Andersen became a source of information about the intrinsically mysterious nature of sex and sex change for a largely ignorant, albeit eager to learn, Spanish audience.[8]

Contrary to general expectation, the transgender role in *Cambio de sexo* was not played by Bibí Andersen, but by Victoria Abril.[9] *Cambio de sexo* deals with the same sex-change topic of *Mi querida señorita,* but there are striking differences between the two films, some of which have to do with the rapid political transformation of Spain during the 1970s, including, importantly, the liberalization of the censorship code. In *Cambio de sexo,* José María (Abril) is a delicate adolescent who endures the humiliations of his provincial milieu and the incomprehension of his own father before undertaking a sex-change operation. The operation, which in *Mi querida señorita* divides the film and the protagonist's life into two halves, is offered here as the culmination of the narrative, and as a happy ending.[10] The fact that the role of the boy is played by an actress represents one of the most interesting aspects of the film, because it is in his/her body that the politics of transformation (under a calculated appearance of ambiguity) is given the physical/visual commentary that the film attempts to articulate. The storyline of *Cambio de sexo* is not based on the sex change, as *Mi querida señorita* indeed was, but rather on being on the wrong side of sex ascription. This explains the film's insistence on issues of homosexuality and conformity to predetermined desires. In one particular episode, José María's father takes him to an all-male night out in Barcelona in an attempt to 'correct' his erotic desires; the father's inquisitive gaze at his reactions to cabaret dancers and prostitutes is all but revealing of the anxiety triggered by the possibility of having a homosexual son. Later in the film, José María himself becomes a cabaret dancer and comes to the forefront of the gaze. In her analysis of *Un hombre llamado Flor de Otoño/A Man Called Autumn Flower* (dir. Pedro Olea, 1978), Isolina Ballesteros makes the point that any subversive value one could expect from transvestism is lost by the fact that it only exists within the limits of the nightclub (Ballesteros 2001: 113). If, in *Mi querida señorita,* the narrative was organized around an 'after' and a 'before' the operation, in *Cambio de sexo* it all centres around the calculated ambiguity of José María's body, thus confirming Jay Prosser's assertion that the transsexual represents a perfect intersection between body and narrative (Prosser 1998: 105). The audience is drawn into the film's strategy of the gaze to the point that José María's exhibition on the nightclub stage becomes synonymous with Victoria Abril's full frontal for the film audience. The sight of Abril's penis (a prosthesis was used to shoot the scene) embodies most of the anxieties associated with a weakened masculinity, but at the same time aptly symbolizes the new levels of sexual tolerance that Spain was rapidly conquering during its transition.

Cambio de sexo is closely related to the documentary *Ocaña, retrat intermitent/Ocaña, an Intermittent Portrait* (dir. Ventura Pons, 1978), about the life and work of a notorious Andalusian drag queen living in the liberal milieu of Barcelona in the 1970s (see Figure 13). Both films are closely linked to the Barcelona School movement of the 1960s, if only because both Aranda and Pons had been involved in it. The scriptwriters, Carlos Durán and Joaquim Jordà, together with Vicente Aranda, had previously been involved in various Barcelona School projects such as *Fata Morgana/Left-Handed Fate* (dir. Vicente Aranda, 1965) and the school's manifesto *Dante no es únicamente severo/Dante is Not Only Rigorous* (dirs Jacinto Esteva and Joaquim Jordà, 1967). Both *Cambio de sexo* and *Ocaña* are also related to the previous Tercera Vía film, *Mi querida señorita*. All these films must be considered somehow elitist, in the sense that they were not intended to fulfil the roles of popular films.[11] *Ocaña, retrat intermitent*, a low-budget documentary that seemed destined to obscurity, received 'apotheosic' reactions in screenings in Cannes, Berlin and worldwide (Smith 2003: 125). Despite the literary script of Ocaña's monologue, the film gestures at a documentary and non-fictional quality: it combines shots of artist José Luis Pérez Ocaña (Cantillana 1947 – Sevilla 1983) speaking about his work and his life, with shots of him performing in the streets and at small locales.[12] Whilst the film seems to be more interested in his art than in his sexuality (Hopewell 1989), it also contains radical remarks

13. Performing gender: José Pérez Ocaña in *Ocaña, retrat intermitent*.

that surely would have been difficult to understand by a mainstream audience in the Spain of 1978 if the film had circulated in broader circles. One of these comments, which is then glossed over by Ocaña, has to do with the difference between identity and performance, 'I like to cross-dress, but I am no transvestite.' Ocaña ties his dressing and his body to the political process that is taking place in the country: it is 'repression' that forces him to use clothes, whilst he opposes the freedom to choose not to use clothes at all. Vilarós describes the final moments of the documentary in Lorquian terms:

> The film ends with the powerful image of Ocaña taking off his bailaora dancing costume, throwing it to the audience, shattered and shouting in a passionate Lorquian crescendo: It was repression that forced these dirty clothes upon me! I am a libertarian! I don't like to be labelled! I don't want clothes! I'd rather give them to my audience! It was repression that forced these clothes upon me! I'd rather be naked! Suddenly, Ocaña begins an intense, orgasmic zapateado; he dances violently, naked except for his shoes and a carnation in his hair. All along, the audience proffers an extended and intense olé, in a spectacular communion bordering on delirium. (Vilarós 1998: 188)

Vilarós quotes several of Ocaña's friends, all of whom insist that Ocaña's transvestism was purely theatrical. Artist Nazario Luque explicitly ties Ocaña's cross-dressing to happenings and street theatre strategies, 'Ocaña used to come cross-dressed to my place at Plaza de San José Oriol, and then we used to get out for a walk and a laugh at the Ramblas; he repeated tirelessly that cross-dressing was for him just a performance and that the Ramblas was a stage' (Vilarós 1998: 195). Despite its underground and niche concept, the film acquired critical relevance to the point of being considered a central piece of Spanish film during the transition, owing to its authenticity, Ocaña's radicalism, the stylistic transparency and documental value.[13] However, Paul J. Smith has convincingly argued that, if the film is still meaningful to contemporary Spanish audiences, 'it is not simply the result of nostalgia for a golden age of transgression, but because *Ocaña's* problematic and oblique politics of performance continues to hold the attention' (Smith 2003: 129).[14] Ocaña's authenticity is in a permanent contradiction to his performances (Fernàndez 2004: 93), but, as Fernàndez has strongly suggested, the Catalanness of this Ventura Pons film relies on Ocaña's drag, which is a form of representing 'Catalan culture in Andalusian drag' (Fernàndez 2004: 96). Ocaña's body becomes, thus, unavoidably semiotized as a multiple signifier of sexual, class, national and countercultural referents.

FEMALING MEN IN CONTEMPORARY SPANISH FILMS

In the Oscar-winning *Belle Epoque/The Age of Beauty* (dir. Fernando Trueba, 1992), young Fernando (Jorge Sanz) finds himself dancing with the lesbian Violeta (Ariadna Gil) in a carnival *verbena* (open-air country dance party) during the Spanish Second Republic. The carnival atmosphere encourages cross-dressing and Fernando is dressed up as a maid with Violeta as a soldier. The context is, in the words of Barry Jordan, that of 'the "anything goes" society', a bucolic paradise that combines '1960s hippy culture, the cult of "make love, not war", plus generous helpings of the 1970s and 1980s feminism, as well as gender-bending and a post-modern taste for blurring political, moral and sexual boundaries' (Jordan 1999b: 155–156). But these doses of libertarianism are not enough to break down the boundaries that separate everyday life from the safely contained transgressive permissiveness of the carnival. Maybe if the characters such as Fernando and Violeta were allowed in the 1930s some of the post-modern taste for blurring sexual boundaries that the *Belle Epoque* audiences were enjoying in the Spain of the 1990s, they would have been allowed to be dressed and represented differently. This scene is a good example of Bakhtin's notion of carnival as a safely contained transgression that reinforces the status quo by presenting the alternatives as confusing and undesirable. In his analysis of the film, Alberto Mira points out that the scene is problematic 'because it uses a lesbian to seek identification with male heterosexual audiences' (Mira 2005a: 206). He argues convincingly that whilst Violeta is fooled by her fantasies about Fernando being a girl, Fernando is aroused by Violeta's true sex, of which he is totally aware. Interestingly, the audience might get an implicit assurance of her heterosexual femininity, but Mira makes the point that the film fails to construct the character of Violeta with a female libidinal gaze whilst the other female bodies are highly sexualized.

The Spanish/Argentine co-production, *Almejas y mejillones/Clams and Mussles* (dir. Marcos Carnevale, 2000), offers a different take on the same juncture (the reference to the earlier film becomes clear through the use of the same actor). Here, Jorge Sanz plays Rolondo, a biologist who runs into Paola (Leticia Brédice), an Argentinean poker player who happens to be a lesbian. The context is, more clearly than in *Belle Epoque*, an anything-goes society, that of the Canary Islands of the millennium. Significant parts of the action take place in gay bars and almost all the main characters are gays or lesbians. The film makes constant references to the renowned Tenerife Carnival, which frames the action in the opening and final scenes. But, unlike *Belle Epoque*, there seems to be no limit to the way the bodies are controlled: when Rolondo falls in love with lesbian Paola, he takes no chances and transforms himself into a woman. The improbable radicalism of this move leaves no one indifferent. Paola's reaction is particularly angry, as she accuses him of merely taking on female clothes to put up a masquerade. Surprisingly, though, Rolondo (now called Diana) leads her and the audience to believe that he has undertaken sex-change surgery, although in the end it will be revealed that such an operation never took place. For a man becoming not only a woman but a lesbian (a possibility much more deeply articulated in Sampedro's novel *El amante lesbiano* – 2000) opens all the possibilities of body manipulation, and therefore the theoretical possibility gestured at in the film represents a significant step forward with respect to *Belle Epoque*. Unfortunately, Sanz's female transformation is marred by some of the most typical pitfalls of this kind of exercise: infelicitous attempts to modulate his voice, his facial expression and his body movements, combined with a feminine dress code that emphasizes his hardest angles. The result is that, in his role of Diana, Sanz's masculinity is even more visible – in a way reminiscent of his sham performance of masculinity in *La niña de tus ojos/The Girl of Your Dreams* (dir. Fernando Trueba) (Perriam 2003: 166).

Peruvian-born Santiago Magill worked in gay-themed films such as *No se lo digas a nadie/Don't Tell Anyone* (dir. Francisco J. Lombardi, 1998) and *Before Night Falls* (dir. Julian Schnabel, 2000) before playing a central role in *I Love You Baby* (dirs Albacete and Menkes, 2001). In the latter Magill plays Daniel, a young gay Latino living in Madrid who meets newcomer Marcos (Jorge Sanz). Their love relationship is truncated by an accident: Marcos's head is hit hard in a disco and he becomes straight. In a desperate attempt to get him back – that echoes the story of the Sanz character in *Almejas y mejillones* and has an earlier Spanish referent in the Carmen Maura character in Almodóvar's *La ley del deseo* – Daniel adopts a female identity to re-conquer the now heterosexual Marcos. This deceptively simple storyline is made even more uninteresting by a predictable ending. Magill's role, however, is made slightly unconventional by means of an imperfect (some would say deliberately clumsy) cross-dressing that renders him more of a farcical transvestite than a credible woman. As a man, his soft-looking face is adorned by a semi-grown beard and a free-flowing, dark-toned, straight hairstyle. As a woman, layers of make-up and bleach turn him into a blonde version of himself. The result of the transformation is so poor that everyone s/he meets can notice something weird about her. If the resulting character is never a convincing woman and the drag elements are never emphasized, it could be seen as an interesting experiment in androgyny at the very least. Perhaps not surprisingly, Daniel is an actor and, presumably, his decision to dress as a woman is influenced by his profession. He is also a fan of Boy George, whose chameleon-like androgyny was a point of fascination for many gay circles in the 1980s. In an unexpected twist, at the film's end Daniel finds a new partner – the very real Boy George – who makes a cameo appearance in the epilogue scene. Androgyny seems to be somehow related to Daniel's acting skills as more than an unreconstructed sense of stable identity. In fact, the film seems unconcerned with the notions of self and authenticity, whilst it favours cultural fusion and *mestizaje*. Music is the best example of this proposition, with Boy George's famous 'Karma Chameleon' being interpreted here by Chacho Carreras with a flamenco swing, and a Japanese karaoke version of a flamenco theme by Paco Ortega. Marcos's story as a migrant in Madrid from the provinces takes place mostly amongst other migrants from the Caribbean and South America. Rather than adopting a social perspective on migration, the film focuses on the apparently seamless interactions of migrants of diverse origins to produce new forms of cultural and social expression. Gender fluidity, androgyny and homosexuality are amongst those forms, together with fusion music, exotic cuisines and mixed couples, pointing out that, potentially, there is an important element of conscious performance in the ethnic identities comparable to that of gender. Unfortunately, the film fails to explicitly develop the connection between body transformation and the fusion of cultures. Perhaps unintentionally, a series of parallels between the main characters (Spaniard Marcos and Latin American Daniel) and the cultures they represent seem to invoke neo-colonial readings (the amnesiac Spaniard, the self-denying colonial subject who masks his own identity) in a sense diametrically opposed to *Almejas y mejillones,* where the Spaniard fakes a sex change to get the erotic attention of the (lesbian) Latin American.

Before his famous cameo appearance in Almodóvar's *Todo sobre mi madre/All About My Mother* (1999) as the promiscuous, provocative, HIV-positive transvestite Lola, former Spanish television personality, Toni Cantó, exploited his feminine side in the gender-bender farce *Pon un hombre en tu vida/Put a Man in Your Life* (dir. Eva Lesmes, 1996). The film partakes of the battle-of-the-sexes tradition that has become associated with the names of directors and scriptwriters, such as Gómez Pereira, Martínez Lázaro, Joaquín Oristrell and Juan Luis Iborra and their comedies of manners around topical arguments (couples in crisis, power struggles, infidelity, sex games and so on).

Many of these comedies display an ensemble approach to characterization, which, in Lesmes's film, adopts the form of an all-male football team and an all-female music band. At the start of *Pon un hombre en tu vida*, Juan (Toni Cantó) and Belinda (Cristina Marcos) have a near-fatal accident in a swimming-pool, which results in a bizarre soul-swap. When they wake up from the coma, Toni Cantó plays Belinda in Juan's body and Cristina Marcos plays Juan in Belinda's body. The effectiveness of the story relies on the huge personality difference: Juan is an aggressive and opinionated football coach, whilst Belinda is a romantic singer who is about to marry the man she loves.[15] Some commentators have focused on the film's modern approach to male identity, but ultimately, it is 'both characters [that] have something to learn from the psychological and behavioural make-up of the opposite gender, demonstrating the positive benefits of a receptive attitude to the fluidity of the "masculine" and the "feminine"' (Jordan and Morgan-Tamosunas 1998: 154). The initial scenes in the film portray a despotic, authoritarian, chauvinist and unpleasant Juan having communication problems with his soccer team and with everyone he contacts. His facial expression is severe and dry. His attire is tasteless and conventional. He shows no care for his looks; he has not shaved for a few days. The swimming-pool accident, in itself, is a powerful sexually charged scene: a man and a woman, both in bathing costumes, use their hotel's indoor pool, and when their bodies collide there is a vital exchange between them. Of course, this exchange is not one of bodily fluids but of the ethereal entities represented on the screen by means of a whitish fluid-like luminosity, but it remains quite clear that the contact of the two young and sexy bodies has changed their lives.

Toni Cantó is much more credible as soft Belinda than as rude Juan. Unlike Francisco 'Paco' Martínez Soria in *La tía de Carlos/Carlos's Aunt* (dir. L.M. Delgado, 1981), he does not try to imitate the effeminate, and, arguably, he does not try to impersonate the perfect woman López Vázquez created for *Mi querida señorita*; instead, his model seems to be the soft new man of the 1990s, made up of a combination of sensitivity, soft manners, empathic communication and a fresh, younger-looking attire. Curiously enough, the spectator is never challenged by this character's sexuality; he is inoffensive for women, because he actually is a heterosexual woman in the fiction, and he is also non-threatening for men because any homosexual undertone is neutralized by the sexual blandness of Belinda's character. All these traits are conveniently highlighted by the constant comparison of this likeable persona with the masculine excess of Cristina Marcos in her version of arrogant Juan.

A particularly interesting scene in which the 'man-playing-man' performance becomes very evident takes place when Cantó's character realizes the enormous self-arousing potential of the new situation. This female character looks at herself in the mirror, and what she sees is the perfectly formed, athletic, sexy and young body of Toni Cantó. The rogue smile on his lips is a clear indication of what is to happen next, but the narrative leaves that to an ellipse that the fantasy of the spectator must, somehow, deal with. There is yet one more twist: when the souls finally return to their bodies (thanks to an ingenious combination of esoterism and coincidence), the newly reconstituted Juan does not go back to the original chauvinist model. Instead, he seems to have learned something from the experience and conducts himself more like the soft man that, as the film seems to suggest, is preferable to the old *macho* version. The film takes some extra risks: soccer-team players (representing the stronghold of Spanish *macho* values) react very positively to Juan's softening, to the point that even some homosexual innuendos are ignored as long as his new manners stay.

In *Corazón de bombón/Sweetheart* (dir. Álvaro Sáenz de Heredia, 2000), Luis (Javier Martín) is not forced by any circumstance or accident to dress as a woman, except in the opening scene: the husband almost catches him having sex with his wife, and he must wear some of her clothes to get away. It is when wearing those clothes that he meets Virginia (Italian actress Valeria Marini), and, in pure melodramatic tone, he saves her from committing suicide. This is the unlikely setting for the beginning of a romantic relationship between the exuberant, Marilyn-Monroesque Virginia, and the, from now on, timid and over-dressed 'Luisa'. There is a mounting sexual tension between the increasingly heterosexual Luis and the growing lesbian self-awareness of Virginia. Luis's cross-gender strategy takes Virginia along a lesbian path and forces him to become not only a woman, but also a lesbian. The film was released a few months after the publication of José Luis Sampedro's novel *El amante lesbiano* (Sampedro 2000),[16] and testifies to a public interest in new dimensions of eroticism that privilege the cerebral over the pornographic. However, whilst Sampedro's novel is an exquisite and morose exploration of the inner labyrinths of sexual identity, *Corazón de bombón* stops at the most superficial and, arguably, heterosexist level. Thus, the storyline is filled with predictable twists, homosexual panics and a happy heterosexual ending. The character played by Javier Martín lacks the authenticity of López Vázquez in *Mi querida señorita* and the commitment of Toni Cantó in *Pon un hombre en tu vida*. The cameo appearance of filmmaker Luis García Berlanga playing himself could be interpreted as a hint towards the erotic tradition in Spanish film, and there is little doubt that *Corazón de bombón* could have been an interesting addition to that tradition if the Luis/Luisa character had been more subtly articulated. There is a scene in which Luis must unexpectedly dress up as Luisa and then as Luis again, in a rapid succession of comic gags clearly reminiscent of the restaurant scene in *Mrs Doubtfire* (dir. Chris Columbus, 1993). This comedic approach does not fit well with the sexual-identity conflict line that, echoing *Tootsie* (dir. Sydney Pollack, 1982), the film seemed to point towards initially. But the most uneven aspect is the lack of consistency in the construction of the Luis/Luisa character, who becomes, from all points of view, two different characters with no common set of attitudes or manners – except, of course, a sexual interest for the female object of desire.[17] Perhaps it should be said in this context that some of Luisa's lines (especially when she counsels Virginia about her relations with men) are extraordinarily similar to the comments of yet another famous man-as-woman in the history of Spanish culture, namely Juan Soto Viñolo, better known as Elena Francis in the famous radio programme that gave domestic and relationship advice to Spanish women during the Franco years.

The first of the many surprises of *20 centímetros/20 Centimetres* (dir. Ramón Salazar, 2005) is that the male-to-female leading role is played by a woman. Mónica Cervera in the role of Adolfo/Marieta gives from the outset a definite positioning to the transitional and unresolved politics of embodiment that seems to be the film's primary point. In fact, Ramón Salazar (a relatively young director with only one long-feature film to his credit prior to this) has gone further than anyone else in Spanish cinema in the radical visual treatment of the body in *20 centímetros*. He offers a full frontal of a pre-operation transgender whose only precedent is *Cambio de sexo*, placing the body of the transgender in a context of other unusual bodies, such as a dwarf (played by Miguel O'Dogherty). The film, *20 centímetros*, goes against the long tradition of the theatrical TG people, but only in part: Marieta is not a cabaret dancer, a transformist or a singer (she is a prostitute and eventually she finds a job as a cleaner), but in her dreams she is always the star of a musical number. As we will see in Chapter 8, reality and dreams are two sharply contrasting worlds in this film, but the character remains the same in both: a pre-operated transsexual who is on hormonal treatment and saves money for the operation (which, as was the case in Aranda's *Cambio de sexo*, represents the end of the narrative). The feminine body of this well-endowed man remains stable through the film; paradoxically, the fact that she is on the verge of the big (surgical) change does not translate, for the duration of the film, into dramatic variations of dress or looks. Her stability as a woman-with-a-penis is strongly reminiscent of La Agrado (Antonia San Juan) in Almodóvar's *Todo sobre mi madre*: both Marieta and La Agrado are seen by other characters as stable (non-transitional) bodies, and are asked to make a sexual use of their penises – although, at least on screen, Marieta does it much more often and much more actively than La Agrado does in Almodóvar's film. In one memorable scene, Marieta penetrates her masculine partner (El Reponedor, played by Pablo Puyol, as discussed in Chapter 8) whilst observed by neighbours from their window. The curious astonishment of the neighbours echoes the astonishment of part of the audience and reinforces the fetishizing of her unimaginable penis – not (only) because of its size, but (mainly) because of her unsuspected ability to actively use it with her hyper-masculine partner. Interestingly, homosexuality is not emphasized in the portrayal of these two men achieving penetration with each other. Contrary to the tendency to connect TG and homosexual stories, both Marieta and El Reponedor are represented as heterosexual, although, in a typically gay manoeuvre, Marieta demands to be penetrated in retribution for penetrating her lover first. Whilst El Reponedor enjoys being penetrated by his girlfriend's huge penis, Marieta knows that the key to her happiness is to become a woman-without-a-penis.

Marieta's character is a refreshing innovation in Spanish cinema for her decisive reformulation of some of the gender/sex roles that became somewhat fixed and even stereotyped during the 1990s. Whilst the films discussed earlier in this chapter show a marked tendency to reduce TG to drag and role inversion, Marieta's pre-surgical condition depends heavily on her ability to avoid any notion of drag and inversion. She successfully manages to give her provisional status the sort of stability she aspires to achieve permanently after her operation, and it is thanks to this utterly credible paradox (which is stretched to the limit by the fact that the character is played by an actress) that Marieta becomes a sympathetic and unexpectedly heroic character.

GOOD EDUCATION: FLUID BODIES IN ALMODÓVAR'S FILMS

TG-related themes feature prominently in the foreground of Almodóvarian literature, owing to the frequency and diversity of his femaling male characters and in part also because of what Smith has referred to as an 'unlimited transvestism', a gender-based deconstructive questioning of identity combined with a cultural promotion of gender fluidity and performance (Smith 1999: 16–17). Characters in different stages of a sex change, from occasional cross-dressers to operated transsexuals, feature in most of his films and are prominent in *La ley del deseo/Law of Desire* (1987), *Tacones lejanos/ High Heels* (1991), *Todo sobre mi madre/All About My Mother* (1999) and *La mala educación/Bad Education* (2004). But the more encompassing and 'unlimited' sort of transvestism that Smith illustrates, amongst other scenes, with the moment in *La flor de mi secreto/The Flower of My Secret* (1996) when husband and wife dress up (fetishized masculinity in his military uniform, iconic femininity in her formal dress) for a re-encounter that has been ritualistically turned into a performance, is, in fact, present everywhere in Almodóvar's films as a matter of style. Taking Smith's argument a step further, it could be argued that the creation of his TG characters (Fabio McNamara in his role as drag queen Roxy in *Pepi, Luci, Bom* and *Laberinto de pasiones*; Tina Quintero in *La ley del deseo*; Femme Letal in *Tacones lejanos*; La Agrado and Lola in *Todo sobre mi madre*; Zahara in *La mala educación*, to name but a few) follows the same logic that Garber applies to general ('unlimited') transvestism: 'The cultural effect of transvestism is to destabilize all such binaries: not only "male" and "female" but also "gay" and "straight", and "sex" and "gender". This is the sense – the radical sense – in which transvestism is a "third"' (Garber 1993: 133). Although, as Butler (1993: 125) rightly points out, not all forms of transvestism achieve or indeed, even aim at, such transgressing or destabilizing effects and in fact there exist reactionary transvestisms that end up reinforcing hegemonic gender binaries. Mark Allinson finds a parodic effect at the very centre of this destabilizing strategy, whether it is the 'carnivalesque' theatricality of drag queens or the authenticity of the transsexuals that can double up as a defence mechanism (Allinson 2001: 90–91). In *La mala educación*, Almodóvar's femaling males are intrinsically different to most of the other examples we have mentioned in this chapter because, in their 'celebration of fluidity and performance [and their] hostility to fixed positions of all kinds' (Smith 2000a: 3), they embody a truly transmodern anti-binarism – that Almodóvar himself has frequently referred to as anti-Manichaean (for example Almodóvar 2004: 13).

The relation between TG and performance – a key element of *La mala educación* – is paramount in *Todo sobre mi madre*, a film Marsha Kinder has linked to *La flor de mi secreto* and *Hable con ella* in what she calls a 'brain-dead trilogy' of films that demand 'an active mode of spectatorship that makes us highly attentive to the fascinating interplay between words and bodies' (Kinder 2004: 247).[18] In *Todo sobre mi madre*, performance, cross-dressing and transsexualism are aptly complemented with the trope of transplanting – of organs between bodies and of people between countries and subjectivities. In fact, as Kinder argues, despite the centrality of the many transvestites, lesbians, morphed fathers and actors/actresses in the film, 'the mobility generated by the story is more a matter of subjectivity than sexuality' (2004: 253), a subjectivity or trans-subjectivity that 'strengthens the alliance among female impersonators of all genders' (2004: 253). In *La mala educación*, Mexican actor Gael García Bernal is transplanted into a Peninsular character who adopts several personalities, cross-dresses several times and has gay sex with several men whilst claiming that he is not gay. The controversy created in Mexico around his disguised accent, his female impersonations and the gay sex scenes missed much of Almodóvar's point about a trans-identitarian transvestism, because, for some critics, García Bernal's physical and linguistic cross-dressing was a form of 'betrayal' to a supposedly fixed identity based on external features.

It should be noted that Almodóvar achieved a similar unsettling effect with the transvestism of pop singer Miguel Bosé in *Tacones lejanos/High Heels* (1991). In the early 1990s, heartthrob Bosé had already released some of his most successful albums (*Bandido*, 1984; *Los chicos no lloran*, 1990) and media speculation about his sexuality was at a high. His role as the transvestite impersonator, Femme Letale, in *Tacones lejanos* was indeed charged with a high sexual drive and was arguably intended to draw on heterosexual female as well as in male gay fantasies about his public persona. In the film, Femme Letale is only one amongst the several fake identities created by a most heterodox judge who deploys extreme tactics in his crime investigation – such as transforming himself into a transvestite singer star at a nightclub where he hopes to find clues. The interest of this impersonation is that it is not just an impersonation or a mere costume: the judge plunges himself into his transvestite role and ends up leading a double life for a while. It is by no means a simple fancy-dress outfit like that of Fernando (Jorge Sanz) in the carnival scene of *Belle Epoque* where, as noted by Mira (2005a: 206–207), Fernando's heterosexual gaze and sexual intentions are made even more explicit in this famous scene with his dancing partner, Violeta (cross-dressed in military uniform), being turned on by his sexual advances. In *Belle Epoque*, both the audience and the other characters are led to interpret the transvestism in this scene as part of a joyful and innocuous fancy-dress ball. But the nightclub persona created by Judge Domínguez in *Tacones lejanos* goes beyond the mere transvestism. His female persona has a proper name (Femme Letale) and the truth of his impersonation is never revealed to the other characters. Miguel Bosé's multiple-identities role in this film is a clear precedent of García Bernal's multiple transvestism in *La mala educación*.

In its original script (an extremely personal and long-postponed project of the director), *La mala educación* was entitled *La visita* (*The Visit*) and the film begins precisely with the intriguing visit that a young actor, Ignacio (García Bernal), pays in 1980 to his boyhood intimate friend and now famous film director Enrique (Fele Martínez).[19] Ignacio carries with him a semi-autobiographical manuscript entitled *La visita* (*The Visit*), partly based on his experiences at a Catholic boarding school in the 1960s – some of them shared with Enrique. Ignacio asks Enrique to make a film out of the story, casting him for the leading role. Enrique agrees to read the manuscript. What happens next is, from a filmic perspective, an extraordinary exercise in visual narrative. It starts very unassumingly with a simple superimposition of Enrique's voice, reading the manuscript, over the first shots of *La visita* story. The fact that Enrique is giving his voice to Ignacio's autobiographical narrative is not particularly emphasized at this stage. The spectator is easily drawn into the time-honoured convention of visualizing a story that, for the characters in the film, is only verbal. And yet, any Almodóvar fan will remember at this point that transsexual Tina Quintero (Carmen Maura) narrated her own back story to her amnesic brother in *La ley del deseo* without any visual flashback. There is something of an element of paradox in the transvestite narratives when a narrator adopts a differently gendered voice. That powerful scene derived much of its fascination from the unexpected gender modulation of Tina's character. From that point onwards, the character became denser, and her story played a bigger role in the narrative. That scene of the transsexual coming-out marked a turning point in the film that required the attentive viewer to mentally rewind and reassess the information about the character in the first half of the film. The same exercise is necessary in the case of *La mala educación*, but on a much larger scale.

The narrative structure of *La mala educación* is non-linear and fragmented. There are several narrative levels as the main story contains at least two other stories – a tale and a film; and, to make things even more complicated, there is no exact correspondence between the actors and the characters – several actors play the same role and conversely, one actor (García Bernal) plays several roles. Given the different narrative levels, at some points of the film we can see a character playing another character. This is what happens in the scene of the film shooting: after some discussions Enrique has decided to allow Ignacio to play the role of himself in his autobiographical story; but, as it will later be revealed, Ignacio is an impostor who has usurped his brother's identity (the real Ignacio), and he has not only appropriated it (like the judge/transvestite in *Tacones lejanos*) but he is also playing it on stage. The complexity of the role(s) played by Gael García Bernal can be summarized as follows, (i) he plays the role of the impostor: his real name is Juan but he pretends to be his brother Ignacio, and because he wants to become a famous actor he begs to be called by his alias, Ángel Andrade, (ii) this impostor plays the role of Ignacio in Enrique Goded's film, (iii) García Bernal also plays the role of the impostor playing the transvestite Zahara in the short story at the beginning of the film, and (iv) he also plays the role of the impostor in the flashback story about the murder of the real Ignacio. This complexity is achieved by two methods: performance and cross-dressing. At the core of the narrative maze of *La mala educación*, we find, once again, the two main constants of Almodóvar's approach to TG.

Despite the apparent artificiality of the narrative structure, however, the film contains a strong emotional component, particularly in those moments where the characters perform other characters. The examples of *¡Átame!*, *La ley del deseo*, *Todo sobre mi madre* and now *La mala educación* confirm that the work of the actor as seen by Almodóvar is intrinsically intense and painful, hence, the fascination of the impostor's role as someone who chooses to transform his life into a permanent performance. In one particularly meaningful scene (discussed in Chapter 8), Enrique Goded and Juan/Ignacio come to confront each other about their true identities. The scene takes place in the swimming-pool at Enrique's house, and is entirely filmed in medium shots and close-ups, with no establishing shot, *sensu stricto*. This scene is central to the film's construction of García Bernal's body as simultaneously and paradoxically powerful and vulnerable. Subject to the objectification of Enrique's homoerotic (and castrating) gaze, García's body is legitimized as male but questions about his feminization derived from his transvestism and anal penetration as Zahara now become more present than ever before.[20] Unfortunately for him, what could be perceived as the 'conventional' masculinity of his physique will become an obstacle for his goal of playing the role of Zahara in Enrique's film, as well as for his plan to successfully adapt the real Ignacio's identity in Enrique's eyes. Crucially, Enrique does not believe that Ignacio/Ángel can play Zahara nor that Ignacio/Ángel is actually Ignacio. They are now out of the water; the sexual tension has been slightly relaxed, but Ignacio/Ángel leaves his jeans unbuttoned in a typically gay erotica fashion. 'Speaking of bodies,' he starts, 'I am very flexible, I can do whatever you want.' He is obviously referring to the role of Zahara. But Enrique keeps looking at him intently. 'I cannot trust you (...).' 'I do not recognize you (....)' 'You are not Ignacio.' Ignacio/Ángel's reaction, 'Who the hell do you think you are to decide who I am and who I am not?' is a succinct version of one of the thematic constants of Almodóvar's career, namely the authority to legitimize one's own identity.

In the last part of *La mala educación*, the real Ignacio appears in a long flashback, played by Francisco Boira. Ignacio is a transgender heavily dependent on hormones and waiting to collect enough money to pay for a sex-change operation. He is addicted to heroin. He wears feminine clothes, has long hair and speaks of himself in the feminine; but he makes no attempt to mask his masculine voice and has mostly manly manners. He represents an androgynous figure that sharply contrasts with the unambiguously masculine figure of his brother and actor-to-be, Juan (played by García Bernal in his version (iv)). In this 'real' version of events, García Bernal's body is now made to incorporate some features of basic masculinity, such as adolescent carelessness, excessive swagger, playful sexuality and an apparent distaste of homosexuality. In this part of the film, the corporality of the characters becomes more central, with Francisco Boira and García Bernal constantly drawing attention to their bodies. One scene is even set in a museum workshop where dozens of giant masks and cartoon characters are stored – a clear reference to the film's underlying TG theme.

Judith Yanof argues that the high level of self-referentiality in *La mala educación* (as exemplified by the fluid relation between art and reality, multi-faceted characters, references to *film noir*, and the film-within-a-film technique, amongst others) is intended to create a clear sense that the film is not reality, just 'pretence'. This way, very much like a child's play and psychoanalysis, the film 'allows forbidden or disturbing ideas to be "tried out" and put out into a transitional space to be "played with"' (Yanof 2005: 1722). In Yanof's reading, these disturbing ideas are instances of perversion – perversion understood in all possible modes: detachment and the lack of reciprocity, sexual addiction, the disavowal of reality, trauma and dissociation, and sadomasochism (Yanof 2005: 1716). From this perspective, it is almost as if *La mala educación* were a practical illustration of all the perversities, and that seems, eventually, to be Yanof's point, despite her final comment about Almodóvar's compassion for his characters and a lack of perversity in his relation to the audience.[21] The ultimate meaning of the metaphoric transitional body could be related to one of these modes of perversion, the disavowal of reality or 'splitting'. Almodóvar's constant play with the idea that nothing is what it seems to be, finds, in the morphed body of the characters played by García Bernal, a graphic and eloquent confirmation.

Almodóvar's filmography is a useful case study in representations of TG fluidity in Spanish (and, arguably, European) cinema. The presence of cross-dressing and transgenderism in his films draws attention to and problematizes issues such as the construction of the body, the artificial nature of identity, the relation between body and self, the antithetical relation between contemporary subjectivities and societal conventions, the relation between performance and authenticity, or the role of personal memories and narratives of the self in the (re)construction of identity. As if trying to encapsulate all these elements of psychology, nature and the body in just one line, Paquita (Javier Cámara) introduces Zahara (García Bernal) to the audience as 'a combination of desert, coincidence and cafeteria'. In *Todo sobre mi madre*, La Agrado's monologue spells out these ingredients in more detail and, in doing so, it becomes one of the most revealing moments of Almodóvar's oeuvre, whose paradigmatic value is obvious in statements such as 'I am not only very agreeable but also very authentic' or 'being authentic is very expensive' – as she itemizes her 'tailor-made body' and the tag-price of her almond-shaped eyes, nose, breasts, silicone-injected lips, forehead, cheeks, hips, and buttocks, jaw filling and laser hair-removal. La Agrado's insistence on her authenticity is remarkable in a TG context because, as we have seen in this chapter, there is a tendency in contemporary Spanish cinema to represent transvestites as performers. Almodóvar's transvestites and transsexuals are more authentic because, in La Agrado's words, they 'resemble what they dream of themselves' when they are performing on stage, on a film set or even in real life. The fluidity of these characters consists, precisely, in the dismantling of the oppositions (gay/straight, male/female, gender/sexuality) mentioned by Garber when describing the destabilizing value of transvestism (Garber 1993: 133).

Whilst Almodóvar's ability to articulate a genuine TG discourse is unquestionable, the same cannot be said about contemporary Spanish cinema at large. The examples of different decades studied in this chapter demonstrate a general tendency to reduce TG to simple cases of cross-dressing with a strong emphasis on costume and disguise. However, a clear evolution can be observed in the last three decades, from the pathological approach of the late-Francoist period, in films such as *El extraño viaje* and *Mi querida señorita*, to the political, during the transition and post-transition years (as exemplified by *Cambio de sexo*, *Vestida de azul* and *Ocaña, retrat intermittent*), to a perkier, more playful spirit in comedies of the 1990s, such as *Pon un hombre en tu vida*, that led quite naturally to the more risqué overtures of *20 centímetros* and the films of Pedro Almodóvar that have been discussed in this chapter. This evolution bears some parallels with the evolution of the cinematic representation of the homosexual (as discussed in Chapter 5), of which the most relevant for our present purposes is the general tendency towards a more authentic representation of the bodies in question – authenticity seemingly based on the avoidance of common stereotypes, the exploration of previously overlooked bodies (bears, pre-op male-to-female TGs) and a revisionist approach to melodrama intent on emphasising the body as 'true' spectacle. This tendency is symptomatic of the fact that Almodóvar's pioneer TG work has been successful in influencing the modes of representation of femaling males in Spanish cinema not least in the core point made by La Agrado in her famous monologue about the real meaning of authenticity.

7

Foreign bodies

THE CONSTRUCTION OF FOREIGNNESS

A relative increase in foreign characters and themes, which is sometimes expressed through multicultural paradigms, has been noticeable in most European national cinemas since the early 1990s. Whilst the Hollywood industry is still going through the combined process of the outsourcing of production and globalization of the contents and distribution, thus making American cinema less obviously American in its thematic constants (Elmer and Gasher 2005), most European national cinemas have embraced co-productions, foreign stars and international topics. On both sides of the Atlantic, national preoccupations have not disappeared, but a new blend of domestic and regional or global issues has transformed the meaning of notions such as 'national' and 'foreign' as well as the identitarian values attached to them. Migrant stars, diasporic filmmakers and nomadic audiences have become a common feature of the contemporary cinema industry, which somehow reflects the increased presence of migrants in Western societies.[1] Migration, however important and massive it might be, is not the only source of foreign influence; in the case of Spanish cinema, international tourism has had a long-standing impact on more than four decades of film history. Yet another source of extra-nationals can be identified around nomadic subjects and experiences (Braidotti 1994: 95–110) commonly associated with young students and self-branded international citizens, temporary expatriates and extended-holiday makers – all of which are common in Spain's main cities and coastal resorts. The presence of migrants, tourists and nomads in contemporary Spanish cinema follows a similar pattern to other European cinemas and their combined 'foreign' effect is palpable. The Spanish case is peculiar not least because of the increased difficulty of defining the national character of the Spanish State and its various internal national configurations. As Jordan puts it, definitions of 'Spanishness' continue to be quickly recycled and subverted whilst, 'at the same time, it is becoming increasingly difficult to distinguish what is Spanish from what is not; indeed, the search for signs of a putative, pre-existing, stable Spanish identity (…) is rather elusive' (Jordan 2000: 76).

In trying to determine, beyond the most obvious levels of national citizenship and cultural ascription, who is a foreigner and what constitutes foreignness, we should be reminded that in both the Cartesian and phenomenological sense, the human body remains a fundamentally foreign entity, which exists outside the mind and which needs to be reconstructed to be apprehended. This applies to all bodies, including, particularly, one's own. Alphonso Lingis, in an attempt to capture and clarify the fundamental foreignness of corporeality, speaks of bodies in the third person ('a body constructed out of the data of external observation and measuring instruments') and bodies in the first person (consisting of 'postural schemas and "body-images" as we ourselves experience them' that only a phenomenological language can describe) (Lingis 1994: 47). Of course, an experiential approach to the body will always demonstrate that there exists a fundamental otherness separating our body from the others. From a filmic viewpoint, the otherness that emanates from the screen is even bigger, albeit of an entirely different nature. An interesting and practical comment about this kind of fundamental otherness is provided by *Fuera del cuerpo/Body Confusion* (dir. Vicente Peñarrocha, 2004), an unsettling thriller about Bruno (Gustavo Salmerón), a *guardia civil* who finds a passageway to a parallel dimension where his body is that of a notorious actor working in a film playing the role of a *guardia civil* – in fact, playing out what in 'this' dimension is real life. This is not a case of split personality: it is the same body that in different dimensions 'belongs' to different persons. Body duplicity and self-estrangement are apt notions to describe this (meta)cinematic approach to the body's radical otherness. This film, with all its uncanny strangeness, fits well with Bauman's (1995) invitation to become foreigners to ourselves as well as Kristeva's emphasis on the need to become aware of the inner foreigner/immigrant in ourselves as a prerequisite to understand external otherness (Kristeva 1991).[2]

Bodies of foreign men tend to be scrutinized with particular interest by domestic audiences regardless of the criteria used to define foreignness (nationality, race, language, religion and so on). Their bodies are the primary vehicles for the transmission of ideological and cultural values in relation to their countries or cultures of origin and domestic audiences are implicitly interpolated by their on-screen presence. Questions of a racial, sexual and cultural nature are posed by their filmic representation to which the audience is prompted to respond. The role of national and cultural stereotypes has been abundantly studied in relation to the figure of the foreigner, in particular in Hollywood cinema (Taylor 1983), and it now seems clear that stereotyping and de-stereotyping play a central role in the way domestic audiences construct meaning in a film. Yet, not enough attention has been drawn to contemporary domestic audiences in Spain and most other European countries with important migrant and nomadic populations whose expectations and stereotypes are different to those of the locals.[3] Contemporary, complex audiences are no longer homogeneous interpretive communities that unquestionably share values and beliefs, but rather groupings of semi-discrete alliances of like-minded spectators whose values and beliefs might have a few commonalities. These fragmented, discontinuous audiences determine the multicultural nature of the films that are made and exhibited to the point of forcing, in extreme cases, the production of different versions or cuts for distribution in different sectors of the market.[4] Audience segmentation is, perhaps, most visible along the racial and broad cultural (language, religion) junctures, but the Spanish case, with an increasingly visible segmentation of its internal market along territorial/regional lines, shows that definitions of 'domestic' and 'foreign' do not depend exclusively on the national.

The marking of foreignness in foreign bodies (tourists, migrants, nomads) is visible in contemporary Spanish cinema through a deliberate visualization of the racial, ethnic, physical or sexual otherness of the foreigner. Whilst foreignness, as any other mark of identity, can be performed (and can thus be faked), the many physical embodiments of foreignness (from the ethnic body of the black African to the 'natural' body of the white European), which are so central to the construction of the self, are concurrently the very masks that non-foreigners can use to simulate foreignness. The possibility of manipulating foreignness through its embodiments means that the markers of nation, race, class, gender and sexuality may be used to impair those bodies' regimes of presence/absence thus invoking a cultural framework which is no longer that of modern radical subjectivity.

The fundamental inscription of foreignness in the foreigner's body makes possible (and, as we shall argue, calls for) an interpretive activity that in the worst cases can degenerate into racism and xenophobia. As Zygmunt Bauman and Isolina Ballesteros have argued, the foreigner is especially unwelcome in times, like the postmodern, of identity anxiety (Bauman 1996: 69; Ballesteros 2001: 209). Spanish contemporary xenophobia might be more diffuse than in other European countries (a political and epistemological ambivalence in its legal and social treatment has been described in Ballesteros 2001: 211) but the fact remains that the presence of the foreigner in Spanish films of all epochs is frequently accompanied by figures of dystopia and anxiety. The foreign body calls for interpretation. The curiosity prompted by its difference derives in an immediate need to read the body in search of a rationale for its being. The urge to interpret, frequently generates 'over-interpretations' of the body; thus, the pervasive construction and constant reinforcement of stereotypes associated with certain embodiments of foreignness (such as the black or the oriental) should be taken as an eminent example of over-interpretation in the same way that, as we have seen in Chapters 4 and 5, the disabled and the homosexual have come to be read as only 'body': here the body in itself becomes the meaning of the foreign person.

FOREIGN BODIES IN SPANISH CINEMA: AN OVERVIEW

Writing on *Bwana* (dir. Imanol Uribe, 1996), a film in which an ordinary Spanish family reacts to an unexpected encounter with a loitering black man with all the precautions and anxieties typically generated by a sexually motivated over-interpretation, Isabel Santaolalla points out that Ombasi (an African black male played by Emilio Buale) is initially reduced to the exuberant sexuality that a widespread social stereotype attributes to his body (Santaolalla 1999a).[5] Conversely, when the body 'other' is assimilated culturally or symbolically into the host society and ceases to excite the interpreting drive, 'under-interpretations' can occur: markers of foreignness become meaningless. In *Rencor/Rancour* (dir. Miguel Albaladejo, 2002) the character played by the Cuban-born actor Jorge Perugorría is never addressed as a Cuban or as a foreigner; his 'Cubanness' is made obvious to the Spanish audiences by his accent, but no character in the film (set in modern-day Spain) ever mentions his national origin, his past life or any other aspect that could be linked to a notion of foreignness. This sort of avoidance has become quite common in the Spanish cinema of the new millennium, in particular, in the case of the Latin Americans. Whilst the common approach in the 1990s focused on the tensions of a local population meeting new migrant arrivals (like the Spanish family in *Bwana*), most recent films portray a society where those migrants have settled in.[6] Spanish films, where foreignness is erased or barely mentioned, display passing bodies of Spanish actors in foreign roles (Toni Cantó playing an Argentinean character in *Todo sobre mi madre/All About My Mother* (dir. Almodóvar, 1999)) or Spanish-American actors in Latino roles using their native Castilian as a factor of domesticity (Argentinean-born Darío Grandinetti playing a perfectly domesticated foreign role in *Hable con ella/Talk to Her* (dir. Almodóvar, 2002) and Mexican Gael García Bernal playing a Spanish character in *La mala educación/Bad Education* (dir. Almodóvar, 2004)). Both possibilities are combined in *Seres queridos/Only Human* (dirs Dominic Harari and Teresa de Pelegrí, 2004), a romantic comedy featuring Guillermo Toledo in the role of a Palestinian resident in Spain who is about to marry the daughter of a middle-class Jewish woman (also resident in Spain) played by the Argentine star, Norma Aleandro.[7]

The confluence of a multiplicity of identity factors in a single character or 'identity saturation' has only been applied to foreign characters in recent years. It has been pointed out that the construction of any national identity is based on 'a system of multiple exclusions (ethnic, racial, cultural, sexual) and therefore modern racism is not concerned with the black or the Moor, but with the black or the Moor as a drug addict, thief, rapist (…) and conversely the rapist (…) as black or Moor' (Balibar and Wallerstein 1991: 81). Earlier examples of male foreigners in Spanish cinema, such as European tourists in *desarrollista* (realist films set against the backdrop of fast economic development during the 1960s) comedies, rarely displayed this kind of complexity: their main concern was with stereotypical representations of the foreigner as just a foreigner and any other circumstance (sexuality or class, for instance) was offered as peripheral to their identity. The tendency not to saturate foreign characters in films prior to the 1990s could explain the absence of nationally or racially diverse characters in gay films of the 1970s and 1980s, such as the Eloy de la Iglesia's work in the 1970s (see Chapter 5 of this book) and Almodóvar's *La ley del deseo/Law of Desire* (1987). However, more recent films have explored saturated foreign characters in diverse ways, from the sexual in the gay comedy *Los novios búlgaros/Bulgarian Lovers* (dir. Eloy de la Iglesia, 2003) – see Chapter 5 – to the political in the documentary *En construcción/Work in Progress* (dir. José Luis Guerín, 2001) to the neo-colonial in the musical *Habana Blues* (dir. Benito Zambrano, 2005).[8]

Whilst saturated foreign identities can be seen as more authentic than the uni-dimensional characters, performed foreignness, which has a long history in cinema, conjures up notions of simulation and unauthenticity not totally disconnected from an intentional vilification of the foreigner on moral or ideological grounds. Discussing the early post-war CIFESA (Compañía Industrial Film Español S.A.) historical dramas, Federico Bonaddio observes that the representation of foreignness lacks verisimilitude: 'since no attempt is made to feign a foreign accent, the figures who appear on screen speak "as Spaniards"' (Bonaddio 2004: 24).[9] Labanyi interprets this spectacular disregard for realism in costume films as 'a self-consciousness bordering on parody, if not the camp' (Labanyi 2004a: 37), an effect particularly evident in the representation of foreign men.[10] Other critics emphasize the political dimension of these misrepresentations; for Ballesteros, 'in Francoist ideology and in its translation to the popular imaginary, the foreigner (mainly French) is automatically transformed in a receptacle of corruption, treachery, perversion, lack of moral principles and liberalism' (Ballesteros 2001: 206).[11] Bonaddio finds a Manichaean and essentialist logic in this kind of representation that contrasts an original, unitary and good Spanishness to an evil foreignness whilst allowing for bad and inauthentic Spaniards 'to be represented as victims of corrupting foreign influence' (Bonaddio 2004: 26).

Contemporary representations of foreign men seem oddly similar to what Bonaddio, Ballesteros and Labanyi describe in relation to the post-war period dramas, at least in one important sense: they reveal less about the reality of the newcomers and more about the Spaniards' anxiety regarding their own identity (Flesler 2004; Nair 2004: 106; Flesler Forthcoming). This effect is particularly visible in certain representations of foreignness performed by Spanish actors. For instance, as we saw in Chapter 3, Javier Bardem embodied a high-impact stereotype of second-degree Spanishness (that is, what an average Spaniard would typically define as a North American vision of Spanishness) in *Boca a boca/Mouth to Mouth* (dir. Manuel Gómez Pereira, 1995), as a would-be actor who fights for the role of his life when a second-rate Hollywood director (Alastair Mackenzie) decides to shoot his next film in Spain.[12] Antonio Banderas is a remarkable case of the representation of foreignness with his Latino roles in Hollywood films from *The Mambo Kings* (dir. Arne Glimcher, 1992) to *The Legend of Zorro* (dir. Martin Campbell, 2005) (Perriam 2003: 44–69; Perriam 2005: 33–37; Smith 2005a). As expected, the physical aspect of the actors who perform foreignness plays a central role in their casting for certain films. Good examples of this are the cases of directors Pedro Almodóvar in the films mentioned above, Icíar Bollaín and her detailed study of the Russian male character (played by Arcadi Levin) in *Hola, estás sola?/Hi, Are You Alone* (1995) and Isabel Gardela's choice of non-professional Zack Qureshi for the role of Muslim character Jalil in the already mentioned *Tomándote/Tea for Two* (dir. Gardela, 2000).

Most of the literature on foreigners in Spanish film focuses strongly on the relationship between the cinema and the social fabric and elaborates on the increasingly central role of migration in Spain (García Domene 2003). In the most comprehensive study to date on the topic, Santaolalla focuses on a number of recognizable foreign figures, such as gypsies ('the domestic other'), Africans and Asians ('the other *par excellence*'), Eastern Europeans ('the masked other') and Hispanic Americans ('the familiar other') (Santaolalla 2005). Santaolalla's work focuses on ethnic and racial differences as instances of otherness. Other figures of otherness and foreignness that are not always present in migration films include the internal foreigner, relatively central to nationalist Basque and Catalan cinema and also central to urban migration *desarrollista* films of earlier decades (Richardson 2002); simulated and erased foreignness, along the lines of the already mentioned cases of Bardem in *Boca a boca* and Perugorría in *Rencor*; modern-day Europeans' domesticated foreignness; and the case of Spaniards abroad, which is conspicuously absent from most studies on recent migration cinema.[13]

The positioning of the Spaniard as a foreigner abroad represents an interesting inversion of subjective roles. In the classic war film, *Los últimos de Filipinas/Last Stand in the Philippines* (dir. Antonio Román, 1945), the highly stereotyped villains/foreigners are reduced in their masculinity to some brutal features and portrayed as non-sexually threatening to the Spanish heroes. Being strongly gendered, the classic war film displays a (mostly) heterosexual male gaze and can only see male foreigners as epiphenomena of martial virility. Modern war films such as *Territorio Comanche/Comanche Territory* (dir. Gerardo Herrero, 1997), tend to use fewer clichés but the heterosexual gaze and the de-sexualization of the male foreigner remain unaltered. The war genre sharply contrasts with female-gaze films such as *La pasión turca/Turkish Passion* (dir. Vicente Aranda, 1994), where, as we will discuss later, the body of the male foreigner is sexualized and over-interpreted along the lines of the Spanish-at-home model. In Aranda's film, the body of the Turkish stallion (Georges Corraface) is never shot fully naked, but it is frequently talked about by other characters and, significantly, the size of his penis and his sexual prowess are meant to explain the behaviour of the female protagonist.

Most contemporary Spanish films about Spaniards abroad avoid the diasporic and migrant experiences, favoured by *desarrollista* films of the 1970s, such as *¡Vente a Alemania, Pepe!/Come to Germany, Pepe!* (dir. Pedro Lazaga, 1971) and *Españolas en París/Spaniards in Paris* (dir. Roberto Bodegas, 1971).[14] In the comedy *Two Much* (dir. Fernando Trueba, 1995), a USA–Spanish co-production, the character played by Antonio Banderas (Art Dodge, a Spaniard in the United States) reproduces some of the most recognisable Latino stereotypes – exoticism, passion, strong physicality. This character functions equally well vis-à-vis American audiences for whom this type of Latin lover is still a recognizable stereotype, and for Spanish audiences for whom the sexualization of the foreigner is also applicable to Spaniards abroad, but the element of the fake identity (he creates an alter ego to flirt with another woman) raises questions of identity and authenticity similar to the old issue of the trustworthiness of the foreigner. In *Habana Blues*, the role of the highly sexualized Latino is represented by two Cubans, Ruy (Alberto Yoel) and Tito (Roberto Sanmartín), whose sexual attractiveness contrasts sharply with the physically innocuous and sexually inactive Spanish male (played by Tomás Cao) in the privileged eyes of the heterosexual Spanish female protagonist (Marta Calvó). In this film, the sexual tension between a Cuban male and a Spanish female is complicated by the power imbalance (in the form of economic affluence and industrial leverage) between the dominant Spaniard and the subjugated Cuban. The intersection of power and desire has an unmistakably neo-colonial flavour in the reduction of the Cuban body to a 'commodity' that, nevertheless, (successfully) resists the controlling machinations of the Spaniard. *Habana Blues* is particularly relevant in the context of an unprecedented hyper-sexualization of male Cubans in Spain and their strong presence in the media as partners of (usually ageing) Spanish female stars.

The representation of gypsies has followed a somewhat different path. As nationally Spaniards but racially other, they occupy an uneasy position on the margins of the symbolic economy and their bodies are frequently taken as emblems of this liminality. Dancer Joaquín Cortés has represented the eroticized male gypsy body in such films as *Flamenco* (dir. Carlos Saura, 1995), *La flor de mi secreto/The Flower of My Secret* (dir. Almodóvar, 1996) and *Gitano/Gypsy* (dir. Manuel Palacios, 2000), thus contributing to a trend of the fashionable gypsy hip that in the last decade has produced titles such as *Alma gitana/Gypsy Soul* (dir. Chus Gutiérrez, 1996), *Historia de Estrella/Estrella's Story* (dir. Manuel Estudillo, 2003), *Papá Piquillo* (dir. Álvaro Sáenz de Heredia, 1998), and *Carmen* (dir. Vicente Aranda, 2003), to name but a few. Paul Julian Smith argues that this trend in gypsy films corresponds to a 'disproportionate presence of the gypsy in everyday Spanish life' (Smith 2000b: 162). In the films chosen by Smith for his study of gypsies,[15] the gypsy is presented as a new, hybrid subject, both strange and familiar, who is at once 'a response to and a displacement of the Spaniards' confrontation with a more radical otherness: that of global immigration to the Spain that was for so long a nation of net emigration' (Smith 2000b: 162). Smith sees the gypsy as combining the roles of alterity, proximity and supplementarity vis-à-vis a mainstream Spanish culture that seems to be taken, once again, as the only benchmark, and that seems to be the origin and justification of the gypsy's hybrid nature.

Spanish thrillers make use of the configurations of masculine foreignness for the creation of suspense and fear. Directors Norberto López Amado (*Nos miran/They're Watching Us*, 2002), Jaume Balagueró (*Darkness*, 2002; *Los sin nombre/The Nameless*, 1999) and Agustí Villaronga (*Tras el cristal/In a Glass Cage*, 1987; *El niño de la luna/Moon Child*, 1989; *El mar/The Sea*, 2000; *Aro Tolbukhin. En la mente del asesino/Aro Tolbukhin in the Mind of a Killer*, 2002) have consistently introduced disquieting foreign men in their films, some of which (like the paralysed, steel-lung dependent, former paedophile Nazi officer played by Günter Meisner in *Tras el cristal*) provide excellent examples of saturated identities.

FOREIGN BODIES IN RECENT SPANISH 'MIGRATION FILMS'

Los sin nombre/The Nameless (dir. Balagueró, 1999), a supernatural thriller about missing persons, suggests that many unexplained cases could have a chilling paranormal dimension: they could inhabit a parallel universe, making themselves visible only to a few. *Los sin nombre* is by no means a migration film, but it can be taken as an eerie metaphor of the phantasmic lives of immigrants in more realist films, people of which mainstream society seems to know very little about, perhaps because their bodies are kept out of sight. Indeed, it exists as a process of standardization and homogenization of all migrant bodies whereby they are 'deprived of individual identity and condemned to anonymity and invisibility within the host society' (Ballesteros 2001: 214). In *La fuente amarilla/The Yellow Fountain* (dir. Miguel Santesmases, 1999) and *Ilegal/Illegal* (dir. Ignacio Vilar, 2003), the ghostly, out-of-sight existence of immigrants is connected to notions of criminality and media exposure in ways that problematize widespread political discourses about integration and asylum in the Spanish State. Both films deal with migration issues and racial minorities in ways that depart from more widely studied migration films. *La fuente amarilla*, a thriller set in the Chinese community of Madrid, outraged that community with its criminalizing storyline featuring ghettoes and people smugglers. Despite Mate Productions' efforts to reassure the Chinese community and the general audience that the film was 'only' a work of fiction, the impression transmitted by the frequent use of a hand-held camera, the subjective POV shots and the references to media representations of the migrants, is that the film made a statement about the pervasiveness of criminal activities within the Chinese community. The thriller *Ilegal* gestures even more clearly towards the documentary by means of a reporter who infiltrates a network of people smugglers to shoot highly compromising footage of illegal migrants. The foreigner's body, as we shall see, is simultaneously erased and reinstated in these films and paradoxically kept at a distance from mainstream society but conspicuously filmed and captured in images.

Isolina Ballesteros characterizes the migration film as a European genre that in the past decade 'has started to focus more or less explicitly on the current phenomenon of immigration and xenophobia' (Ballesteros 2005: 4) using identifiable patterns in terms of authorship, ideology, cinematography and spectatorship. She traces the origins of the migration genre back to *Angst essen Seele auf/Ali, Fear Eats the Soul* (dir. Fassbinder, 1974), which 'anticipated a common pattern that linked race, masculinity and class and that can be found in subsequent films made since the 1990s that focus on the first and mostly male immigration' (Ballesteros 2005: 4), but she also notices that, following a first wave of mainly masculine migration films, a focus on women is stronger in recent films, 'as a response to the feminization of migration flows and the political mobilization by ethnic-minority women' (Ballesteros 2005: 5).[16] Commenting on canonical migration films such as the already mentioned *Bwana*, *Las cartas de Alou/Letters From Alou* (dir. Montxo Armendáriz, 1990), *Saïd* (dir. Llorenç Soler, 1999), *En construcción/Work in Progress* (dir. José Luis Guerín, 2001) and *Poniente/Sunset* (dir. Chus Gutiérrez, 2002), Parvati Nair rightly observes that most Spanish examples of the genre focus on men's bodies and experiences. She acknowledges that many of these films open, in different ways, semiotic spaces for migrant subjectivities, but at the same time 'the categories of gender, place and ethnicity are seen to be both mutually implicated and traversed by complex mechanisms of social domination and subordination' (Nair 2004: 105).[17] Given the rising levels of anxiety in European societies about the presence of large migrant communities (a fact that seems to indirectly validate Balibar's idea that racism is closely linked to nationalism – Balibar and Wallerstein 1991), it is hardly surprising that immigration cinema tends to emphasize issues of xenophobia and racism, often drawing on media stories that relegate immigrants to the position of 'passive, poorly qualified subjects, downgrading the public perception of them, homogenizing them in categories constitutive of the racist stereotype, and thus affecting legalization policies' (Ballesteros 2005: 3). Film and media discourses cannot be disassociated from the 'invasion psychosis' and other psycho-social dysfunctions associated to xenophobia and in many cases could well be in the origin of the stereotyping of foreigners. Spanish media often conveys the idea that an invasion is taking place from the South, suggesting that 'there are hordes of unskilled, poor, black, Arab or Latin-American immigrants who are destitute and desperate to reach the European Promised Land by way of Spain' (Molina Gavilán and Di Salvo 2001).

The credits sequence of *Ilegal* shows camcorder footage of a beached boat, presumably used by illegal migrants to reach European soil, seen through the camera's own screen. The mediation of the camcorder's screen symbolizes the huge power of the media in determining public perceptions of immigrants. The film's storyline, which combines a media plot to secure and publish footage of African migrants being smuggled into Europe with the progressive uncovering of a Galician mafia involved with drug trafficking and people smuggling, is narrated from the perspective of Luis (Chisco Amado), a Galician reporter who has no qualms about obtaining and then exploiting images of migrants against their will. At the film's end, he realizes that the very existence of those images has caused too many deaths, including that of the group of migrants they were supposed to document, and, in an unexpected moral move, he destroys the tapes without making them public.

Ilegal features almost exclusively young men. At the very beginning of the film, Luis visits one of the many temporary camps in Northern Morocco of young men waiting to cross over into Europe. As he turns his camcorder on, we can see the camp partly through its screen. Amidst the detritus, a group of men wash themselves, lie down and wander purposelessly. Most of them are black; the camera captures their naked, hard upper torsos to suggest youth and strong virility. Only a few are not black (presumably North Africans) and they are seen fully dressed. The setting, the characters and the cinematography (instances of a hand-held camera and POV shots combined with a documentary-style diegetic camera) strongly reminds one of the three features of Third Cinema as defined by Robert Stam: hybridity, chronotopic multiplicity and the redeeming of detritus (Stam 2003: 32). The contrast between the dressed whites and the semi-naked blacks suggests a subtle sexualization of the racialized body that is nevertheless not followed up by the heterosexual male gaze of the reporter. When the reporter speaks to one of the black men, he chooses one who is fully dressed, crouching and eating some food. It is, perhaps, not coincidental that this Senegalese young man is played by Emilio Buale, the actor whose hard body and strong physical presence was central to the success of Uribe's *Bwana* (1996) (see Figure 14). Making it clear that the game of domination and submission is not going to be played out this time, the nameless Senegalese in *Ilegal* stands up when addressed by the reporter. Both men share the frame looking at each other; despite their diametrically opposed geographical and social origin, their clothes look remarkably similar with their light hues against the backdrop of garbage and detritus. In this marginal and almost unreal setting, the black successfully resists being manipulated or dominated by the white; the reporter is here to buy information and footage, and the black is ready to sell all that for a price. Intercalating camcorder images with the diegetic camera, we follow both men to an 'ad hoc' shed where two other fully dressed Senegalese wait. When they start recounting their (admittedly conventional) story for the camera, a group of angry and violent-looking men burst in, destroy the reporter's tape and expel him from the camp.

The microcosm of the camp reveals a stratification of migrant society visually defined by race and dress. Those who are ready to negotiate with whites are shown fully dressed with incongruously white and clean shirts and pants. The rest are seen semi-naked and wearing non-Western clothes. In one particular instance, one of the black men wearing a loose jumpsuit is seen cooking or burning what could be a ram. Making a spectacle of these young men is achieved not only by means of the camcorder, but also by contrast with the two white Europeans in the camp (the reporter and a people smuggler who speaks with a Galician accent), who both have clearly exploitative intentions. The gaze of the reporter mirrors, up to a certain point, the gaze of an audience familiar with migrants on European soil but not about their lives in Africa.

In *Ilegal*, there is a marked dividing line that separates foreigners (North Africans and black Africans) from non-foreigners (referred to as 'Europeans' rather than 'Spaniards'). Not only does the film concern itself with the avatars and vicissitudes of the Europeans, relegating the Africans to the role of background figures with no name (something common to most Spanish immigration films, in which the locals seldom care about learning foreign names), but it also relocates the migrant experience to a white European subjectivity, implicitly suggesting that the experience of being smuggled into Europe in an illegal fishing ship could only be rendered interesting or meaningful to European audiences through the eyes of another European. The reduction of Africans to mere background figures is further reinforced throughout the film by the frequent use of simple stereotyping mechanisms such as untranslated conversations in foreign languages, exotic food and clothes, and the suggestion of ghetto structures. Therefore, the title of the film ends up being deceptive: it does not refer (only) to the illegal African migrants, but (mainly) to the various illegal activities of the Europeans, including the reporter's dubious methods and the smugglers' mafias. It could be argued that the film has a positive attitude towards migrants, because they are portrayed as the unwilling victims of unscrupulous local interests; but ultimately, Ballesteros's hypothesis about the migrants' deprivation of individual identities through exoticism,

14. Undressed: Emilio Buale in *Bwana*.

objectification, homogenizing and victimization (Ballesteros 2001: 214) receives strong confirmation.

La fuente amarilla offers itself as a particularly interesting example of xenophobia in the context of the Chinese migrant community in Madrid, whilst simultaneously providing a revealing alternative position to more numerous migrant communities, such as the Latin American, the Maghrebi and the black African, all of which have been scrutinized by better-known Spanish migration films. The focus of *La fuente amarilla* on the Chinese community is problematic from the outset because the Chinese are a relatively small minority in Spain, numerically insignificant in comparison with the Moroccan and the Latin American and strongly concentrated in the major capital cities. And yet, the stereotype of the devious Chinese (as succinctly seen in the first minutes of *El amante bilingüe/The Bilingual Lover* (dir. Vicente Aranda, 1993) in the figure of Joan Marés's father, who as a young man used to perform the Chinese stereotype in post-war Barcelona) has produced xenophobic discourses of distrust and fear. The earlier-mentioned (see Chapter 1) *Torrente: el brazo tonto de la ley/Torrente, the Stupid Arm of the Law* (dir. Santiago Segura, 1998) offers a caricature of the extended misconception of the Chinese as drug-traffickers who would use a restaurant as a cover-up for their dealings. The thriller *La fuente amarilla*, however, makes no deliberate use of humour: its representation of the Chinese migrants is presented as realist, almost documentary, to the point that one of the characters has been collecting press clippings about missing Chinese persons in Spain for years, and offers comments about the socio-demographics of the group. During the shooting of the film in 1998, the Madrid Chinese community was deeply concerned about the negative impact this film could have on the way they were perceived by the rest of society. Sixteen community groups, with the support of the Chinese Embassy, lodged a court injunction to get the film stopped on the grounds of xenophobia and racism, and some of the 27 Chinese actors abandoned the film under pressure from the Chinese groups (Korean, Japanese and Vietnamese actors were called in as replacements). Director and producer insisted that the film was not racist, that it was a mere fiction, that it was supported by the Ministry of Culture, the RTVE and the European Union, and that, in any case, violence was not absent from many Chinese and Hong Kong film traditions. A spokesman for the Chinese replied that the film was not comparable to any by Bruce Lee and that the sort of 'lies' contained in the film would be equivalent to the Chinese speaking in China of Spaniards as if they all belonged to ETA (Juan Carlos Xu quoted in Ahrens 1998: 3).

The key 'lie' that mobilized the Chinese migrant community was the existence, central to the story told in the film, of *triadas* or local mafias. Through his press-clipping collection, Sergio (Eduardo Noriega) had come to realize that, despite the triads' constant growth, the number of deceased Chinese was minimal. He suspects the visas and passports of the dead are used by a network of people smugglers. This information, together with his unique archive of names and dates, is instrumental in helping Lola (Silvia Abascal), half-Chinese half-Spanish, whose parents were killed by compatriots when she was a child. Her goal is to break into the local mafia and avenge the death of her parents. As the story unfolds, the camera confirms Sergio's and Lola's suspicion (presumably shared by a large segment of the audience, although emphatically denied by the Chinese) that a people-smuggling mafia does indeed exist in Madrid, and that it operates, as it was the case in *Torrente*, using a network of Chinese restaurants as a cover-up. Lola's journey into the gang follows a traditional three-stage structure, from its outer layer to its core. In each of the three stages, Lola meets a different Chinese man, whilst maintaining a friendship/romance relation with the nerd, Sergio. Lola's struggling relations with these men at times adopt sexual overtones that, in turn, contribute to the sexualization of the Chinese. Migration films (and *La fuente amarilla* is no exception) operate an overt sexualization of the foreigner, and, as we will see, they frequently make use of interracial or intercultural romance stories. The sexualization of the Chinese male in *La fuente amarilla* shares some elements of exoticism with the North African, the black and the Latino, but, unlike them, it follows a path of its own, arguably because of the absence of a clear and immediate visual referent. The film should be credited for having avoided the physical stereotyping of the Chinese in martial-art films (from Bruce Lee to Jackie Chan). Rather than proposing the hyper-lean martial-art body as a model for the representation of the average Chinese, Santesmases uses three actors whose physicality is inflected by class and social position.

As mentioned earlier, contemporary Spanish migration films reveal less about the reality of the newcomers and more about the Spaniards' anxiety regarding their own liminal location in Europe (Flesler 2004: 106).[18] This hypothesis, according to which the foreign male body performs a specular function in relation to the Spanish male body, seems to receive unexpected confirmation from East Asian quarters in *La fuente amarilla*. According to director Santesmases, the first idea for the film consisted of the romance story between a courageous young lady and a cowardly young man (Torregrosa 1999). The Chinese element, which would eventually become central to the film, was originally conceived as a somewhat unusual backdrop. From this perspective, it can hardly be surprising the choice of heartthrob Noriega for the role of Sergio, a Spanish character whose shyness and self-repression (to the point of self-denial) is diametrically opposed to the kind of seductive masculinity with which he had become associated. Noriega's construction of Sergio is sober and contained: his glasses, his speech impediment and his nervous movements represent adequate somatizations of his trauma (later in the film we will learn that as a young boy he was falsely convicted of rape). He becomes defensive in his first encounter with the Chinese/Spanish Lola, who is perfectly bilingual and behaves purposefully and decidedly. The bookish, introverted Sergio will see himself dragged in to Lola's dangerous world – a Chinese world of which he knows next to nothing, a violent world he is not prepared to deal with, but maybe an underworld based on secrecy might not be totally dissimilar to Sergio's own traumatized experience of life. In fact, trauma, more than anything else, helps make the emotional connection between Lola and Sergio.

Wayne (Carlos Wu) is the first of the three Chinese men Lola will meet on her journey. Young, confident and extroverted, he is portrayed as the negative of Sergio (Eduardo Noriega). That he also happens to be Lola's cousin is no obstacle to his sexual interest in her; the fact that he shares a tiny apartment with 'thirty or forty' other Chinese does not seem to be an obstacle either. Apart from his early sexualization, Wayne plays the role of informing Lola about some of the secrets of the Chinese ghetto, including the existence of a Big Uncle, a top boss who controls everything in the community. Lola meets then Liao Peng (Tony Lam), a well-dressed, well-spoken man who offers her a temporary job as a translator. Liao Peng is also the local leader of the Chinese mafia. His powerful position, which allows him to exert some effective control over Lola, is immediately contrasted with Sergio's weakness. In a particularly intense scene, Lola, standing, confronts Sergio, seated, and asks him whether he is afraid of her because she has a gun or because she is half-Chinese or because she is just a woman. Liao Peng, unlike Sergio, will not be afraid of an armed (phallic) Chinese woman.

Whilst the black body is ostentatiously shown fully naked in films mentioned earlier such as *Las cartas de Alou* and *Bwana*, in *La fuente amarilla* the foreign body is not displayed naked. In the only scene a Chinese body is displayed in *La fuente amarilla*, all we get to see is a timid and partial nude of Wayne in his derailed sexual advances with Lola. His abdomen and upper torso are not lean or muscular and have nothing to do with the naked model of Bruce Lee. The scene, in which Wayne unsuccessfully tries to have sex with Lola, is shot primarily from her point of view, with the camera set at a low angle. Wayne's soft body is sexualized in an undesirable and suffocating way that contrasts vividly with Sergio's presumed hard and lean (but inaccessible) body. In this scene, Wayne's body is marked with negative connotations that are explicitly linked to his foreignness: whilst Lola is mixed-race, in this instance she chooses to privilege her Spanishness, which Wayne acknowledges this way, 'You half-Chinese half-Western but more Western, a whore as all Western women, no wonder you mother left with a foreign devil.' Ironically, his use of the Chinese xenophobic expression 'foreign devil' (he uses words *Wai Guo Ren*, 'foreigner' in Chinese Pinyin) runs parallel to his own sudden reconstruction, in Lola's eyes, as truly a foreigner whose repulsiveness is associated with his negatively sexualized body.

La fuente amarilla represents an ambivalent approach to the mixed romance narrative. On the one hand, the film flirts with the idea that Lola and her cousin Wayne could develop a mono-cultural Chinese romantic story; on the other, Lola is definitely more interested in her Spanish boyfriends (the security guard of the prologue scene, then Sergio). Lola's ambivalence as a borderline woman makes her very similar to the Moroccan migrant men identified by Nair as the agents of the identification of Spanish anxieties (Nair 2004: 106–110), and the fact that she is able to adopt a fluid approach to her Spanish-Chinese identity continuum makes her not only a powerful agent, but also a catalyst that makes gender, power/class and nation paradigms eminently visible. Lola's extraordinary position in the symbolic and erotic economies of the film, and the positions therefore assigned to the weak Spanish man and the powerful but ultimately defeated Chinese men, contradicts most of Flesler's observations in relation to the intercultural romance. In particular, her point about the contrast between liberated women and conservative men, which is central to her reading of Muslim–Western romances (Flesler 2004: 106–110), seems to become irrelevant in the dialogue between China and Europe. *La fuente amarilla* is representative, then, because the fluid identity of nomadic subjects such as Wayne, the ambivalence of bi-cultural subjects such as Lola (often called by her Chinese name, Yellow Moon, in the film), and the insecurity that has become associated with some forms of Western cultural identity, as aptly represented in the film by Sergio, are all crucial to its core narrative.

THE FOREIGN MALE LOVE OBJECT

In classic Hollywood narrative cinema, the body of the male foreigner was sexualized in different ways to the female body. On the one hand, given the implicit masculinity of the gaze (Mulvey 1992), the foreign female body was sexualized as an object of desire and the foreign male body was sexualized as a threatening rival. Replicating this model, Spanish sexy comedies of the 1970s showed female Europeans as highly desirable and male Europeans as sexually apt and active – usually as formidable competitors for the relatively disempowered locals (as we have seen in Chapter 1 of this book). The fact that these sexually active Europeans were also tourists and economically superior to the locals helped to perpetuate an inferiority complex in the minds of many Spaniards. The same could be said of the blacks and the Caribbeans, with the particularity that, whilst the sexualization of the European faded away progressively during the late 1980s and early 1990s (coinciding with the official acceptance of Spain's European status and entry to the CEE in 1986), those racially marked foreigners remained subject to a stereotypical over-interpretation that can still be observed in the films of this new century. The increased presence of blacks, Latinos and Eastern Asians in major Spanish cities does not seem to have changed the deep need for rendering their bodies readable; however, one important reversal from the cross-cultural practices of the previous decades seems to be that the onus is now on the locals to understand the foreigner, rather than on the foreigner to make himself understood.

The sexualization of the European has its origins in the sexual repression of the Franco years and the consequent eroticization of well-off European tourists whose economic superiority was perceived by the locals to be just an emanation of other superiorities – cultural, physical, sexual. In *Juana la Loca/ Mad Love* (dir. Vicente Aranda, 2001), as discussed in Chapter 3 of this book, the sexualization of the European is put in a remote historical context (corresponding to the early sixteenth century), but the fascination of the Spanish woman (Pilar López de Ayala) with the strong virility of the Flemish man (played by Italian actor Daniele Liotti) contains the same passionate undertones that can be found in more modern renditions of the same theme, and in the animal sexualization of non-European males such as the Turkish stallion in *La pasión turca*. For instance, in *Menos que cero/Less Than Zero* (dir. Ernesto Tellería, 1996), the Romanian male migrant (Roman Luknár) is subjugated by a Spanish vamp who obtains pleasure from sexually objectifying his body. Luknár's body is not as muscular, tanned or well-defined as that of Liotti's, but that does not seem to be the point in a process of sexualization marked by foreignness and a (sadistic) female gaze, rather than by the foreign body's physical attributes. A similar sort of sexualization can be seen in *Los novios búlgaros*, although in this case the body of the Bulgarian migrant is given a more attentive (voyeuristic) gaze both by his Spanish gay lover and by the non-less-gay gaze of the camera (as we discussed in Chapter 5).

Torremolinos 73 (dir. Pablo Berger, 2003) re-creates the sexual insecurities of the Spanish male prior to the Europeanization of the country, and the consequent hyper-sexualization of the European male. The film is an amusing commentary not only on the dramatic evolution of sexual mores that took place in Spain in the last three decades of the last century, but also on the contrast between the national body and the European body, which, in the 1970s, epitomized many of the average male Spaniard's sexual anxieties. In relation to the sexy comedies of the 1960s and 1970s and drawing on Shaviro (1993), Pavlović makes the point that they were profoundly sexualized films and that the very notion of masculinity was at their core, with 'voluptuous foreign women' (typically branded as 'Swedish') who offered a sharp contrast with a Spanish male protagonist, usually portrayed as sexually and physically mediocre (Pavlović 2003: 81–82). Interestingly, the conservative public morality of the late Franco period associated the naked foreign (female) body with pornography, and reserved it for international versions of Spanish-made films containing liberal images of Spain (usually female bodies and sunny beaches) aimed at the potential foreign tourists (Pavlović 2003: 67).[19] All these themes featured in Berger's film with the perspective of those three decades.[20] Alfredo López (Javier Cámara) embodies the bland domestic masculinity of the times: he is in his mid-thirties and his middle-sized moustache somehow compensates for his half baldness; he uses thick-framed reading glasses and has a foot-odour problem. When Alfredo and his wife Carmen (Candela Peña) are chosen for a film feature euphemistically described as the 'reproductive practices of the Spaniards' to be marketed in the Scandinavian countries, they receive specific training in film and erotic techniques from a Danish married couple. Quick and easy money help them overcome the moral anxiety caused by the pornography and they become assiduous, enthusiastic and imaginative stars in their home-made pornographic films. The contrast between the Spanish and the foreigner (North European) is constant in the film, in particular when Alfredo and Carmen get involved in a much more ambitious shooting: nothing less than a Spanish–Danish co-production.

Magnus (Mads Mikkelsen), the leading Danish actor, is a likeable, blonde and attractive young man, who takes on the leading male role in the sex scene in place of Alfredo. The sex is real, and Carmen becomes pregnant whilst shooting a pornographic film with her husband as director and camera operator. The contrast between the seemingly sterile Spanish husband and the fertile foreigner who impregnates Carmen at the first attempt could not be sharper; and, as happens in similar cases (such as Aranda's *La pasión turca*, which we will briefly discuss later in this chapter), it is an unambiguous way of signalling the inferiority of the Spanish male body.

European integration and the sudden increase of migrants from non-European countries have combined to produce a sense of racial and cultural sameness that has contributed to the domestication (and de-sexualization) of the white European body. As a point of comparison, the French/Spanish multilingual co-production *L'Auberge Espagnole/Una casa de locos/Euro Pudding/The Spanish Apartment* (dir. Cédric Klapisch, 2002) displays a gallery of European students sharing an apartment in Barcelona. Arguably, none of them feels the need to read the bodies of the others, despite some apparent differences in personality and sexual life. A similar situation in the migrant film *Las cartas de Alou*, with Arab and black African characters sharing accommodation, prompts a much higher level of interpreting activity: racially different bodies need to be properly decodified before they can circulate socially.

In her study of Moroccans in Spanish cinema, Flesler identifies as common traits in the Spanish migration films the locals' fear of racial or cultural contagion, their anxiety regarding their peripheral location in Europe, and the unfolding of a narrative of intercultural romance which usually ends up in failure (Flesler 2004). Whilst Muslim male migrants occupy a unique position in Spain (they are the most numerous migrant group and have contributed to reintroduce into Spain the question of its hybrid national identity), their filmic representation can be taken as representative of the way other migrants are portrayed in Spanish cinema.[21] Interestingly, mixed romances are a frequent occurrence in films that include the presence of a foreigner, be it a North African migrant or other foreign nationality; but, unlike the films of the 1970s in which a Spanish man fantasized about foreign women, contemporary films display Spanish women having real romances with foreign men. Perhaps surprisingly, mixed romances occur not only in migration films set in Spain but also in films where a Spanish woman travels abroad. Mixed romances, in these cases, do not always end up in failure. As we shall see, Flesler (2004: 112) is right in her hypothesis that failure is most common when one of the partners is Moorish.

One of the characteristics of the Spanish–Arab mixed romance, according to Flesler, is that it offers a deferred commentary about Spanishness and not about 'Otherness' (2004: 106). This would correspond to the specular function of the foreign body that we discussed earlier in this chapter. In her analysis of *Bwana* and *En la puta calle/Hitting Bottom* (dir. Enrique Gabriel, 1997), Santaolalla identifies the same effect in relation to black African and Latin American men, confirming the view that the migrant in these films is only a catalyst for the actions and reactions of the Spaniards (Santaolalla 2003: 155). But here Santaolalla makes a most relevant point about the nature of the catalyst role: if the foreigner becomes just a mirror of the Spaniard, then the spectacularization of the foreigner's body as the object of display devoid of psychological or emotional depth renders him an almost exclusively physical entity. This is why in mixed-romance films and in interracial buddy films, the male body is so often sacrificed or mutilated. Whilst *Bwana* and *En la puta calle* are set in modern-day Spain, *La niña de tus ojos/The Girl of Your Dreams* (dir. Fernando Trueba, 1998) is set in Germany at the dawn of the Second World War – and yet, the point made by Flesler and Santaolalla about the specular role of the foreign male body is still perfectly valid. Moreover, if, according to Santaolalla, the migration films she analyses 'scrutinize and condemn outdated models of domestic Spanish masculinity' (Santaolalla 2003: 161), the same can be said about a Spaniards-abroad film such as *La niña de tus ojos*. In the film, a group of actors travel from Spain to the UFA studios in Berlin during the Second World War to work in a co-production musical. In the context of an oppressive (albeit comically distorted) Nazi Germany, the group of actors and actresses find themselves in some limbo space between the controlling German and the subjugated Jews and Russians who are brought in from a concentration camp to work as extras in the film.

La niña de tus ojos reveals some of the anxieties that have been described in relation to Spanishness and foreignness, such as their European liminarity. This sense of dislocated identity could explain the passive-aggressive response of the leading actor Julián Torralba (Jorge Sanz) to the (homo)sexual proposition of his German counterpart (Götz Otto). The contrast of the bodies of both actors could not be more eloquent: the Spaniard is relatively short, his (heterosexual) relations seem to be more platonic than real, his body is wounded (he falsely pretends it is a heroic war wound), he is bitten by dogs, and he ends up being tortured in a concentration camp. The German is tall, muscular, blond (an unambiguous embodiment of Aryan physical supremacy), and his approach to homoeroticism seems to be unashamed and direct. Moreover, the way the German tries to seduce the Spaniard shows total physical control and domination – a physical control the Spaniard constructs both as the internalized inferiority and as the naturalized heterosexuality of his Spanish body. The episode in which the German tries to seduce the Spaniard mobilizes many of the common assumptions of modern Spanish audiences about their own past, some of which are openly paradoxical. For instance, the German is (ironically) constructed by the film as physically 'superior' and morally 'more advanced' in contrast with the Spaniard's unreconstructed masculinity, but concurrently the German is put in the surrogate position of 'imitating' the Spaniard in the double version of the Spanish theme they are working on (a seemingly neo-romantic melodrama set in an idealized Andalucía). Thus, the German embodies simultaneously some of the German values that the Spaniards used to admire (perfectionism, progress) and some of the Germans' defects the Spaniards used to put forward in defence of their own national pride. Despite the German's weakened position in relation to the Spaniard (he not only imitates him, but also feels attracted to him and is eventually rejected by him), the scene closes with the sense that the Spaniard has been (comically) constructed as 'inferior'.

The relation of the inferior male to the national body is explored elsewhere in the film. The character of Goebbels (Johannes Silberschneider) plays abject games of control and domination with the Spanish leading actress, Macarena (Penélope Cruz), and his maimed body is used to emphasize his abjection, not his sexuality. Goebbels is heavily contrasted both visually and at the narrative level with one of the Russian prisoners forced to work as extras (Karel Dobry). The Russian is sexualized in a positive light: he does not display the abjection that seems to be monopolized by the Germans, he is seen affectionately by the Spaniards, and his lean and flexible body ultimately provides his own salvation (being a professional contortionist he is able to hide in a small coffer and thus escape his German captors). His slim, tall, resilient body contrasts markedly with the shorter, bulkier, more rigid bodies of the Spaniards. It is significant that this character, with his combination of national inferiority as a POW and a physical advantage, is chosen as Macarena's romantic partner in the film, because he represents a kind of 'illegal' foreignness not totally dissimilar to the subaltern subjects of the migration films and yet, contrary to what Flesler (2004) observes for Arab–Spanish mixed romances, this one has a happy ending.

Another Russian–Spanish romance with a happy ending occurs in *Hola, estás sola?* Whilst Flesler (2004) justifies the success of mixed romances other than the Arab–Spanish alluding to a meaningful cultural compatibility that simply does not exist between Muslims and Christians, in the case of *Hola, estás sola?*, it would be difficult to argue that (between El Ruso (Arcadi Levin) and La Niña (Silke)) a meaningful cultural compatibility exists at all. Amongst other issues, El Ruso does not speak Spanish. El Ruso is constructed as a case of radical foreignness or, in other words, as someone who does not know the language of the other characters, cannot communicate his own values and beliefs, and has been physically displaced from his country of origin. His dislocation is somatized from his first appearance in the film: La Niña sees him dancing in a disco, surrounded by a uniform mass of presumably domestic bodies: 'On the dance floor, dancers are totally uniform, like a dancing group in harmony – harmony broken by a huge man who is jumping and gesticulating in total asynchrony' (Bollaín and Medem 1997: 42). His asynchrony is made even worse by his excessive corporality when La Niña invites him to spend the night in the tiny apartment she shares with her friend Trini: 'El Ruso stands by the bed. His huge body makes the apartment appear even smaller. He looks around and says something incomprehensible yet again' (Bollaín and Medem 1997: 44). The sexualization of this foreign character is achieved by means of La Niña's gaze, whose dominant role is emphasized by her body language,[22] and by the physical injuries inflicted later in the film to El Ruso (as discussed in Chapter 8, the medicalization of the male body is frequently associated with a loss of phallic power). The film's last scene, unspoken, is described this way in the script:

> In a hospital room, with a bed and a few chairs. La Niña walks towards the bed, by the window, where someone is sleeping. It is Olaf. He wears a surgical collar; his torso is bandaged, both arms in a cast. La Niña watches him sleeping. Very slowly, quietly, she moves a chair closer to the bed and sits down. We can see her face. La Niña gazes at Olaf, almost motionless, speechless. La Niña closes her eyes again. (Bollaín and Medem 1997: 99)

Both *La niña de tus ojos* and *Hola, estás sola?* feature Russian males in successful romantic narratives involving Spanish women. In both films, women are presented with a choice between a Spaniard and a foreigner, thus making it clear that the Russianness of the successful male must be interpreted as an alternative to the Spaniards, and that their inability to speak or understand Spanish signals their radical otherness. In *La niña de tus ojos* the defeated Spanish male is played by Antonio Resines; in *Hola, estás sola?* the Spanish male (played by Daniel Guzmán) is not defeated but, rather, abandoned by La Niña before meeting El Ruso. These cases do not confirm the tendency in other intercultural romances for the Spanish male to intervene as the protector 'of a hegemonic sexual order in which Spanish women should not attempt to choose any other but a Spanish male as sexual romantic partner' (Flesler 2004: 106).

In the earlier-mentioned *La pasión turca/Turkish Passion* (dir. Vicente Aranda, 1994), another film about a Spanish woman abroad, the presence of the Spanish 'protector' is marked more strongly in the figure of Ramiro (Ramón Madaula), the sterile and seemingly impotent Spanish husband of Desideria (Ana Belén). In the film, Ramiro's emasculation is emphasized by various means: visually, he often occupies an inferior part of the frame when shot together with his wife; his body is always fully dressed; his weak libidinal drive leads to unsatisfactory sex; he reluctantly gives in to fathering the baby his wife has from another man; and, when the baby suddenly dies, he is abandoned by Desideria. Ramiro is never a 'protector' in the literal sense, but he is instrumental in building the film's deliberate opposition between Desideria's two worlds: the received universe of traditional Spain (described as ritualistically Catholic, Castile-centred and sterile) and the newly found universe of traditional Turkey (described as a heaven of pleasures and long-held hedonistic traditions).

Yamam (Georges Corraface), Desideria's Turkish lover is described by the camera in the first half of the film as a resourceful lover who lingers between shades and lights in his erotic encounters with Desideria in mosques and bazaars. Whilst Desideria's body is shot fully naked on several occasions, Yamam's is constantly fragmented; he is first seen from Desideria's POV shot from behind, in a tourists bus, his lips sensually reflected in a rear-view mirror. The sex scenes between Yamam and Desideria are shot in close-ups that usually focus on Desideria's facial expressions and naked body; in one of these scenes, the camera follows Desideria's head in her exploration of Yamam's body scents from his armpit to his pubis and back, again in close-up. The most explicit shot of a well-lit Yamam's body, a frontal upper torso, takes place on the only occasion he is having sex with someone other than Desideria.[23] The prudish shooting of Corraface's body in *La pasión turca* contrasts markedly with the more daring cinematography employed with Daniele Liotti in a similar stud role in *Juana la Loca* (see Chapter 3). In ways that fit the representational economy of the male genitals that will be discussed in the next chapter, the size of Yamam's penis is only talked about by other characters but never visualized, despite its importance in the unfolding of Desideria's story.[24] It is also somehow surprising that the most risqué scene involving male sex (an ejaculation, with a potent shot of sperm crossing the screen in front of Desideria's face) does not involve Yamam, but a secondary character of little importance in the narrative.[25]

Indeed, the parallels between *Juana la Loca* and *La pasión turca* about female out-of-control passionate sexual love are strikingly clear in the treatment of the female character and the narrative. However, the treatment of the male character is rather different in the way their bodies are filmed and also in the way they relate to their cultures of origin: whilst there is little that connects Philip the Handsome to his native Flanders in *Juana la Loca*, Yamam is presented as a quintessential Turk in his agreeable combination of Orientalism and Europeanism.[26] The failed romance between Desideria and Yamam has a tragic finale: Desideria's long-suspected phallic potential is suddenly realized when she gets hold of a gun and shoots Yamam in his crotch. The stud's castration and Desideria's ambiguous liberation resonate strongly in the context of the Muslim-European mixed-romance genre, which very often incorporates a discussion about the contrast between the liberated European women and oppressive Muslim men. According to Flesler, at times these mixed romances explore the idea that 'these relationships are not "natural" and are not "meant to be", that they would involve, for the women, an abandonment of their "true" identity' (Flesler 2004: 112). *La pasión turca* seems to confirm the difficulty of naturalizing an intercultural romance with its unhappy ending (Yamam castrated, Desideria leaving Istanbul purposelessly).[27]

Spanish contemporary cinema has departed quite markedly from previous modes of the representation of the foreign man in an evolution that in many ways mirrors that of Spanish society itself, vis-à-vis a greatly increased presence of foreigners in the country. Whilst there is an undoubtedly strong connection between the evolution of the social fabric and the new representational mechanisms deployed in films, the male foreigner does not always translate into a migration film with a definite social moral. As we have shown in this chapter, the foreigner is an important archetype in other genres, particularly in comedies and thrillers, and serves specific generic roles in each of those. The foreigner is also a strongly gendered character type and the bodies of male foreigners tend to be sexualized according to a template of domestic female fantasies and domestic male anxieties. This subjugation of the foreigner to the domestic remains a largely unchanged tendency of Spanish cinema to use foreigners as an excuse to rethink Spanishness. More specifically, in the examples discussed in this chapter, the body of the foreigner is explicitly compared to the body of the Spaniard. Some serious discourses about the specific instances of foreignness have featured in relation to Latin Americans and North Africans; films about Eastern Europeans and Asians remain less numerous and more two-dimensional in their construction of foreignness. Race has often been used as a strong signifier of foreignness, which, on the one hand, has opened Spanish cinema to specific issues of body representation, such as the semiotization of skin colour or the hyper-sexualization of certain types of body but, on the other hand, has also been exploited with racist undertones. Mixed-romance stories involving a foreign man and a Spanish woman (the reverse remains much less common despite an increased presence of foreign women in the more recent films) still tend to be portrayed as painful when an Arab male is involved; but the general tendency is towards a greater implication with foreigners of all cultures and conditions, including the possibility of the Spaniards themselves becoming foreigners and assuming migrant, nomad and tourist roles.

8

The genitals

DEALING WITH THE OBVIOUS?

In his influential book on masculinity and the representation of the male body, Peter Lehman sets out to challenge the silence and mystery that has surrounded discourses of male nudity with regards to the genitals. He argues that many such discourses are focused on demonstrating that 'everything else in the image other than the genitals is important' (1993: 24). His remarks on the reasons behind this silence and its effects provide a good starting point for this chapter on the representation of the male genitals:

> In addition to presuming that we are dealing with the obvious, the arts have yet another way of skirting the issues of explicitness – good taste. It is impolite to notice such things or, more accurately, to talk about them. This climate of silence perpetuates, rather than challenges, patriarchal assumptions about the sexual representation of the male body. (1993: 24)

Lehman explains that, beyond the threat to deflate the symbolic (phallic) power often equated with the penis, there are two other reasons why it is difficult to represent the penis in our culture: 'men may fear that the representation of the penis gives women a basis for comparison and judgement' and it 'creates a great deal of anxiety for homophobic men who may become intensely disturbed at finding themselves fascinated by it or deriving pleasure from looking at it' (2000: 27). In response to such challenges, the easiest option, Lehman argues, is not to represent the penis at all or to carefully regulate its representation. His examples are drawn from pornography, medical discourses and penis-size jokes: in pornography the representation of the penis is limited to 'the large, ever-present, long-lasting erection', in penis-size jokes 'the small penis is the butt of the joke', and the twentieth-century medical discourse 'virtually fetishizes the normal, average penis' (2000: 27). For Lehman, strategies of representation of the male genitals from the late twentieth century onwards are similar to those concerning the female genitals in the past and have resulted in a new representational category, 'the melodramatic penis':

> The dominant ideological drive to retain the awe and mystique surrounding the penis is crumbling before the journalistic and artistic drive to break down the final taboo. The melodramatic penis is the result. The melodrama surrounding the representation of the penis paradoxically cries out to reaffirm the spectacular importance of the penis even as the very assault on the taboo seeks to dislodge that importance. The melodramatic penis can, on the one hand, be read in a positive manner as avoiding such simple structuring dichotomies as the large, awesome phallic spectacle versus its pathetic comic collapse (…). On the other hand, the melodramatic penis continues to insist that the very act of representing the penis is somehow monumental. (2000: 39 – see also 2004: 202)

Whilst the recent attention paid to the penis in contemporary Western culture may seem relatively new, from Ancient Egypt (Osiris) and Greece (Dionysus) to contemporary rituals in Japan or New Guinea, the display of the male member has been, and still is, a central part of many cultural manifestations, some of which are close in terms both of time and space to the sociocultural contexts of the films that we are about to discuss.[1] Susan Bordo found that some best-selling American romance novels include countless accounts of penis-worshipping episodes conveyed by female narrators (1999: 45–46). Clarissa Smith (2003) also identified the importance that the display of the penis has for female consumers of the so-called 'women's magazines' that proliferated in Britain in the 1990s. As Lehman further suggests (2000), the 1990s was a decade in which more open discussions about the penis also became more prominent in Western film and mass media. His point is perhaps best illustrated with the success of the revealing male underwear ads (made prominent by the Calvin Klein mass campaigns in the early 1990s but then followed by many other major designers) and television series that celebrated female and queer perspectives on sexuality such as *Sex and the City* (HBO, 1998–2004) or *Queer as Folk* (UK Channel 4, 1999–2000 and then US Showtime, 2000–2005). Other events such as the growth of the porn and sex-toy industry (aided by the rapid advancement of new technologies and the Internet), the commercialization of the Viagra pill and the popularization of cosmetic surgery and implants amongst other developments, might be said to have contributed to an apparent demystification of the penis, which seems (metaphorically) to have found its way into many coffee-table conversations.[2] Nonetheless, as many scholars have pointed out, there is a danger that 'the desire to render the penis visible can be read as an attempt to stabilize rather than to destabilize constructions of masculinity' (Spongberg 1997: 20). Bordo's study of Viagra advertisements sheds some light on this debate: rather than focusing on its medical benefits as a way to restore the reproductive function of the penis, or on its potential enhancement of female sexual pleasure, the ads sell the pill as a means for the man to live up to the 'cultural standards and expectations of masculinity' (1999: 41–42). In other words: the emphasis is drawn away from the issues that make the pill necessary in the first place (the malfunctioning of the male sexual organ) towards the need to restore the organ's symbolic and physical prowess. This example illustrates the usual discrepancy between the imagery used to represent the penis and its reality. As García Cortés has argued, it is ironic that although 'male genitals are fragile, delicate and vulnerable, needing permanent protection, symbols associated with them are always hard, heavy and rigid objects that suggest aggression', adding that 'despite being flaccid and calm most of the time, men have a predilection for showing it erect and aggressive' (2004: 189).

As we shall see in our analysis of recent Spanish films later in this chapter, this new 'unveiling' of the penis in popular culture may be deceiving in many other ways. In the study of women's glossy magazines mentioned earlier, Clarissa Smith has described how the UK-based *For Women* magazine, which was initially sold on a promise to 'show more', avoided images of erect penises altogether. After a while, even flaccid penises had to be covered up with strategically positioned towels and hands in order to 'get the magazine off the top shelf and thereby increase circulation and advertising revenue' (2003: 137). This argument could apply to many of those very suggestive and increasingly revealing underwear ads mentioned above: the vast majority of them avoid full-frontal nudity (models are shown nude but from behind) and instead tease the viewer with a game of hiding and displaying. On the other hand, as Pérez Gauli has argued, the gaze of the semi-nude male models suggests a high level of narcissistic self-sufficiency and genetic superiority reminiscent of fascist imagery, reaffirming a sense of masculine superiority (2000: 73 – see also García Cortés 2004: 195): their hard bodies are a direct visual reference to phallic power, an insinuation of that other hardness that we cannot directly see but, we are led to think, is there. Equally surprising is the fact that the aforementioned unconventional conversations about the male organ in television series such as *Sex and the City* somehow managed to verbally scrutinize it without ever showing it.[3] With the exception of more recent and more revealing adverts and other images coming mainly from France (such as the famous ad for Lacoste perfume or the even more famous calendar of the French National Rugby team – *Dieux du stade*) it seems that, far from eradicating the patriarchal connotations of the phallic discourse, the presence of the penis in these ambiguous contexts has contributed to the maintenance of that discourse either by insisting on its phallic quality or by showing less than audiences might have been led to expect, thus maintaining its mystique (Dyer 1992).[4]

A NEW '*DESTAPE*': UNCOVERING THE PENIS IN SPANISH CINEMA

In the first chapter of this book we discussed the *destape* phenomenon as a way to illustrate the contrast between the levels of male and female nudity seen in some mid-1970s Spanish comedies. Whilst still not as common as female nudity, male frontal nudity in Spanish cinema of the last three decades has become increasingly frequent. Ballesteros refers to the close-up shot of Jorge Sanz's flaccid penis in the moderately explicit film *Amantes/Lovers* (dir. Aranda, 1991) as 'probably the first in Spanish cinema' (2001: 188). She argues that, despite the novelty of such focus on the male organ, the visual narrative avoids the exhibitionism of the male body and that the visual pleasure in the film is biased towards the heterosexual male spectator. It is true that the close-up attention on the male organ was relatively unusual until the 1990s, and yet there is a surprisingly high number of examples of frontal male nudity that go back as far as 1978 (a year after censorship was abolished). As mentioned in Chapter 1 and according to Ponce (2004: 17), the first example of non-frontal, male nudity in mainstream Spanish cinema was passed by Francoist censors. In *El libro de buen amor/The Book of Good Love* (dir. Tomás Aznar, 1974), the star Patxi Andión became the first male actor to appear nude on the screen (albeit only from the back). Long shots of penises are seen in a number of Spanish films released immediately after the end of censorship, notably the already discussed (Chapter 6) *Ocaña, retrat intermitent/Ocaña, an Intermittent Portrait* (dir. Ventura Pons, 1978) but also *Arriba Hazaña/Long Live Hazaña* (dir. Gutiérrez Santos, 1978) and two films of Eloy de la Iglesia released in 1978: *El diputado/Confessions of a Congressman* (see Chapter 5) and *El sacerdote/The Priest*. In the first two of these films, frontal nudity becomes doubly symbolic of the relative liberalization of the early years of the transition. The pupils' revolt against the stern ways of the priest teachers in *Arriba Hazaña* seems symptomatic of the political transition. More interesting for our purposes is the symbolic gesture made by one of the students (played by Quique Sanfrancisco) to mark his own protest against compulsory attendance to mass: he pulls down his trousers and underwear. The sight of his penis was perhaps surprising for audiences used to strict censorship, but the film was very popular, doing even slightly better at the box office than Buñuel's controversial *Cet obscur objet du désir/Ese oscuro objeto de deseo/ That Obscure Object of Desire*, which was released in Spain only two days later.[5] The pupils' revolt, then, becomes symbolic not only of the declining power of the Church in the new democracy (the film is set in a strict Catholic school), but also of the recent end of censorship. In *El diputado*, Nes's (Ángel Pardo) penis is seen in long shot and in a medical but still highly homoeroticized context (it is being checked out by a doctor while in prison, but admired by Roberto (José Sacristán)). Remarkably, in *El sacerdote*, a priest unable to resist sexual temptations (Simón Andreu) decides to cut his penis as a desperate measure. Although the actual excision is not shown (a close-up shot of his blood-splattered hands is used instead), there is a medium shot of his genitals as he wraps around them a large pair of pruning scissors in preparation. The castration is a direct critique to the Catholic Church's take on sexuality (the film expresses a cynical view of the issue of chastity): in a later scene, the priest 'talks' to a sculpture of Jesus on the cross and points out how images such as this place so much attention on the symbols of pain (crown of thorns, nailed hands and feet) and yet his genitals are always covered up, adding: 'Perhaps, like me, you have been castrated by the Church.' The castration is also a commentary on 1970s Spain, as suggested by the conversation that the priest has with a (formerly married) female admirer in the previous scene: 'It is too late for me, but not for you (…) It is very hard to be free in this country, but you have to try and be free above all things.'

As we have seen in various examples outlined throughout this book, for Spanish film audiences of the last three decades male frontal nudity is no longer a taboo. Most major male stars have agreed to full-frontal exposure albeit often only from a distance in medium-long or long shots. These include cases already discussed such as the late Antonio Flores in *Colegas* (see Chapter 2) or Jorge Sanz in *Amantes* – as discussed earlier in this chapter. The list includes key contemporary actors such as Antonio Banderas (his first full-frontal exposure was, as Perriam notes (2003: 52), in *Pestañas postizas/ False Eyelashes* (dir. Belloch, 1982)), Jordi Mollà (in *La buena estrella/Lucky Star* (dir. Ricardo Franco, 1997)) or Javier Bardem (in *El detective y la muerte/ The Detective and Death* (dir. Gonzalo Suárez, 1994)). Other films of the past three decades, such as those discussed in the Almodóvar case study that follows or Bigas Luna's films of the early 1990s (discussed in Chapter 1) are perhaps less casual in their approach to male frontal nudity. These films place the erect or semi-erect member visually and narratively at the centre of certain episodes whilst strategically avoiding its actual display.

The penis has enjoyed an unprecedented period of visibility in the Spanish cinema produced this side of the millennium. *Lucía y el sexo/Sex and Lucia* (2001) (Julio Medem's most commercially successful film to date in Spain) was marketed, particularly abroad, on its sexually explicit content. Interestingly, as Paul Julian Smith has noted, despite the abundant female nudity, it was the close-up shots of two erect penises that seemed to strike some audiences (2005b: 243). As Smith argues, the contrast between Lucía's (Paz Vega) and Lorenzo's (Tristán Ulloa) striptease scenes (hers is sensual, his is comic) could suggest that, despite the emphasis on Lucía's sexuality in the title, the film's main concern is heterosexual male desire, given the degree of visual investment in female bodies (not only Lucía's, also Belén's (Elena Anaya), her mother (Diana Suárez) and Elena (Najwa Nimri)). Interestingly, issues of authenticity problematize what could have been otherwise 'natural' close-up shots of the penis: the first of the two, supposed to be Lorenzo's penis fondled by Lucía is in fact not Ulloa's but David Bulnes's (who plays the minor role of a porn actor working with Belén's mother, appearing in various scenes that are shown on a television screen). The second close-up of a penis, supposed to be Carlos's (Daniel Freire) could be, as Smith points out (2005b: 243), a prosthesis. Yet, the action leading up to these shots does not contribute to a 'melodramatic' effect, to use Lehman's (2000: 39) term. In the first instance, the body-double's shot is inserted as part of a passionate sex scene between the characters involved whilst the second one comes as a surprise: Lucía bumps into Carlos on the beach: he lies naked but covered in mud, his large penis stands out first flaccid in a long shot, then in close-up as it becomes erect when he smears Lucía's sex with mud. Elena had talked to Lucía about the proportions of Carlos's member (her lodger), directly equating the size factor with enhanced sexual gratification for her (adding that she was using him just for sex) and increasing Lucía's (and the audience's) curiosity about it. Importantly, unlike the examples mentioned earlier, here the audience is allowed to see the 'object' of the discussions between the two females, thus doubly demystifying it: not only is the audience invited to see and perhaps judge for themselves but the female characters are the subjects whilst the penis becomes an object for their gratification.

Frontal nudity has also become increasingly common and unapologetic in some of the more recent gay-themed films that have been discussed in Chapters 5 and 6 of this book. *Los novios búlgaros/Bulgarian Lovers* (dir. Eloy de la Iglesia, 2003), *Cachorro/Bear Cub* (dir. Albaladejo, 2004) or *20 centímetros/20 Centimetres* (dir. Salazar, 2005) are amongst the most recent and most representative examples. The opening scene of *Cachorro* deserves a special mention: it is refreshing to have a medium close-up shot of an erect penis in the context of gay sex, which mainstream cinema seems to accept only as long as it is not explicit or between men with the kind of toned body that has become stereotypically associated with gay men (Mercer 2003; Pronger 1990: 272–276). As we have seen in Chapter 5, this is a scene that celebrates not only sex between men but also between bodies that do not conform to the social expectations of the body beautiful (the men are middle-aged, overweight and hairy, a type known as 'bears' in the gay scene). The medium close-up shot of the penis is all the more relevant here as it shows the act of putting on a condom – a crucial gesture in the context of HIV consciousness that permeates the film's narrative. Thus, whilst showing an erect penis in the second minute of the film could be seen as a stunt (in our personal experience, this was the scene that most people referred to when discussing the film), it is far from anecdotal and, in our view, an effective way to invite audiences to reflect on one of the key themes of the film from the very start.[6]

Salazar's *20 centímetros* was one of the most awaited Spanish films of 2005, attracting much media coverage from the start of filming in the summer of 2004. As the title suggests, the penis is a key element of the narrative, although the reasons could not be more different than those discussed so far: here the large penis becomes a burden and the main motivation of the protagonist is to get rid of it. Unlike the castration episode in *El sacerdote* discussed earlier, doing away with the penis here is an issue of liberation, not repression. Marieta is a transsexual prostitute (played by Salazar regular actress Mónica Cervera) and, by all accounts a very convincing female. In a series of close-ups, the opening scene fetishizes those parts of her body that are most clearly female: her breasts; her bright red, meaty lips; her feet (toenails painted in bright red, high heels) whilst her excessive femininity is immediately reinforced in the first musical number of the film.[7] Following the steps of Lars von Trier's *Dancer in the Dark* (2000), colourful dream sequences (the musical numbers, which are also highly influenced by the aesthetics of the pop-music video) provide a sharp contrast with the harshness of Marieta's reality.

Whilst in the opening scene she lay unconscious on the floor having been pushed out of a van by a client in a desert-like land 40 kilometres away from the city, in her first dream she is the queen of Madrid's Gran Vía. In a series of camp dance routines she impersonates several queer icons, including Marilyn Monroe, whose excessive femininity facilitates an appropriate masquerade for the character. Characterized by a carnival atmosphere, the capital's busiest street comes to a standstill to watch her perform on top of a double-decker bus: the neighbourhood joins in the routine from the windows, passersby, policemen and street sweepers happily become part of her troupe just as the bus reaches the Chueca end of the Gran Vía (Chueca is Madrid's gay centre). However, the dream comes to an abrupt end just as she adopts a Marilynesque pose, her skirt lifted above knee-height by the air produced by an underground ventilation shaft and sings the verse 'Yo soy toda una mujer' ('I am all woman'). The dancers look under the skirt and are shocked by what they see. The music stops before she can finish her line: contrary to what her iconic femininity and the lyrics of the song might suggest, she is by no means 'all woman'. Even though her 20 centimetres of male flesh are not actually seen at this moment, the scene's dynamics are in line with Lehman's 'melodramatic penis' (2000: 39). Not only does the music stop, the dancers sigh loudly and exclaim to each other: 'don't look, don't listen, don't speak', a critical presentiment, perhaps, of the ways in which others will react on finding out Marieta's sex.[8]

Throughout the film other characters pointedly remind her of her biological sex: her neighbour, a single mother, even asks her to show it to her son, who is learning the reproductive system at school and, unlike his peers, does not have a father who can show him what a penis looks like. Having a penis is certainly an advantage in her profession: indeed, her friend 'La Frío' (Rossy de Palma) warns Marieta that she lost clients after her (La Frío's) operation and customers often ask her if she has a dick (on one occasion two men ask her to perform fellatio on one of them whilst fucking the other one). Crucially, far from being put off by her penis, her heterosexual boyfriend Raúl (played by heartthrob Pablo Puyol) is fascinated by it. During their first date he performs fellatio and asks her to fuck him. This is repeated later on in a famous scene in which they have sex at his parents' home (whilst they watch television right next door) and are seen by some neighbours across the patio.

Despite the emphasis that the film puts on the large penis of the title and, in the making of the film, the much talked about practical difficulties that the actress had to go through to wear the prosthesis,[9] it is only barely seen twice: slightly out of shot during the first sexual encounter with Raúl (as she positions it to penetrate him) and then in a long shot (and briefly in close-up) during a masturbation scene, partly obscured by the distance, the darkness of the room and what appears to be a filter that conceals her body in a misty dream-like visual effect. Notably, it was the brief medium shot full frontal of co-star Puyol (coming out of the shower) that attracted most press attention. Yet, in all the sex scenes Marieta uses her penis to penetrate others: one of her clients in a car, then Raúl twice and on two other occasions she masturbates with her male organ, once graphically cumming all over the bathroom mirror. Beyond the film title and the sex scenes, the narrative also highlights the importance of the penis. In a scene at the job centre, she touches it and partly reveals it to an administrator who refused to offer her a job for not fulfilling the gender requirements of the post (they wanted to appoint a male cleaner). Later, when Raúl tries to persuade her not to have the sex-change operation because 'she is already a woman', she explains that she cannot possibly be a woman with such a large 'rabo' ('tail') and adds that she has always dreamt of having a huge vagina.

Refreshingly, the film presents the male organ as a burden and its elimination as a liberation for the central character: the sex-change operation at the end of the film is illustrated with another musical number which she dreams up whilst lying unconscious on the operating table. The song is Queen's 'I Want to Break Free', and the dance routine involves most of the film's characters emulating the scissors movement with their fingers. Yet, as we have seen, other characters do not seem to share her view, constantly warning her not to get rid of her penis and reminding her of its attraction whilst the abundant phallic imagery in the film seems to act as a constant reminder of the phallocentric society she lives in. In clear homage to one of the most memorable Almodóvar transsexuals – played by Maura in *La ley del deseo* – one of the dream sequences includes a man refreshing Madrid's streets with a large hose.

It seems ironic that the piece of unwanted flesh became a central element of the promotional campaign, with Cervera appearing on the front cover of gay magazine, *Shangay*, two weeks before the film's première, topless and in male underwear, in a crotch-grabbing pose, highlighting the length and apparent hardness of the fake penis. In a further example of penis fixation, Cervera's co-star Puyol also appeared naked on the cover of the Friday cultural supplement of Spain's best-selling newspaper (*EP3*) on the day of the première, his penis used as a hat hook (that conveniently covers it whilst emphasizing its length and hardness) under the title 'El chico "Upa" se pone duro' ('The "Upa" guy gets hard').[10]

Other recent Spanish films such as *Amor idiota/Idiot Love* (dir. Ventura Pons, 2004) or *XXL* (dir. Sánchez Valdés, 2004) have also exploited the presence of the penis in their narratives directly (in the title) or indirectly (in the media) as a way of publicizing the film. *Amor idiota* will be remembered by the few seconds at the beginning of the film in which Pere (played by television personality Santi Millán), drunk at a party, puts his penis on a dish next to a large sausage, and threatens to stick a fork in it. This brief scene undoubtedly provoked castration anxiety amongst male audiences (perhaps concealed under the nervous laughter also encouraged here), but it is also a good metaphor of phallic power. Pere's large penis was a key factor in the seduction of an apparently happily married woman (played by Cayetana Guillén Cuervo) whom he stalks for the first part of the film and with whom he performs no less than 18 sexual acts (some of these edited in one long sequence). Like Pere the character, Millán the actor also metaphorically served his main assets on a plate to promote the film, as suggested by co-star Guillén Cuervo's insistence during television appearances at the time of the film's première that people should not miss the actor's full-frontal.[11]

Teen comedy *XXL* is, to some extent, a copy of the male-chauvinist and phallocentric comedy for which Bigas Luna's 'Iberian Portraits' trilogy became famous (see Chapter 1). Here the aptly named protagonist Fali (Óscar Jaenada) is a present-day Raúl (Javier Bardem's character in *Jamón, Jamón*) whilst the actor could arguably be considered a new Bardem. Jaenada became famous mainly for his work on television but, like Bardem, it was the nudity involved in his first role as a protagonist (in *Lisístrata* (dir. Bellmunt, 2002)) which launched his career. Since then he has won the Best Actor award at the Spanish Goya for his leading role in *Camarón* (dir. Chávarri, 2005). Like Raúl in *Jamón*, the male protagonist of *XXL* is a delivery man, but renowned amongst female customers for his 'packet'. He also likes to eat garlic and his ambition is to own a BMW or a Mercedes – the same car that Raúl aspired to in *Jamón*. Like Bardem's character in *Huevos de oro*, Fali likes to smoke cigars 'because cigarettes are for losers', and like *Jamón*'s Raúl, Fali is also hired by an older character to seduce a younger woman but, in the process, ends up seducing an older woman too (who happens to be his boss's wife), ultimately becoming a victim of his own excessive sexuality. Visually, Fali is also reminiscent of the iconic *macho ibérico* embodied by Bardem in *Jamón*, wearing similar clothes. Fali's erection is, like that of Raúl in *Jamón*, only visible underneath his jeans. However, *XXL* is even more obvious than the Bigas Luna film in its use of phallic imagery and its phallocentrism.

Apart from the title (a direct reference to Fali's large penis), the poster and the film's opening credits serve both to emphasize and conceal the protagonist's large penis: the 'L' of the title is shown as a ruler emerging from Fali's genital area as he lies in bed talking to his penis (which he irreverently calls '*la poderosa*' – the 'all mighty', a term associated with the hand of God in Roman Catholic iconography), asking it to 'go down'. Humorously, the film was playfully promoted as 'a comedy of great proportions' and yet despite the visual and verbal emphasis on Fali's organ, it is never shown in the film. Instead, its size is discussed by friends, lovers and middle-aged female customers (who circulate Fali's contact details and request his services as a 'delivery man' – actually giving him a 30-Euro 'tip' for his sexual favours). It is also humorously emphasized in the soft sex scenes by the facial expression of his sexual partners (and, in one particularly hilarious case, by the frightened reaction of a cat when he sees him strip down) or by appreciative comments made by his satisfied lovers ('The next time someone says that size does not count I will crack up laughing'). In a weak effort to deflate the phallocentrism celebrated by the film, the protagonist's immaturity is suggested by the fact that he prefers to live with his mum and hang around with his mates than to settle down with a girlfriend.

Other films such as *Isi & Disi: Amor a lo bestia/Isi & Disi Beastly Love* (dir. de la Peña, 2004), *Fin de curso/School is Out* (dir. Miguel Martí, 2005) or *Semen: una historia de amor/Semen: A Love Story* (dirs Daniela Fejerman and Inés París, 2005) make a big issue of the mockery of what in porn is known as 'the money shot': the release of semen. In both *Isi & Disi* and *Fin de curso* the release of semen is a key comic element linked to a specific character in each case and associated with freakiness (due to the amount of semen they produce and the incontrollable way in which it is released). In *Semen* the substance is linked to its primary function of reproduction: a biologist working in an artificial insemination clinic ends up having to secretly use his own semen to aid a patient with whom he eventually falls in love. In all three films the comic context in which the release of semen is produced, oddly overrides its sexual element (there is no sexual intercourse as such and the penis is never seen) whilst still emphasizing the sexual potency of the respective male characters and making a spectacle out of it. Perhaps surprisingly, as we shall see in the next section, it seems that the approach taken to the representation of the penis in Almodóvar's filmography is not radically different from what we have seen so far.

FROM GENERAL ERECTIONS...TO SHRINKING LOVERS: HIDING AND DISPLAY OF THE PENIS IN PEDRO ALMODÓVAR'S FILMOGRAPHY

Widely acknowledged by critics as a 'women's director',[12] Pedro Almodóvar has himself expressed preference for the feminine world, arguing that it is 'more fascinating' and that 'women are more interesting, richer, more varied, more surprising (…) men are all one thing' (Rouyeur and Vié 2004: 78). The titles of some of his films would seem to substantiate this.[13] A long list of so-called 'chicas Almodóvar' who, in differing degrees, have remained faithful to the director on and off screen (such as the now internationally renowned actresses Carmen Maura, Victoria Abril or Marisa Paredes) contribute to this label.[14] Crucially, as Victor Fuentes has argued, Almodóvar's narratives also 'celebrate the declining power of masculine discourse and the Father's Law' and 'reveal a general feminisation of culture' (Fuentes 1995: 163), often inviting identification with the female protagonists to a degree that 'openly and self-consciously' question 'the voyeuristic and sadistic tendencies inherent in cinema' (Allinson 2001: 81). Yet, one aspect that stands out in Almodóvar's entire filmography is also the visual investment in the masculine body, and we will devote the rest of this chapter to an analysis of some of the key moments of his work in which the male body is foregrounded, in an attempt to analyse Almodóvar's approach to the representation of the male nude and, in particular, the display of the genitals.

Almodóvar's first long feature film *Pepi, Luci, Bom y otras chicas del montón/Pepi, Lucy, Bom and Other Girls on the Heap* (1980) has become somewhat iconic of the Spanish Transition and the Madrid *movida*. One of the film's most famous scenes parodies the then young democracy through a penis-size contest which the characters call 'general erections'. What some might regard as a marginal scene in the film became one of the most memorable and controversial episodes of Almodóvar's debut. This scene was probably intended as the film's centrepiece. Indeed, 'the general erections' was the working title in the original script (see Allinson 2001: 10 and 36). Paul Julian Smith has interpreted the episode as '[not only] a parodic pointer to the plebiscite recently celebrated when the script was written, but also a blatant assertion of the autonomy of pleasure and of the triumph of libidinal anarchy over the pieties of political progressives' (2000a: 16). Beyond the strictly socio-political insight that the scene provides, a close analysis also reveals Almodóvar's gender politics and his approach to the filmic representation of the male body in much of his work to date.

There is little doubt that, in the context of the overexposure of breasts and other female body parts that characterized the *destape* films of the years prior to the release of this film (Chapter 1), the apparent visual emphasis that this scene places on the male genitals stands out. This unusual narrative and visual investment in the male organ could be seen as an attempt to deflate phallocentrism. One of the premises of Lacan's thinking is that the concept of the phallus only applies when veiled and that any display of the male organ would appear as feminine, a notion developed in the field of visual culture by Dyer (1992: 261–264), Lehman (1993: 28) and Thomas (2003: 249) amongst others. As the young men line up in front of an audience which is multi-layered (the young men and women watching the contest live and the voyeur looking from his apartment's window in the film as well as the camera and the cinema spectators), waiting for their penises to be measured, it seems clear that Mulvey's mid-1970s argument that 'the male figure cannot bear the burden of sexual objectification' (1992: 28) is negated by the gaze encouraged here.[15] Two further issues problematize the film's use of the male body as spectacle: not only are the men measured and judged by another male (played by Almodóvar himself) who openly celebrates the 'breathtaking' proportions of the winner's organ (his words), but the contest itself appears to have been orchestrated by a married male voyeur – the one watching with binoculars from his apartment's window whilst having sex with his wife – thus problematizing not only the gaze but also older hegemonic conceptions of gender and sexuality.

Further to these visual aspects, the fact that this contest focuses on the size of the men's penises underlines the implicit critique both of phallocentrism and of the primitive instinct of competitiveness, supposedly inherent in all – heterosexual – men, and which is inescapable in the political contest that it parodies.[16] On the other hand, the fact that the winning contender will have the audience (quite literally) at his service adds to the political dimension, suggesting that, behind the façade of modernity and gender equality, the long-awaited democracy is firmly rooted in the workings of patriarchy and phallocentrism and that the newly implemented system is, in that specific sense, not that different from the previous one, nor indeed far removed from those tribal cultures that Western democracies would regard as primitive or inferior. Yet, with all its implicit political criticism, the *erecciones generales* episode could also be read as a glorification of the penis, suggesting a potential reinforcement of phallic superiority. Indeed, despite all the talk and excitement about the male penises, these are never shown to the film audience. Whilst the humorous atmosphere is already de-eroticising and distracting from the matter at stake, the lighting and camera positions draw the cinema audience's attention further away from the male object of desire by either obscuring the genitals or focusing on the contestants' behinds instead. Notwithstanding the subversiveness of such close focus on the male buttocks (which, as Easthope 1990: 52 has argued, are also highly unusual and draw attention to the vulnerability of the male body by pointing to one of its most prominent orifices and its penetrability), the concealment of the penis reinforces the phallic mystique that the scene had arguably set out to mock. The camera teases the audience with a game of presence (suggested by the dialogue and gazes of characters in the film) and absence (we never get to see what the characters see).

In his discussion of *¿Qué he hecho yo para merecer esto?/What Have I Done to Deserve This?* (1984), Lehman argues that the sight of a flaccid and small penis in the famous shower sex scene (involving a – dressed – cleaning lady played by early Almodóvar regular Carmen Maura and a – naked – martial artist in the changing rooms of the gym where she works and he practices) is at once a departure from 'the compulsive need to make a powerful, phallic spectacle of the penis' and a confirmation that 'the small penis is somehow a sign of weakness and failure' (1993: 10). This is especially persuasive in this context since the sexual encounter in the shower is far from satisfactory for the woman. Indeed, there is nothing less phallic than the sight of a small, flaccid penis that fails to deliver sexual pleasure (Bordo 1999: 45) and in the scene that follows, Gloria gets over the frustration by enacting some martial arts movements with a kendo pole, held up at waist height.

In a later scene, in many ways related to the shower incident, Gloria is asked by her prostitute neighbour Cristal (Verónica Forqué) to watch her have sex with an exhibitionist client (a cameo role played by famous director Jaime Chávarri). Before they start, the man improvises a striptease and 'shows off' his body to the two women, explaining that it is not as scrawny as it at first seems. He flexes his arms, sticks out his chest, fishing for compliments. Despite his claim that the size of his dick is the cause of his having to resort to prostitutes for sex (their sex, in his view, being more slack 'due to usage'), Cristal's fake facial expressions during the sexual act suggests that the man's penis is small and, more importantly, unable to satisfy her (see Figure 15). Thus, this scene mocks the equation of a muscular body with a hard penis (muscles being an impersonation of the phallus, as argued by Bordo (1999: 49); Easthope (1990: 54); Ian (1995: 79) and others). The comic male striptease scene in ¿Qué he hecho yo para merecer esto? and the sex scene that follows, then, both mock and confirm this theory since, despite the man's distorted self-image, his body is clearly not as hard as he makes out. Consequently, it seems that his dick will not be as large as Cristal had been led to expect. It is as if the apparently phallic and confident but ultimately pitiful man of these scenes is painfully aware of the phallic power that he lacks, an awareness that appears to have been transferred to the 'knowing' women. Gloria witnesses in awe the pathetic spectacle of the scrawny male and Cristal having sex, as he holds her brand-new and unmistakably phallic curling iron, an equivalent of the kendo pole in the scene that followed the shower episode, reinforcing the above-mentioned appropriation of the film's inescapable phallic imagery.[17]

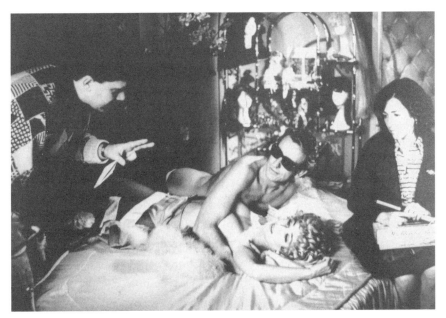

15. Phallic matters: Pedro Almodóvar, Jaime Chávarri, Verónica Forqué and Carmen Maura on the set of ¿Qué he hecho yo para merecer esto?

Yet, towards the end of the film, Cristal tells the inspector in charge of investigating the death of Gloria's husband – who happens to be the one Gloria had sex with in the shower at the beginning of the film – that Gloria 'desperately needs some dick', adding (ironically in the context of earlier events of which Cristal is unaware) that he should 'sort out' his erectile problems and do her a favour. As with the *erecciones generales*, the significance of phallic power is reiterated and in this apparent role-reversal, as Epps argues with reference to Gloria, the women 'remain in a phallic economy even as [they are] beside it' (1995: 111).

Other 1980s Almodóvar films such as *Laberinto de pasiones/Labyrinths of Passion* (1982) and *Matador* (1986) include notorious close-ups of male crotches from (presumably heterosexual) female and (presumably gay) male points of view and employ similar tactics. The close-up shots put the men and their private parts in the spotlight and under the scrutiny of non-hegemonic gazes at the same time that they perpetuate (visually and narratively) the myth of male superiority and the association of virility and social/sexual success with penis size (as Jackson notes 1995: 171). In a fashion similar to the earlier films, the masturbation scenes that open both *Matador* and *La ley del deseo* (1987) avoid focusing on the male genitals by displacing the attention away from it to other visual elements such as, in *Matador*, the close-up shots of the man's face, long shots of his body or POV shots of the slasher-movie footage that he is watching on television and, in *La ley*, close-up shots of various other parts of the body, long and medium shots of the actor's backside and close-ups of the faces of the film dubbers (the masturbation scene is part of a film-within-a-film). Moreover, as Jackson notes, the masturbatory fantasy of *La ley* in fact includes a second invisible penis: the one that is supposed to penetrate the man (1995: 165–168). The hiding of the penis in both films is compensated with the ever-present phallic imagery. *Matador*'s Diego (Nacho Martínez) masturbates furiously whilst watching what appears to be an edited tape of climatic scenes of various slasher movies in which there is explicit violence done to female bodies. In some cases, the violence is unambiguously executed by men whose face is either out of frame or covered up, in stark contrast with the close-ups of the terrified faces of the objectified and brutalized women. In the context of the film's narrative and, given Diego's profession as a matador, these images serve to emphasize the parallelism between the bullfight, sexual penetration and violence that is insistently played out visually in the narrative and that, it would appear, perpetuate men's active and penetrative role.[18] However, as Smith (1997: 183) and Allinson (2001:

82) note, in the next sequence, shots of Diego's explanation of 'the art of killing' at a bullfighting school are cross-cut with shots of the real (sexual) hunt and killing of a man who is picked up, seduced and killed by María (Asumpta Serna) who penetrates a sharp hairpin into his neck during the sexual act. This sets the mood for the rest of the film, which will end with Diego's death by the same method. The men seduced and killed by María are seen as objects, dissected in close-ups of body parts during the sexual act and then in the photographs of their corpses seen at the police station. Such images are the equivalent of the images of dissected and hurt female bodies seen at the start of the film. For Evans (1993: 333) María could be seen as an 'avenger' of the type of male degradation of women seen at the start of the film.

Many critics have focused on the fetishization of Diego's body (see, for instance, Allinson 2001: 83; Davies 2004; Smith 1997: 185 and 2000a: 73), firstly by María – who obsessively collects *corrida*-related objects that remind her of him – but also by means of frequent close-up shots of different parts of his body (notably his eyes and lips) that, as Lev notes, 'inscribe him with "feminine" cinematic features' (1995: 81 – see also Davies 2004: 14). The mentioned shot of the students' crotches is also fetishizing, offering a (presumably) gay male point of view which, for Smith, makes the fetishization of the male body possible since, in terms of gender, a gay man, unlike a woman, still belongs to 'the dominant regime of visibility' (2000a: 73). As in *¿Qué he hecho yo para merecer esto?* and, as we shall see later, *Kika* (1993), *Matador* also deflates the phallic awe of penetrative sex by turning a rape scene that would traditionally inspire contempt and hatred for the attacker into a comic situation in which the rapist becomes himself victim: Ángel (Banderas) ejaculates before managing to penetrate his victim. He then confesses his action to the police, but they seem reluctant to believe him, thinking that it was he who was raped. This character, as Smith has argued, is defined by inactivity and, in that sense, 'he corresponds more consistently than María to the fetishized, feminine object of narrative cinema' (2000a: 72).

The opening scene of *La ley del deseo* justifies the claim that the film is 'Almodóvar's self-reflexive paean to the male body and homosexual desire' (Morris 1995: 94). A young, athletic man is seen undressing slowly as he follows the orders of an anonymous deep male voice. In one of the most memorable male stripteases of Spanish cinema, he keeps his underwear on until the last moment whilst carefully touching his body, kissing himself in the mirror or rubbing his crotch against it, dutifully obeying orders. Still commanded by the voice, he then masturbates with his back to the camera, facing the bed and reluctantly asking to be fucked – as instructed. Following the conventions of soft-porn, the master/slave role-play enacted in this scene serves to emphasize but also subvert the phallocentric active/passive binary. Half-way through this sequence and through a series of cross-cut shots, we learn that this voice belongs to an actor who is adding the voiceover to an erotic film in a studio. Importantly in the context of Spanish audiences who are used to watching dubbed foreign films, this familiarity is deconstructed by separating the image from the voice and adding a revealing twist when we learn that the man dubbing the 'athletic' lad belongs to an overweight and balding middle-aged man with thick glasses who sweats heavily whilst moaning and repeating the words 'fuck me' into the microphone (something that triggered the laughter of some – gay – audiences Arroyo 1992: 38). As the scene comes to an end, the actor is paid for his work by an anonymous, faceless man (apparently the one who was instructing him) who walks into the frame. To further elaborate the film-within-a-film structure of the sequence, there is a cut to a close-up of film tape in the editing room and then to the theatre where the film première is taking place as the audience watch that very (final) scene and applaud. The way in which the actor counts his cash with satisfaction contrasts with his awkward body language whilst masturbating earlier on. What might have looked like a rough-cut of the film for dubbing purposes (which included the moment at which the actor is paid for his work) was in fact already part of the narrative of the porn film that ends as *La ley* opens.

Once again, here the male body is multiply objectified: the model is manipulated by the voice and obeys orders, putting various parts of his body on display as instructed, including its most vulnerable part (the buttocks), 'offered' to the camera during masturbation, drawing further attention to its visual penetrability by the words that he is asked to declaim. He is then paid for 'the show'. The gaze here is emphasized through a succession of layers. The first two layers originate in Almodóvar's script and camera, both of which clearly make a spectacle of the male body (as Arroyo has noted (1992: 38)). The third layer comes with the film-within-the-film as evidenced by the dubbers who scrutinize the scene for professional purposes but also with perceptible sexual arousal. The fictional cinema audience add an extra layer with their energetic applause. Finally, there is the reaction of an individual member of that fictional audience with the Antonio Banderas character – also called Antonio. He goes to the cinema's toilets and masturbates whilst repeating the words enunciated by the athletic man in the film 'fuck me'. Antonio's own body becomes fetishized at his very first appearance, by means of a close-up of that other male orifice, the mouth, thus anticipating the penetration of his own body by no other than the director of the film. Interestingly, as Smith (1997: 186) notes, the masturbation scene avoids shots of the man's penis. Following the trend of what we have discussed so far, the camera focuses on the man's behind instead, thus somewhat preserving the phallic mystique. This approach to the representation of the male body applies to most of the film, where, whilst there is a high exposure of naked men and close-ups of male body parts, the genitals of the male leads are kept well out of sight by long shots, dark lighting, towels (Pablo – played by Poncela) or potted plants (Antonio) amongst other strategies. The notable exception is the 'utilitarian' nudity, to use Bordo's term (1999: 28), of one shot in which Pablo's flaccid penis is shown whilst he gets dressed after a shower. The male body is displayed mainly from the perspective of other males in a homoerotic visual economy that, as in other Almodóvar films, does not necessarily exclude women spectators (see Morris 1995: 89). The lack of focus on male genitalia in this film is perhaps best illustrated in the lavish celebration of the curvy 'female' body of Pablo's transsexual sister Tina (Maura again) and, as in the cases discussed earlier, arguably compensated for with an ever-present phallic imagery (notably in the key lighthouse scene – examined by Arroyo 1992: 42), which Tina herself cannot escape. In one famous scene, she asks a street cleaner to drench her with a large and powerful hose as a means of liberating herself.

As Smith has noted (2000a: 109), the objectification of the male body is also remarkable in *¡Átame! / Tie me up! Tie me down!* (1990) (see Figure 16). Yet, despite the apparent emphasis on the body of the Banderas character, visual attention to him is in no way comparable in quality or quantity to that of his female counterpart, whose body is voyeuristically and frequently observed from the perspective of both Ricky (Banderas) and Máximo (Francisco Rabal), offering close-ups of her various body parts, including breasts and genitals. Marina (Victoria Abril) is seen undressing, wearing revealing clothes, or naked in various scenes and is penetrated on various occasions: from behind in an old porn film (that Máximo watches at home); in the bath by a toy scuba-diver and during the sex scenes with Ricky. Famously, in the climatic sex scene between Ricky and Marina, Banderas's buttocks can be observed from five different angles, as they are reflected in an octagonal mirror in the ceiling that is partially shown. Yet his 'missionary' position contributes to the avoidance of frontal nudity. Crucially, however, the sexual act refreshes Marina's memory; she could not remember at first that she had already had sex with her admirer on a previous occasion (this motif would recur in *Carne trémula*). As

Almodóvar put it in a DVD re-issue of the film (released by El Deseo in 2002), it is 'through Ricky's dick' that she finally recognizes the man. The same strategy is used in *Tacones lejanos/High Heels* (1991), where the multiple identities of the undercover detective played by Miguel Bosé are partly unveiled due to the unmistakable appearance of his penis which is recognized in a photograph by a character (interestingly also played by Abril). The audience may never get to see them, but these penises are of crucial relevance for the narratives and, indeed, a key part of the men's identities.[19]

One of the titles considered for *Kika* (1993) was *Raboterapia* (*Dick Therapy*), in reference to one of the porn flicks starring Paul Bazzo (Santiago Lajusticia), the film's insatiable rapist (and also fugitive). Undoubtedly, such a title could inspire politically incorrect readings, such as the suggestion that the apparently never-ending rape that takes place in the film could have done the victim some good. It is perhaps no coincidence that the actress who plays Kika (Verónica Forqué) also played the prostitute that, as earlier mentioned, at the end of *¿Qué he hecho yo para merecer esto?*, asks one of her clients to 'sort out' her neighbour who is 'in need of some dick'. It is hardly surprising that *Raboterapia* was discarded as a title, not only for its 'lack of seriousness', as Almodóvar claims in the 'film notes' published in his official website

16. The hurt male body on display: Antonio Banderas and Victoria Abril in *¡Átame!*

(www.pedroalmodovar.es), but also for the implications that such a title would have had for real rape victims, although, as the director has pointed out, both characters are figuratively 'raped' by the media, which broadcasts to the masses a recording of the act.[20] Yet, the film does celebrate the phallic mystique of the insatiable sex machine that is Paul. To add to his porn-star credentials, his nickname 'Paul Bazzo' emphasizes his sexual prowess ('*polvazo*' means 'great fuck' in Spanish); he can have several orgasms in a row 'without coming out of her body' and it is suggested that his insatiable sexual appetite does not know any boundaries. Indeed, he finds casual relief with members of his family (his sister, his cousin) and it is suggested that he also had sex with men whilst in prison and with animals in his village. Further to this, references are made in the news programme to his low IQ and he is referred to by other characters (including his sister) as a 'brute', thus emphasizing those beastly features that will contribute to his animalization and, indirectly, to his objectification. On the other hand, the context of the religious procession of 'Los Picaos' emphasizes the religious iconography of the male body previously seen in Almodóvar and which equates the character's body with that of Christ during the Passion (famously in the homosexual *Pietà* at the end of *La ley del deseo*).[21] In this procession, as shown in the images of mock sensationalist television programme *Lo peor del día* ('Worst of the day'), penitents cover their head with a hood (with holes just for the eyes) and their bodies with a tunic, leaving a large square of bare skin at the back so that it can be flagellated and pricked with various torture instruments in a ritual that is supposed to mark the suffering of the Passion. Pablo's back is still bleeding from these wounds when he removes his (red) shirt before the sexual act, thus emphasizing both the masochistic side of the religious ritual and his physical strength (of beastly proportions). Some of these associations are applicable, as we have seen, to earlier films such as *Matador* or *¡Átame!*, all of which emphasize the links between pain and pleasure and the resilience of the hurt male body, as well as casually providing an opportunity for its display.

The rape scene in *Kika* follows the scheme described so far, by which phallocentrism is apparently mocked but also indirectly exalted. Kika's body language is reminiscent of Forqué's own prostitute Cristal in *¿Qué he hecho yo para merecer esto?* when having penetrative sex with her exhibitionist 'huge' client (as Martin-Márquez 1999: 30–31 notes). Her apparent dissatisfaction is not only a product of the act of rape but also the result of a woman sexually frustrated by her voyeuristic partner and overall disappointed by the selfishness embedded in *machista* sexuality. Yet, this uncomfortably comic rape scene also suggests that, apart from the obvious unpleasantness of rape, Pablo's sexual reputation is not fully deserved. As argued by Smith, he seems 'unable to distinguish between a fictional and an authentic sexual performance' (1996: 40). The scene plays out the aesthetic conventions of porn by making a spectacle of the man's cumming ('the money shot'). Far from being put off by the arrival of the police, the rapist (concentrating fully on the sexual act) refuses to stop his action and, when forced away from his victim, he runs to the balcony and still manages to reach an orgasm, his semen running all the way down to the street, accidentally reaching the face of the television programme's female reporter. Linda Williams's (1999) observations on 'the money shot' (based on pornography) seem particularly apt for this former porn star, whose special trick had undoubtedly earned him the nickname of 'Paul Bazzo': apart from the sexual connotations in Spanish of *polvazo* earlier discussed, the expression '*echar un polvo*' refers specifically to the release of semen.[22]

Despite the noticeable stylistic differences of the films that followed in the second half of the 1990s (discussed in Smith 2003: 144–168), the more recent films have retained this characteristic attention to the masculine body.[23] The predominantly female narratives of *La flor de mi secreto/The Flower of My Secret* (1996), *Todo sobre mi madre/All About My Mother* (1999) and, arguably, *Hable con ella/Talk to Her* (2002) make the important presence of the male body in all three films all the more striking whilst *Carne trémula/Live Flesh* (1997) was aptly hailed as 'Almodóvar's rediscovery of masculinity' (Smith 2000a: 183). In *La flor*, the trim and toned body of writer Leo's (Marisa Paredes) absent husband Paco (a NATO officer in Bosnia played by 1980s heartthrob Imanol Arias) is seen nude for a considerable part of his brief time on screen (although avoiding full-frontal nudity before, during and after taking a shower by means of a towel and his underwear) and contrasted with the chubby figure of Leo's new man, a newspaper editor appropriately named Ángel (Juan Echanove). The disciplined, phallic body of the officer seems to suit not only his job but also his cold and *macho* personality, whilst the rounder shape of Ángel contributes to his feminization.[24]

The much talked about frontal nudity of Víctor (Liberto Rabal) in *Carne trémula* (1997) (discussed in Chapter 4) is far from gratuitous: he emerges out of the shower and rushes to the kitchen to put out a fire caused by Clara's (Ángela Molina) absentmindedness. The scene might seem an opportunistic, even exploitative invitation to admire the naked and glistening body of Rabal (the effect conveniently achieved by a combination of the wetness from the shower and sweat provoked by the intensity of the fire, as both Smith 2000a: 163 and Perriam 2003: 187 note). Yet, crucially, it provides a visual reminder of the cocky character's own physical vulnerability, a factor that his disabled opponent David (Bardem) will take advantage of by punching his genitals as a response to Víctor's malicious comment on David's physical disadvantage. Notably, as Smith (2000a: 184) points out, the sexual scene involving David transcends the obsession with penetration (the character was impotent in the Ruth Rendell novel that inspired the film) by focusing on oral sex instead. Yet, one of the striking differences between this scene and the passionate sexual re-encounter between David's wife and Víctor will be the focus on that part of Víctor's body that has become dysfunctional for her husband: the all-important and unambiguously phallic legs that are further emphasized in the film's official poster and in the use of the mannequin's broken leg scene from Buñuel's *Ensayo de un crimen/Rehearsal for a Crime* (1955) that Elena (Francesca Neri) watches on television just before the shooting that would make her future husband dependent on a wheelchair.[25]

In *Todo sobre mi madre*, where the absence of male characters is such that two of the key biological males are transsexuals and where, as Acevedo-Muñoz argues (2004: 29), even some of the potentially phallic imagery is denied and turned into symbolic maternity (his comments relate to the structurally crucial trains and tunnels that separate/unite Madrid and Barcelona), references to the male genitals also stand out. Agrado (a transsexual played by Antonia San Juan) admits that her pre-op status was highly valued in her former job as a prostitute and one of the scenes that celebrates the comradeship between the four main female characters (including Agrado) peaks with a joke about how long it had been since the last time they had a dick in their mouths.

For some critics like Smith (2002: 26) *Hable con ella* marks a new return to masculinity in Almodóvar's work. Here, the focus shifts to the male characters as the female leads remain comatose for most of the film. The characteristics of the friendship that develops in the hospital between journalist Marco (Darío Grandinetti) and nurse Benigno (Javier Cámara) is reminiscent of many female friendships in previous films and, as Smith also notes, one of Almodóvar's favourite female traits (weeping) is here transferred to Marco, in the moving opening scene. The attention paid to the female body of the female leads is clear: not only do we witness how they are undressed, washed and fed whilst unconscious in hospital, but before their hospitalization the women had physically demanding jobs that relied on their fit bodies to a large extent (one was a dancer, the other a bullfighter).[26] The obvious phallic imagery returns, with a scene in which bullfighter Lydia (Rosario Flores) reveals her phobia of snakes and requires Marco's assistance to go into her house and kill one.

Further to this, a key sequence inspired by one of the many films that Benigno watches regularly in Madrid's Filmoteca and then retells to dormant patient Alicia (Leonor Watling), the pretend silent classic *Amante menguante* (*The Shrinking Man*), shows how a man drinks a potion produced by his scientist girlfriend that accidentally makes him shrink to the extent that he is able to walk into his lover's vagina. Seemingly a perfect metaphor for the male discovery of 'the dark continent' (possibly inspired by Niki de Saint Phalle's *Nanas*),[27] but one which will also turn out to represent Benigno's rape of his unconscious patient. The tension during this scene is punctuated by the increasing intensity of the music and by the alternation of extreme close-up shots of the silent-film actress's various body parts and face, whilst asleep, indicating her pleasure (and by implication Alicia's). When describing the film to the dormant patient, Benigno compares himself to the shrinking man (Alfredo) saying that he was a bit overweight 'just like me'. The man's scientist girlfriend also resembles Alicia, not just in features but also in posture during the key moment of penetration, as revealed by the cut from head of the sleeping scientist in the black-and-white film to Alicia's lying in the hospital bed. The links between the story and the act it symbolizes become increasingly clear through a series of close-up shots of the red shapes in the lava lamp which stands on Alicia's bedside table (a metaphor for her ovulation) just as Benigno ends his story with the words 'and the man would stay inside her forever' as indeed a part of him would stay in Alicia's womb. Despite the comic and potentially anti-phallic image of the little man, the consequences of the rape (it turns out to be a double trigger of life resulting in the pregnancy of the comatose victim and her consequent recovery) could suggest a phallocentric orientation. As in the previous Almodóvar films analysed so far, it could be argued that the hiding of the penis (which here remains wrapped up in humour and metaphoric representation) and the coded references to its indispensability to women's lives (the sleeping beauty awakes with the intervention of the not-so-charming prince) are problematic. Conversely, in *Volver* (2006) the male organ is symbolically loaded with negativity. Raimunda's (Penélope Cruz) gaze at the corpse of her dead husband Paco (Antonio de la Torre) and the amount of blood apparently emanating from his genital area could suggest that Raimunda's daughter Paula (Yohana Cobo) castrated her mother's partner in an act of self-defence against a rape attempt. The excessive sexuality embodied by Paco (and by Raimunda's incestuous father before him) disturbs the mother–daughter relationship and, arguably threatens the all-female relationships that the film so vividly celebrates. In contrast, male subjectivity is literally frozen up or burnt for most of the film – Paco's corpse is kept in the freezer and eventually buried in it, while Raimunda's father dies in a fire.

Although *La mala educación/Bad Education* (2004), arguably surpasses the levels of attention to the male body as spectacle reached with *La ley, ¡Átame!* or *Carne*, it pointedly avoids the full-frontal nudity of the latest 'chico Almodóvar' Gael García Bernal, whose naked body is explicitly referred to in the script as 'a spectacle' (Almodóvar 2004: 86).[28] In one key scene – referred to in Chapter 6 – director Enrique Goded (Fele Martínez) and aspiring actor Juan/Ángel (Bernal) discuss the latter's casting for Goded's new film at the director's house. The homoerotic tension increases when they decide to have a swim in the pool, with the director plunging in first, completely naked. Apart from the familiar symbolic value of water as sexuality, the image of men bathing together in the nude reinforces the homoerotic quality of this episode by playing with an iconic scene familiar in many queer literary classics from Whitman to E. M. Forster (also celebrated in films such as the 1980s Merchant-Ivory adaptations of Forster or, more recently, 'coming out movies' such as *Get Real* (dir. Shore, 1999)).[29] In that scene, Goded watches Juan/Ángel get undressed. As if the implications of the low-angle shot were not clear enough, the script spells out that, from the pool, 'Ángel's figure acquires idolesque dimensions' (Almodóvar 2004: 86). Interestingly, in the context that we have been discussing in this chapter so far, on perceiving Enrique's admiring gaze, Ángel decides to leave on one piece of clothing only: his underpants, thus interrupting Enrique's (and the audience's) visual pleasure at such a 'spectacle'. Teasingly, the effect is further exploited first with a series of extreme close-ups of Enrique's wet pants as he comes out of the water and then when, with his back to the camera, he puts his jeans back on without underwear and leaves the top buttons undone, revealing his pubic hair.[30] As the script adds later, 'the genitals stick to the wet underwear provoking a more obscene effect than if (Ángel) were completely naked' (Almodóvar 2004: 87), a statement that, as is typical in the work of Almodóvar to date, appears to support the hypothesis of the visual representation of the penis with which we opened this chapter, that 'the phallic mystique relies on either keeping it hidden from sight (…) or carefully regulating its representation' (Lehman 1993: 28). Yet, as we have seen in the other examples analysed in the first half of the chapter, the more overt display of the penis does not necessarily undo the phallic mystique that so clearly dominates most of the narratives studied. It is perhaps the most casual and/or justified display of the penis, either flaccid or erect, as we have seen in *Cachorro*, that could contribute to deflate its phallic connotations. It is only on the rare occasions in which the display of the penis in a film is not presented as a big issue (either diegetically or in the promotion of the film) that such connotations can be truly overcome.

Notes

CHAPTER 1

1   See Pavlović (2003: 84–85), Jordan 2003a and Martínez-Expósito 2004a for recent readings of this film in the context of *landismo*. The film is also briefly discussed in the context of gender and sexuality in Chapters 5 and 6 of this book.

2   Earlier, in *El año de las luces/Year of Enlightenment* (dir. Trueba, 1986) Sanz's body had been equally portrayed as the desirable centre of attention of young and older women alike in the repressed environment of the post-Civil War years. As Perriam notes, in the film Manuel's (Sanz) body is 'monitored, measured, self-recorded, sized-up and eventually spelled' (2003: 148). In *La niña de tus ojos/The Girl of Your Dreams* (dir. Trueba, 1998) with the backdrop of Nazi Germany, he plays a Spanish actor who unwontedly becomes the object of desire of a homosexual German counterpart (see Chapter 7). Critics have argued that some of these films use present-day gender and sex politics to re-interpret older Iberian approaches to gender (see Evans 1999; Jordan 1999a and 1999b or D'Lugo 1998).

3   As Perriam has found, however, this objectification is kept within the 'safe' boundaries of heterosexuality and 'homophobia (...) rises to the surface when Sanz's character finds himself in some extreme situation that is demanded of him as performer' (2003: 164).

4   This road-movie type of film, narrating the adventures of a group of friends in a long stag party, is a clear precursor of Santiago Segura's *Torrente* saga, given the film's exploitation of scatological humour (one of the key motivations of the characters is to get back the groom's wedding ring, accidentally 'lost' in the anus of a prostitute) and politically incorrect vocabulary.

5   The other two films of the trilogy are *Huevos de oro/Golden Balls* (1993) and *La teta y la luna/The Tit and the Moon* (1994). See Fouz-Hernández 1999 for a discussion of the male body in *Huevos de oro* and D'Lugo 1997, Smith 2000b and Martínez-Expósito 2002 for *La teta y la luna*. The trilogy was immediately followed by another trilogy in which female stereotypes were more clearly explored.

6   Famously, in a friendly challenge prior to the release of *Torrente 1*, Segura and Bajo Ulloa agreed to have the title of the film with the highest audience figure tattooed on the body of the loser (Salgueiro 1998: 50).

7   See Rabalska 1999 for an interesting study of the taste for the grotesque in Spanish cinema. Pavlović 2003 is also a thorough study of the 'transgressive

body' in Spanish cinema during Franco and especially in relation to director Jess Franco.

8   See Fouz-Hernández (2005a) for a comparative analysis of Bardem's roles in *Before Night Falls* and *Jamón, Jamón*.

9   It must be noted that, despite the apparently obvious American connotations of the Coke ring, Bigas Luna has declared that 'today one cannot talk about Coke as a symbol of invasion. Coke has become a typical drink in any typical Spanish bar and therefore is part of our everyday lives' (Rafat 1992: 131).

10 This control is not necessarily a reflection of the narrative control which, for critics such as D'Lugo (1995: 70), Deleyto (1999) or Evans (2004: 94), belongs to the women. Others like Isolina Ballesteros condemn the film's emphasis on phallic order and stereotyping of women (2001: 197) or note the typically homosocial framework by which 'the women remain vehicles through which the men measure and examine their effectiveness in relations between each other' (Jordan and Morgan-Tamosunas 1994: 62).

11 As Evans notes, both the Osborne bull's genitals and the similarly shot and equally chipped sign of the road sex club insist on the concept of love and sex as commercial transactions (2004: 40).

12 Bigas Luna was one of the loudest defenders of the bull, arguing that it was a symbol that had trespassed its originally commercial message to become part of Spanish history and 'of similar interest that a Romanic church might have' (Lorenzo 1994: 98). When the authorities announced the removal of all the remaining silhouettes from Spanish hilltops, he offered to buy them and plant them on a specially created theme park at Los Monegros (where *Jamón* was shot) so that people could see them (Estrada 1994: 50).

13 The story of the so-called '*indulto del toro*' ('pardon of the bull') is proudly recounted in great detail in the Osborne website <http://www.osborne.es>. Ironically, and despite its Spanish design of the bull and markedly Spanish connotations, the Osborne company itself was founded in the late eighteenth century in Cádiz by an Englishman.

14 As noted by Sánchez Vidal (quoted in Deleyto 1999: 282) and Marvin D'Lugo (1995: 75) bullfighters come traditionally from humble origins and their success can also be interpreted as a symbol of the cross-class quality so characteristic of Spanish society. Indeed, the history of bullfighting is also revealing here: originally associated with royalty and aristocracy (one of the earliest references comes from the *Poem of the Cid* in the context of a royal wedding), it then became part of religious and academic rituals and its origins as a spectacle with large paying crowds can be traced to the mid-eighteenth century in what Shubert regards as a modern form of commercialized mass leisure comparable to those emerging elsewhere in the West (1999: 7–15). There is an element of cross-class aspirations in Raúl's identity, who indirectly 'sells' his body to businesswoman Conchita in order to get a Yamaha bike and a Mercedes car, both also symbols of globalizing consumerism and metaphors for the commodification of his own body.

15 The notion that the close-up shots of the male genitals serve to reinforce the men's virility whilst similar shots of female body parts work to undermine the female body is not fully justified by Aguilar (1998: 128). As we shall see in Chapter 8 such attention to the male parts is extremely rare and often disempowering.

16 These are perhaps some of the answers to Aguilar's question as to 'why do films take for granted that women's buttocks are of interest to audiences (including female spectators) and do not consider that male buttocks can be equally attractive?' (1998: 131). Here, her assumption of the heterosexuality of the audience seems to work against the contestation of the (male) gendered gaze.

17 As Deleyto notes, José Luis finally tears off the bull's genitals when he breaks up with Silvia, who then uses them to protect herself from the rain as she walks away from him and towards Raúl (1999: 282). Interestingly, the slot machine that Raúl is playing with when Silvia finally gives in to his advances is considerably larger than the one that José Luis uses in his room in the company of his mother in the bedroom scene discussed earlier. This comparison is paralleled in the final fight scene in which Raúl accidentally kills José Luis by hitting him with an appropriately big and thick phallic ham, which is also bigger than the thin ham bone seized by his victim (as noted by Holder 1998: 35). Incidentally, José Luis's blow on Raúl's genitals further emphasises the parallelism with the (now castrated) bull.

18 'The Spanish Hero is Back' was the ironic slogan used to promote *Torrente 2*.

19 We are aware that these figures are based on national film audiences and, as we have argued, the importance of the Bigas Luna's films lies in their relative success abroad and also to their consumption on video and DVD.

20 The Miró Law was underpinned by a subsidy system that supported the production of 'quality' art films and sought to improve the impact of Spanish cinema within Europe (see Jordan 2003b: 194–195 and Esquirol and Fecé 2001: 37–39).

21 Although Bardem's days as a *macho ibérico* typecast had long been over by 1998, his mother remembers that one of the actor's happiest memories was the day he was asked to paint his teeth black for a role in *Días Contados/Running Out of Time* (dir. Uribe, 1994). Such fictional deterioration of his physique proved to be a milestone for his career beyond the Bigas Luna roles that made him famous (Castellano and Elola 1997: 38) such as the overweight unemployed man he plays in *Los lunes al sol /Mondays in the Sun* (dir. León de Aranoa, 2002).

22 *Españolada* is a term often used to refer to the popular Spanish films of the 1950s and 1960s.

23 References to the dictatorship are frequent: Torrente and some other characters make dismissive remarks about the Spanish Constitution and autonomous system. There are jokes about the Spanish King (Torrente gets a fancy for a portrait of the king but only because he was interested in the frame and wants to replace it with a picture of a naked woman) and nice remarks made about the Francoist-style Spanish flag. In *Torrente 2* the detective's dog is called Franco. When he dies (killed by some criminals) Torrente has a monument made for him in sand, in the shape of the Valle de los Caídos where the Spanish dictator is buried.

24 Similar scenes of physical violence and abjection are also common in *Torrente 2* where a man also loses his ear due to (Torrente's) gunshot, another man is crushed by his motorbike (it falls from a tree after an accident) and another one crashes onto the floor from a hotel balcony, to mention but a few examples. This violence is often directed at non-Spanish men, such as the Chinese men in *Torrente 1* or the Korean men that are used as human targets to try out a professional hit-man in *Torrente 3*.

25 For a Freudian reading of this scene see Triana-Toribio 2004: 154–155, where she analyses the fetishization of Amparito's 'Spanish' body in conjunction with 'the fetishistic nature of nationalism and allegiance to football clubs' (154).

26 Torrente is less successful in his advances to a beautiful singer (Inés Sastre), who expresses loud and clear that she finds him repulsive. However, at the beginning of the film he is seen constantly surrounded by women (until he loses all his money at a Bingo hall).

27 Marbella is a Spanish holiday resort frequented by the rich and famous and more recently known for the corruption of its administration (a large number of high-ranking council officials were incarcerated during 2006). It is also associated with the city's late mayor Jesús Gil y Gil (and also manager of the Atleti) and a controversial figure on Spanish media. Arguably some aspects of Torrente are inspired by him.

28 This reading of Segura can be taken more literally in one of the many incarnations that were to come. In *El asombroso mundo de Borjamari y Pocholo/The Amazing World of Borjamari and Pocholo* (dirs Cavestany and López Lavigne, 2004) he plays a forty-something posh kid has-been stuck in the 1980s, still reading for the degree he started twenty years earlier and living at home with his parents and inseparable brother.

CHAPTER 2

1 Baca Lagos points out that whilst youth represented only 24.4% of the total Spanish population in 1991, young people featured on 67% of Spanish advertising and 59% of Spanish television programmes (1998: 39–40).

2 Data based on the 2001 census (see Aguirre Gómez Corta 2005: 26).

3 The emphasis of the *Revista* is largely sociological, although, more recently, an issue (64) has been devoted to Spanish youth cultures (Freixa 2004). Authors such as Gil Calvo (1985) or Baca Lagos (1998) have also addressed issues of youth culture and its representation in the Spanish mass media.

4 On early Almodóvar and 1980s Spanish youth culture see Allinson 2000 and Triana-Toribio 2000.

5 See Ballesteros 2001: 232–269 for a thorough analytical review of key Spanish films about youth in the 1980s and 1990s.

6 'Generation X' is a North American term used to describe the baby-boomers in the early 1990s but also applied to the Spanish coetaneous generation and particularly writers such as Mañas or Ray Loriga – see Perriam, Thompson, Frenk and Knights

2000. The film and the novel are discussed in detail in Deveny 1999: 212–217; Fouz-Hernández 2000; Ballesteros 2001: 256–262; Moreiras Menor 2002: 214–229; Faulkner 2004: 67–72 or (mainly the film) Smith 2006: 75–90.

7 Whilst there is little room to discuss the issue of clubbing and dancing here, we should nonetheless note the relevance of dance and other types of physical movement for the study of the young body (see Malbon 1998).

8 Stanley also discusses the importance of speed as a marker of youth resistance which, like certain forms of dancing, works as a unifying resistance to the fixing gaze of society (Stanley 1995: 113).

9 See Martínez-Expósito (1998a: 42) for a discussion of Fierro (Pedro's name in Mañas's novel) in relation to homosexuality, weakness and illness. This argument is also developed with regards to other films in Chapter 5 of this book.

10 *Barrio* and *El Bola* had audiences of over 700,000, *Krámpack* just under 200,000 – very few Spanish films reach audiences over one million. Both *Barrio* and *El Bola* received Spanish academy awards – three and four respectively – as well as other awards in the prestigious San Sebastián film festival, whilst *Krámpack* received two awards at the Málaga Festival and various recognitions abroad.

11 León de Aranoa was born in 1968, Gay in 1967 and Mañas in 1966.

12 In the words of the director, *Krámpack* is an untranslatable and non-existent word that refers to an act of intimate friendship – not necessarily physical (Armengol 2003).

13 Unaccomplished pleasure is a running theme in *Barrio*, also symbolized by the jet ski and the constant contrast that is established between fantasy and reality.

14 Edley and Wetherell (1996: 100) make the first of these points in relation to male violence about their female partners.

15 One of the most striking similarities between these three films is the prominent presence of the rail tracks and the railway system in all three of them: shots of the tracks open and close *El Bola*, the rail station is the setting of the opening and one of the final scenes of *Krámpack* and the tracks also appear in the opening credits of *Barrio* (see Fouz-Hernández 2006 for an interpretation of the track imagery in the three films and Marsh 2003 for a reading of the city and tracks in *Barrio*).

16 We are aware that the old-fashioned active/passive hierarchy runs against post-modern conceptions of fluidity celebrated by queer movements. As Mercer has argued, the potential active connotations of the so-called 'passive' sexual role should not be underestimated (2003: 286).

17 Another classic element of the Hollywood teen movie, the romantic story, is also developed here: Dani – Gorka Moreno – and anorexic girl Gloria – Maite Jauregui – show their commitment to each other with a pact: she will eat as long as he agrees to have the chemotherapy treatment that he so much fears.

CHAPTER 3

1   For Jeffords, the metaphorical value of the Hollywood hard male body as being indicative of the nation's international power and strength was undeniably linked to US foreign policy during the Reagan administration (1994: 25). The metaphorical relationship between hard body and powerful image of the nation could be traced to the Spanish Crusade films of the 1940s; but, as we shall discuss later in this chapter, this metaphor works very differently in a Spanish contemporary film, partly because that nation is rarely perceived as 'powerful' in the techno-military sense, partly because the American appropriation of the metaphor was received by Spanish audiences with sarcasm (a reaction not disconnected from a critical view of 'muscular cinema' as 'dumb movies for dumb people', as Tasker has put it – 1995: 230).

2   Chris Holmlund studies different kinds of impossibility in Hollywood bodies, such as the outrageous Schwarzenegger's muscles, Rosie Perez's mouth, the constrained and the invisible bodies of Asians, Latinos, old-age men (she recalls that for decades muscular Swedish actors have played Asian, Russian or Eastern European roles, but never Swedish). She rightly points out that normal, let alone ideal, bodies are far from being the statistical social average, and that that might be the origin of the desire inspired by Hollywood's impossible bodies (2002: 3).

3   For muscular masculinities in the action film of the 1980s, see Holmlund on 'masculinity as masquerade', Tasker on the marketability of the commodified male body, and Jeffords on the turn from the 1980s focus on muscularity to the 1990s focus on fatherhood (all three in Cohan and Hark 1995). These three highly coherent visions indirectly demonstrate that the way muscular masculinities are deployed in Hollywood films of the Reagan era depended largely on the national idiosyncrasy and political context of the time.

4   In Chapter 2, we referred to Vilches's acrobatic body in the context of the adolescent; in *Guerreros*, however, the reference frame is that of adult military life, and his body offers an interesting contrast with the more solid Eduardo Noriega.

5   See Chapter 1 for a discussion of this film in the context of the 'stereotypical body' and Chapter 5 in the context of homosexual representation.

6   The success of the *cuerpo Danone* campaign in Spain was such that the expression entered the common parlance as a synonym for a perfect-looking young body. The television spot presented a group of young men and women in tight gym attire, lazily savouring their yoghurts in an immaculately abstract interior that could well be a unisex changing room. Relaxing background music, slow camera movements, and a lateral bluish light that emphasized the perfectly toned, hairless bodies contributed to create a statuesque quality to the bodies, which seemed untouchable and out of reach. Part of the campaign's success was due to the growing popularity of fitness programmes and the increasingly acceptable notion that the body could be sculpted at will.

7   In *¡Átame!/Tie Me Up! Tie Me Down!* (dir. Almodóvar, 1990) there is an allusion to muscularity through the masochistic layout of the movie-within-the movie directed by Máximo Espejo (Francisco Rabal). The excessive body of the Phantom in that setting has been subjected to a multiplicity of readings, but, according to Harmony Wu, codes of genre and desire are 'insistently re-framed and frustrated' in the film (2004: 264).

8   The physical contrast established between Bardem's character and the American hunk in *Huevos de oro* is discussed in Chapter 1.

9   The topicality of the couple is highlighted by the slightly comic POV shot of Coronado at the worksite.

10 There are frequent allusions to iconic examples of the fantasy genre, such as the Indiana Jones trilogy (dir. Steven Spielberg, 1981, 1984, 1989), *Conan* (1982 and 1984), *Red Sonja* (dir. Richard Fleischer, 1985), *Hercules* (dir. Luigi Cozzi, 1983 – starring bodybuilder Lou Ferrigno, who played Hulk in several TV shows in the 1970s), *Blade Runner* (dir. Ridley Scott, 1982), and the Lara Croft character from the *Tomb Raider* videogame released in 1996 and its film adaptations in 2001 and 2003.

11 Other contemporary films that deal with conspiracy theories include *Atilano, presidente/Atilano for President* (dirs Santiago Aguilar and Luis Guridi, 1998) and *Más de mil cámaras velan por tu seguridad/More Than a Thousand Cameras are Working for your Safety* (dir. David Alonso, 2003).

12 Other Quixotic elements include the identification with his alter ego Beldar to the extent of considering his 'other' identity more real than his ordinary one; his confidence in fighting a moral battle against evil; his resorting to supernatural powers to explain what is happening to him; his awareness of having a simultaneous existence in more than one world; the presence of a Sancho Panza-type best friend; the invention of a Dulcinea (albeit a physical one); the fact that those evil forces he claims to fight do actually exist, although in a different form and shape; and the fact that he is eventually defeated.

13 The same troubled, vulnerable air was used for his second feature, *Carreteras secundarias/Backroads* (dir. Emilio Martínez Lázaro, 1997) and in *Krámpack* (dir. Cesc Gay, 2000) – see Chapter 2.

14 A second mirror scene takes place later on in the film, when Ramón sees the image of Beldar in the reflection of a glass-panelled bus stop. This time, all the shyness and incredulity of the earlier bathroom scene has gone, being replaced with a sense of pride and self-reassuring complicity between warrior and boy. Interestingly, the bus-stop scene includes an observer in the figure of an old lady waiting for her bus, who looks nervously at the seemingly extravagant boy, thus highlighting the gap between Ramón's complex solipsism and conventional reality.

15 The script was co-written by Aranda and Antonio Larreta. This co-production (Spain 70%, Italy 20%, Portugal 10%) had an official budget of 800 million pesetas (€49 million). It was a huge success, both in reception and in box-office results, in Spain in the 2001–2002 season. It won three Goya Awards and was considered as Spain's nomination for 'Best Foreign Film' at the Oscars.

16 The first time Felipe uses the term 'mad' against Juana is in the scene when Juana is breastfeeding her baby daughter. He insists that no princess does that, and that her behaviour is just startling. The second time, Felipe uses 'madness' as a shield to protect him from Juana's imprecations at having discovered him having sex with another woman. Clearly, both uses differ substantially from any psychological definition of madness according to modern usage.

17 Juana's animalization has not gone unnoticed. Martín Pérez (2004: 76) mentions several key episodes in this regard, such as Juana's sniffing of Felipe's bed and also one of her ladies-in-waiting, Juana's licking the sores on Felipe's dying body, several instances of sex devoid of romantic love, and her giving birth to a baby in a toilet with no assistance whatsoever – prompting one of the ladies to say that 'her Highness is like a cow' (Fernández Santos 2000: 76).

18 Martín Pérez's final assessment of Aranda's film is therefore cautionary: 'the representation of women in *Juana la Loca* can be viewed as possibly reactionary and regressive, in the sense that it returns to the old derogatory concepts of womanhood and is very far from being the "feminist" cinema in which Aranda would claim his films can be located' (2004: 82).

19 Owing to Cucinotta's popularity in Italy, the version of *Juana la Loca* released in Italy included more close-ups of her face during the Moorish dance scene.

CHAPTER 4

1   The following films offer examples of configurations of disability. Wheelchairs: *El Cochecito/The Wheelchair* (dir. Marco Ferreri, 1960), *El jardín de las delicias/The Garden of Delights* (dir. Carlos Saura, 1970), *Carne trémula/Live Flesh* (dir. Almodóvar, 1997); hospital beds: *La ley del deseo/Law of Desire* (dir. Almodóvar, 1987), *Solas/Alone* (dir. Zambrano, 1999); body paralysis: *Tras el cristal/In a Glass Cage* (dir. Agustí Villaronga, 1987), *Mar adentro/The Sea Inside* (dir. Amenábar, 2004); seriously injured or diseased: *El techo del mundo/World's Ceiling* (dir. Felipe Vega, 1995), *El mar/The Sea* (dir. Villaronga, 2000).

2   In October 2004, victims of the March 11 train bombings in Madrid demanded that major TV channels stopped showing images of the attacks. In the United States, images of wounded military personnel in Iraq have been tacitly banned.

3   Parvati Nair (2000: 91–94) has argued that García Berlanga's 'ambivalent' male characters representing the ordinary man could be read as an antidote against the rigid, erect, heroic heroes embodied by Alfredo Mayo and Alberto Closas.

4   See Leonard (2004) for a reading of gender issues in this film.

5   Allusions to ETA and Basque violent groups is inescapable from the logo of the '*Acción Mutante*' terrorist/disabled group (sketching a male figure in a wheelchair brandishing a shotgun, all in black against a five-point red star), and also from the graffiti that decorates some of the urban settings and the violent behaviour of the police forces wearing Spanish-flag badges against an unidentified mob. The televised

appearances of the '*Acción Mutante*' gang are also highly reminiscent of media coverage of ETA.

6   Whilst Conway's (2000) attempt to position the film within a modern paradigm of a disabled-friendly culture has the potential to inspire radical readings, de la Iglesia himself is far less optimistic: 'you make your movie thinking that it is going to anger many people who will recognize themselves in it and then it turns out that (...) no one notices anything and everybody applauds' (Heredero 1997: 483).

7   Carolina Otero, 'The Beautiful Otero', a Galician-born music-hall dancer, became an erotic legend in Europe during the *Belle Époque*. Kings of Spain, Belgium, Monaco, Russia, as well as many noblemen and aristocrats were known to be her lovers. She disappeared from public life at age 46 for fear of being seen aging. Mexican actress María Félix played that role in *La bella Otero/La Belle Otéro* (dir. Richard Portier, 1954).

8   Snuff movies are amateur horror films in which the victim is tortured and killed for real. Amenábar has said that a news item about this type of film found in a newspaper inspired the script (Rodríguez Marchante 2002: 49).

9   At least by this type of media, which is parodied throughout Amenábar's oeuvre. In *Tesis*, through the closing scene but also in the mock video message of Bosco (Noriega) to his missing friend Vanessa (whom, in fact, he had tortured and killed); in *Abre los ojos*, through the sensationalist report on 'crionization' and in *Mar adentro* through the manipulative news items about Sampedro's case.

10   Interestingly, Sofía and César are only framed together in the scenes in which Noriega's face is not deformed – with the exception of the scene which apparently opens the virtual reality part of the narrative in which Sofía picks him up from the street and gives him a kiss.

11   For an interpretation of the mirror in this film, see Perriam (2004a: 218–219).

12   Sampedro's story was prominent in the media throughout the mid and late 1990s, particularly in Galicia. The media attention persisted after his death owing to the legal battle that followed. Months after the events that ended his life, a document signed by over thirteen thousand people (all declaring their involvement to avoid the imposition of legal responsibilities on anyone in particular) was submitted to the court that instructed the case by a representative of the DMD (Asociación del Derecho a Morir Dignamente – Association for the Right to a Dignified Death) on 17 June 1998. This media interest was revived in 2004 by the film and continued during 2005 as a result of the film's success at home and abroad but also, because of an unexpected turn of events, Ramona Maneiro (dramatized as Rosa – the character played by Lola Dueñas – in *Mar adentro*), declared on live television that it was she who had assisted Ramón's suicide, thus temporarily re-opening the legal case (only closed on 17 March 2005 when it was confirmed that the case for prosecution had expired).

13   The release of *Mar adentro* in late 2004 provoked a controversial and yet productive and much-needed discussion of tetraplegia in the Spanish media (later renewed with the film's Oscar success and commercial DVD release in the first quarter of 2005).

The interview with Javier Romañach, President of the '*Foro de la Vida Independiente*' ('Forum for Independent Living') shown on the Spanish TVE-1 chat show 'Las Cerezas's on 22 March 2005 is a particularly interesting example. The purpose of the Forum for Independent Living struggle is ideologically opposed to the Asociación Derecho a Morir Dignamente (Association for the Right to Die with Dignity) that appears in the film. Romañach (a fairly independent IT graduate and technology specialist who has been living with tetraplegia for over 13 years) was defined in the show's website as 'the antithesis of Ramón Sampedro' (http://www.rtve.es/ tve/b/lascerezas/ last visited in June 2006). The show '*Las Cerezas*' ('The Cherries') was hosted by Julia Otero for one season only (November 2004 to June 2005).

14 Marsh attributes this particular feature of Liberto Rabal (his lips) to his character's echo of Marlon Brando (2004: 64). Note how Rabal, like Banderas before him and García Bernal since, was also labelled 'chico Almodóvar' by the Spanish media at the time of the film's release (as noted by Perriam 2003: 185).

15 The complicated structure of the two triangles involving Víctor and David with Clara and Elena is also susceptible to a queer interpretation following the Sedgwick (1985, 1991) model applied to *Historias del Kronen* in Chapter 2. The bond between the two rival men seems stronger than the one they separately establish with the woman. Clara's job as a teacher provides the perfect role as mediator through a process of teaching and learning that involves both men. Also, as Morgan-Tamosunas notes (2002) there is a clear Oedipal element in the relationship between Clara and Víctor established through a direct physical resemblance between Clara and Víctor's late mother (they met at the cemetery where he was visiting his mother's grave).

16 As Marsh notes, the 'Champion' billboard could be read as an ironic reference to the poster that in *Jamón, Jamón* used a close-up of Bardem's crotch to advertise underwear (Marsh 2004: 64) – see Chapter 1.

17 As we shall discuss in Chapter 8, muscle-flexing and press-ups are used by Almodóvar throughout his filmography, often as a way to mock the construct of masculinity implied by such demonstrative exercises but which the films arguably celebrate and perpetuate by making them part of the spectacle of the male body. This is the case of the exhibitionist client of Cristal in *¿Qué he hecho yo para merecer esto?* or Paul in *Kika*. In *La mala educación*, Enrique's press-ups accentuate his attractiveness, in one instance attracting the attention of an older admirer. On the phallic qualities of hard bodies see, for example, Easthope (1990) and Ian (1995).

18 There is an interesting visual parallelism between the television footage of David's Paralympics match – as watched by Víctor from jail – and the televised football match that David and Víctor watch together in this scene. It could be argued that this deconstructs the hatred contained in Víctor's gaze in the first of these instances through this shared interest in sport, whilst reinforcing their homoerotic attraction.

19 A parallel could be established with the other wheelchair-bound character in Almodóvar's filmography: in *¡Átame!* Máximo (Francisco Rabal) arguably gains artistic freedom because of his disability (Almodóvar interviewed in Pally 2004: 89).

20 As Morgan-Tamosunas also notes, the link established between Víctor's vulnerability and Elena's final infatuation with him (as well as the story of the initial rejection followed by the courtship and victory) is one of the factors that adds to the comparison often established between *Carne*'s Víctor and *¡Átame!*'s Ricky (2002: 192, 198 n 5).

21 It is worth mentioning that Bardem was replaced by Diego de Paz (a genuine paraplegic basketball player) for some of the difficult scenes.

22 As noted by Arroyo (1998: 50) and Perriam (2003: 109). Morgan-Tamosunas notes the fact that David ends up broken-hearted in Miami, thus providing a further link to Bardem's character in the Bigas Luna film (2002: 191).

CHAPTER 5

1 The book quoted is *La Mala Vida en Madrid. Estudio Psico-sociológico con dibujos y fotograbados de natural* by C. Bernardo de Quirós and J. M. Llanas Aguilaniedo (1901).

2 Interestingly, such features became associated with HIV-positive people (and particularly homosexuals) in the late twentieth century.

3 Simon LeVay (1996) reviews the history of scientific research into sexual orientation that goes from Ulrichs's and Hirschfeld's 'Third Sex' theory through to LeVay's own controversial findings about the relationship of 'brain structure' and sexual orientation.

4 *Party* was founded in April 1977 to be followed by other titles, such as *Hombre erótico* in 1979 or *Coverboy* as well as several magazines edited at the J.M.R. studios in Barcelona, such as *Visado, Código 4, ¿Qué?, ¿Te va?, Punto Rojo o Chicos*. These would eventually disappear and become replaced by Spanish translations of French and North American magazines (Petit 2004: 71–101).

5 The medicalization of homosexuality, as we pointed out earlier in this chapter, appears obliquely in de la Iglesia's films. At the beginning of *El diputado*, for instance, Roberto Orbea has a stomach problem and is taken to a hospital, where he meets a younger gay man with a testicular condition. Homosexuality itself is not the pathology they are shown to be suffering from.

6 Virtually the same narrative formula had already proved successful in the British hit *Shallow Grave* (dir. Danny Boyle, 1995), released a year earlier.

7 Spanish reviewers have consistently accused these films of opportunistic attempts to exploit the successful Almodóvar formula but devoid of the latter's work's subversive potential (see, for example, reviews from *El País* (Torreiro 1997: 32) or *El Periódico* (C., Q. 1997: 51)).

8 Interestingly, in contrast with the 'promiscuous' Dani, who is made to feel guilty owing to his sexual hyper-activity, Lucas's many sexual encounters with women are only gradually revealed towards the end.

9 The three gay flatmates are seen gazing at Lucas together moments after they meet him for the first time (they watch him leave the flat after their interview), then they voyeuristically observe him whilst he is asleep and finally, when he is lying dead in bed.

10   Early discourses on sexual inversion in a Spanish context are discussed by Cleminson 1995: 19–23 and 37–45.

11   These characters address each other in the feminine with a complicity that is common in some sectors of the Spanish gay scene.

12   Bardem gay roles include *Boca a boca/Mouth to Mouth* (dir. Pereira, 1995) and his Oscar-nominated performance in *Before Night Falls* (dir. Schnabel, 2000). Mollà had performed a series of gay roles in the mid-1990s, including the by now familiar *Historias del Kronen* (see Chapter 1) or *Perdona Bonita, pero Lucas me quería a mí*, discussed earlier in this chapter.

13   As Perriam notes, the X-rays of the opening credits are used to emphasize the film's promise to be 'an X-ray of the hidden issue of homosexuality' (2003: 114). The body silhouettes include a female one, but notably, the two men are seen embracing and touching their own and each other's bodies.

14   It should be noted that the English subtitles of the Spanish commercial DVD used for this analysis (Manga Films 1999) offer a misleading translation of the original 'me voy y vuelvo cuando esté bien', which is translated as 'I will come back when things get better' instead of 'I will leave and come back *when I am* better'.

15   *Amic/Amat* is an adaptation of Josep Maria Benet i Jornet's play *Testament*. See Zatlin (2001) for an analysis of the adaptation process.

16   The father/son relationship between Jaume and David is intensively played out. Beyond the obvious circumstances of Jaume's inability to have a child and the traumatic memory of David's father (who committed suicide), Jaume openly tells David, 'I fantasize that you are my son.' There is also an interesting visual parallelism established between these two characters and David's girlfriend with her mother. Scenes between mother and daughter are often immediately followed by similar shots of Jaume and David and similar conversations. On one occasion, just after the mother tells her daughter, 'I can help you,' Jaume repeats the exact same words to David. This parallelism is also a reminder of the huge age difference between the two men: Jaume could indeed be David's father.

17   It is ironic that the same actor would play the role of a priest strongly opposed to the idea of assisted death, in Amenábar's *Mar adentro* (see Chapter 4).

CHAPTER 6

1   For stereotyping, see Chapter 1. Some of these films, in particular *No desearás al vecino del quinto* have been the object of renewed critical interest in recent times (Jordan 2003a; Martínez-Expósito 2004a).

2   Marjorie Garber reminds us that the overestimation of cross-dressing 'as a phenomenon of our time' occurs equally in high culture and low (1993: 5).

3   Mirizio (2000) offers an analysis of the subversive values of transvestism, cross-dressing and transsexualism in contemporary Western societies.

4   Later in this chapter, we discuss the casting of this transsexual in the iconic film *Cambio de sexo*.

5   The most immediate effect of casting well-known non-transgender actors in transgender roles is the one of 'lack of authenticity'; in the more severe cases, unauthenticity can be seen as mere transvestism, but in a few cases an extraordinarily gifted actor has been able to make credible a character of the opposite gender (as was the case of José Luis López Vázquez as Doña Adela in *Mi querida señorita*). When a well-known actor is cast for an opposite-gender role (López Vázquez in *Mi querida señorita*) or a different sexuality (Fernando Esteso playing a camp homosexual in *Celos, amor y Mercado Común/Jealousy, Love and the EEC* (dir. Alfonso Paso, 1973)), the audience reacts to the public persona primarily, and takes notice of the character only in second place.

6   Commenting on the nature of transvestism in Almodóvar's films, Smith points out that as a distinctive sign of contemporary culture, transvestism has become ubiquitous and re-centred. 'A paradox arises, if transvestism has become ubiquitous, it has also remained invisible: the transvestite is not looked at, but rather looked through, thus erasing his/her own existence' (Smith 1999: 17).

7   As Garber points out, transvestism is, consciously or not, 'bound up with the story of homosexuality and gay identity' and 'homosexuality, itself taboo in many contexts, might be viewed as the repressed that always returns' (1993: 4–5).

8   Andersen's cinematic career has been marked by her iconic transsexualism and by the tendency (observable both in production techniques and in audience reactions) to interpret herself. In *Cambio de sexo* (already mentioned) and *La noche más hermosa/ The Most Beautiful Night* (dir. Manuel Gutiérrez Aragón, 1984), she plays characters that bear her own name. Andersen became one of the most recognizable 'chica Almodóvar' in the 1980s, featuring in *Matador* (1986), *La ley del deseo/Law of Desire* (1987), *Tacones lejanos/High Heels* (1991) and *Kika* (1993). She has also worked in post-Almodóvar comedies such as *Acción mutante/Mutant Action* (dir. Álex de la Iglesia, 1993) – discussed in Chapter 4, *Más que amor, frenesí/Not Love, Just Frenzy* (dirs Albacete, Bardem and Menkes, 1996) - discussed in Chapter 5 – and *Atómica/Atomic* (dirs Albacete and Menkes, 1997).

9   Interestingly, Bibí Andersen was not even considered by Vicente Aranda for the transsexual role in *Cambio de sexo*.

10   As Jordan and Morgan-Tamosunas argue, 'although Aranda regrets the imposition of a "happy ending" on this film, a 1990s re-reading of this resolution is perhaps more tragic and illustrative of the pernicious effects of the imposition of rigid models of gender and sexuality' (1998: 148).

11   As we shall argue later in this chapter, Pedro Almodóvar was more successful than his Tercera Vía predecessors in his attempt to fill the gap between high and popular genres.

12   The ambiguous documentary/fictional nature of some Spanish Transition films has also been observed in relation to *Vestida de azul/Dressed in Blue* (dir. Giménez-Rico, 1983), a transgenders' film which, according to Garland, 'plays with widely accepted

but problematic conventions of cinema (Documentary? Fiction?), proclaiming at the beginning, for instance, that all "the characters in this film are real. What you are about to see really happens to them," but then crediting the protagonists in titles à la star actors. As do the featured transsexuals, the film takes what it needs, mixing and matching, often foregrounding boundaries to question and transcend them' (Garland 1991: 100).

13 Smith has emphasized the unexpected iconic value that the film has achieved in retrospect: 'It is curious indeed, then, that such a marginal film, devoted to a niche market as minute as that of immigrant drags in the Catalan capital, should come to bear the symbolic charge of representing the entirety of the Spanish state at a crucial historical moment' (Smith 2003: 127).

14 *Ocaña* has been explicitly linked to Almodóvar's *Todo sobre mi madre*, in which 'Agrado's performance on-stage in Barcelona evokes the figure of Ocaña, but the Catalonian context is all but effaced in the film, and the political overtones of authenticity and spectacle so central to Ocaña's performances on the Ramblas are removed' (Garlinger 2004: 131 n.3).

15 The similarities of this plot line with the comedy *Switch* (dir. Blake Edwards, 1991), in which a chauvinist *macho* man (Steve Brooks) is killed by one of his girlfriends and then sent back from heaven to earth in the body of a woman so that he can see how women are treated by men like the one he once was, have not gone unnoticed. A more remote antecedent is *Goodbye Charlie* (dir. Vincente Minnelli, 1964), based on the homonymous 1959 play by George Axelrod. Marilyn Monroe rejected the leading role in Minnelli's film as 'not feminine at all' – a comment echoed three decades later by Cristina Marcos in reference to the Spanish film. The storyline is still exploited in recent English-language films such as the teen comedy *It's a Boy/Girl Thing* (dir. Hurran, 2006).

16 No English translation of this novel seems to exist; the title could be translated as *The Male Lesbian Lover.*

17 In this context, it is useful to recall that many of the interpretations of *Tootsie* deliberately focused on the nature and validity of its critique of the Western gender system. Marjorie Garber opens up her influential book *Vested Interests* with a necessary observation about the extent to which a popular comedy such as *Tootsie* could generate a relevant debate – an observation that could be easily extrapolated to some of the Spanish comedies mentioned in this chapter: 'the film, say detractors, is slick, mainstream, unthreatening, not really a critique of gender roles, opportunistic and exploitative, a cop-out (...). If it is not a critique of gender roles, that may be because it is a critique of gender itself as a category' (Garber 1993: 9).

18 Allinson agrees that this film typifies Butler's assertion that all gender is performatively constituted, but he also advances that the humour in Almodóvar's TG characters might be 'a protective mechanism against potentially hostile reactions' (Allinson 2005: 236).

19 In the prologue to the script book, Almodóvar confesses that the first draft was written in 1973 (Almodóvar 2004: 11). Smith places a description of the plot in the

frontispiece of his authoritative collection of Almodovariana, with a note about the source (copyrighted material deposited at the Biblioteca Nacional in Madrid, dated 1975), and a reference to Almodóvar's first attempt to use this material in *La ley del deseo* (Smith 2000a: 1).

20 For the purpose of this study of García Bernal's body it is not relevant for establishing a distinction between Zahara and Juan/Ignacio, although they belong to different narrative levels and Enrique Goded, logically, has never visualized Juan/Ignacio playing Zahara because he has only read the tale.

21 It should be noted, however, that perversion has been frequently used by many conservative critics to attack Almodóvar on moral grounds and the legitimacy of the term as an objective notion has therefore been seriously tarnished.

CHAPTER 7

1 Examples of increased academic interest are the Migration and Diaspora Cultural Studies Network (University of Manchester) and the numerous conferences about diasporic film, of which 'The Transnational in Iberian and Latin American Films' (University of London, April 2006) is but one example.

2 *Extranjeros de sí mismos/Aliens to Themselves* (dirs José Luis López Linares and Javier Rioyo, 2000) deals with the topics of internationalization and the reasons why young men to go abroad and fight for, presumably, ideals. Adopting a documentary format, it contains interviews with International Brigadists, Italian Fascists, and members of División Azul José Luis Pinillos, Miguel Ezquerra, Luis Ciges and Luis García Berlanga, and chronicles 'the probable reasons for a nationless combat, the meaning of wars in foreign soil by men who left their countries willing to pay with their lives' (Heredero 1999: 244). A similar attempt, albeit with passive rather than active émigrés, can be found in another documentary, *Los niños de Rusia/The Children of Russia* (dir. Jaime Camino, 2001), a series of interviews on the survivors of the Spanish republican diaspora.

3 A North African character labelled as 'foreign' by a native Spanish audience might be used as a cultural mirror by a North African migrant audience. Similarly, a Spanish-produced film with Latin American characters and themes might be branded 'foreign' by native Spaniards, even if set in a Spanish city, but perfectly 'domestic' by local Latinos who will derive pleasure from recognizing part of themselves on the screen. As examples of the first case, we could think of *Tomándote/Tea for Two* (dir. Gardela, 2000) (for an audience analysis see Flesler 2004) and *La fuente amarilla/The Yellow Fountain* (dir. Miguel Santesmases, 1999). *Cosas que dejé en La Habana/Things I Left in Havana* (dir. Gutiérrez Aragón, 1997) and *Flores de otro mundo/Flowers From Another World* (dir. Icíar Bollaín, 1999) or *Princesas/Princesses* (dir. Fernando León de Aranoa, 2005) are classical examples of the second.

4 This practice, common in modern Hollywood global products, is not entirely dissimilar from the Spanish practice during the last years of Franco's dictatorship,

when the need to export films was at odds with the regime's vigilance of domestic public morality.

5   We would avoid equating over-interpretation with more blatant cases of foreigner exploitation, which frequently leads to racism or xenophobia as demonstrated by the gross chauvinism of the *Torrente* saga (see Chapter 1), degrading neo-nazi racism in the tele-film *Diario de un skin/A Skinhead's Diary* (dir. Jacobo Rispa, 2005), and the surrealism of a French petoman in *La teta y la luna/The Tit and the Moon* (dir. Bigas Luna, 1994).

6   There is a clear evolution in the way Spaniards perceive foreigners in films. In the 1950s foreigners were seen as objects of desire and admiration; in the 1960s an ambivalent attitude of rejection and admiration arose towards Western tourists; in the 1980s, Europeans became a model whilst Gypsies and Moors were labelled as anti-models; in the 1990s the concept of foreignness was replaced by the more specific phenomenon of immigration (Ballesteros 2001: 206–207; Santaolalla 2005).

7   The presence of foreign actors in Spanish cinema has been well documented by Borau. Having been a prerequisite of many European and North American co-productions in the 1950s and 1960s, in more recent times the success of Spanish–Cuban co-productions has produced a more visible presence of Latin American stars such as the Cuban Jorge Perugorría and the Argentinean Federico Luppi (Borau and Heredero 1998).

8   Basque director Julio Medem has made of character saturation one of his distinctive auteur signatures. In his 1992 debut film *Vacas/Cows*, the third generation of the Basque Irigibel family is represented by Peru, who migrates to America only to come back years later showing obvious signs of Americanization, as a journalist to cover the Civil War in his native land. The character is played by the same actor, Carmelo Gómez, who also plays his father and his grandfather. In *Los amantes del círculo polar/The Lovers of the Arctic Circle* (dir. Medem, 1998), a similar device is used in the construction of the main characters (three actors for one character, as opposed to three characters for one actor in *Vacas*). On Medem, see Stone (2002: 158–182) and Stone (2007).

9   He gives a number of examples: 'whenever lack of verisimilitude leads us to see the performance of foreignness for what it is, a *performance*, the foreignness denoted by role or plot becomes merely nominal. If, in this context, the display of "foreignness" is perceived to be anything other than artificial, then such a perception may owe much to prejudices lying beyond the film's diegesis and in the spectators themselves' (Bonaddio 2004).

10   Among several examples, Labanyi examines *La Princesa de los Ursinos/Princess of the Ursinos* (dir. Luis Lucía, 1947), in which 'modern French fashions masculinize women (seductively) and feminize men (ridiculously)' (Labanyi 2004a: 41).

11   The recent evolution of the representation of the French, from an oppositional foreignness to a domestic other can be traced in films such as *La teta y la luna* (dir. Bigas Luna, 1994); *París Tombuctú* (dir. García Berlanga, 1999), and the Spanish–French co-production *L'Auberge Espagnole* (dir. Cédric Klapisch, 2002).

Evans points out that the French in films about the Peninsular War such as *Agustina de Aragón/Agustina of Aragon* (dir. Juan de Orduña, 1950) and *Lola la piconera/ Lola, the Coalgirl* (dir. Luis Lucía, 1951) could have been read in Francoist Spain as an instance of internal (Republican) as well as external otherness (Evans 1995: 217).

12 Bardem played Latino roles in *Perdita Durango* (dir. Álex de la Iglesia, 1997) and, in Hollywood, *Before Night Falls* (dir. Julian Schnabel, 2000) and *The Dancer Upstairs* (dir. John Malkovich, 2002).

13 The almost unanimous critical attention to the migrant issue in detriment to other forms of foreignness might have its explanation in the huge media pressure that, since the mid-1990s, has characterized the treatment of immigration. Sensationalist media stories about migrants' substandard living conditions, social tensions and criminality focus exclusively on migrants from Latin America, Africa and Eastern Europe, while Spain's patrolling responsibility for the Southwest border of the European Union receives unparalleled media coverage with stories of African nationals dying in the Gibraltar Straits and the Canary Islands (Molina Gavilán and Di Salvo 2001).

14 An interesting commentary about the republican diaspora can be found in *Soldados de Salamina/Soldiers of Salamina* (dir. David Trueba, 2003). The character of Miralles (Joan Dalmau) is a magical combination of memory and amnesia, willingness and forgetfulness. His sick, aged body is a palimpsest of mementos and lacunae. This film also makes an important contribution to the historical rehabilitation of lesbianism in contemporary Spanish culture (Martínez-Expósito 2006).

15 *Tierra/Earth* (dir. Medem, 1996), *La flor de mi secreto/The Flower of My Secret* (dir. Almodóvar, 1996), *El efecto mariposa/The Butterfly Effect* (dir. Fernando Colomo, 1995) and *Alma gitana/Gypsy Soul* (dir. Chus Gutiérrez, 1996).

16 In her analysis of *Flores de otro mundo* (1999), *Poniente* (2002) and *Extranjeras/ Foreign Girls* (dir. Helena Taberna, 2003), Ballesteros argues that these films undo negative assumptions about migrant women and avoid sexualizing them (2005: 9).

17 Nair explores the relation between gender and migration, in the belief that cultural memory, dislocation, disempowerment and Third/First-world differences may have an impact in the way gender is performed (Nair 2004: 105–106). Thus, in *En construcción*, a documentary about a radical transformation of Barrio Xino, one of Barcelona's inner city districts, 'post-colonial representations are weighted with the metaphorical and historical experience of displacement, relocation and mobility' (Nair 2004: 106).

18 This point is also developed by Nair (2004), Santaolalla (2005) or Molina Gavilán and Di Salvo. In reference to migration films of the 1990s, Molina Gavilán and Di Salvo point out that 'focusing on Spain's conversion from an exporter to a receiver of migrant workers, these films function as a fictional mirror in which Spaniards can critically look at themselves face to face with the racial, economic, national, political, religious and gendered Other' (2001). The connection between the films of the Spanish emigrants and the immigrants to Spain has been explored in some detail by Eduardo Moyano (2005) and Richardson (2002).

19 According to Pavlović, the first female nude in the cinema of the dictatorship occurred in the foreign version of *La pecadora/ The Sinner* (dir. Ignacio F. Iquino, 1954), with a Spanish actress, Carmen Lirio. The film represented, in the words of Pavlović, the 'contradictions and connections among secrecy, cinema, pornography, and sexuality' (2003: 68).

20 References to the 'sexy' comedies of the 1970s are made explicit in the film, e.g. *Adiós, cigüeña, adiós/Goodbye, Stork, Goodbye* (dir. Manuel Summers, 1971), *No desearás al vecino del quinto/Thou Shalt Not Covet Thy Fifth Floor Neighbour* (dir. Ramón Fernández, 1970), *Lo verde empieza en los Pirineos/Smut Starts at the Pyrenees* (dir. Vicente Escrivá, 1973).

21 For instance, Flesler (2004) establishes a chronological evolution in the Muslim migration film from the main preoccupation with stories of difficult arrival in films of the 1990s such as the already-mentioned *Las cartas de Alou*, *Bwana* and *Saïd*, to a focus on the migrants' daily life in more recent films, such as the also-mentioned *En construcción*, *Poniente*, *Tomándote*, and *Susanna* (dir. Antonio Chavarrías, 1996).

22 She is always on top; the script is clear about it: 'La Niña embraces him. They kiss each other against the wall, la Niña always on top' (Bollaín and Medem 1997: 42).

23 In one of the scenes eliminated from the final cut (included in the DVD edition included in the 'Cine Español' series of Lola Films – released in 2005), Yamam is on top and allows for a medium shot of his buttocks with a slow pan camera movement. It is the only sex scene in which Yamam's body is given more prominence than Desideria's.

24 Some commentators make inferences about Yamam's penis. At their first encounter in the mosque, for instance, he puts her hand in his crotch; one Spanish critic concludes that she discovers 'the erect member' which represents 'a world beyond her husband's limitations' (Colmena 1996: 235–239).

25 This character, however, provides Desideria with the gun she will eventually use to shoot Yamam and, in the film's alternative ending, to kill herself. The minuscule size of the gun contrasts with the man's oversized, obese body, but also with the presumed size of Yamam's penis, and with the symbolic size of Desideria's desire/passion. There is ultimately a preoccupation with 'size' in the film that suggests a clear connection with unreconstructed, traditional notions of masculinity (as discussed in a wider context in Chapter 8).

26 According to Flesler, characters in migration films embody the cultures they come from; thus, Muslim men are 'conservative, oppressive to women' and Spanish women are 'liberated, modern, secular' (Flesler 2004: 108).

27 For the purposes of this commentary, it is irrelevant that Aranda shot an alternative ending in which Desideria ritualistically shoots herself in the mouth with the same gun she shot Yamam's crotch. However, the controversy in Spain about the director's cut was considerable; in recent DVD editions of the film (Lola Films 2005) both endings are included.

CHAPTER 8

1   A 'penis day' is still held every April 15th at Wakamiya Hachimangu Shrine in Kawasaki, and in New Guinea some tribesmen see the possession of a large penis 'as a sign of sexual prowess or status' (Dutton 1995: 236).

2   For a discussion of the Calvin Klein male underwear ads see Bordo (1999: 168–171). See also Jobling (2003) for a detailed analysis of male underwear advertising campaigns in the twentieth century.

3   For a discussion of *Sex and the City* see Akass and McCabe (2004).

4   Our point about the famous calendar of the French National Rugby team *Dieux du stade* (which, in its recent editions has had 'guest appearances' from other European teams) is that, whilst the bodies of the players are expectedly hard and the lighting and studied postures often contribute to reinforce their hardness and muscularity, many of the photographs seem to challenge phallocentric notions of male nudity. In full frontals the penises are flaccid and not particularly large. The setting, visual aesthetic and the poses are extremely homoerotic, particularly in those cases in which players pose in pairs. Phallic imagery is often used teasingly to imply that their bodies are less impenetrable than their hardness may appear to otherwise suggest. Pérez Gauli found that the famous 'Yacaré aftershave' telephone box posters were the first advertisements to use male nudity in Spain. The adverts caused a great impact by displaying life-size images of apparently full-frontal male nudity in very public and then frequently used spaces and yet, as Pérez Gauli demonstrates, the images created the illusion of full-frontal nudity: from a distance the genitals appeared to be visible since the upper and lower body were divided at waist height into two separate images pasted onto the upper and lower panes of glass. However, close up, it became clear that the genital area was not visible at all: it was obscured by the metal structure that provided a frame support for the glass in the old-fashioned Spanish phone box (2000: 51).

5   According to official figures released by the Spanish Ministry of Culture (www.mcu.es), *Arriba Hazaña* had an audience of 1,236,071 and *Ese oscuro objeto de deseo* 1,076,250.

6   Later on in this scene, a second penis is shown, flaccid and in long shot as a third man comes into the bedroom, fresh from the shower. The casual display of the penis of the third 'bear' in a flaccid state and removed from the sexual intercourse of his two friends deflates both the arguably phallic spectacle of the penetrative sex scene and also its eroticism (he rushes them to finish quickly and leave as he is expecting a family visit).

7   The musical numbers represent Marieta's many dreams and mostly involve her life as a woman, in excessively 'feminine' poses and situations. Marieta's narcolepsy provides an opportunity to give way to the dream sequences and musical numbers but it is also an appropriate reference to the gay classic *My Own Private Idaho* (dir. Gus Van Sant, 1991), where the character played by River Phoenix, also a male prostitute, suffers from the same illness. In both cases the illness also emphasizes the fragility of the

characters and their dependence on others (on a discussion of the phallus in *My Own Private Idaho* see Tinkcom 2005: 235–239).

8 This type of reaction is later exemplified by the job centre assistant or the neighbours who watch in amazement as Marieta has penetrative sex with her boyfriend later on in the film.

9 According to the actress, fitting the prosthesis (which had to be reduced to 17 centimetres) was a two-hour daily process. She described the prosthesis as 'disgusting' (Gómez Cascales 2005: 10).

10 Upa Dance is the name of the pop group that made Puyol famous (the band was tied in with a television series). The connotations of 'getting hard' here are both metaphorical (in reference to a new, hard-edge performance in his big break into film) but also, of course, a pun with the hardness of his penis, as suggested by the picture that illustrates the headline. In the interview he discusses his views on nudity and on being penetrated in the film (see Villa 2005).

11 We are referring to Guillén Cuervo's appearance in the popular late night TV show *Buenafuente* (Antena 3 television, 9 February 2005), where Santi Millán is a regular.

12 See, for example, Vernon (1995: 62); Smith (2000a: 2); Allinson (2001: 72) or Marsh (2004: 54). Almodóvar himself has frequently acknowledged this (see interviews by Llauradó 2004: 23–24 and Pally 2004: 90).

13 Mark Allinson – writing before the release of *Hable con ella* and *La mala educación* – refers to *Matador* and *La ley del deseo*, together with *¡Átame!* and *Carne trémula*, as the only films in which 'male characters really compete for the attention of the audience' (2001: 72). Perriam singles out *La ley del deseo*, *La flor de mi secreto* and *Carne trémula* as films in which Almodóvar 'pa[ys] unusual attention to the eroticized male body' of Banderas, Joaquín Cortés and Liberto Rabal respectively (Perriam 2003: 187).

14 It is important to point out, as Colmenero Salgado has done (2001: 38–39), that the label '*chica* Almodóvar' places too much emphasis on the director's 'agency' over the success of these actresses who, in most cases, already had a successful career before – and after – working with Almodóvar. It could be argued that the director owes them at least as much as they owe him. It is also worth noting here that, although the media has also used the term '*chico* Almodóvar' to refer to some of the actors that have worked with him, the male leads tend to change in every film with the notable exception of Antonio Banderas (who starred in five films in the 1980s and is rumoured to be working with Almodóvar again in the near future) and perhaps Imanol Arias (who appears in two films). Interestingly, two of the Spanish heartthrobs who have appeared in Almodóvar films (Miguel Bosé in *Tacones lejanos* and Toni Cantó in *Todo sobre mi madre* – rumoured to have been lovers in real life) play transvestite roles – see Chapter 6.

15 Although, as we have seen, Mulvey's theory has been largely superseded and it is perhaps not relevant for most contemporary films, *Pepi*, remarkably, was released only five years after the original publication of Mulvey's hugely influential article.

16 We are leaving gay men out of the equation in agreement with Dollimore's view that gay men 'opt out' of the competitive issue (1995: 237).

17 Beyond the unmistakably phallic curling iron and kendo pole (both in terms of shape and context), phallic imagery in this film is remarkable and includes, amongst other objects, 'mops and brooms, a rough wooden stick (...) a ham bone and a boom microphone' (see Epps 1995: 111).

18 The theme of bullfighting and sexual intercourse is developed in the first chapter of this book. Smith (2000a: 66) and Perriam (2003: 49) also make this connection in their respective readings of this film.

19 On phallic imagery and gender performance in this film, see Shaw (2000).

20 Almodóvar has argued that the media rape is even worse than the sexual rape itself. See Troyano (2004: 102). See also Martin-Márquez (1999: 32–33) on the narrative links with Powell's *Peeping Tom* (1960). Interestingly, she also discusses the issue of media exploitation as a form of rape not only in the fictional context of the film (in Andrea's programme), but by Almodóvar himself (37–39).

21 The procession of 'Los Picaos' exists in real life and has formed part of the Easter celebrations of San Vicente de la Sonsierra in the Northern Spanish region of La Rioja for the last five centuries. See Martínez-Expósito 2000 and 2004b: 195–213 for a discussion of the 'damaged body' in Almodóvar's films.

22 Notably, in the central sex scene of *¡Átame!* mentioned earlier, Banderas's character also has more than one orgasm in a row. However, unlike in this case, the semen is never seen because Marina asks him 'to stay inside'. In the light of Williams's theory, whilst *Kika* fulfils the expectations of hardcore porn (i.e. the audience is given proof that the orgasm has taken place for real), the sexual climax in *¡Átame!* draws attention to the impossible representation of the real thing: it is contained within the woman's body and therefore cannot be shown to the audience, becoming just another figure of lack (Williams quoted in Tuck 2003: 270).

23 We are by no means suggesting that the only interest in men in Almodóvar's work is of a physical nature but, rather, we want to draw attention to the aspect of his work that is most relevant here.

24 The process of Ángel's feminization was acknowledged by Almodóvar in an interview with Smith (2000a: 179). As Kinder notes (1997: 17), the physical identification of Leo and Ángel is pointed out by Leo's mother and is later illustrated by the fact that Ángel adopts Leo's pseudonym and writes for her in order to liberate her from a publishing contract.

25 Although according to Almodólvar's film notes (pedroalmodovar.es), the choice of Buñuel's classic *Ensayo de un crimen* (which is showing on Elena's television during the shooting scene) was accidental and due to purely bureaucratic and financial reasons (it was the final on his list of five), this reference has received much critical attention because its storyline has many parallels with *Carne* (Allinson 2001: 152). Buñuel's fetishist interest in legs and feet provides a visual reference to the accident that will result in David's disability just before it happens (the broken leg of the mannequin). The visual match of the broken leg in the film and Elena also anticipates the start of her relationship with a paraplegic by the end of the night. During Elena and Víctor's night of passion, she holds on to his legs. In his notes,

Almodóvar pre-empts any fetishistic reading of this by saying that it is a natural reaction of someone who is deprived of legs in her everyday sex life. However, the interest in Víctor's legs is clear: even one of the children at the home is told off by one of the teachers for holding on to Víctor's legs, jokingly suggesting that he is obsessed with them.

26 See Kinder (2004) for a detailed analysis of the female body in *La flor de mi secreto*, *Todo sobre mi madre* and *Hable con ella*.

27 The monumental *Nana* figure created by Niki de Saint Phalle, Jean Tinguely and Per Olof Ultvedt was inspired by the very same concept and with similar effects. The figure called *Hun* (Swedish for 'Her') measured 6.10 x 28.70 x 9.15 metres and was exhibited during the summer of 1966. Visitors could literally walk into *Hun*'s vagina and explore the inside of her body, which included a small cinema (in the left arm) showing Garbo's first film, a planetarium (in the breast), a 'Gallery of Fakes' (in one leg) and a payphone amongst other things (see Hulton 1995: 60–72). We are grateful to Christian Mieves for bringing this to our attention.

28 The label 'chico Almodóvar' was applied by the Spanish media to the Mexican actor at the time of the release. The weekend supplement of *El País* newspaper used the label on its front cover, playfully illustrated with a photograph of the actor... in drag (he plays a transsexual in the film-within-the-film). See Villoro (2004: 30–37).

29 This iconography is reinforced with a flashback in which we are shown a group of children bathing in a river – again, highly associated with sex and, in this case, sexual abuse of children by a priest.

30 As observed in the previous films, the absence of penis shots contrasts with the presence of close-up shots of the character's buttocks.

Bibliography

Acevedo-Muñoz, Ernesto R. (2004) 'The Body and Spain: Pedro Almodóvar's *All About My Mother*', *Quarterly Review of Film and Video* 21(1), 25–38.

Aguilar, Pilar (1998) *Mujer, amor y sexo en el cine español de los 90*. Madrid: Fundamentos.

Aguirre Gómez Corta, Marta (2005) 'El porcentaje de jóvenes católicos practicantes cae a la mitad en cuatro años', *El País* (19 de enero), 26.

Ahrens, J. M. (1998) 'La colonia china boicotea el rodaje de una película sobre la mafia oriental', *El País* (20 de febrero), 1 and 3.

Akass, Kim and Janet McCabe (2004) *Reading Sex and the City*. London and New York: I.B.Tauris.

Alas, Leopoldo (1997) 'No existió el Edén, no hubo ni serpiente ni pecado original', *El Mundo* (1 de marzo), 47.

Alegre de la Rosa, Olga María (2003) *La discapacidad en el cine*. Barcelona: Octaedro.

Alfeo Álvarez, Juan Carlos (2000) 'El enigma de la culpa: la homosexualidad y el cine español 1962–2000', *International Journal of Iberian Studies* 13(3), 136–147.

Aliaga, Juan Vicente and José Miguel G. Cortés (1997) *Identidad y diferencia: sobre la cultura gay en España*. Barcelona and Madrid: Egales.

Allinson, Mark (1997) 'Not Matadors, not Natural Born Killers: Violence in Three Films by Young Spanish Directors', *Bulletin of Hispanic Studies* (Liverpool) 74, 315–330.

Allinson, Mark (2000) 'The Construction of Youth in Spain in the 1980s and 1990s' in Barry Jordan and Rikki Morgan-Tamosunas (eds) *Spanish Contemporary Cultural Studies*. London and New York: Arnold, pp. 265–273.

Allinson, Mark (2001) *A Spanish Labyrinth: The Films of Pedro Almodóvar*. London and New York: I.B.Tauris.

Allinson, Mark (2005) '*Todo sobre mi madre/All About My Mother*' in Alberto Mira (ed.) *The Cinema of Spain and Portugal*. London and New York: Wallflower Press, pp. 229–237.

Almodóvar, Pedro (2004) *La mala educación: guión cinematográfico*. Madrid: Ocho y Medio and El Deseo.

Armengol, Joseph M. (2003) '*Krámpack* o La Iniciació a la Masculinitat', unpublished conference paper presented at the Primera Convenció Catalana sobre masculinitats, diversitat i diferència conference, Barcelona (March).

Arnalte, Arturo (2003) *Redada de violetas. La represión de los homosexuales durante el franquismo*. Madrid: La esfera de los libros.

Arroyo, José (1992) '*La ley del deseo: a Gay Seduction*' in Richard Dyer and Ginette Vincendeau (eds) *Popular European Cinema*. London and New York: Routledge, pp. 31–46.

Arroyo, José (1998) '*Live Flesh*', *Sight and Sound* 8(5), 50–51.

Baca Lagos, Vicente (1998) *Imágenes de los jóvenes en los medios de comunicación de masas*. Madrid: Instituto de la Juventud.

Balibar, Etienne and Immanuel Wallerstein (1991) *Race, Nation, Class: Ambiguous Identities*. London and New York: Verso.

Ballesteros, Isolina (2001) *Cine (ins)urgente: textos fílmicos y contextos culturales de la España postfranquista*. Madrid: Fundamentos.

Ballesteros, Isolina (2005) 'Embracing the Other: Feminization of Spanish "Immigration Cinema"', *Studies in Hispanic Cinemas* 2(1), 3–14.

Bauman, Zygmunt (1995) 'The Stranger Revisited – and Revisiting' in Zygmunt Bauman (ed.) *Life in Fragments: Essays in Postmodern Morality*. Oxford and Cambridge, Mass.: Blackwell, pp. 126–138.

Bauman, Zygmunt (1996) 'Making and Unmaking of Strangers' in Sandro Fridlizius and Abby Paterson (eds) *Stranger or Guest? Racism and Nationalism in Contemporary Europe*. Stockholm: Göteburg University, pp. 59–79.

Belategui, Oscar L. (1998) 'Vecinos del éxito', *El Correo Español del Pueblo Vasco*, 'Viernes de evasión' section 190 (2 de octubre).

Benito Gil, Jesús (1987) *Entre el terror y la soledad: minusválidos en el cine*. Madrid: Editorial Popular.

Berthiers, Nancy (2001) 'Splendeurs et miseres du male hispanique: *Jamón, jamón, Huevos de oro* et *La teta y la luna*' in Nancy Berthiers (ed.) *Le Cinéma de Bigas Luna*. Toulouse: Publications Universitaires du Mirail, Cinespaña, pp. 53–72.

Bhabha, Homi (1994) *The Location of Culture*. London: Routledge.

Bingham, Dennis (1993) 'Warren Beatty and the Elusive Male Body in Hollywood Cinema', *Michigan Quarterly Review* 32(4), 148–176.

Bollaín, Iciar and Julio Medem (1997) *Hola, estás sola?* (Guión), Viridiana 15, 8–99.

Bonaddio, Federico (2004) 'Dressing as Foreigners: Historical and Musical Dramas of the Early Franco Period' in Antonio Lázaro-Reboll and Andrew Willis (eds) *Spanish Popular Cinema*. Manchester and New York: Manchester University Press, pp. 24–39.

Borau, José Luis and Carlos F. Heredero (1998) *Diccionario del cine español*. Madrid: Alianza Editorial, Sociedad General de Autores y Editores, Fundación Autor, Academia de las Artes y las Ciencias Cinematográficas de España.

Bordo, Susan (1999) *The Male Body: A New Look at Men in Public and Private*. New York: Farrar, Straus and Giroux.

Bou, Núria (2000) *El tiempo del héroe: épica y masculinidad en el cine de Hollywood*. Barcelona: Paidós.

Braidotti, Rosi (1994) *Nomadic Subjects: Embodiment and Sexual Difference in Contemporary Feminist Theory*. New York: Columbia University Press.

Butler, Judith (1993) *Bodies That Matter: On The Discursive Limits Of 'Sex'*. New York and London: Routledge.

C., Q. (1997) 'Tres amores imposibles', *El Periódico* (2 February), 51.

Califia, Pat (1997) *Sex Changes: The Politics of Transgenderism*. San Francisco: Cleis Press.

Calleja, Pedro (1993) '*Huevos de oro*', *Primera Línea* (agosto), 60.

Calleja, Pedro (1998) 'Torrente: policía, pervertido, racista, alcohólico, hincha del Atleti', *Primera línea* (marzo), 34–37.

Cash, Thomas F. (1997) *The Body Image Workbook: An 8-Step Guide for Learning to Like Your Looks*. Oakland: New Harbinger.

Castellano, Koro and Joseba Elola (1997) 'Javier Bardem: la sensibilidad tiene cara de bruto', *El País Semanal* 1100 (26 October), 32–42.

CIS (1999) *Los jóvenes de hoy*, Centro de Investigaciones Sociológicas, Boletín 19.

Clark, Kenneth (1960) *The Nude: A Study of Ideal Art*. Hardmondsworth: Pelican.

Cleminson, Richard (1995) *Anarquismo y homosexualidad. Antología de artículos de La Revista Blanca, Generación Consciente, Estudios e Iniciales* (1924–1935). Madrid: Huerga & Fierro Editores.

Cleminson, Richard and Francisco Vázquez García (2000) '"Los Invisibles": Hacia una historia de la homosexualidad en España, 1840–2000', *International Journal of Iberian Studies* 13(3), 167–181.

Cohan, Steven and Ina Rae Hark (eds) (1995) *Screening the Male: Exploring Masculinities in Hollywood Cinema*. London and New York: Routledge.

Collins, Jacquie and Christopher Perriam (2000) 'Representation of Alternative Sexualities in Contemporary Spanish Writing and Film' in Barry Jordan and Rikki Morgan-Tamosunas (eds) *Contemporary Spanish Cultural Studies*. London and New York: Routledge, pp. 214–222.

Colmena, Enrique (1996) *Vicente Aranda*. Madrid: Cátedra.

Colmenero Salgado, Silvia (2001) *Todo sobre mi madre Estudio Crítico*. Barcelona: Paidós.

Connell, R. W. (1990) 'An Iron Man: The Body and some Contradictions of Hegemonic Masculinity' in Michael A. Messner and Donald F. Sabo (eds) *Sport, Men, and the Gender Order: Critical Feminist Perspectives*. Champaign: Human Kinetics, pp. 83–96.

Conway, Madeline (2000) 'The Politics and Representation of Disability in Contemporary Spain' in Barry Jordan and Rikki Morgan-Tamosunas (eds) *Contemporary Spanish Cultural Studies*. London: Arnold, pp. 251–259.

D'Lugo, Marvin (1995) 'Bigas Luna's *Jamón, Jamón*: Remaking the National in Spanish Cinema' in José Colmeiro, Christina Duplae, Patricia Greene and Juana Sabadell Dartmouth (eds) *Spain Today: Essays on Literature, Culture and Society*. Hanover: Dartmouth College, pp. 67–80.

D'Lugo, Marvin (1997) 'La teta i la lluna: The Form of Transnational Cinema in Spain' in Marsha Kinder (ed) *Refiguring Spain: Cinema/Media/Representation*. Durham and London: Duke University Press, pp. 196–214.

D'Lugo, Marvin (1998) 'Vicente Aranda's Amantes: History as Cultural Style in Spanish Cinema' in Jenaro Talens and Santos Zunzunegui (eds) *Modes of Representation in Spanish Cinema*. Minneapolis and London: University of Minnesota Press, pp. 289–300.

D'Lugo, Martin (2004) 'El extraño viaje alrededor del cine de Almodóvar', *Journal of Spanish Cultural Studies* 5(3), 287–300.

Davies, Ann (2004) 'The Spanish Femme Fatale and the Cinematic Negotiation of Spanishness', *Studies in Hispanic Cinemas* 1(1), 5–16.

Davis, Lennard J. (1995) *Enforcing Normalcy: Disability, Deafness, and the Body*. New York and London: Verso.

Davis, Lennard J. (1997) 'Constructing Normalcy: The Bell Curve, the Novel, and the Invention of the Disabled Body in the Nineteenth Century' in Lennard J. Davis (ed.) *The Disability Studies Reader*. New York: Routledge, pp. 9–28.

Deleyto, Celestino (1999) 'Motherland: Space, Femininity, and Spanishness in *Jamón, Jamón* (Bigas Luna, 1992)' in Peter Evans (ed.) *Spanish Cinema: The Auterist Tradition*. Oxford: Oxford University Press, pp. 270–285.

Deveny, Thomas G. (1999) *Contemporary Spanish Film from Fiction*. Lanham, Maryland, and London: The Scarecrow Press.

Diario 16 [Unatributted] (1997) 'Bardem: paralítico por Almodóvar', *Diario 16* (12 de enero), 47.

Dollimore, Jonathan (1995) *Sexual Dissidence: Augustine to Wilde, Freud to Foucault*. Oxford: Oxford University Press.

Donapetry, Maria (2005) 'Juana la Loca en tres siglos: de Tamayo y Baus a Aranda pasando por Orduña', *Hispanic Research Journal: Iberian and Latin American Studies* 6(2), 147–154.

Dutton, Kenneth R. (1995) *The Perfectible Body: The Western Idea of Physical Development*. London: Cassell.

Dyer, Richard (1983) 'Seen to Be Believed: Some Problems in the Representations of Gay People as Typical', *Studies on Visual Communications* 9(2), 2–19.

Dyer, Richard (1992 [1982]) 'Don't Look Now: The Male Pin-Up' in *The Sexual Subject: A Screen Reader in Sexuality*. London and New York: Routledge, pp. 265–276.

Easthope, Anthony (1990) *What a Man's Gotta Do: The Masculine Myth in Popular Culture*. New York and London: Routledge.

Edley, Nigel and Margaret Wetherell (1996) 'Masculinity, Power and Identity' in Máirtín Mac and Gahill (ed.) *Understanding Masculinities: Social Relations and Cultural Arenas*. Buckingham: Open University Press, pp. 97–113.

Edwards, Tim (1994) *Erotics and Politics: Gay Male Sexuality, Masculinity and Feminism*. London and New York: Routledge.

Ekins, Richard (1997) *Male Femaling: A Grounded Theory Approach to Cross-Dressing and Sex-Changing*. London and New York: Routledge.

Elmer, Greg and Mike Gasher (eds) (2005) *Contracting Out Hollywood: Runaway Productions and Foreign Location Shootings*. Lanham, MD: Rowman & Littlefield.

Epps, Brad (1995) 'Figuring Hysteria: Disorder and Desire in Three Films of Pedro Almodóvar' in Kathleen M. Vernon and Barbara Morris (eds) *Post-Franco, Postmodern: The Films of Pedro Almodóvar*. Westport, Connecticut and London: Greenwood, pp. 99–124.

Esquirol, Meritxell and Josep Lluís Fecé (2001) 'Un freak en el parque de atracciones: *Torrente, el brazo tonto de la ley*', *Archivos de la filmoteca* 39, 26–39.

Estrada, Cristina (1994) 'El cine para mí es ficción, es mentira', *Ya* (5 de octubre), 50.

Evans, Peter (1993) '*Matador*': Genre, Subjectivity and Desire', *Bulletin of Hispanic Studies* 70 (3), pp. 325–335.

Evans, Peter (1995) 'Cifesa: Cinema and Authoritarian Aesthetics' in Helen Graham and Jo Labanyi (eds) *Spanish Cultural Studies: An Introduction*. Oxford: Oxford University Press, pp. 215–222.

Evans, Peter (1999) 'The Dame in the Kimono: *Amantes*, Spanish Noir and the Femme Fatale' in Robin Fiddian and Ian Michael (eds) *Sound on Vision: Studies on Spanish Cinema*. Bulletin of Hispanic Studies (Glasgow) 76(1), 93–100.

Evans, Peter (2000) 'Victoria Abril: The Sex Which Is Not One' in Jo Labanyi (ed.) *Constructing Identity in Contemporary Spain*. Oxford and New York: Oxford University Press, pp. 128–137.

Evans, Peter (2004) *Jamón, Jamón Estudio Crítico*. Barcelona: Paidós.

Faulkner, Sally (2004) *Literary Adaptations in Spanish Cinema*. Rochester: Tamesis.

Featherstone, Mike (ed.) (2000) *Body Modification*. London: Sage.

Fernàndez, Josep-Anton (2004) 'The Authentic Queen and the Invisible Man: Catalan Camp and its Condition of Possibility in Ventura Pons's *Ocaña, Retrat Intermitent*', *Journal of Spanish Cultural Studies* 5(1), 83–99.

Fernández Santos, Angel (1998) 'Javier Bardem' in 'Nuestro cine', *El País Semanal* (25 de enero), 1113, 20–49.

Fernández Santos, Elsa (2000) 'Vicente Aranda recrea los engaños y los celos que enloquecieron a Juana de Castilla', *El País* (22 de noviembre), 76.

Figueras, Jaime (2004) 'Javier Bardem: "tengo los pies sobre el suelo, calzo un 45"', *Fotogramas* (septiembre), 74–79.

Flesler, Daniela (2004) 'New Racism, Intercultural Romance, and the Immigration Question in Contemporary Spanish Cinema', *Studies in Hispanic Cinemas* 1(2), 103–118.

Flesler, Daniela (Forthcoming) *An Analysis of Spanish Responses to Current North African Immigration through Film, Literature and the Media*. West Lafayette, Indiana: Purdue University Press.

Foucault, Michel (1990 [1978]) *The History of Sexuality Volume I*, trans. Robert Hurley. London: Penguin.

Foucault, Michel (1991 [1975]) *Discipline and Punish: The Birth of the Prison*, trans. Alan Sheridan. London: Penguin.

Foucault, Michel (1992) *The Use of Pleasure (The History of Sexuality Volume II)*, trans. Robert Hurley. Penguin: London.

Fouz-Hernández, Santiago (1999) 'All that Glitters is not Gold: Reading Javier Bardem's Body in Bigas Luna's *Golden Balls*' in Rob Rix and Roberto Rodríguez-Saona (eds) *Spanish Cinema: Calling the Shots*. Leeds: Trinity and All Saints, pp. 47–66.

Fouz-Hernández, Santiago (2000) '¿*Generación X*? Spanish Urban Youth Culture at the End of the Century in Mañas's/Armendáriz's *Historias Del Kronen*', *Romance Studies* 18(1), 83–98.

Fouz-Hernández, Santiago (2003) 'Sociedad, Cultura, política y teoría gay en España: Entrevista con Ricardo Llamas', *Tesserae: Journal of Iberian and Latin American Studies* 9(1), 81–97.

Fouz-Hernández (2004) 'Identity without Limits. Queer Debates and Representation in Contemporary Spain', *JILAS: Journal of Iberian and Latin American Studies* 10(1), 63–82.

Fouz-Hernández, Santiago (2005a) 'Javier Bardem: Body and Space' in Wendy Everett and Axel Goodbody (eds) *Revisiting Space: Space and Place in European Cinema*. Oxford: Peter Lang, pp. 187–207.

Fouz-Hernández, Santiago (2005b) 'Male Bodies That Matter: Masculinity and Trauma in the Films of Alejandro Amenábar' in Robert Archer, Valdi Astvaldsson, Stephen Boyd and Michael Thompson (eds) *Proceedings of the AHGBI Annual Conference 'Antes y después del Quijote: en el cincuentenario de la Asociación de Hispanistas de Gran Bretaña e Irlanda'*. València: Biblioteca Valenciana, pp. 523–530.

Fouz-Hernández, Santiago (2006) 'Boys will be Men: Teen Masculinities in Recent Spanish Cinema' in Timothy Shary and Alexandra Seibel (eds) *Youth Culture in Global Cinema*. Austin: Texas University Press, pp. 222–237.

Fouz-Hernández, Santiago and Chris Perriam (2000) 'Beyond Almodóvar: "Homosexuality" in Spanish Cinema of the 1990s' in David Alderson and Linda Anderson (eds) *Territories of Desire in Queer Culture: Refiguring Contemporary Boundaries*. Manchester and New York: Manchester University Press, pp. 96–111.

Freixa, Carles (ed.) (2004) *De las tribus urbanas a las culturas juveniles. Revista de estudios de la juventud* 64 (March). Madrid: Instituto de la juventud.

Fuentes, Víctor (1995) 'Almodóvar's Postmodern Cinema' in Kathleen M. Vernon and Barbara Morris (eds) *Post-Franco, Postmodern: The Films of Pedro Almodóvar*. Westport, Connecticut and London: Greenwood, pp. 155–170.

Garber, Marjorie (1993) *Vested Interests: Cross-Dressing and Cultural Anxiety*. New York: Harper Collins.

García Cortés, José Miguel (2004) *Hombres de mármol. Códigos de representación y estrategias de poder de la masculinidad*. Madrid y Barcelona: Egales.

García Domene, Juan Carlos (2003) *Inmigración en el cine*. Murcia: Foro Ignacio Ellacuría.

Garland, David (1991) 'A Ms-take in the Making?: Transsexualism Post-Franco, Post-Modern, Post-Haste', *Quarterly Review of Film and Video* 13(4), 95–102.

Garlinger, Patrick Paul (2004) 'All About Agrado, or the Sincerity of Camp in Almodóvar's *Todo sobre mi madre*', *Journal of Spanish Cultural Studies* 5(1), 117–134.

Gil Calvo, Enrique (1985) *Los depredadores audiovisuales. Juventud urbana y cultura de masas*. Madrid: Tecnos.

Gómez Cascales, Agustín (2005) 'Mónica Cervera y Ramón Salazar: A escasos 20 centímetros el uno del otro', *Shangay* (23 de mayo), 10–12.

Graham, Helen and Jo Labanyi (eds) (1995) *Spanish Cultural Studies: An Introduction*. Oxford: Oxford University Press.

Guasch, Òscar (1995 [1991]) *La sociedad rosa*. Barcelona: Anagrama.

Halberstam, Judith (2005) *In a Queer Time and Place: Transgender Bodies, Subcultural Lives*. New York: New York University Press.

Haraway, Donna (1985) 'A Manifesto for Cyborgs: Science, Technology and Socialist Feminism in the 1980s', *Socialist Review* 15(2), 65–107.

Haste, Helen (1993) *The Sexual Metaphor*. Cambridge, Mass: Harvard University Press.

Heredero, Carlos F. (1997) *Espejo de miradas: entrevistas con nuevos directores del cine español de los años noventa*. Alcalá de Henares: Fundación Colegio del Rey.

Heredero, Carlos F. (1999) *20 nuevos directores del cine español*. Madrid: Alianza Editorial.

Hocquenghem, Guy (1993) *Homosexual Desire*. Durham: Duke University Press.

Holder, John D. (1998) 'Pata Negra: Goya's Cudgel Motif in Two Contemporary Spanish Films', *Donaire* (April), 31–36.

Holmlund, Chris (2002) *Impossible Bodies: Femininity and Masculinity at the Movies*. London and New York: Routledge.

Hopewell, John (1986) *Out of the Past: Spanish Cinema after Franco*. London: British Film Institute.

Hopewell, John (1989) *El cine español después de Franco, 1973–1988*. Madrid: El Arquero.

Hulton, Pontus (1995) *Niki de Saint Phalle* (exhibition catalogue). Bonn: Kunst- und Ausstellungshalle der Bundesrepublik Deutschland GmbH.

Ian, Marcia (1995) 'How do you Wear your Body? Body Building and the Sublimity of Drag' in Monica Dorenkamp and Richard Henke (eds) *Negotiating Lesbian and Gay Subjects*. London and New York: Routledge, pp. 71–90.

Jackson, Earl (1995) *Studies in Gay Male Representation*. Bloomington and Indianapolis: Indiana University Press.

Jacobi, Lora and Thomas F. Cash (1994) 'In Pursuit of the Perfect Appearance: Discrepancies among Self Deal Percepts of Multiple Physical Attributes', *Journal of Applied Social Psychology* 24(5), 379–396.

Jagodzinski, Jan (2003) 'Women's Bodies of Performative Excess: Miming, Feigning, Refusing, and Rejecting the Phallus', *Journal for the Psychoanalysis of Culture & Society* 8(1), 23–41.

Jeffords, Susan (1994) *Hard Bodies: Hollywood Masculinity in the Reagan Era*. New Brunswick and New Jersey: Rutgers University Press.

Jobling, Paul (2003) 'Underexposed: Spectatorship and Pleasure in Men's Underwear Advertising in the Twentieth Century' in Judith Still (ed.) *Men's Bodies, special issue of Paragraph* 26(1/2), 147–162.

Jordan, Barry (1999a) 'Promiscuity, Pleasure, and Girl Power: Fernando Trueba's *Belle Epoque* (1992)' in Peter Evans (ed.) *Spanish Cinema: The Auteurist Tradition*. Oxford: Oxford University Press, pp. 286–309.

Jordan, Barry (1999b) 'Refiguring the Past in the Post-Franco Fiction Film: Fernando Trueba's *Belle Epoque*', *Bulletin of Hispanic Studies* (Glasgow) 76(1), 139–156.

Jordan, Barry (2000) 'How Spanish is It? Spanish Cinema and National Identity' in Barry Jordan and Rikki Morgan-Tamosunas (eds) *Contemporary Spanish Cultural Studies*. London and New York: Arnold, pp. 68–78.

Jordan, Barry (2003a) 'Revisiting the comedia sexy ibérica: No desearás al vecino del quinto (Ramón Fernández, 1971)', *Internacional Journal of Iberian Studies* 15(3), 167–186.

Jordan, Barry (2003b) 'Spain's "New Cinema" of the 1990s: Santiago Segura and the Torrente Phenomenon', *New Cinemas: Journal of Contemporary Film* 1(3), 191–207.

Jordan, Barry and Mark Allinson (2005) *Spanish Cinema: A Student's Guide*. London and New York: Hodder Arnold.

Jordan, Barry and Rikki Morgan-Tamosunas (1994) '*Jamón, Jamón*: A Tale of Ham and Pastiche' in *Donaire* 2, 57–64.

Jordan, Barry and Rikki Morgan-Tamosunas (1998) *Contemporary Spanish Cinema*. Manchester and New York: Manchester University Press.

Jordan, Barry and Rikki Morgan-Tamosunas (2000) *Contemporary Spanish Cultural Studies*. London and New York: Arnold.

Kemp, Martin and Marina Wallace (2000) *Spectacular Bodies: The Art and Science of the Human Body From Leonardo to Now*. Berkeley, Los Angeles and London: University of California Press.

Kinder, Marsha (1993) *Blood Cinema: The Reconstruction of National Identity in Spain*. Berkeley and London: University of California Press.

Kinder, Marsha (1997) (ed.) *Refiguring Spain: Cinema/Media/Representation*. Durham and London: Duke University Press.

Kinder, Marsha (1997) 'Introduction' in Marsha Kinder (ed.) *Refiguring Spain: Cinema/Media/Representation*. Durham and London: Duke University Press, pp. 1–32.

Kinder, Marsha (2004) 'Reinventing the Motherland: Almodóvar's Brain-Dead Trilogy', *Journal of Spanish Cultural Studies* 5(3), 245–260.

Kristeva, Julia (1991) *Strangers to Ourselves*. New York: Columbia University Press.

Labanyi, Jo (ed.) (2002) *Constructing Identity in Contemporary Spain: Theoretical Debates and Cultural Practice*. Oxford: Oxford University Press.

Labanyi, Jo (2004a) 'Costume, Identity and Spectator Pleasure in Historical Films of the Early Franco Period' in Steven Marsh and Parvati Nair (eds) *Gender and Spanish Cinema*. Oxford and New York: Berg, pp. 33–51.

Labanyi, Jo (2004b) 'Lo andaluz en el cine del franquismo: los estereotipos como estrategia para mejorar la condición', *Documento de trabajo* H2004.02. Sevilla: Junta de Andalucía.

Lahti, Martti (1998) 'Dressing Up in Power: Tom of Finland and Gay Male Body Politics', *Journal of Homosexuality* 35(3–4), 185–205.

Laqueur, Thomas (1990) *Making Sex: Body and Gender from the Greeks to Freud*. Cambridge Mass and London: Harvard University Press.

Lázaro-Reboll, Antonio (2005) '*Torrente: el brazo tonto de la ley, Torrente: The Dumb Arm of the Law/ Torrente 2: misión en Marbella Torrente 2: Mission in Marbella,*' in Alberto Mira (ed.) *The Cinema of Spain and Portugal*. London: Wallflower Press, pp. 218–227.

Lehman, Peter (1993) *Running Scared: Masculinity and the Representation of the Male Body*. Philadelphia: Temple UP.

Lehman, Peter (2000) 'Crying Over the Melodramatic Penis: Melodrama and Male Nudity in the Films of the 90s' in Peter Lehman (ed.) *Masculinity: Bodies, Movies, and Culture*. London and New York: Routledge, pp. 25–41.

Lehman, Peter (2004) '"They Look so Uncomplicated Once They are Dissected"': The Act of Seeing the Dead Penis with One's Own Eyes' in Phil Powrie, Ann Davies and Bruce Babington (eds) *The Trouble with Men: Masculinities in European and Hollywood Cinema*. London and New York: Wallflower Press, pp. 196–206.

Leonard, Candyce (2004) 'Solas and the Unbearable Condition of Loneliness in the Late 1990s' in Antonio Lázaro-Reboll and Andrew Willis *Spanish Popular Cinema*. Manchester: Manchester University Press, pp. 222–236.

Lev, Leora (1995) 'Tauromachy as a Spectacle of Gender Revision in *Matador*' in Kathleen M. Vernon and Barbara Morris (eds) *Post-Franco, Postmodern: The Films of Pedro Almodóvar*. Westport, Connecticut and London: Greenwood, pp. 73–86.

LeVay, Simon (1996) *Queer Science: The Use and Abuse of Research into Homosexuality*. Cambridge MA: MIT Press.

Lingis, Alphonso (1994) *Foreign Bodies*. New York and London: Routledge.

Llamas, Ricardo (1995) 'La reconstrucción del cuerpo homosexual en tiempos de Sida' in Ricardo Llamas (ed.) *Construyendo Sidentidades. Estudios desde el corazón de una pandemia*. Madrid: Siglo Veintiuno, pp. 153–189.

Llamas, Ricardo (1997) *Miss Media. Una lectura perversa de la comunicación de masas*. Barcelona: Ediciones de la Tempestad.

Llamas, Ricardo and Francisco Javier Vidarte (2000) *Homografías*. Madrid: Espasa.

Llauradó, Anna (2004 [1983]) 'Interview with Pedro Almodóvar: *Dark Habits*' in Paula Willoquet-Maricondi (ed.) *Pedro Almodóvar Interviews*. Jackson, Mississippi: University of Mississippi, pp. 17–25.

Lloréns, Antonio and Pedro Uris (1996) 'Centímetros de cuerpo humano', *Academia. Revista del cine español* 13 (enero), 36–42.

Lombroso, Cesare (1876) *L'uomo delinquente in rapporto all'antropologia, alla giurisprudenza ed alle discipline economiche*. Milano: Hoepli.

Lorenzo, Javier (1994) 'Me interesa mucho la eñe', *Época* (24 de octubre), 98.

Lury, Karen (2000) 'Here and Then: Space, Place and Nostalgia in British Youth Cinema of the 1990s' in Robert Murphy (ed.) *British Cinema of the 1990s*. London: BFI, pp. 100–108.

Malbon, Ben (1998) 'The Club: Clubbing: Consumption, Identity and the Spatial Practices of Every-night Life' in Gill Valentine and Tracey Skelton (eds) *Cool Places: Geographies of Youth Cultures*. London and New York: Routledge, pp. 266–286.

Mangan, J. A. (2000) *Making European Masculinities: Sport, Europe, Gender*. London: Frank Cass.

Marsh, Steven (2003) 'Tracks, Traces and Common Places: Fernando León de Aranoa's *Barrio* (1998) and the Layered Landscape of Everyday Life in Contemporary Madrid', *New Cinemas* 1(3), 165–177.

Marsh, Steven (2004) 'Masculinity, Monuments and Movement: Gender and the City of Madrid in Pedro Almodóvar's Carne Trémula (1997)' in Steve Marsh and Parvati Nair (eds) *Gender and Spanish Cinema*. Oxford and New York: Berg pp. 53–70.

Marsh, Stephen and Nair, Parvati (eds) (2004) *Gender and Spanish Cinema*, Oxford and New York: Berg.

Martín Pérez, Celia (2004) 'Madness, Queenship, and Womanhood in Orduña's *Locura de amor* (1948) and Aranda's *Juana la loca* (2001)' in Steven Marsh and Parvati Nair (eds) *Gender and Spanish Cinema*. Oxford and New York: Berg, pp. 71–85.

Martin-Márquez, Susan (1999) *Feminist Discourse and Spanish Cinema: Sight Unseen*. Oxford: Oxford University Press.

Martínez, Antonio (2005) 'Fantasías homosexuales', *El País, Suplemento del domingo* (19 de junio), 15.

Martínez-Expósito, Alfredo (1998a) *Los escribas furiosos: configuraciones homoeróticas en la narrativa española*. New Orleans: University Press of the South.

Martínez-Expósito, Alfredo (1998b) 'Metáforas enfermizas: la representación del sujeto homoerótico en el cine español' in Túa Blesa (ed.) *Mitos: Actas del VIII Congreso Internacional de la Asociación Española de Semiótica*. Zaragoza: Anexos de Tropelías 1, pp. 169–174.

Martínez-Expósito, Alfredo (2000) 'Contempla mis heridas: el cuerpo mancillado en Almodóvar', *AUMLA: Journal of the Australasian Universities Language and Literature Association* 94 (December), 83–108.

Martínez-Expósito, Alfredo (2002) 'Ambivalencia, performatividad y nación en *La teta y la luna*, de José Juan Bigas Luna', *Garoza 2*, 16–85.

Martínez-Expósito, Alfredo (2004a) 'Visibility and Performance in the Anti-gay Sexy Spanish Comedy: "No desearás al vecino del quinto" (1970)' in Stewart King and Jeff Browitt (eds) *The Space of Culture: Critical Readings in Hispanic Studies*. Newark: University of Delaware Press, pp. 12–28.

Martínez-Expósito, Alfredo (2004b) *Escrituras torcidas: ensayos de crítica 'queer'*. Barcelona: Laertes.

Martínez-Expósito, Alfredo (2004c) 'Construcción visual de la homosexualidad en el cine español de los años noventa' in Roy Osegueda Boland (ed.) *Place, Memory, Identity: Australia, Spain and the New World*. Melbourne: La Trobe, pp. 113–126.

Martínez-Expósito, Alfredo (2006) 'Signification et fonction du lesbianisme dans Les Soldats de Salamine (2003) de David Trueba', *Inverses 6*, 145–162.

Mazzara, Bruno M. (1999) *Estereotipos y prejuicios*, trans. Olga Pinasco. Madrid: Acento Editorial.

Melero Salvador, Alejandro (2004) 'New Sexual Politics in the Cinema of the Transition to Democracy: de la Iglesia's *El Diputado*' in Steven Marsh and Parvati Nair (eds) *Gender and Spanish Cinema*. Oxford and New York: Berg, pp. 87–102.

Méndez, Lourdes (2004) *Cuerpos sexuados y ficciones identitarias: ideologías sexuales, reconstrucciones feministas y artes visuales*. Sevilla: Instituto Andaluz de la Mujer.

Mendicutti, Eduardo (1993) *Los novios búlgaros*. Barcelona: Tusquets.

Mercer, John (2003) 'Homosexual Prototypes: Repetition and the Construction of the Generic in the Iconography of Gay Pornography' in Judith Still (ed.) *Men's Bodies, Paragraph* 26(1/2), 280–290.

Mericka Etxebarría, Antón (1994) 'Javier Bardem: el cine en vena', *El Correo Español* (2 de octubre), 4.

Michalko, Rod (1946) *The Difference That Disability Makes*. Philadelphia: Temple University Press.

Mira, Alberto (2004a) *De Sodoma a Chueca: una historia cultural de la homosexualidad en España en el siglo XX*. Madrid: Egales.

Mira, Alberto (2004b) 'Spectacular Metaphors: The Rethoric of Historical Representation in Cifesa Epics' in Antonio Lázaro-Reboll and Andrew Willis (eds) *Spanish Popular Cinema*. Manchester: Manchester University Press, pp. 60–75.

Mira, Alberto (2005a) '*Belle Epoque*' in Alberto Mira (ed.) *The Cinema of Spain and Portugal*. London and New York: Wallflower Press, pp. 198–207.

Mira, Alberto (2005b) '*El extraño viaje/ Strange Journey*' in Alberto Mira (ed.) *The Cinema of Spain and Portugal*. London and New York: Wallflower Press, pp. 119–128.

Mirizio, Annalisa (2000) 'Del carnaval al drag: la extraña relación entre masculinidad y travestismo' in Marta Segarra and Angels Carabí (eds) *Nuevas masculinidades*. La Coruña: Icaria, pp. 133–150.

Mitchell, David T. and Sharon L. Snyder (2000) *Narrative Prosthesis: Disability and the Dependencies of Discourse*. Ann Arbor: University of Michigan Press.

Molina Gavilán, Y. and T.J. Di Salvo (2001) 'Policing Spanish/European Borders: Xenophobia and Racism in Contemporary Spanish Cinema', *Ciberletras 5*, http://www.lehman.cuny.edu/ciberletras/

Monterde, José Enrique (1993) *Veinte años de cine español* (1973–1992): *un cine bajo la paradoja*. Barcelona: Paidós.

Moreiras Menor, Cristina (2002) *Cultura herida: literatura y cine en la España democrática*. Madrid: Libertarias.

Moreno, Francisco (1997) '*Perdona bonita, pero Lucas me quería a mí*', *Reseña 282* (abril), 15.

Morgan-Tamosunas, Rikki (2002) 'Narrative, Desire and Critical Discourse in Pedro Almodóvar's *Carne Trémula* (1997)', *Journal of Iberian and Latin American Studies* 8(2), 185–199.

Morris, Barbara (1995) 'Almodóvar's Laws of Subjectivity and Desire' in Kathleen M. Vernon and Barbara Morris (eds) *Post-Franco, Postmodern: The Films of Pedro Almodóvar*. Westport, Connecticut and London: Greenwood Press, pp. 87–97.

Moyano, Eduardo (2005) *La memoria escondida: cine y emigración*. Madrid: Tabla Rasa.

Mulvey, Laura (1992 [1975]) 'Visual Pleasure and Narrative Cinema' in Screen (eds) *The Sexual Subject: A Screen Reader in Sexuality*. London and New York: Routledge, pp. 22–34.

Muñoz, Diego (1998) 'Mi película es un vómito sobre la España cutre que llevamos todos dentro', *La Vanguardia* (9 de marzo), 36.

Nair, Parvati (2000) 'Displacing the Hero: Masculine Ambivalence in the Cinema of Luis García Berlanga' in Diana Holmes and Alison Smith (eds) *100 Years of European Cinema: Entertainment or Ideology?*. Manchester: Manchester University Press, pp. 88–99.

Nair, Parvati (2004) 'Borderline Men: Gender, Place and Power in Representations of Moroccans in Recent Spanish Cinema' in Steven Marsh and Parvati Nair (eds) *Gender and Spanish Cinema*. Oxford and New York: Berg, pp. 103–118.

Navarro, Rafael (1999) 'Un "árbrito" lidiará entre los toros de Osborne y Lois', *El Mundo*, edición Alicante (29 de mayo), 12.

Neale, Steve (1992 [1983]) 'Masculinity as Spectacle' in *The Sexual Subject: A Screen Reader in Sexuality*. London and New York: Routledge, pp. 277–287.

Nieto, Marta (1998) 'El hijo de la España casposa', *El País de las tentaciones* (6 de marzo), 4.

Norden, Martin F. (1994) *The Cinema of Isolation: A History of Physical Disability in the Movies*. New Brunswick: Rutgers University Press.

Oltra, Roberto J. (1993) 'Javier Bardem: en la vida no todo es cuestión de huevos', *Tiempo* (4 de octubre), 99.

Pally, Marcia (2004) 'The Politics of Passion: Pedro Almodóvar and the Camp Esthetic' in Paula Willoquet-Maricondi (ed.) *Pedro Almodóvar: Interviews*. Jackson, Mississippi: University Press of Mississippi, pp. 81–91.

Parrondo Coppel, Eva (2004) 'A Psychoanalysis of La mujer más fea del mundo (1999)', in Steven Marsh and Parvati Nair (eds) *Gender and Spanish Cinema*. Oxford and New York: Berg, pp. 119–134.

Pavlović, Tatjana (2003) *Despotic Bodies and Transgressive Bodies: Spanish Culture from Francisco Franco to Jess Franco*. Albany: State University of New York Press.

Pavlović, Tatjana (2004) 'Gender and Spanish Horror Film' in Steven Marsh and Parvati Nair (eds) *Gender and Spanish Cinema*. Oxford and New York: Berg, pp. 135–150.

Pérez Gaulí, Juan Carlos (2000) *El cuerpo en venta: relación entre arte y publicidad*. Madrid: Cátedra.

Perriam, Chris (1999) 'A un dios desconocido: Resurrecting a Queer Identity under Lorca's Spell', *Bulletin of Hispanic Studies* (Glasgow) 76(1), 77–91.

Perriam, Chris (2003) *Stars and Masculinities in Spanish Cinema: From Banderas to Bardem*. Oxford: Oxford University Press.

Perriam, Chris (2004a) 'Alejandro Amenábar's *Abre los ojos/Open Your Eyes* (1997)' in Antonio Lázaro-Reboll and Andrew Willis (eds) *Spanish Popular Cinema*. Manchester: Manchester University Press, pp. 209–221.

Perriam, Chris (2004b) 'Heterosexuality in *Segunda Piel* (Gerardo Vera, 2000) and *Sobreviviré* (Alfonso Albacete and David Menkes, 1999): Strong Women or the Same Old Story?' in Steven Marsh and Parvati Nair (eds), *Gender and Spanish Cinema*. Oxford and New York: Berg, pp. 151–163.

Perriam, Chris (2005) 'Two Transnational Spanish Stars: Antonio Banderas and Penélope Cruz', *Studies in Hispanic Cinemas* 2(1), 29–45.

Perriam, Chris, Mike Thompson, Susan Frenk and Vanessa Knights (2000) *A New History of Spanish Writing, 1939 to the 1990s*. Oxford: Oxford University Press.

Petersen, Alan (1998) *Unmasking the Masculine: 'Men' and 'Identity' in a Sceptical Age*. London, Thousand Oaks and New Delhi: Sage.

Petit, Jordi (2004) *Vidas del arco iris. Historias del ambiente*. Barcelona: DeBolsillo.

Piña, Begoña (1997) 'Ruth Rendell no va a matar', *Diario 16* (18 de febrero).

Pisano, Isabel (2001) *Bigas Luna: sombras de Bigas, luces de Luna*. Madrid: Sociedad General de Autores y Editores.

Pitts, Victoria (2003) *In the Flesh: The Cultural Politics of Body Modification*. New York: Palgrave Macmillan.

Pleck, Joseph H. (1987) 'The Theory of the Male Sex-Role Identity: Its Rise and Fall, 1936 to Present' in Harry Brod (ed.) *The Making of Masculinities: The New Men's Studies*. London, Sydney and Wellington: Allen & Unwin, pp. 21–38.

Pomerance, Murray and Frances Gateward (2005) 'Introduction' in Murray Pomerance and Frances Gateward (eds) *Where the Boys Are: Cinemas of Masculinity and Youth*. Detroit: Wayne University Press, pp. 1–18.

Ponce, José M. (2004) *El destape nacional. Crónica del desnudo en la transición*. Barcelona: Glénat.

Ponga, Paula (2004) 'Amenábar nos cuenta su película más íntima', *Fotogramas* (septiembre), 80–81.

Powrie, Phil, Ann Davies and Bruce Babington (eds) (2004) *The Trouble with Men: Masculinities in European and Hollywood Cinema*. London and New York: Wallflower Press.

Pronger, Brian (1990) *The Arena of Masculinity. Sports, Homosexuality and the Meaning of Sex*. London: GMP.

Prosser, Jay (1998) *Second Skins: The Body Narratives of Transsexuality*. New York: Columbia University Press.

Quart, Alissa (2002) *Branded: The Buying and Selling of Teenagers*. Cambridge, MA: Perseus.

Rabalska, Carmen (1999) 'A Dark Desire for the Grotesque' in Rob Rix and Roberto Rodríguez-Saona (eds) *Spanish Cinema: Calling the Shots*. Leeds: Trinity and All Saints, pp. 91–111.

Rafat, Ahmad (1992) 'España es hoy una mezcla de jamón y ordenador', *Tiempo* (21 de septiembre), 131–132.

Requena, Miguel (2002) 'Juventud y dependencia familiar en España', *Revista de estudios de juventud* 58, 1–13.

Richardson, Nathan E. (2002) *Postmodern Paletos: Immigration, Democracy, and Globalization in Spanish Narrative and Film, 1950–2000*. Lewisburg: Bucknell University Press.

Richardson, Niall (2004) 'The Queer Activity of Extreme Male Bodybuilding: Gender Dissidence, Auto-eroticism and Hysteria', *Social Semiotics* 14(1), 49–65.

Rigalt, Carmen (1997) 'Javier Bardem: el deseado', *La Revista de El Mundo 96* (17 de agosto), 12–20.

Rivera, Alfonso (1994) 'Un paso adelante', *El País de las Tentaciones* (23 September), 5.

Rodríguez Marchante, Oti (2002) *Amenábar: vocación de intriga*. Madrid: Páginas de Espuma.

Rouyeur, Philippe and Claudine Vié (2004 [1988]) 'Interview with Pedro Almodóvar' in Paula Willoquet-Maricondi (ed.) *Pedro Almodóvar Interviews*. Jackson, Mississippi: University of Mississippi, pp. 70–80.

Rutherford, Jonathan (1992) *Men's Silences: Predicaments in Masculinity*. London and New York: Routledge.

Salgueiro, J. B. (1998) 'Ni yo mismo hubiera escrito unas críticas tan buenas', *Faro de Vigo* (25 de marzo), 50.

Sampedro, José Luis (2000) *El amante lesbiano*. Barcelona: Plaza y Janés.

Sampedro, Ramón (2004) *Cartas desde el infierno*. Barcelona: Planeta.

Sánchez, Mariano (1997) 'Almodóvar en su nuevo mundo', *Extra: Revista Airtel* (Otoño), 18–21.

Sangrador García, José Luis (1996) *Identidades, actividades y estereotipos en la España de las autonomías*. Madrid: CIS.

Santaolalla, Isabel (1999a) 'Close Encounters: Racial Otherness in Imanol Uribe's Bwana', *Bulletin of Hispanic Studies* (Glasgow) 76(1), 111–122.

Santaolalla, Isabel (1999b) 'Julio Medem's Vacas (1991): Historicizing the Forest' in Peter William Evans (ed.) *Spanish Cinema: The Auteurist Tradition*. Oxford: Oxford University Press, pp. 310–324.

Santaolalla, Isabel (2003) 'Behold the Man! Masculinity and Ethnicity in Bwana (1996) and En la puta calle (1998)' in Guido Rings and Rikki Morgan-Tamosunas (eds) *European Cinema: Inside Out: Images of the Self and the Other in Postcolonial European Film*. Heidelberg: Universitätsverlag Winter, pp. 153–163.

Santaolalla, Isabel (2005) *Los 'Otros': etnicidad y 'raza' en el cine español contemporáneo*. Zaragoza and Madrid: Prensas Universitarias de Zaragoza and Ocho y Medio.

Sartori, Beatriz (1993) 'Bigas Luna: huevos con jamón', *El Mundo* (7 de abril), 39.

Satué, Francisco J. (1996) 'Nunca es triste', Academia: Revista del cine español 13 (enero), 56–62.

Schneider, Steven Jay (2005) 'Jerkus Interruptus: The Terrible Trials of Masturbating Boys in Recent Hollywood Cinema' in Murray Pomerance and Frances Gateward (eds) *Where the Boys Are: Cinemas of Masculinity and Youth*. Detroit: Wayne University Press, pp. 377–393.

Sedgwick, Eve K. (1985) *Between Men: English Literature and Male Homosocial Desire*. New York: Columbia University Press.

Sedgwick, Eve K. (1991) *Epistemology of the Closet*. London and New York: Penguin.

Shakespeare, Tom (2001) '*The Secret Passion of Disabled People*', unpublished conference paper presented at the Film Festival and Short Film Competition, Ateneum Hall, Helsinki.

Shary, Timothy (2002) *Generation Multiplex: The Image of Youth in Contemporary American Cinema*. Austin: University of Texas Press.

Shary, Timothy (2005) 'Bad Boys and Hollywood Hype: Gendered Conflict in Juvenile Delinquency Films' in Murray Pomerance and Frances Gateward (eds) *Where the Boys Are: Cinemas of Masculinity and Youth*. Detroit: Wayne University Press, pp. 21–40.

Shaviro, Steven (1993) *The Cinematic Body*. Minneapolis and London: University of Minnesota Press.

Shaw, Deborah (2000) 'Men in High Heels: The Feminine Man and Performances of Femininity in *Tacones lejanos* by Pedro Almodóvar', *Journal of Iberian and Latin American Studies* 6(1), 55–62.

Shubert, Adrian (1999) *Death and Money in the Afternoon. A History of the Spanish Bullfight*. Oxford and New York: Oxford University Press.

Silverman, Kaja (1992) *Male Subjectivity at the Margins*. London and New York: Routledge.

Simpson, Mark (1994) *Male Impersonators: Men Performing Masculinity*. London: Cassell.

Sinfield, Alan (1994) *The Wilde Century: Effeminacy, Oscar Wilde and the Queer Moment*. London and New York: Cassell.

Smith, Clarissa (2003) 'Fellas in Fully Frontal Frolics: Naked Men in For Women Magazine' in Judith Still (ed.) *Men's Bodies*, special issue of *Paragraph* 26(1/2), 134–146.

Smith, Paul (1995) 'Eastwood Bound' in Maurice Berger, Brian Wallis and Simon Watson (eds) *Constructing Masculinity*. New York and London: Routledge, pp. 77–97.

Smith, Paul Julian (1992a) *Representing the Other: Race, Text, and Gender in Spanish and Spanish American Narrative*. Oxford: Oxford Clarendon Press

Smith, Paul Julian (1992b) *Laws of Desire: Questions of Homosexuality in Spanish Writing and Film, 1960–1990*. Oxford, Clarendon Press.

Smith, Paul Julian (1996) *Vision Machines: Cinema, Literature and Sexuality in Spain and Cuba, 1983–1993*. London and New York: Verso.

Smith, Paul Julian (1997) 'Pornography, Masculinity, Homosexuality: Almodovar's Matador and La ley del Deseo' in Marsha Kinder (ed.) *Refiguring Spain: Cinema/ Media/Representation*. Durham and London: Duke University Press, pp. 178–195.

Smith, Paul Julian (1999) 'Un travestismo sin límites: el cine de Pedro Almodóvar', *Antípodas: Journal of Hispanic and Galician Studies* 11/12, 15–22.

Smith, Paul Julian (2000a) *Desire Unlimited: The Cinema of Pedro Almodóvar*. London and New York: Verso.

Smith, Paul Julian (2000b) *The Moderns: Time, Space, and Subjectivity in Contemporary Spanish Culture*. Oxford: Oxford University Press.

Smith, Paul Julian (2002) 'Only Connect', *Sight and Sound* 12(7), 24–27.

Smith, Paul Julian (2003) *Contemporary Spanish Culture: TV, Fashion, Art and Film*. Cambridge: Polity Press.

Smith, Paul Julian (2005a) 'Dangerous Intimacies', *Sight and Sound* 15(3), 26–29.

Smith, Paul Julian (2005b) '*Lucía y el sexo/ Sex and Lucía*' in Alberto Mira (ed.) *The Cinema of Spain and Portugal*. London: Wallflower Press, pp. 239–246.

Smith, Paul Julian (2006) *Spanish Visual Culture: Cinema, Television, Internet*. Manchester: Manchester University Press.

Spencer, Colin (1995) *Homosexuality: A History*. London: Fourth Estate.

Spongberg, Mary (1997) 'Are Small Penises Necessary for Civilisation? The Male Body and the Body Politic', *Australian Feminist Studies* 12(25), 19–28.

Stam, Robert (2003) 'Beyond Third Cinema: The Aesthetics of Hybridity' in A.R. Guneratne and W. Dissanayake (eds) *Rethinking Third Cinema*. London: Routledge, pp. 31–48.

Stanley, Christopher (1995) 'Teenage Kicks: Urban Narratives of Dissent Not Deviance', *Crime, Law & Social Change* 23, 91–119.

Stavans, Illán (1998) 'The Latin Phallus' in Antonia Darder and Rodolfo D. Torres (eds) *The Latino Studies Reader: Culture, Economy and Society*. Oxford and Malden: Blackwell, pp. 228–239.

Stone, Rob (2002) *Spanish Cinema*. London and New York: Longman.

Stone, Rob (2004) '¡Victoria? A Modern Magdalene' in Steven Marsh and Parvati Nair (eds) *Gender and Spanish Cinema*. Oxford and New York: Berg, pp. 165–182.

Stone, Rob (2007) *Julio Medem*. Manchester: Manchester University Press.

Strauss, Frédéric (2001) *Conversaciones con Pedro Almodóvar*. Madrid: Akal.

Strick, Philip (1993) '*Jamón, jamón*', *Sight and Sound* 3(6) (June), 57–58.

Stryker, Susan (2006) '(De)Subjugated Knowledges: An Introduction to Transgender Studies' in Susan Stryker and Stephen Whittle (eds) *The Transgender Reader*. New York: Routledge, pp. 244–256.

Tasker, Yvonne (1993) *Spectacular Bodies: Gender, Genre and the Action Cinema*. London and New York: Routledge.

Tasker, Yvonne (1995) 'Dumb Movies for Dumb People' in Steven Cohan and Ina Rae Hark (eds) *Screening the Male: Exploring Masculinities in Hollywood Cinema*. London and New York: Routledge, pp. 230–244.

Taylor, John R. (1983) *Strangers in Paradise: the Hollywood Émigrés, 1933–1950*. London: Faber and Faber.

Thomas, Calvin (2003) 'Racing Forms and the Exhibition(ist) (Mis)Match' in Judith Still (ed.) *Men's Bodies*, special issue of *Paragraph* 26(1/2), 245–262.

Thompson, J. Kevin (2004) 'Body Image, Bodybuilding, and Cultural Ideals of Muscularity', *Think Muscle* online <http://www.thinkmuscle.com/ articles/ thompson/body-image-and-bodybuilding.htm>. Last consulted in August 2006.

Thompson, J. Kevin, Leslie J. Heinberg, Madeleine Altabe and Stacey Tantleff-Dunn (1999) *Exacting Beauty: Theory, Assessment, and Treatment of Body Image Disturbance*. Washington and London: American Psychological Association.

Thomson, Rosemarie Garland (1997) *Extraordinary Bodies: Figuring Physical Disability in American Culture and Literature*. New York: Columbia University Press.

Tinkcom, Matthew (2005) 'Out West. Gus Van Sant's *My Own Private Idaho* and the Lost Mother' in Murray Pomerance and Frances Gateward (eds) *Where the Boys Are: Cinemas of Masculinity and Youth*. Detroit: Wayne University Press, pp. 233–245.

Toro, Suso de (2004) 'Bardem/Amenábar: una pareja comprometida', *El País Semanal* (22 de agosto), 32–29.

Torregrosa, Ana (1999) 'Entrevista con Miguel Santesmases, director de cine: "La polémica con la comunidad china perjudicó a mi película"' *El País* (13 de junio).

Torreiro, M. (1997) 'Una propuesta modestita', *El País* (10 de february), 32.

Torres, Maruja (1992) 'La estrella es… Javier Bardem' in '*Jamón, Jamón*, Un film de *Bigas Luna*' (booklet accompanying a special edition of the video published in Spain). Lola Films.

Trenzado Romero, Manuel (1997) 'La imagen de la juventud y la familia en el reciente cine español', *Revista de estudios de juventud* 39, 93–106.

Trenzado Romero, Manuel (1999) *Cultura de masas y cambio político: el cine español de la transición*. Madrid: Centro de Investigaciones Sociológicas, Siglo XXI.

Triana-Toribio, Núria (2000) 'A Punk Called Pedro: La Movida in the Films of Pedro Almodóvar' in Barry Jordan and Rikki Morgan-Tamosunas (eds) *Spanish Contemporary Cultural Studies*. London and New York: Arnold, pp. 274–282.

Triana-Toribio, Núria (2003) *Spanish National Cinema*. London and New York: Routledge.

Triana-Toribio, Núria (2004) 'Santiago Segura: Just When You Thought Spanish Masculinities Were Getting Better…', *Hispanic Research Journal* 15(2), 147–156.

Triviño, Mentxu (1997), 'Ruido de fondo', *Deia* (12 de agosto), 8.

Tropiano, Stephen (1997) 'Out of the Cinematic Closet: Homosexuality in the Films of Eloy de la Iglesia' in Marsha Kinder (ed.) *Refiguring Spain: Cinema/Media/Representation*. Durham: Duke University Press, pp. 157–177.

Troyano, Ela (2004 [1994]) 'Interview with Pedro Almodóvar: *Kika*' in Paula Willoquet-Maricondi (ed) *Pedro Almodóvar Interviews*. Jackson, Mississippi: University of Mississippi, pp. 102–109.

Troyer, John and Chani Marchiselli (2005) 'Slack, Slacker, Slackest: Homosocial Bonding Practices in Contemporary Dude Cinema' in Murray Pomerance and Frances Gateward (eds) *Where the Boys Are: Cinemas of Masculinity and Youth*. Detroit: Wayne University Press, pp. 264–276.

Trujillo, Nick (1995) 'Machines, Missiles and Men: Images of the Male Body on ABC's Monday Night Football', *Sociology of Sport Journal* 12(4), 403–423.

Tuck, Greg (2003) 'Mainstreaming the Money Shot: Reflections on the Representation of Ejaculation in Contemporary American Cinema' in Judith Still (ed.) *Men's Bodies*, special issue of *Paragraph* 26 (1/2), 263–279.

Tyler, Carol-Anne (1991) 'Boys will be Girls: The Politics of Gay Drag' in Diana Fuss (ed.) *Inside/Out: Lesbian Theories, Gay Theories*. New York and London: Routledge, pp. 32–70.

Umbral, Francisco (1977) 'Bibí Anderson', *El País* (28 de octubre).

Vernon, Kathleen M. (1995) 'Melodrama Against Itself: Pedro Almodóvar's What Have I Done to Deserve This?' in Kathleen M. Vernon and Barbara Morris (eds) *Post-Franco, Postmodern: The Films of Pedro Almodóvar*. Westport, Connecticut and London, Greenwood, pp. 59–72.

Vilarós, Teresa M. (1998) *El mono del desencanto: una crítica cultural de la transición española (1973–1993)*. Madrid: Siglo XXI.

Villa, Manuela (2005) 'El chico "Upa" se pone duro', *El País EP3* Friday supplement (10 de junio), 10–14.

Villoro, Juan (2004) 'El nuevo "chico Almodóvar"', *El País Semanal* (22 de febrero), 30–37.

Waugh, Thomas (1993) 'The Third Body: Patterns in the Construction of the Subject in Gay Male Narrative Film' in Martha Gever, John Greyson and Pratibha Parmar (eds) *Queer Looks: Perspectives on Lesbian and Gay Film and Video*. New York and London: Routledge, pp. 141–161.

Williams, Linda (1999) *Hard Core: Power, Pleasure and the 'Frency of the Visible'*. Berkeley, Los Angeles and London: University of California Press.

Wu, Harmony (2004) 'The Perverse Pleasures of Almodóvar's *¡Átame! (Tie Me Up! Tie Me Down!)*', *Journal of Spanish Cultural Studies* 5(3), 261–271.

Yanof, Judith A. (2005) 'Perversion in *La mala educación* [*Bad education*] (2004)', *International Journal of Psychoanalisis* 86(6), 1715–1724.

Zatlin, Phyllis (2001) 'From Stage to Screen: *Amic/Amat*', *Anales de la literatura española contemporánea* 26(1), 239–253.

Zunzunegui, Santos (1993) '"Vida corta, querer escaso" o los felices 60 según Fernando Fernán-Gómez' in Jesús Angulo and Francisco Llinás (eds) *Fernando Fernán-Gómez. El hombre que quiso ser Jackie Cooper*. San Sebastián: Patronato Municipal de Cultura, pp. 39–58.

Zunzunegui, Santos (1999) *El extraño viaje: El celuloide atrapado por la cola o la crítica norteamericana ante el cine español*. Valencia: Episteme.

Filmography

20 centímetros/20 Centimetres (dir. Ramón Salazar, 2005)

¡A mí la legión!/Follow the Legion! (dir. Juan de Orduña, 1942)

A mí las mujeres, ni fu ni fa/Women Don't Do it for Me (dir. Mariano Ozores, 1971)

Abre los ojos/Open Your Eyes (dir. Alejandro Amenábar, 1997)

Acción mutante/Mutant Action (dir. Álex de la Iglesia, 1993)

Adiós, cigüeña, adiós/Goodbye, Stork, Goodbye (dir. Manuel Summers, 1971)

Agustina de Aragón/Agustina of Aragon (dir. Juan de Orduña, 1950)

Airbag (dir. Juanma Bajo Ulloa, 1997)

Al salir de clase/After School (television series Tele 5, 1997–2002)

Alma gitana/Gypsy Soul (dir. Chus Gutiérrez, 1996)

Almejas y mejillones/Clams and Mussels (dir. Marcos Carnevale, 2000)

Amante bilingüe, El /The Bilingual Lover (dir. Vicente Aranda, 1993)

Amantes/Lovers (dir. Vicente Aranda, 1991)

Amantes del círculo polar, Los /The Lovers of the Arctic Circle (dir. Julio Medem, 1998)

American Pie (dir. Paul Weitz, 1999)

American Pie 2 (dir. James B. Rogers, 2001)

American Pie Presents Band Camp (dir. Steve Rash, 2005)

American Wedding (dir. Jessy Dilan, 2003)

Amic/Amat/Beloved/Friend (dir. Ventura Pons, 1999)

Amor de hombre/The Love of a Man (dirs Yolanda García Serrano and Juan Luis Iborra, 1997)

Amor idiota/Idiot Love (dir. Ventura Pons, 2004)

Angst essen Seele auf/Ali, Fear Eats the Soul (dir. Rainier Werner Maria Fassbinder, 1974)

Anita no perd el tren/Anita Takes a Chance (dir. Ventura Pons, 2001)

Año de la garrapata, El /The Year of the Tick (dir. Jorge Coira, 2004)

Año de las luces, El /Year of Enlightment (dir. Fernando Trueba, 1986)

Ardilla roja, La /The Red Squirrel (dir. Julio Medem, 1993)

Aro Tolbukhin: En la mente del asesino/Aro Tolbukhin in the Mind of a Killer (dir. Agustí Villaronga, 2002)

Arriba Hazaña/Long Live Hazaña (dir. Gutiérrez Santos, 1978)

Asombroso mundo de Borjamari y Pocholo, El /The Amazing World of Borjamari and Pocholo (dirs Juan Cavestany and Enrique López Lavigne, 2004)

¡Átame!/Tie Me Up! Tie Me Down! (dir. Pedro Almodóvar, 1990)

Atilano, presidente/Atilano for President (dirs Santiago Aguilar and Luis Guridi, 1998)

Atómica/Atomic (dirs Alfonso Albacete and David Menkes, 1997).

Barrio/Neighbourhood (dir. Fernando León de Aranoa, 1998)

Batman Returns (dir. Tim Burton, 1992)

Baywatch (television series NBC, 1989–2004)

Before Night Falls (dir. Julian Schnabel, 2000)

Bella Otero, La /La Belle Otéro (dir. Richard Portier, 1954)

Belle Epoque/The Age of Beauty (dir. Fernando Trueba, 1992)

Ben-Hur (dir. William Wyler, 1959)

Birdcage, The (dir. Mike Nichols, 1996)

Blade Runner (dir. Ridley Scott, 1982)

Blue Velvet (dir. David Lynch, 1986)

Boca a boca/Mouth to Mouth (dir. Manuel Gómez Pereira, 1995)

Bola, El /Pellet (dir. Achero Mañas, 2000)

Boys Don't Cry (dir. Kimberly Peirce, 1999)

Braveheart (dir. Mel Gibson, 1995)

Buena estrella, La /Lucky Star (dir. Ricardo Franco, 1997)

Buena vida, La / The Good Life (dir. David Trueba, 1996)

Bwana (dir. Imanol Uribe, 1996)

Cabeza, La / The Head (dir. Alejandro Amenábar, 1991)

Cachorro/Bear Cub (dir. Miguel Albaladejo, 2004)

Camarón (dir. Jaime Chávarri, 2005).

Cambio de sexo/Forbidden Love (dir. Vicente Aranda, 1977)

Carmen (dir. Vicente Aranda, 2003)

Carne trémula/Live Flesh (dir. Pedro Almodóvar, 1997)

Carreteras secundarias/Backroads (dir. Emilio Martínez Lázaro, 1997)

Cartas de Alou, Las /Letters From Alou (dir. Montxo Armendáriz, 1990)

Celos, amor y Mercado Común/Jealousy, Love and EEC (dir. Alfonso Paso, 1973)

Cet obscur objet du désir/Ese oscuro objeto de deseo/That Obscure Object of Desire (dir. Luis Buñuel, 1977)

Chulos, Los (dir. Mariano Ozores, 1981)

Cid, El/The Cid (dir. Anthony Mann, 1961)

Cochecito, El /The Wheelchair (dir. Marco Ferreri, 1960)

Colegas/Pals (dir. Eloy de la Iglesia, 1982)

Compañeros/Peers (television series Antena 3, 1998–2002)

Conan the Barbarian (dir. John Milius, 1982)

Conan the Destroyer (dir. Richard Fleischer, 1984)

Corazón de bombón/Sweetheart (dir. Álvaro Sáenz de Heredia, 2000)

Corazón del guerrero, El /Heart of the Warrior (dir. Daniel Monzón Jerez, 2000)

Cosas que dejé en La Habana/Things I Left in Havana (dir. Manuel Gutiérrez Aragón, 1997)

Crónicas Marcianas (television show Tele 5, 1997–2005)

Crying Game, The (dir. Neil Jordan, 1992)

Cyborg (dir. Albert Pyun, 1989)

¡Dame un poco de amor!/Bring a Little Lovin' (dirs José María Forqué and Francisco Macián, 1968)

Dancer in the Dark (dir. Lars von Trier, 2000)

Dancer Upstairs, The (dir. John Malkovich, 2002)

Dante no es únicamente severo/Dante is Not Only Rigorous (dirs Jacinto Esteva and Joaquim Jordà, 1967)

Darkness (dir. Jaume Balagueró, 2002)

Detective y la muerte, El /The Detective and Death (dir. Gonzalo Suárez, 1994)

Día de la bestia, El / The Day of the Beast (dir. Álex de la Iglesia, 1995)

Diario de un skin/A Skinhead's Diary (dir. Jacobo Rispa, 2005)

Días contados/Running Out of Time (dir. Imanol Uribe, 1994)

Días de fútbol/Football Days (dir. David Serrano, 2003)

Die Hard (dir. John McTiernan, 1988)

Diferente/Different (dir. José María Delgado, 1962, re-released 1978)

Diputado, El /Confessions of a Congressman (dir. Eloy de la Iglesia, 1978)

Dirty Harry (dir. Don Siegel, 1971)

Edades de Lulú, Las /Ages of Lulu (dir. Bigas Luna, 1990)

Efecto mariposa, El / The Butterfly Effect (dir. Fernando Colomo, 1995)

Elephant (dir. Gus Van Sant, 2003)

En construcción/Work in Progress (dir. José Luis Guerín, 2001)

En la puta calle/Hitting Bottom (dir. Enrique Gabriel, 1997)

Ensayo de un crimen/Rehearsal for a Crime (dir. Luis Buñuel, 1955)

Españolas en París/Spaniards in Paris (dir. Roberto Bodegas, 1971)

Espinazo del Diablo, El / The Devil's Backbone (dir. Guillermo del Toro, 2001)

Extranjeras/Foreign Girls (dir. Helena Taberna, 2003)

Extranjeros de sí mismos/Aliens to Themselves (dirs José Luis López Linares and Javier Rioyo, 2000)

Extraño viaje, El /Strange Journey (dir. Fernando Fernán Gómez, 1964)

Face/Off (dir. John Woo, 1997)

Fata Morgana/Left-Handed Fate (dir. Vicente Aranda, 1965)

Fin de curso/School is Out (dir. Miguel Martí, 2005)

First Blood (dir. Ted Kotcheff, 1982)

Flamenco (dir. Carlos Saura, 1995)

Flor de mi secreto, La / The Flower of My Secret (dir. Pedro Almodóvar, 1996)

Flores de otro mundo/Flowers From Another World (dir. Icíar Bollaín, 1999)

Fuente amarilla, La / The Yellow Fountain (dir. Miguel Santesmases, 1999)

Fuera del cuerpo/Body Confusion (dir. Vicente Peñarrocha, 2004)

Gente pez/Fish People (dir. Jorge Iglesias, 2001)

Get Real (dir. Simon Shore, 1999)

Gitano/Gypsy (dir. Manuel Palacios, 2000)

Gladiator (dir. Ridley Scott, 2000)

Glen or Glenda (dir. Edward D. Wood, 1953)

Golfos, Los / The Delinquents (dir. Carlos Saura, 1962)

Goodbye Charlie (dir. Vincente Minnelli, 1964)

Gran familia, La / The Big Family (dirs Fernando Palacios and Rafael Salvia, 1962)

Gran hermano/Big Brother (television show Tele 5, since 2000)

Guerreros/Warriors (dir. Daniel Calparsoro, 2002)

Habana Blues (dir. Benito Zambrano, 2005)

Hable con ella/Talk to Her (dir. Pedro Almodóvar, 2002)

¡Harka! (dir. Carlos Arévalo, 1941)

Henry, Portrait of a Serial Killer (dir. John McNaughton, 1986)

Hercules (dir. Luigi Cozzi, 1983)

Historia de Estrella/Estrella's Story (television) (dir. Manuel Estudillo, 2003)

Historias de la puta mili/Tales of the Stinking Military Service (dir. Manuel Esteban, 1994)

Historias del Kronen/Stories from the Kronen (dir. Montxo Armendáriz, 1995)

Hola, estás sola?/Hi, Are You Alone (dir. Icíar Bollaín, 1995)

Hotel y domicilio/In Calls and Out (dir. Ernesto del Río, 1995)

Huevos de oro/Golden Balls (dir. Bigas Luna, 1993)

I Love You Baby (dirs Alfonso Albacete and David Menkes, 2001)

Ilegal/Illegal (dir. Ignacio Vilar, 2003)

Indiana Jones trilogy (dir. Steven Spielberg, 1981, 1984, 1989)

Isi & Disi: Alto voltaje/Isi & Disi: High Voltage (dir. Miguel Ángel Lamata, 2006)

Isi & Disi: Amor a lo bestia/Isi & Disi: Beastly Love (dir. Chema de la Peña, 2004)

It's a Boy/Girl Thing (dir. Nick Hurran, 2006)

Jamón, Jamón (dir. Bigas Luna, 1992)

Jardín de las delicias, El / The Garden of Delights (dir. Carlos Saura, 1970)

Johnny Got His Gun (dir. Dalton Trumbo, 1971)

Juana la Loca/Mad Love (dir. Vicente Aranda, 2001)

Kickboxer (dirs Mark DiSalle and David Worth, 1989)

Kika (dir. Pedro Almodóvar, 1993)

Krámpack/Dani and Nico (dir. Cesc Gay, 2000)

L'Auberge Espagnole/Una casa de locos/Euro Pudding/The Spanish Apartment (dir. Cédric Klapisch, 2002)

Laberinto de pasiones/Labyrinths of Passion (dir. Pedro Almodóvar, 1982)

Lara Croft: Tomb Raider (dir. Simon West, 2001)

Last Seduction, The (dir. John Dahl, 1994)

Legend of Zorro, The (dir. Martin Campbell, 2005)

Lethal Weapon (dir. Richard Donner, 1987)

Ley del deseo, La / Law of Desire (dir. Pedro Almodóvar, 1987)

Libro de buen amor, El / The Book of Good Love (dir. Tomás Aznar, 1974)

Liga no es cosa de hombres, La / League/Garter is Not For Men (dir. Ignacio F. Aquino, 1972)

Lisístrata (dir. Francesc Bellmunt, 2002)

Lo verde empieza en los Pirineos/Smut Starts at the Pyrenees (dir. Vicente Escrivá, 1973)

Lobo, El/Wolf (dir. Miguel Courtois, 2004)

Locura de amor/Love Crazy (dir. Ricardo de Baños, 1909)

Locura de amor/The Mad Queen (dir. Juan de Orduña, 1948)

Lola la piconera/Lola, the Coalgirl (dir. Luis Lucía, 1951)

Lucía y el sexo/Sex and Lucia (dir. Julio Medem, 2001)

Lunes al sol, Los /Mondays in the Sun (dir. Fernando León de Aranoa, 2002)

Mad Max (dir. George Miller, 1979)

Mala educación, La/Bad Education (dir. Pedro Almodóvar, 2004)

Mambo Kings, The (dir. Arne Glimcher, 1992)

Mar adentro/The Sea Inside (dir. Alejandro Amenábar, 2004)

Mar, El /The Sea (dir. Agustí Villaronga, 2000)

Más de mil cámaras velan por tu seguridad/More Than a Thousand Cameras are Working for your Safety (dir. David Alonso, 2003)

Más que amor, frenesí/Not Love, Just Frenzy (dirs Alfonso Albacete, Miguel Bardem and David Menkes 1996)

Matador (dir. Pedro Almodóvar, 1986)

Matrix, The (dirs Andy and Larry Wachowski, 1999)

Menos que cero/Less Than Zero (dir. Ernesto Tellería, 1996)

Mi querida señorita/My Dearest Senorita (dir. Jaime de Armiñán, 1972)

Monja alférez, La /The Lieutenant Nun (dir. Javier Aguirre, 1987)

Mrs Doubtfire (dir. Chris Columbus, 1993)

Mujer más fea del mundo, La /The Ugliest Woman in the World (dir. Miguel Bardem, 1999)

My Own Private Idaho (dir. Gus Van Sant, 1991)

Niña de tus ojos, La /The Girl of Your Dreams (dir. Fernando Trueba, 1998)

Niño de la luna, El /Moon Child (dir. Agustí Villaronga, 1989)

Niños de Rusia, Los /The Children of Russia (dir. Jaime Camino, 2001)

No desearás al vecino del quinto/Thou Shalt Not Covet Thy Fifth Floor Neighbour (dir. Ramón Fernández, 1970)

No se lo digas a nadie/Don't Tell Anyone (dir. Francisco J. Lombardi, 1998)

Noche más hermosa, La /The Most Beautiful Night (dir. Manuel Gutiérrez Aragón, 1984)

Nos miran/They're Watching Us (dir. Norberto López Amado, 2002)

Novios búlgaros, Los /Bulgarian Lovers (dir. Eloy de la Iglesia, 2003)

Novios de la muerte/The Betrothed of Death (dir. Rafael Gil, 1975)

Ocaña, retrat intermitent/Ocana, an Intermittent Portrait (dir. Ventura Pons, 1978)

Olvidados, Los /The Young and the Damned (dir. Luis Buñuel, 1950)

Operación Triunfo/Fame Academy (television series TVE-1 since 2001 and Tele 5 since 2005)

Otro barrio, El /The Other Side (dir. García Ruiz, 2000)

Otros, Los /The Others (dir. Alejandro Amenábar, 2001)

Palo, El /The Hold-Up (dir. Eva Lesmes, 2001)

Papá Piquillo (dir. Álvaro Sáenz de Heredia, 1998)

París Tombuctú (dir. J.L. García Berlanga, 1999)

Pasión turca, La /Turkish Passion (dir. Vicente Aranda, 1994)

Pau i el seu germà/Pau and His Brother (dir. Marc Recha, 2001)

Pecadora, La /The Sinner (dir. Ignacio F. Iquino, 1954)

Peeping Tom (dir. Michael Powell, 1960)

Penalti más largo del mundo, El/The Longest Penalty in the World (dir. Roberto Santiago, 2005)

Peores años de nuestra vida, Los / The Worst Years of Our Lives (dir. Emilio Martínez Lázaro, 1994)

Pepi, Luci, Bom y otras chicas del montón/Pepi, Luci, Bom and Other Girls on the Heap (dir. Pedro Almodóvar, 1980)

Perdita Durango/Dance with the Devil (dir. Álex de la Iglesia, 1997)

Perdona Bonita, pero Lucas me quería a mí/Excuse Me Darling, but Lucas Loved Me (dirs Félix Sabroso and Dunia Ayaso, 1997)

Pestañas postizas/False Eyelashes (dir. Enrique Belloch, 1982)

Placeres ocultos, Los / Hidden Pleasures (dir. Eloy de la Iglesia, 1977)

Planta cuarta/The Fourth Floor (dir. Antonio Mercero, 2003)

Pon un hombre en tu vida/Put a Man in Your Life (dir. Eva Lesmes, 1996)

Poniente/Sunset (dir. Chus Gutiérrez, 2002)

¿Por qué lo llaman amor cuándo quieren decir sexo?/Why Do They Call It Love When They Mean Sex? (dir. Manuel Gómez Pereira, 1993)

Portero, El / The Goalie (dir. Gonzalo Suárez, 2000)

Princesa de los Ursinos, La /Princess of the Ursinos (dir. Luis Lucía, 1947)

Princesas/Princesses (dir. Fernando León de Aranoa, 2005)

Psycho (dir. Alfred Hitchcock, 1960)

¿Qué he hecho yo para merecer esto?/What Have I Done to Deserve This? (dir. Pedro Almodóvar, 1984)

Queer as Folk (television series UK Channel 4, 1999–2000 and US Showtime, 2000–2005)

Rambo: First Blood Part II (dir. George P. Cosmatos, 1985)

Raza/Race (dir. José Luis Sáenz de Heredia, 1942)

Red Sonja (dir. Richard Fleischer, 1985)

Rencor/Rancour (dir. Miguel Albaladejo, 2002)

Reservoir Dogs (dir. Quentin Tarantino, 1992)

Robocop (dir. Paul Verhoeven, 1987)

Rocky (dir. John G. Avildsen, 1976)

Sacerdote, El / The Priest (dir. Eloy de la Iglesia, 1978)

Saïd (dir. Llorenç Soler, 1999)

Salsa rosa/Pink Sauce (dir. Manuel Gómez Pereira, 1992)

Scanners (dir. David Cronenberg, 1981)

Segunda piel/Second Skin (dir. Gerardo Vera, 1999)

Semen: una historia de amor/Semen: A Love Story (dirs Daniela Fejerman and Inés París, 2005)

Séptimo día, El / The Seventh Day (dir. Carlos Saura, 2004)

Seres queridos/Only Human (dirs Dominic Harari and Teresa de Pelegrí, 2004)

Sex and the City (television series HBO, 1998–2004)

Shallow Grave (dir. Danny Boyle, 1995)

She's the Man (dir. Andy Fickman, 2006)

Si te dicen que caí/If They Tell You I Fell (dir. Vicente Aranda, 1989)

Sin nombre, Los / The Nameless (dir. Jaume Balagueró, 1999)

Sixth Sense, The (dir. M. Night Shyamalan, 1999)

Slam (dir. Miguel Martí, 2003)

Sobreviviré/I Will Survive (dirs Albacete and Menkes, 1999)

Solas/Alone (dir. Benito Zambrano, 1999)

Soldados de Salamina/Soldiers of Salamina (dir. David Trueba, 2003)

Some Like it Hot (dir. Billy Wilder, 1959)

Superman (dir. Richard Donner, 1978)

Susanna (dir. Antonio Chavarrías, 1996)

Switch (dir. Blake Edwards, 1991)

Tacones lejanos/High Heels (dir. Pedro Almodóvar, 1991)

Tarzan of the Apes (dir. Scott Sidney, 1918)

Tarzan the Ape Man (dir. W.S. van Dyke, 1932)

Te doy mis ojos/Take my Eyes (dir. Icíar Bollaín, 2003)

Techo del mundo, El /World's Ceiling (dir. Felipe Vega, 1995)

Ten Commandments, The (dir. Cecil B. DeMille, 1956)

Terminator 2: Judgment Day (dir. James Cameron, 1991)

Terminator, The (dir. James Cameron, 1984)

Territorio Comanche/Comanche Territory (dir. Gerardo Herrero, 1997)

Tesis/Thesis (dir. Alejandro Amenábar, 1996)

Teta y la luna, La / The Tit and the Moon (dir. Bigas Luna, 1994)

Tía de Carlos, La /Carlos's Aunty (dir. Luis María Delgado, 1981)

Tierra/Earth (dir. Julio Medem, 1996)

Tigres de papel/Paper Tigers (dir. Fernando Colomo, 1977)

Todo sobre mi madre/All About My Mother (dir. Pedro Almodóvar, 1999)

Tomándote/Tea for Two (dir. Isabel Gardela, 2000)

Tootsie (dir. Sydney Pollack, 1982)

Torremolinos 73 (dir. Pablo Berger, 2003)

Torrente, el brazo tonto de la ley/Torrente, the Stupid Arm of the Law (dir. Santiago Segura, 1998)

Torrente 2: Misión en Marbella/Torrente 2: Mission Marbella (dir. Santiago Segura, 2001)

Torrente 3: El Protector/Torrente 3: The Protector (dir. Santiago Segura, 2005)

Transamerica (dir. Duncan Tucker, 2005)

Tras el cristal/In a Glass Cage (dir. Agustí Villaronga, 1987)

Troy (dir. Wolfgang Petersen, 2004)

Twins (dir. Ivan Reitman, 1988)

Two Much (dir. Fernando Trueba, 1995)

Últimos de Filipinas, Los /Last Stand in the Philippines (dir. Antonio Román, 1945)

Un hombre llamado Flor de Otoño/A Man Called Autumn Flower (dir. Pedro Olea, 1978)

Un paso adelante/One Step Ahead (television series Antena 3, 2002–2005)

Una de zombis/Zombi Adventure (dir. Miguel Ángel Lamata, 2003)

Una señora llamada Andrés/A Lady Called Andrés (dir. Julio Buchs, 1970)

Vacas/Cows (dir. Julio Medem, 1992)

¡Vente a Alemania, Pepe!/Come to Germany, Pepe! (dir. Pedro Lazaga, 1971)

Verano Azul/Blue Summer (television series TVE-1, 1981–1982).

Vestida de azul/Dressed in Blue (dir. Antonio Giménez-Rico, 1983)
Victor/Victoria (dir. Blake Edwards, 1982)
Volver (dir. Pedro Almodóvar, 2006)
Willy/Milly (dir. Paul Schneider, 1986)
XXL (dir. Sánchez Valdés, 2004)
Yo soy ésa/I'm the One (dir. Luis Sanz, 1990)
Yoyes (dir. Helena Taberna, 2000)

Index